A PALER SHADE OF RED

Memoirs of a Radical

W. E. GUTMAN

**CCB Publishing
British Columbia, Canada**

A Paler Shade of Red: Memoirs of a Radical

Copyright ©2012 by W. E. Gutman
ISBN-13 978-1-927360-96-5
First Edition

Library and Archives Canada Cataloguing in Publication
Gutman, W. E., 1937-
A paler shade of red : memoirs of a radical / written by W. E. Gutman.
ISBN 978-1-927360-96-5
Also available in electronic format.
Additional cataloguing data available from Library and Archives Canada

Cover design by the author.
Photograph on the front cover is in the public domain.

This book is printed on acid-free paper.

Extreme care has been taken to ensure that all information presented in this book is accurate and up to date at the time of publishing. The publisher cannot be held responsible for any errors or omissions. Additionally, neither is any liability assumed by the publisher for damages resulting from the use of the information contained herein.

All rights reserved. No part of this publication may be reproduced, stored in a retrieval system or transmitted in any form or by any means, electronic, mechanical, photocopying, recording or otherwise without the express written permission of the author. Printed in the United States of America, the United Kingdom and Australia.

Publisher: CCB Publishing
             British Columbia, Canada
             www.ccbpublishing.com

IN MEMORY OF IONEL

Also by W. E. Gutman

JOURNEY TO XIBALBA:
The Subversion of Human Rights in Central America
Reporter's Notebook, © 2000 (Out of print)

***NOCTURNES* -- Tales from the Dreamtime**
Fiction, © 2006

FLIGHT FROM EIN SOF
Fiction, © 2009

THE INVENTOR
Historical fiction, © 2009

***ONE NIGHT IN COPÁN* -- Chronicles of Madness Foretold**
Short stories, © 2012

ONE LAST DREAM
Screenplay (Registered with the American Writers' Guild), © 2012

UN DERNIER RÊVE
Screenplay (French-language version), © 2012.

CONTENTS

ix FOREWORD

x PROLOGUE

xii THIS I BELIEVE

1 PART ONE -- THE SOURCE
The seminal years

227 PART TWO -- MIDSTREAM
Against the current

293 PART THREE -- THE ESTUARY
Muddy waters

407 PART FOUR -- THE OPEN SEA
In hindsight

465 PART FIVE -- TREADING WATER
Onward to the past

475 POSTSCRIPT -- THE NAME OF THE GAME
Learn your lines

479 ACKNOWLEDGEMENTS

WHEN THERE'S DOUBT THERE'S HOPE

DON'T BELIEVE ANYTHING UNTIL ITS' BEEN OFFICIALLY DENIED
John Pilger

FOREWORD

By Alan Riding, author of
And The Show Went On: Cultural Life in Nazi-Occupied Paris

W. E. Gutman's life has been so crammed with twists-and-turns -- some unwelcome, many unexpected, a few stubbornly pursued -- that his moving and lyrical memoir has the punch of an epic novel, both fast-paced and reflective. Driven successively by a need to survive occupied France, by an intense curiosity, by an instinct for rebellion and a taste for adventure, Gutman has collided all too often with the shortcomings of humanity. But in *A Paler Shade of Red*, he finds solace in the power of words, free at last to display the idealism that explains his simmering fury with the world.

PROLOGUE

Say what you will but not all rivers run to the sea. Only those whose beds are deep and wide, whose waters swell with winter snows and summer rains will ever stream unhindered into Mother Sea's embrace. Nor do the fountainheads from which they spring share common beginnings. Some come to life in silent majesty where ice-encrusted granite reaches for the sky. Others dribble out of a mossy cleft or scatter from a rocky crevice like strands of quicksilver. Brook, rivulet and creek merge at random. Tributaries join the headlong race and carve mighty waterways. They will all return to the source one day, transmuted by nature's alchemy, ready for yet another cycle of endless self-renewal.

Some would-be rivers are stunted at birth. Their channels lack depth or vigor. Others bubble and billow for a while then vanish, never to be seen again. Exhausted, disheartened, others yet die of thirst along the way on some arid plain. A few meander without cause. They don't seem to know where they're headed, or why. They just obey their own life force, rushing heedlessly toward an estuary and surrendering at last to the rapture of the deep.

•

You are about to embark on a journey brimming with reminiscences. Reflected in its paces is the deepest dimension of self. Revelation is the fruit of foreknowledge. It entails a sense of *déjà vu*. It also evokes an anticipatory awareness of life's looming exactions. Yet, all is serendipity, the result of some casual chain reaction, an intertwining of haphazard events. The trick is to seize the moment. Time recedes, never to be replenished. Life is an adventure. To revel in its actuality, to love it as we wince from the low blows it delivers along the way, is to exalt it.

For all its expectations, this narrative is little more than a sketch. Spanning seven decades, many of its basic pen strokes rely on memory -- dimmer as I rummage through the distant past, clearer as powers of recall increase with the vividness of more recent events. Likewise, long periods of self-inquiry have yielded a few mismatched but pertinent fragments. Some events, too faint to recollect with any certainty, may be inadvertently out of sequence; I strove toward spontaneity, not the rigors of linear history. Others, as relates to some aspects of my work, especially in Central America, were deliberately reversed or transposed to cover compromising tracks or protect valued sources. Lastly, too painful to relive, even vicariously, too personal for public consumption or too fragmentary, some details were synopsized or ultimately excised from an over-exuberant first draft. Whenever possible, I've endeavored to reconstruct events, recapture feelings and echo dialogues long since blunted by time. Legitimized by indelible recollections, notes, faded photographs, family anecdotes, yellowed documents and recorded history, this narrative also relies on insights and perspectives apprehended long after the fact. They are laid bare without pedantry or false modesty. I vouch for their candor. I offer no apology should they lack wisdom, civility or virtue.

THIS I BELIEVE

"*Solitude knocks at the door only when invited,*" my grandmother used to say. She suffered neither fool nor whiner gladly. My uncle, a hopeless romantic, asserted that *"flirting is a science; loving is an art."* An aunt, a notorious adulteress, justified her innumerable trysts by pleading that *"never to lie, never to deceive is a feat only an imbecile can perform."* My father, a country doctor who lacked a scintilla of entrepreneurial spirit, warned that *"the transaction that brings the highest dividends is the one not yet concluded."* My maternal grandfather, an electrical engineer and amateur humorist, liked to say that *"intelligence is a battery that can be recharged only when plugged into someone else's intelligence."* And, shortly before she died, in a moment of agonizing self-awareness, his daughter -- my mother -- whispered, *"To live with death in one's soul is to die alive."*

For all their pithiness, poignancy or devilish wit, aphorisms evoke what is already there in the glaring light of day. It's the hyperbolic nature of subjective truth that transforms perceived reality into a grotesque parody of itself. But the essential lessons they convey, even metaphorically, speak volumes about those who coined them, about their lives and times, about the hopes, joys and sorrows that inspired them. More profoundly, what emerges from their confluent parts is the culture of cynicism, circumspection and stoicism that favored their survival.

Crafted over the generations by members of my clan, countless aphorisms were already common currency when I was a boy. They may have influenced the man I would become:

Avoid the arbitration of those who call themselves "neutral."

Man discards the debris of his subconscious by dreaming.

Society jettisons the detritus of its conscience
by eliminating dreamers.

Only fools think they're always right.

One tolerates more readily the meanness of an idiot than the stupidity of a cruel man.

Society censures abortion not because it robs it of a genius or a virtuoso, but because it deprives the state of a taxpayer and the church of a hostage.

Money is like fire. It can warm your feet or burn your socks.

A political slogan is tripe in pill form that only imbeciles swallow whole.

Never honest with itself, history unfolds while historians deform it.

One starts out being a portrait; one ends up being a caricature.

Men are by nature ungovernable, which is why they clamor for laws they're unfit to obey.

When politicians keep pointing fingers at each other, it's the voters who eventually give them the finger.

The pernicious spirit of religion is that it considers temptation as much of a sin as the misdeed it invites.

To appreciate exile one must have endured the indignities of the regime that inflicted it.

Eat today if you hope to be hungry tomorrow.

Beware of those who haven't yet betrayed you.

Always get even in advance.

If you can't afford a hired killer, try blasphemy.

Words have the right to be, even if they sting.

To be credible, journalism can't afford to be harmless.

PART ONE
THE SOURCE

The seminal years

FUTURE PERFECT

Proverbs and aphorisms and in-your-face wisecracks are the legacy of the Jewish people. We wouldn't know how to ride the stormy swells of life or countenance calamity without invoking some quaint saying that warms the soul, or chases away the blues or restores faith in divine providence:

Life is the greatest of all bargains; we get it for nothing.

The clever repartee that lifts the spirit --

Live; you can always hang yourself later.

The age-old counsel that warns against rumor-mongering --

What your eyes don't see, don't invent with your mouth.

The sarcasm that demolishes absurd assumptions --

If my grandmother had testicles, she'd be my grandfather.

The sardonic rejoinder to airs of mawkish nostalgia --

If you want to talk about the good old days, wait a while.

The subversive one-liner that encapsulates and concretizes the Jewish ethos --

To be Jewish is not a circumstance; it's a state of mind.

Jews are by nature restive, skeptical. Encrypted in the Jewish psyche, the greater truths and lesser lights our Biblical heroes bequeathed are course-plotting aids, not endpoints. We recognize their fallibility.

Adrift on a sea of perplexity, we don't follow them without engaging in endless soul-searching or endless debate. It's our nature to spin then reject hermetic concepts. We are, therefore we doubt. Everything is relative, unfinished, highly debatable, often contentious. We owe this paradox both our longevity and our vulnerability. Reality is a many-sided gem. It's impossible to glimpse all the facets without being blinded in the process. To see *everything* is to see nothing. So we improvise.

There's a question to every answer.

The closer you get to the altar, the farther God retreats.

Sometimes, we switch from the declarative to the interrogative. When we respond to a question by asking another -- an acquired reflex -- what emerges is neither witticism nor affront, but the synthesis of a cardinal reality in which the sublime and the ridiculous come together and mate. It takes very little to create an alternate reality -- or to endow it with a seductive oddness.

One day, in Tel Aviv -- I was about twelve -- I asked a passerby for the time.

"Why do you care," he retorted and walked away. A few days later, as I rummaged in search of shoelaces at a Jerusalem bazaar, the merchant informed me with studied indifference that he'd run out but would be happy to sell me toothpaste. I could have demurred but I didn't. This sort of pluck, this archetypal chutzpah, would teach me, as my ancestors called their "pedagogics" -- two basic lessons:

Time swallows everything; then it swallows itself. To know the time is a nuisance. It does nothing to alter its course.

Without a trace of irreverence, malice or lunacy, wit is humorless.

I would seize the moment one day and get even. Call it atavism or chromosomes on speed. In 1956, shortly after I immigrated to

America, I enlisted in the U.S. Navy. The recruiter asked if I could swim.

"Why," I asked without a trace of irony, "don't you have ships?" I no longer wonder whether the recruiter had ever, even for a moment, envisaged the rib-splitting perspective of a fleet bereft of vessels.

"Why are you enlisting in the Navy?"

"So I don't have to swim across the Atlantic."

I know the martial soul of the military. It's a soul that asks itself few questions. Its optic reveals a grimness and narrowness of mind that forbids it to ponder abstractions or hypotheticals. My deadpan baiting would qualify me as an "agitator" in U.S. Navy files. I would later be branded a gadfly, a muckraker, a heretic, and worse.

RULES OF THE GAME

By the age of thirteen I could recite tens of dictums, epigrams and barbs. Their origin is lost in time. I imagine each had sprouted spontaneously in response to some stimulus or vexation, all the echo of the sardonic genius, the iconoclasm of my dynasty. Surely some go back centuries. Recast, amended and fine-tuned over the years, others exude a scent of faded modernity. I've since retouched and rejuvenated those that needed to harmonize with the vagaries of my era. I've added many more of my own:

ACQUAINTANCE (1): *Someone we know sufficiently well to borrow from but not well enough to lend to.*

ACQUAINTANCE (2): *Degree of friendship dismissed as insignificant if the subject is poor but described as intimate if he is rich or famous.*

ADMIRE: *To recognize oneself in the object of our infatuation.*

ALLIANCE: *In politics, the union of two crooks whose hands are so deeply buried in each-other's pockets that they're incapable of robbing a third.*

AMBITION: *The uncontrollable urge to be scorned by those who have none.*

BACK: *That part of a friend's anatomy we can admire when we're down and out.*

BEGGAR: *Someone who once relied on his friends.*

BIRTH: *The beginning of the end.*

BORDER: *In geopolitics, an artificial line between two regions that separates the imaginary rights of one from the fictitious claims of the other.*

BRAIN: *Organ that allows humans to pretend that they're capable of thought.*

BREASTS: *Milky ways.*

CLEAN CONSCIENCE: *Faulty memory.*

CANNON: *Instrument used to redraw borders.*

CONGRATULATE: *To cloak jealousy in garments of gallantry.*

CONVICTION: *Inflexible belief, generally absurd.*

COWARD: *Someone who thinks with his legs.*

CYNICISM: *To see things as they really are.*

DEMOCRACY: *Self-destructive political system that tolerates the existence of undemocratic institutions.*

DIGESTION: *The process that reminds us what we're really made of.*

DICTATOR: *Statesman who turns to despotism when anarchy threatens him.*

DIPLOMACY: *The art of lying on behalf of one's country.*

EGOTIST: *Someone who cares more about himself than about me.*

EXCUSE: *Ruse that paves the way for a future affront.*

FAILURE: *Virtual success.*

FAITH: *The illogical belief in the occurrence of the impossible.*

FELLOW MAN: *Mythical being we are ordered to love as ourselves and who does everything to make us disobey.*

FRIENDSHIP: *Invitation to ingratitude.*

FUTURE: *The refuge of optimists.*

GIFT: *Investment without guarantee of dividends.*

HOPE: *Antidote against reality.*

KILL: *To create an opening without naming a successor.*

LIFE: *Nightmare of the wide-awake.*

LOYALTY: *Virtue of those who have not yet been betrayed.*

NATIONALISM: *Flag-draped racism and xenophobia.*

NEUTRALITY: *Crime of indifference; aloofness further sullied by cowardice and opportunism.*

OPINION: *Second-hand conviction often modified according to need.*

OPPORTUNITY: *Prospect susceptible to disappointment.*

OPTIMISM: *Baseless faith in intangible results.*

ORPHAN: *Someone whose parents' death prevents him from being ungrateful.*

PATIENCE: *Waste of time.*

PATRIOTISM: (See NATIONALISM).

PEACE: *Brief intermission between wars.*

PESSIMIST: *Someone who is never disappointed.*

PHILOSOPHY: *Speculative art whose objective is to render all things simple complicated or incomprehensible.*

PLAN: *Method that leads to unintended consequences.*

POLITENESS: *Two-faced courtesy.*

PRAGMATISM: *Selfishness disguised as realism.*

PUBLICITY: *Mass-deception.*

RHINE: *Eau de Cologne.*

SOLITUDE: *In the best of company.*

SPECIALIST: *Amateur who knows almost everything about very little and nothing about the rest.*

TRUTH: *A lie we can believe in.*

USURY: *Crime of interest.*

WISDOM: *Form of intuition and circumspection that blossoms with age; the conscious but reluctant control of reckless instincts.*

NEVER FAR FROM THE TREE

I descend from a long line of mavericks, thinkers, would-be prophets, and utopians, each the originator of essential truths that their descendants would dutifully record and trumpet with oracular verve. A ham at the age of three or four, I'd memorized several ancestral precepts. I recited them at will when we had company. My parents beamed with pride. When a child doesn't quite understand adults, he apes them:

> *The young want to add wings to the chariot of time; the old want to remove its wheels.*
>
> *One is more often unjust through carelessness than bad faith.*
>
> *Life is absurd; only death is logical.*
>
> *Happy is he who doesn't take himself seriously.*
>
> *Politics is the art of exploiting events for the benefit of the dominant class while persuading the populace that they're profiting from their leaders' intrigues.*
>
> *When two people agree on anything, one of them is tired, in a hurry or confused.*

Coined by my father, two axioms would guide the rest of my days:

> *You were given life; now fashion yourself.*
>
> *When you talk about nothing, you say too much.*

•

I was eighteen when I landed in America, alone, with the fifty dollars my mother had sewn in the lining of my overcoat. The avatar of Babeuf, the 18th century French revolutionary agitator and journalist, would soon replace Sacha Guitry, the early 20th century playwright and ham actor of my childhood. The iron was hot; it was time to strike it.

•

My ancestors, natives of Spain, the Guzmán (a German surname they had the wisdom to modify once settled in Burgos), almost certainly also had the prudence to convert to Christianity -- a precaution they might not have taken a century earlier. Indeed, under the enlightened rule of King Alfonso X *"the Learned,"* Jews occupied positions of influence and privilege at the court. Alfonso surrounded himself with Jewish doctors, diplomats, scribes, astrologers, tax collectors and bankers. A major Jewish cultural and commercial center since the 11th century, Burgos had already suffered the defection of Solomon Halevy, later re-christened Paul of Burgos. In 1390, Halevy, the son of a rabbi, abjured Moses, kneeled before Christ, became bishop of Cartagena, then archbishop of Burgos, and spent the next forty-five years orchestrating savage pogroms against his fellow Jews. He dispossessed and exiled those he couldn't convert by force. Others paid with their lives. According to historian Jeremy Cohen, the century marked a disastrous abandonment of Augustinian tolerance and the onset of modern anti-Semitism.

Halevy had an able and zealous confederate, Vincent Ferrer, a Dominican friar venerated as a saint by the Catholic Church. Ferrer engineered the mass conversion of Jews, more often by questionable means. He made their lives so miserable that they surrendered their synagogues and "dedicated" them to the Church. One of his early converts was Solomon Halevy himself. Anti-Semitism spread in Spain under Ferrer who fomented violence in towns where Jews lived. He promulgated various anti-Jewish laws banning Jews from trading with Christians, prohibiting them from changing residence and, so they would stand out, from cutting their hair or trimming their beards. In 1391, he preached to mobs whose riots led to the transformation of the synagogue in Toledo into the Santa Maria la Blanca Church.

The defection of the Guzmán, a widespread practice among Jewish subjects of their "very Catholic" majesties, Ferdinand and Isabel, and despite the minor rewards and privileges it brought, would elicit -- posterity would claim -- our most memorable epigram:

Conversion is a despicable act of disloyalty only Jews are apt to commit.

Despite its cynicism and distinctive Guzmán cachet, this imputation may be apocryphal but it lingered for many years in popular lore. The accusation is also specious: Moors fared no better during and after the "Reconquista" and most were coerced to forsake Allah the Compassionate and genuflect before his cantankerous and vengeful Judeo-Christian twin. Halevy's more notorious copycats would include Spain's Grand Inquisitor, Tomás de Torquemada, the descendant of converted Jews. The apostasy of the late Cardinal Jean-Marie Lustiger (né Aaron), the archbishop of Paris from 1981 to 2005], would lend a certain legitimacy to the incendiary saying my ancestors devised and circulated well into the 20th century. Unlike the others, Lustiger, a vocal opponent of anti-Semitism who considered himself a Jew until the end of his life, evoked hesitant sympathy: "Poor man, he's misguided but not unlikable."

The Guzmán would expiate their impiety (and ditch the Castilian lisp) soon after their expulsion from Spain. They trekked to Worms, in Germany's Palatinate, dropped the *z* from their Iberian surname and restored the virile *t* of their forebears. The men regrew their beards and side curls, changed from doublets and hose to kaftans and fur hats, and the women took ritual baths, groused and gossiped, this time in Yiddish or Ladino.

Known in Medieval Hebrew as Vermayza, Worms was an important Jewish center whose origins go back to the 10th century. The first synagogue was erected in 1034. In 1096, 800 Jews were murdered by Crusaders and the local rabble. The Jewish Cemetery, dating back to the 11th century, is believed to be the oldest in Europe. The Rashi Synagogue, which dates back to 1175 and was lovingly rebuilt after its desecration on *Kristallnacht* in 1938, is the oldest in Germany. Worms today has a very small Jewish population and any semblance of an established Jewish community can only be found in the buildings of the Jewish Quarter which were renovated in the 1970s and 1980s and now serve as an outdoor museum.

In 2010 the synagogue was fire-bombed. Eight corners of the edifice were set ablaze and a Molotov cocktail was tossed through a window for good measure.

Some say that if you scratch your family tree you'll find strands of Jewish DNA in the bark, the sap, the leaves, the fruits. And if you dare dig down to the roots, you might discover generations of scorned Maranos (Jewish converts to Christianity) or, earlier yet, reviled Khazars (converts to Judaism). We're very popular that way.

•

Soon enough, wanderlust still coursing through their veins, my clan pulled up stakes and set out for Poland, Ukraine, Russia and Romania where my parents were born. It's in Romania, where I spent four years as a child that I discovered the mind-bending quirkiness of paradox. I would long revel in its incendiary potential.

Cynicism is honesty with a grudge.

A circle fancies itself sexier than a square; a trapezoid thinks it's nimbler than a triangle.

An upright mind, like vertical surfaces, gathers less dust.

Common sense is more Cartesian than logic -- and less corruptible.

Memorizing incongruities and reciting them as Allied bombs rained on Bucharest and, later, as Fascist Romania turned overnight into a communist state would prove useful to the boy of seven I was at the time.

•

I often imagine my ancestors gathered around a large table festooned with plates of sliced stuffed derma and sizzling *latkes,* saucers brimming with *gefilte fish*, *kishka* and vine leaves filled with rice, large platters of fried *mamaliga* squares daubed with sour cream and sprinkled with goat cheese, and tureens overflowing with piping hot *cholent,* an indescribable but savory mishmash of potatoes, barley, beans, carrots, garlic, mushrooms and fried onions. They are no doubt downing fermented cider, schnapps and plum brandy. At Purim, they scoff *hammentashen,* bite-size raspberry, apricot, and prune tartlets shaped like the ears of the dastardly Persian vizier Haman, the appendages by which, so legend says, he was hanged to avenge his genocidal plot against the Jews.

Jews celebrate victory or flight from persecution by eating. They mourn catastrophe and death and expiate sin with a fast. Our history is filled with feasts, abstinence and famine. Every calamity is seen as divine retribution, God's payback for the debauchery and impiety of his people. No disaster, no torment, however inscrutable and cruel is deemed trivial because every event, every setback, every tragedy is the manifestation of Yahweh's will. Upheavals and grief and misery are tolerated, if not subconsciously foretold, precisely because they herald purification and redemption and are encoded by God himself. God has decreed that Jews may not defy their own destiny by repudiating Moses' legacy without unleashing upon themselves the fires of hell. This is why Jews, to this day, live in a state of controlled anxiety -- the Diaspora's assimilated ones subliminally, the new Canaanites with a sense of urgency and fatalism.

Some believe they can circumvent fate by calling it coincidence.

"When will it ever end?" I can hear my great-great-grandfather Abraham asking rhetorically, readjusting his prayer shawl around his shoulders, his bright blue eyes fixed heavenward, his right fist hammering softly the left side of his chest, unaware that his grandson, his wife and several of their children would perish and become mere statistics in the nihilistic calculus of the Final Solution. No one has the heart to tell him. Or maybe he forgot. This form of self-induced amnesia spares men the trauma of storing up too much knowledge which, everyone knows, can render them mad. Everyone at the table looks quizzically at each other for a moment then continues to eat.

"Never," I reply, breaking several generations of leaden silence. "We're the *Chosen People*." My father, who catches the bitter irony of my words, smiles and pours himself another jigger of *Tsuica*. My mother looks at me, a grown man, as she always had, like a hen admiring her newly hatched chick. It's a look that had caused me great embarrassment as a boy but whose reassuring tenderness I would miss when she died, still young, of pancreatic cancer.

"Everything is convention," she had sighed, "except pain."

●

In *"All Rivers Run to the Sea,"* Elie Wiesel, a distant relative, wrote:

> *"Why is it that my town [Sighet] still enchants me so? Is it because in my memory it is entangled with my childhood? In all my novels it serves as background and vantage point. In my fantasy I still see myself in it."*

From all accounts, my father, also a native of Sighet, neither felt enchantment for his town, nor saw himself in it, in fantasy or otherwise. Sighet was the embodiment of a niggardly heredity, a childhood filled with misery and privation, an adolescence overflowing with unattainable dreams long surrendered by his own forefathers.

A shattered dream is like a broken vase; you can cement the pieces but you can never hide the fracture lines.

LIKE FATHER, LIKE SON

My great-great-grandfather, Abraham Gutman, was also born in Sighet, a small town in northern Transylvania, not far from the Hungarian border. His grandfather may have migrated from Poland or the Ukraine. Abraham's son Fabian, my father's grandfather, lost his mother when he was just a child. Thirty days after his wife's death, having complied with tradition by engaging in histrionic displays of mourning, lamentations, breast-beatings and tearful one-way dialogues with God, Abraham remarried. His new spouse, Rivka, a pretty, young orphan he'd been screwing when his wife wasn't looking, produced three children. Fabian was just a teen when he was apprenticed to a soap and candle factory many kilometers from home. He carried bitter memories of his childhood well into adulthood and once told my father, tears streaming from his eyes, of the indignities he suffered at the hands of his father's new wife. When he went home for brief visits he would be fed leftovers and forced to sleep in the attic in the stifling heat of summer or on bitter winter nights. His stepmother made him do degrading chores and took pleasure in humiliating him in front of her own children.

"Like his Biblical namesake, my father Abraham," Fabian claimed until the day he died of a heart attack in the arms of his mistress, "gave in to his wife's frivolity and meanness. He never intervened. I was not cast out into the desert, like Ishmael; I was abandoned in a barren field of desolation where love and tenderness did not grow."

Calumny or cry from the heart? The truth would turn out to be more sinister.

Memory may have holes, be short, sometimes even blocked. In the end it is always deformed.

•

Conscious of his heritage, painfully chained to his lot, my father would neither seek nor find comfort in the very device that gave Jews their identity, favored their survival -- religion. As a child he complied with its elaborate rituals and conformed to its stringent mandates, brutishly and without reaping the slightest spiritual gratification.

"I waited for the high holy days, not as re-affirmations of the Jewish ideal but in anticipation of a better meal."

Like other Jewish children, he'd worn *peyes* and attended C*heder*, the elementary Hebrew school where he was taught to read the Pentateuch and other sacred works -- a formality to which he submitted without eagerness or fervor out of filial piety, along with a hundred other daily conventions and obligations.

"Impoverished parents show love by providing food and clothing. Caresses, kisses and embraces are in very short supply, dispensed on rare occasions and with extreme parsimony. Impoverished children redeem themselves by obeying their parents and submitting to their lot with cheerful self-effacement. Suffering dilutes a child's capacity to love. I did what I was told to do. We all did. Conformity and measured indifference, I learned, will get a child through anything: boredom, endless chores, long hours of rote study, not enough sleep, even the nagging urge to turn tail and run as far as your legs will take you."

"Did you ever run away," I asked.

Absconding would have been out of character for my father, an inconceivable act of betrayal against his parents and siblings. They needed each other "the way parasites need their host." Each fed on an enormous well of collective emotion when his or her own was depleted. It was his family's sole defense against the vast and incomprehensible universe that stretched beyond the walls of their little town.

"No," he sighed. "But I thought about it with nagging frequency. I dreamed of places I'd only read about. Late at night, in the glow of a small kerosene lamp, I thumbed through picture books, fascinated, lusting for the wonders that unfolded with every page: Budapest, Vienna, Rome, Paris, New York. I longed to be delivered from the stifling sameness of my life. I would eventually earn my independence by getting an education. It was one hell of a long shortcut to nowhere."

"What do you mean by 'nowhere'?"

My father looked away.

"It's hard to explain. I don't know if you'd understand."

I understood perhaps better than he could ever imagine, with a keenness and sensitivity only heredity, empathy and similarity of circumstance can inspire. *Like father, like son.* I too had taken shortcuts. Some led straight to a precipice. Unlike my father, I'd defied reason and sidestepped convention, veering away from a course I knew I was not qualified to navigate. Fearing failure, I'd circumvented well-trodden lanes and cut my own footpaths. (I often boasted that I thrived on adventure when, in fact, it was a fear of commitment or a lack of faith in the constancy of my own objectives that catapulted me from one castle-building venture to another). Insufficiently schooled, ill-suited for commerce, undisciplined and ferociously eclectic, I would drift into journalism less by conscious choice than a happy confluence of wishful thinking and naiveté, youthful immodesty and self-created opportunities. Necessity, in my case, *was* the mother of invention. I enjoyed writing -- no, I liked to test the limits of forbearance, to indict, to bait. I was seduced by controversy, polemics, and I would invent myself bit by bit: part-chronicler, part agitator. The pleasure I derived from telling inconvenient truths surpassed any possible urge to inform or enlighten. I treated facts as props, words as projectiles; I relied on the mood they're apt to convey. I am and have always been a good visualizer and words evoke strong images. I used surreal colors. I savored the vibes they were meant to provoke. It was the disquiet or indignation that my essays might elicit that found me pen in hand. I cared little for the Fourth Estate or the public it serves. I had one objective: to cause unease and discomfiture, to unnerve, to remind the gullible and the smug that the emperor was still naked, and to parade the son of a bitch bare-assed and trembling in his imaginary brocades and gold-embroidered silk robes for all to see.

To be credible, journalism can't afford to be harmless.

One day I wrote a tract in which I examined the link between political conservatism and the spirited patronage the death penalty seems to gain in times of recession and popular discontent. I suggested that no one likes to squeeze through the narrow door of austerity -- especially the rich. I added that the fans of capital punishment surely harbor in their soul of souls the terrifying fear that they themselves might be murderers. I called capitalism a dogma that sacrifices the masses at the altar of personal profit -- I called it a form of legal cannibalism. These convictions, which I continue to embrace, did not prevent me from describing "communism" as a doctrine that recruits the maladjusted and the malcontent and sacrifices them at the altar of the Party.

"How else do you awaken a dormant conscience," I once fired back at an editor, "if not by prying eyes open and dousing them with acid? If man does not peer into the heart of darkness, if he refuses to confront evil and crush it, why should God?" The editor had responded by tearing up my essay. This would not be the last affirmation that "freedom of the press" belongs to those who own the presses.

Later, in my novels, I would tell truths that only fiction can safely exhume and ventilate. I would continue to pay dearly for indulging this vice: it cost me jobs and friendships, it pissed off some of my relatives and earned me warnings and threats. But I remained habituated, less for the fleeting high it produced than out of regard for all the unpopular causes I had espoused, some out of conviction, others out of spite. I was also fearful of losing the modest notoriety I had worked so hard to achieve. I was getting published. At last, I had a byline, an audience. Protecting such ego-boosting assets would exact an effort all out of proportion with the satisfaction they produced. Instead of catering to my craft, I was now busy feeding an insatiable momentum of self-renewal-by-retaliation. No sooner had one of my columns created the desired effect -- shock, indignation or sheer horror at the medley of human miseries I chronicled -- than I would fire off a riposte. I took no prisoners. Eventually, a youthful fantasy -- a Faustian pact -- would shackle a once happy dilettante to a tiresome reflex. Having to earn a living at a hobby, in my case, would eventually spoil the fun. But I kept going just to see how far it would get me. I lay down my arms when age, decrepitude and nausea toward society turned the agent provocateur into an exhausted hermit.

•

Ironically, an education had delivered my father into another kind of servitude, one that would call for an even greater degree of devotion and submission than the disciplines endured in his childhood's confining theocratic milieu. Proud, principled, mindful of his reputation, he would spend the rest of his life obeying the Hippocratic Oath. He was indeed an excellent physician. He would have been an excellent astronomer, tailor or blacksmith if that's what he'd aimed to be. An unwavering sense of duty would have given dignity and worth to any task he undertook. He would have worked long and hard to refine needed skills. He would have peered into the blackness of space until his eyes gave out, crafted the smartest apparel, fashioned the finest horseshoes until exhaustion had weakened his grip. But I know of no occupation that could have filled him with lasting satisfaction. Medicine did not. The career that was to free him from the bonds of destitution would become an encumbrance, a liability and a moral constraint he would scrupulously endure for more than fifty years. When my mother died of pancreatic cancer in 1973, my father exclaimed, "Fuck medicine" and retired. Uttered with equal doses of despair and relief, the expletive epitomized his frustration at the frailty of life and the maddening inexactitude of medical science. It also summed up the emotional toll daily issues of life and death had claimed on a restless man convinced of the futility of existence.

"Humanity is an absurd happenstance and a calamity. If Sisyphus weren't so busy rolling his rock up the hill he'd be laughing his head off at us. But wait, he *is* us."

A lifetime of empathy, repaid with indifference or unkindness, had found him exhausted, depleted. Caring too deeply, he'd discovered, can bruise the heart and harden the soul. The "long shortcut to nowhere" had turned him inside out and left him empty and vulnerable.

•

Unlike Wiesel, my father invested neither pride nor mysticism in his origins. He first toyed with the idea that Jews may have been predestined to martyrdom. He quickly rejected that notion and concluded that suffering is universal and indiscriminate, and begins at birth for both man and beast. Although he would never think of himself as anything but a Jew, his Jewishness was circumstantial, utterly devoid of affectation; it lacked the visceral transcendentalism his father and grandfather had attached to their faith.

An ant doesn't wonder why it isn't a butterfly.

"I didn't ask why I'm a Jew. I still don't. It would be 'un-Jewish' of me to ask such an absurd question. I am what I've created. My whole is larger than the sum total of my hereditary parts."

It was this repudiation of an unalterable fate, of a fixed and inevitable future -- bolstered by his view of the world as a godless and irrational affair of ceaseless striving and affliction -- that led my father to shake the last congenital remnants of religiosity. He would also abjure the Kabbalah, in which he had dabbled in his youth. Like his father before him, he'd spent countless hours "meandering in stupefied fascination" through its cerebral minefields. Ultimately, it was the Kabbalah's hyper-deterministic character that prompted my father to dismiss this, the most arcane of all Jewish mystical systems as "a disquieting pastime for the idle, borderline monomaniacs or candidates for lunacy." The Kabbalah, he would conclude, not only trivializes human hopes, knowledge, dreams and the legitimacy of voluntary action or inaction, it effectively discourages rational and deliberate action of any kind. Any system that pledges to temper human perplexities and lead to enlightenment through occultism, he held, delivers false hope and culminates in disillusionment.

"A real man doesn't submit to his maker's caprices. He takes risks; he defies them." In this bitter admonition I recognized both a veiled rebuke of his own father, a theosophist who fought boredom and sought refuge from his own inadequacies in the Kabbalah's vaporous realm, and a warning to his only son -- me -- to stand tall and yield to no one.

•

Suspended midway between waning faith and waxing reason, an old friend, a Southern Christian, had once wistfully mused that "people seem to need religion. Who knows, society might collapse without it."

Coming to his senses, he'd quickly added, "Of course, the more hocus-pocus and melodrama religion delivers, the more persuasive its canons become."

Yes, I reckoned. The grand spectacle of religious rituals, the trance-like paroxysms of Hassidic worship, the necromantic melodrama of the Catholic Mass, the boisterous exuberance of "born-again" evangelical revivals, the numinous meditation of Muslim devotion -- all enthrall the faithful and they keep coming back for more. *Need* is often the product of habituation. Religion is a one-way dialectic, a maudlin soliloquy. Our incantations and histrionics are met with a stone-cold silence from which echoes, we are told, the sum total of all truths.

Religion punishes the present to expiate the future.

"Faith" is first infused in an unsullied psyche then reinforced through repetition, the discipline of fear and the expectation of otherworldly rewards. I doubt mankind would wander in a spiritual desert without God, but this was one assumption my friend was not quite ready to accept. He still believes in the existence of a "God molecule," an inbred predisposition woven into our DNA that makes us look heavenward not only for our roots but for our salvation. I would have gladly toyed with my friend's proposition were it not for the nagging fact that I and many people I know don't seem to possess the slenderest wisp of spirituality in our genes.

•

I was brought up in an ambiance utterly lacking religious affectations. An absence of casual or ritualistic spirituality at home did not create a void in my life and, as I tell anyone willing to listen, I found the concept of an omnipotent, unseen and ineffable, unknowable creator/judge/destroyer preposterous even as a child. Yes, I would embark on my own "mystical journey" and immerse myself in the study of Zen, the Tao, Tantric Buddhism, Hinduism, Shinto. Like my father before me, I'd spent countless hours *"meandering in stupefied fascination"* through the Kabbalah's cerebral minefields. The leaps of comprehension, not to mention the leaps of faith the Kabbalah demands, would leave me exhausted and confused. However enthralling, my excursions were inspired by a need to know, not a need to belong.

"I think, therefore I doubt," I'd exclaimed at last when I awoke from a blinding sleep and shed the last vestiges of forbearance for senseless beliefs. Nine-tenths of my family had perished in Hitler's gas chambers and the "inscrutability of God's designs," at best an offensive rationale, had since acquired the stench of a loathsome affront. I rejected the notion that man is born sullied by some "primal offense," that pain ennobles the soul and that sentient beings need to be ruled by an arbitrary system of faith-based values and protocols. In religion's imaginary goodness, I discovered not a path to enlightenment but an instrument of deceit and emotional enslavement. The transformation from fence-straddler to mutineer was gradual, filled with misgivings. At first, I found religion's mystique inscrutable. I'd meandered through its occluded allegories and bizarre canons like an explorer in a strange, uncharted wasteland. I'd glimpsed the very faint light that religion claims to shed but found only vast and gloomy shadows. It is in the shadows that my senses, now accustomed to the darkness, caught sight of a glow, a radiant luminosity that rinsed my pupils free of the gritty debris of credulity. I now understood that blind faith, not truth; prejudice and fear, not common sense, threaten humankind and condemn it to bondage.

Like others before me, I'd absent-mindedly tolerated sundry propositions and viewpoints along the way, some of which I even peddled, parrot-like, out of stupidity or intellectual sloth, not for the intrinsic virtues with which they were ostensibly endowed.

Assembly-line rearing, fashionable in the days of my youth, had instilled a value system that seemed strange if not utterly without merit. I'd been coached by otherwise doting parents to defer to authority with robot-like reverence. Be polite; do not innovate. Honor your elders. Respect your teachers. Salute your superiors. Obey the boss. Comply with the mandates of the public order. In short, I was to idolize or at least yield to all species of adults of dubious pedigree who had by now forgotten what it feels like to look at a very menacing world from three feet off the ground.

In school, I'd been programmed by coldhearted masters to smile or fight back the tears, to subdue, sometimes to smother very raw feelings under the pretext that such perfunctory bearing is what society expects of a good little boy and later, of a *mensch*. Precocious and sly, I knew I was not and could never be a good little boy. Nor did I aspire to *menschhood*, a status not clearly defined or imagined at the time. But I understood that pretending to do what others anticipate -- feigning religion, simulating approval of orthodox concepts, conforming to time-honored trends -- can bring on small rewards or, at the very least, shield one from censure, reprimand or retribution -- all of which I eventually incurred when I tired of pretending and transitioned at last from conciliation and irresolution to open defiance.

Later, as my peripheral vision improved and my depth perception sharpened, I began to ask questions: Why are we susceptible to pain and defenseless against the fury of disasters -- natural and manmade -- that, religion insists, are wrought against us "for mysterious reasons" by some fickle supernatural force? Who is this "maker" who inflicts (or tolerates) atrocities for "the good that comes from them"? What cunning and irreducible absolute orchestrates without apparent aim -- or turns a blind eye to -- the paroxysms that convulse his realm? What "intelligent designer" remains stone-silent while the sobs of his creation are never heard? What "ineffable" entity is this, whose ear is inattentive and whose breast is unfaithful to the throngs who call on him and seek his succor? What perverted despot decrees that his subjects will recite words not their own, that they will blindly obey the injunctions of self-anointed envoys, tremble at their threats and admonitions, mouth off supplications and jeremiads and parrot guilt-ridden prayers of indebtedness and veneration, all repeated *ad nauseum*, day after day, to a God who never shows his face, never bares his heart, never sheds a tear, never says he's sorry, a God who grants life and, with it, the fear of death?

The questions, mulled over when I was still very young, were in fact declaratory statements conjugated in the interrogative. This I believe: at best, religion is divisive, repressive, irrational and detrimental to the pursuit of harmony among men. It belongs, if at all, in houses of worship or at home. It has no place in the bedroom, schools and government, much less in the crafting of a national psyche or the shaping of policy. At its worst, it's a form of psychosis.

Karl Marx was right. *"Religion is the opiate of the people."* But unlike opium, which surrenders users to a state of blissful lethargy, religion inflames passions and brings the worst in man. The sectarian hatreds and paroxysms of ferocious religiosity that convulse the planet epitomize religion's toxic character. Eventually, I would conclude that "God" is a useless and costly hypothesis with which I could dispense. And crypto-agnosticism turned into overt atheism.

Atheists don't wage wars to protect their right not to believe. There may come a time when they must.

•

Late in life, overwhelmed and bewildered by the Kabbalah's abstruseness, repelled by "the effeminacy of mysticism," my father sought succor and guidance from the "undeviating honesty of realism." In time, he would also turn away from the rich Yiddish literature he had savored in his youth, describing it as "insular, ethnocentric and self-absorbed." Told and retold, Hassidic tales, with their subtle masochism, their sly subordination to divine will and fatalism toward human evil, seemed to magnify and reaffirm the Jewish *"shtettel"* [small-town] mentality he had fought so hard to escape. He would continue to read the Bible, however, until the end of his life. Far from seeking comfort, he was looking to discredit hallowed heroes -- Abraham, David and Joshua (he called them "thugs"), to challenge cherished convictions by pointing to the recorded lies, the betrayals, the greed, the violence, the cruelty, the bestial godlessness of man, the insufferable inhumanity of God. Proclaiming that all human actions and "godly edicts" are motivated by abject self-interest, he would find in the ancient texts the ammunition he needed to launch vitriolic attacks against the very lore that had suffused his childhood. Among his most contentious compositions was a stinging pastiche in which he lampooned the

Biblical Abraham for his lack of moral fiber -- "the man had no balls" -- and derided his wife, Sarah, for her conceit and heartlessness. He characterized their ingratitude toward their host, the Pharaoh, as "harlotry."

Having concluded that man is stimulated by instinct, selfishness and greed, and that "divine edicts" are "fantastical aberrations," he attacked the beliefs and traditions of his people. The piece was published in a Jewish periodical in New York, drawing instant fury from scores of readers.

Accused of heresy by fellow Jews, many of them fellow Sigheters, my father would find further evidence of human vanity and intolerance in their attitude, a revelation that inevitably engendered fresh assaults -- and earned him further scorn and alienation.

A short time before he died, reflecting on his own metamorphosis, no doubt troubled by mine, he counseled against reckless pursuits and glib conclusions.

Seeking the truth is not a spectator sport. Do it in private, alone with your conscience, shielded from partisan influences and purged of all acquired knowledge.

The truth he'd referred to was several orders of magnitude removed from mine. I can only imagine how painful it must have been for him to watch the comforting warmth of imparted beliefs irrevocably replaced by the chilling emptiness of reason. In the end, hollowed out, he had sought asylum in a vacuum that could never be filled. I must find comfort in the hope that he may have died at odds with the world but at peace with himself.

Thought cannot distance itself from its point of origin. The mind is incapable of self-scrutiny.

•

I come from a household where the word "God" was never uttered -- except as an exclamation -- and death or the hereafter had no place at the dinner-table, either in a mystical or existential context. I was never given a religious education, nor deprived of such, and the notion of an invisible, omnipotent creator/arbiter/destroyer seemed ludicrous to me even as a boy. By the time I was old enough to reflect on the enormity of my parents' suffering, especially during the German occupation of France, their indifference to religion had turned to embittered antagonism -- my father's early childhood religious upbringing and my mother's genteel, pseudo-assimilation into a Christian mainstream notwithstanding. Struck with pancreatic cancer, my mother had endured several months of martyrdom and died convinced that religion is a travesty and a fraud. Heartbroken, my father, a physician, grieved at the fragility of the human body and railed against the staggering imperfection of medical science. He spent the rest of his days in the company of a cantankerous cat mourning my mother and perusing and annotating the Bible -- the Old Testament (he considered the New Testament a preposterous fantasy, its final chapter, the Book of Revelation, the ghastly hallucinations of a psychopath) -- not to seek inspiration or comfort, but to vilify it, to find the contradictions and highlight the aberrations, to poke a wrathful finger at God's unfathomable cruelty, to denounce man's limitless taste for evil.

My father and I had often chatted long into the night about religion. We were not in pursuit of salvation; our tête-à-têtes were simply exercises in pure reasoning. We agreed that the underpinnings of religion -- mysticism, the supernatural, the *credo quia absurdum* (I believe *BECAUSE* it is absurd), faith in an invisible entity, the rituals, the taboos, the hellish penalties -- had all been contrived to enslave man, not to free him. We acknowledged the outwardly chivalrous but simplistic precepts of the "Golden Rule," or Ethic of Reciprocity, present in Judaism, Christianity and Islam (but probably of more ancient Buddhist provenance) but pointed at man's inclination to ignore it, even violate it, in the name of Yahweh, Theo and Allah. We quoted from Hillel the Elder, the 1st century BCE rabbi who summed up the Torah with the command, *"What is hateful to you do not do to your neighbor."* We read Luke (6:31), which teaches, *"Treat others as you want them to treat you."* Last, we turned to the Koran's lofty counsel, *"No one of you is a believer until he desires for his brother that which he desires for himself."*

But "others," "neighbor" and "brother," we surmised, have a parochial meaning that, history has shown, signifies "those of *our* own kind -- *us*, not *them*."

This dichotomy would be astutely dissected two decades later by journalist Christiane Amanpour in CNN's *God's Warriors: The Clash Between Piety and Politics*. Rebroadcast several times since its first airing in August 2007, the three-part award-winning documentary offers a disturbing rendering of the three major religions' penchant for violence in the service of deity. It also lays bare their unceasing effort to manipulate civil society through indoctrination, intimidation, civil disobedience and, all else failing, swift, copious bloodshed.

Carried to its extremes, *God's Warriors* had shown, religion is a dangerous eccentricity that will render men insane. Only religious delirium could inspire a Muslim to plot the "honor killing" of his own daughter, or to bomb a disco filled with Jewish youths. Only mystical rapture could lead a self-styled Christian to murder doctors performing legal abortions. Only a Jewish zealot could violate the Torah, slaughter Muslims gathered in prayer in their mosque, torch cars on the Sabbath or assault members of a peaceful Gay Pride parade and threaten violence if the Jerusalem police chief allowed the pageant to proceed.

This is the bare face of religion, my father and I had concluded. This is how religion transforms men into zombies, societies into citadels of intolerance, incubators in which simmers the hatred of heretics -- those who, according to the Vatican, "hold different beliefs" or grant themselves the inalienable right to hold none. Within that conflict rests the unresolved tension between the command to "love one's enemies" and the equally strong injunction to reject and eradicate any alien or divergent dogma. In the final analysis, my father and I had reasoned, neither Jew, nor Christian or Muslim knows which of the two directives to follow at any given time. By attacking "heretics" as tools of Satan, religious fanatics seize the rhetorical high ground and shift the focus from embracing one's fellow man to the escapist option of waging war against an imaginary but prescriptive source of evil.

This catch 22 was the preeminent rationale for a succession of gruesome confrontations in which only Yahweh, Theo or Allah could triumph: the Crusades, the St. Bartholomew's Day massacre, the

Inquisition, the 30-Years War, the centuries-old strife in Northern Ireland, the Armenian and Jewish Holocausts, the Hutu-Tutsi reciprocal slaughter, the Hindu-Moslem-Sikh rivalries in India and Kashmir, the bloodbath in Sudan and the cyclic carnage between Shia and Sunni Muslims.

•

It was soon after my father's death -- I was 50, he was 83 -- troubled by his stormy apostasy and anxious to jettison some of my own dismissive preconceptions that I ventured for the first time in the Kabbalah's arcane realm. Enthralled and bewildered at first, often driven to mental exhaustion, I eventually tired of its multilayered circularity, contradictions and maddening esotericism. I was not being ushered into some liberating "beyond." Rather, I was being shoved and jostled and inveigled to probe the "nothingness" that dwells within. I found such mental pirouettes more taxing than I'd imagined. Faced with the imponderable -- the very essence of Kabbalah -- I bowed out, humbled by the magnificence of paradox. All in all, my brief but intense foray into Kabbalah was not in vain. Careful, measured readings yielded fresh insights on the magnitude of the Mosaic ideal and the depth of Jewish thought. I would later marvel at the influence it would have on the works of Pico Della Mirandola, Baruch Spinoza, Gottfried Leibniz, Emmanuel Swedenborg, Franz Kafka, Jorge Luis Borges, Walter Benjamin and Jacques Derrida. I would also discover that the root of Kabbalistic doctrine had been enunciated, much earlier and in considerably simpler language, in the Tao and other Buddhist teachings. No matter the originality of a concept -- *"There is nothing new under the sun"* (King Solomon; Ecclesiastes, 1.9) I must believe that I too was transformed, however imperceptibly, by the Kabbalah's awesome and wrenching cerebral exactions.

When the distinction between material reality and mysticism become muddled, faith loses its mythical pretenses and one quickly dispenses with God.

•

Imagination is not inventive; it only perceives the latency of an eventuality.

JOURNALIST OR GRAVEDIGGER?

It was a winter dawn heavy with clouds the color of pewter. Frost had formed overnight and patches of rime speckled the railing where I stood, an unknown emptiness now claiming a share of my jumbled emotions.

I'd awakened early and gone up on deck to see the Statue of Liberty, ready to weep with ritual if unfelt reverence, eager to surrender like a pilgrim at a holy shrine to its symbolism and physicality. But the androgynous, vacant-eyed stone-faced monolith had loomed across the bow; it had risen against the drab grayness of New York's concrete piers, fuming smokestacks and decaying wooden hangars, then receded on the port side.

To my dismay, the titan elicited none of the prescribed passions or susceptibilities. I found it stiff, almost intimidating: it lacked the stirring vigor or mythic grace I had envisioned. I'd often glimpsed its diminutive twins, one under the chestnut trees in the Jardin du Luxembourg where I played as a child, the other perched on a battlement overlooking the Seine. Both, I thought -- my sense of observation now in doubt -- exuded more charm, if not splendor, than the square-jawed icon with the sphinxlike gaze towering above New York Harbor.

"America! America!" cried out a man as he surveyed the unfolding scene. He was at my elbow by the railing. I'd not seen him draw near. His hands were clasped against his chest the way people hail a miracle or flinch before a great calamity, and he was shaking his head from side to side as if his eyes and his soul were not yet in sync. Gaunt, weather-beaten, a week-old ashen stubble adding age to his years, he seemed to be inhaling the colossal spectacle, the unimaginable enormity that is New York. Every pore, every crevice on his brow spoke of life endured, hopes deflected, fears surmounted and, now, it seemed, dreams fulfilled.

I would have given anything to know his exhilaration, to share in his feelings of redemption, to consecrate with tears of gratitude my own ascension to the Promised Land.

"Yes. America," I echoed without joy, startled and dismayed to find myself at its gates. Idealized and reinvented, perhaps as a hedge against its unfathomable essence, half lusted, half feared like a forbidden fruit, America had been but one of a thousand islands in a huge archipelago of youthful fantasies. Yesterday, in the unbroken vastness of the steel-blue sea, America had been the future. Yesterday, there was a tomorrow to anticipate, a reality as yet unconsummated among a stockpile of nebulous expectations. It was an indwelling, irreducible *now* that I faced as the colossus dissolved into a nether realm of vapor and shadows and ghostlike vessels heaving in the channel's inky waters.

The man grabbed my wrist and repeated, "America. Can it be? I've waited so long."

"Now look, sir," I wanted to tell the man, "it's adventure I seek, not sanctuary. Yes, I'm nomad, restless vagrant, drifter, a wandering Jew beguiled by locomotion, a gypsy craving new horizons, a vagabond enlivened not by landings but by ceaseless migrations, a wayfarer steering not toward the nearest port of call but chasing after the open sea on a journey without end. I'm all that, I grant you. Like my father before me, I roam, seeking both uniformity and self-regeneration through change, finding constancy and coherence in mutability, endlessly coveting a foretaste of the things only anticipation hint at. But I am no refugee, I tell you, no battered remnant of war, and I resent that I might be mistaken for one. Unhand me, please."

But I said nothing. I didn't have the heart. A youthful insolence still percolating in my veins, traumatized by the inexplicable reality in which I'd suddenly been drawn, I wanted to distance myself from this tempest-tossed wretched refuse who like millions, had reached the golden door of America's promise. I ambled instead to the starboard side, the overcoat my parents had purchased a fortnight earlier no match against the arctic chill. Manhattan's skyline rose before me, a monochrome carcass, unreal, like a theater backdrop, grotesque in its breadth and bulk, and rendered all the more forbidding as memories of Paris, my beloved Paris, submerged my mind's eye with tears. I blamed the wind. I didn't want the man to think that they were tears of relief or elation.

•

Montmartre. Frame by frame, I relive the moment: A cobbled courtyard. Madame Muche, the concierge, is there, ruddy-cheeked, feinting peevishness but susceptible to gallantry. A blue denim apron girds her opulent rotundity. She is mopping the portico's weather-worn stoop. A vague odor of fried onion wafts from her unshaven armpits.

"*Bonjour, Madame Muche.*"

"*Bonjour, jeune homme. Alors, l'école, ça va?*"

"*Tout va très bien, merci.* And how are things with you?"

"*Bof*, as you see, a million chores, little time, only ten fingers." Josephine Muche props the broom handle against a broad, sallow cleavage and shows me the palms of her hands. "Just look at them. Have you ever seen anything so pathetic?"

I mumble words of commiseration and offer her some chocolate. She blushes like a schoolgirl then scolds me softly.

"You shouldn't. I'm on a diet. My liver, you know." But she takes the offering and devours it all the same and the sugar triggers another burst of irascibility, this time aimed at her husband, Maurice, a burly, warmhearted Paris gendarme, who is pumping air in their six-year-old son Lucien's bicycle.

"Some people have it easy," Josephine demurs, raising her eyebrows. "He's off today. You'd think he'd use his big muscles, the lunkhead, and help a little.

"Pay her no heed, *mon petit*," rejoins Maurice, grinning. "It's pure theater. She should have been on stage, the woman. She's got enough talent for two, *n'est-ce-pas?*" Maurice spreads his arms, draws two semi-circles in the air and cups his enormous hairy hands on the downward curve as if to enfold an imaginary pair of buttocks. Mortified, Madame Muche bites her lower lip, peers over her glasses and shakes an outraged finger at her husband. But outrage gives way to amusement and she surrenders a good-natured smile.

"*Ah, les hommes!* Men. They're all the same."

Emboldened, Maurice aims the bicycle pump at his wife's behind.

"We can't let the air out of such talent, can we?"

Little Lucien squeals with delight.

"Do it, papa, do it."

His mother parries, raises the broom and threatens to hit her husband over the head.

"Now, now, *mon amour*." Maurice cowers with feigned terror. "Who loves his little Fifine? Her little Momo, *non*?" Madame Muche melts. They lay down their weapons and embrace. Monsieur Muche grabs Madame's generous posterior and declares with Gallic showmanship, "if that's not talent, I don't know what is...."

"Run for your life," Madame Muche exhorts. "This man is incorrigible. I'm liable to.... *Oh, la la!*"

I retreat, laughing, and scale four flights up a steep, creaking wooden stairway sagging from a century or more of clambering feet. Each narrow landing gives onto two small apartments with tiny rooms and eccentric plumbing. I'm embarked on a dizzying voyage up a spiral gullet resonating with discordant sounds and reeking with disparate exhalations, all vying for dominance. The fullness of their vitality haunts me still: I can smell Mademoiselle Vauclair's Friday fare -- cabbage soup, chicken gizzards and fried leeks. Madame Jabois' tremulous renditions of Mistinguett's classic, *Mon Homme*, later reprised by Fanny Brice in *My Man,* echo as she sloshes twice weekly in her Empire brass tub. Monsieur Vacheron's stentorian voice thunders like a summer storm as he barks at his eight-year-old daughter, Monique, over some petty infraction. Next door, Sylvie Lefèvre, unkindly favored by nature, stridently denies her husband's absurd accusations of infidelity with the butcher's errand-boy. Eugène Lefèvre knows his wife is incapable of disloyalty but morbid suspicion sharpens his libido and they eventually bury their sham conflict in furious and sonorous make-up sex.

Mornings bring the redolence of croissants, evenings the aroma of freshly baked baguettes. Radios hum in cacophonous unison, summarizing soccer scores, blasting the latest popular hits or reporting on some faraway conflict. I can hear the Golaud children repeating their verses in an exhausting drone as the garlic in Madame Morabito's *ailloli* and the commingling vapors of hearty wines and pungent beers waft and settle in mid-air.

In this olfactory and sonic Babel also lived Wanda, her presence foretold by the heavy perfume she wore -- Mitsouko by Guerlain -- and the lugubrious wails she emitted at odd hours of the day and night, compliments of a mercifully discreet assortment of suitors. She had an unpronounceable Polish name so everyone called her "La Vanda" or "*l'anglaise*," even though she hailed from Steubenville, Ohio, via Tangiers and other Byronic locales, all tested and abandoned in favor of Paris. Wanda was a tall, cadaverous middle-aged expatriate, the living caricature of many a castaway I would chance upon in Hamburg and Tegucigalpa, Marseilles and Port-of-Spain. Bedaubed with funereal make-up, she had an incurable American twang and a weakness for gin. I'd vainly tried to sharpen my English and often engaged her in conversation about Chicago and gangsters and cowboys and Indians and Hollywood and skyscrapers and the mighty Mississippi -- pretty much all I knew about America. But "*l'anglaise*" was either too drunk to contribute useful intelligence or she'd invariably insist on trading sex for the education I yearned. I never took her up on it. I'd often wandered what it might be like to fuck an American but a mixture of pity and revulsion made such commerce unlikely.

There are women one hungers for even after; others from whom one is sated well before.

Only the Bredoux brothers -- Bernard and Bertrand -- veterans of *La Grande Guerre*, never married and subsisting on their pensions, lived in unsettling silence amid the dissonance and ubiquitous effluvia. They were kind-hearted souls with gentle smiles and simple truths, not given to idle chatter but always ready to comfort or encourage. I could see them now, their tall, lanky frames bent by age, a vague mustiness exuding from their taupe-colored cardigans, as they read the papers by the window -- *France Soir* and old copies of *Le Petit Parisien*. They'd been generous with their baskets of green Normandy apples and steaming chestnuts. They'd offered me other gifts along the way -- a small plaster bust of Hector Berlioz, a tortoise shell cigarette case, a gold-tipped fountain-pen, an illustrated first edition of Jules Verne's Voyage to the Center of the Earth.

I'd objected politely but they'd insisted. "It'll be that much less to dust," they'd quipped, winking at each other. "You're doing us a favor, my boy." It was a hint that held, in its subtlety, the promise of some impending finality I did not have the maturity to decipher. I continued to do errands for them on rainy days or when the pain in their joints flared up. They never spoke about the Great War. I never asked. All wars, I surmised, possess a prosaic commonality, a tragic redundancy that makes explication quite useless. It is the mark of great soldiers never to reminisce. Bernard and Bertrand committed suicide, I later learned, when life, irrelevant and joyless, ceased to be worth living. They were found in bed, their medals and ribbons lying at the bottom of chamber pots in which they had dutifully -- and with studied scorn for the military establishment, La République and posterity -- taken their last shit. It was a scene straight out of Louis-Ferdinand Céline: blasphemy exalted by contempt.

Above the din and the scents, tucked away at the top of a narrow wooden corkscrew staircase, was home at last. It was in the nurturing silence of this sparsely furnished mansard that I withdrew after work and school. Delivered from the world below, I'd hasten to the dormer, part the chintz curtains and gape at my city the way a boy covets a woman. Under me were the streets. I could read in their cadence like from an open diary and I reveled in their pantomimes. In the distance, Paris spread like a tapestry of gilded domes, verdant parks, esplanades, and ancient spires, and I'd marvel at the loveliness, the grace, long after twilight had draped the city in a star-studded mantle of lilac and periwinkle blue.

I'd then turn to my books. In their pages, I explored the unrevealed nature of things, unearthing strange and wondrous emotions, toying with enticing abstractions. I wanted to conquer everything that is known and, if possible, to understand all that is unknowable. Such quest, I would discover, was as self-defeating as it was all-consuming. Alluring as they were, the voices behind the words (or was it the echo of my own ruminations?) invariably raised more questions than they answered. Curiosity is a long hallway filled with an infinite number of doors. Most never swing open, even at the loudest rap. I would settle on the notion that to *seek* knowledge is *to know*. In prospecting the unknown, I would also later concede, I was not so much interested in acquiring new insights (I was even less impressed with their utility or application) as in how they played on my imagination, how they kindled certain longings. Once digested, essential knowledge and fresh perspectives opened up a world into which I withdrew the better to savor the transcendent realms they evoked. I was intent at all cost, and with each newly apprehended truth, to let my subconscious roam free. Knowledge was in vain unless it had the capacity to stir, touch, shock or stupefy.

"The totality of all action culminates in knowledge…"
-- The Bhagavad-Gita

Surrealism, still in vogue in post-war Paris, played a pivotal role in this frenetic self-scrutiny. The eccentric cultural movement of the 1920s might have eluded me altogether had I not heard it panned as "intellectual snobbery" and "spiritual degeneracy," or dismissed as "a hoax perpetrated by petty artists bent on scandalizing the purist mainstream." Condemnation of an idea, much more than praise, tended to arouse my curiosity and, in some cases, earn my support.

Fierce criticism strengthens a cause more than high praise.

To have talent, imagination, or technique is not enough to be Arp, Dali, Duchamps, Ernst, Klee, Magritte, Miró, Picabia, Picasso or Tanguy. One must also have a grain of madness, daring and irreverence.

One embraces a cause to challenge the status quo; one discards it to challenges oneself.

Distracting society from its utilitarian yoke and reconciling irrationality with the rigors of conscious thought, a fundamental aim of Surrealism, found immediate favor with the wayward, nonconformist-in-training that I was becoming. The works I read, the avant-garde paintings, sculptures and musical compositions I discovered along the way, produced an immediate and lasting euphoria, and I eagerly surrendered to their spell. They still enchant me to this day.

It was Baudelaire, my mother's favorite poet -- and one of France's most revered literary icons -- who initiated me to Surrealism. Aroused, I would acquire an enduring appreciation for the genre. The formidable bard lavished not only the perfect harmony of his verse on a young, hungry mind; read with quasi-liturgical fervor, *Les Fleurs du Mal* also seemed to legitimize and vindicate my most visceral inclinations. Trusting neither man nor God, Baudelaire takes refuge in primordial chaos, in the flesh, in orgiastic sin. His verses crawl with monsters and freaks and pitiable *bas-monde* creatures all too reminiscent of ourselves. To set us at ease, to ensnare and disarm us perhaps, he strips himself to the bone in a poignant display of self-deprecation. Like Saint Sebastian, he flaunts the crimson gashes that score his naked breast, to arouse not pity but indignation. He then agitates our own demons, the ghouls that doze or stir within us, those we can never disavow. Shunned and lonely, the poet finds redemption in the anonymity of crowds, among beggars, cripples, harlots, drunkards. In sad or worn faces, he discovers traces of fathomless drama, in ephemeral smiles a twinkling of hope deferred. His is the voice of all who love unrequitedly, suffer inconsolably, savor rare joys with moving intensity and endure the sorrows, the longings and broken dreams that clutter the deepest regions of our being. Unloved, perhaps unlovable, he craves tenderness and quietude, longing for a faceless maiden to shine upon his winter years the golden warmth of an early autumn sky. He drowns his wrath and his agony in alcohol and hashish, and he dies, still waiting for that which he knows never comes.

If Rimbaud and Poe -- Baudelaire's contemporaries and partners-in-rhyme -- gave madness a lyrical hue, it was Cocteau, France's alchemical man, who urged me up the winding stairway of Surrealism, who shepherded me across its portals, and eased me into its strange and wondrous inner sanctum. Cocteau's fairy tales, opium-induced phantasms and hallucinatory incantations imparted unique life to ambiguity, purpose to paradox.

"I am a lie doomed to always tell the truth."

I gamboled and drowsed with Cocteau in fragrant fields of poppy only to awaken, sprinting in place in a relay race with myself. Forever seeking to jolt men out of their torpor as he himself prowls at the edges of delirium and paranoia, Cocteau's trails are strewn with mockery toward the zealot, scorn for the hypocrite and disdain for the uninspired, pity -- dark, raging, agonizing pity. I often set sail on the wings of his allegories, just to keep in shape. Every time I alit from these fantastic voyages I was reminded that rationality is no match for intuitiveness, that the imponderable can only be hinted at by appealing to the imagination, not common sense. No, Surrealists do not live in ivory towers, as their critics suggest. They take careful aim instead and, with mordant wit and disarming irreverence, topple them and scatter their sordid debris for all to see. With the dismal fragments of their own intolerance now strewn at their feet, victims of reality no longer recoil from it but acknowledge its ineffable absurdity. Once fathomed, Surrealism encourages its disciples to seek within themselves new dimensions, hidden planes of awareness. Surrealism is the language of free spirits, the idiom of free thought.

Disquieting as my enthusiasm for Surrealism might have seemed (I would exploit this perceived eccentricity to discomfit those who were vexed by it), and in spite of a growing interest in the abstruse, I was still very much a boy and, like all French boys, I read Alexandre Dumas. In the flip of a page I became D'Artagnan and Edmond Dantès and Cagliostro. I wooed fair maidens with chivalry and selfless devotion. I rode noble steeds in pursuit of miscreants. I fought desperate duels on the side of the just, against despots, scheming aristocrats, and perfidious clergy. I escaped from dungeons, eluded the gallows, exposed dastardly cabals, and restored the good and the worthy to their rightful stations.

Mark Twain's landscapes and perspectives evoked settings and locales of an America now long gone, of mores and prejudices that are not. Wanderlust and a craving for the hinterlands of exoticism would be further whetted by Joseph Conrad, James Fenimore Cooper, Jack London, Pierre Loti, Herman Melville, James Michener, Marco Polo, Robert Louis Stevenson and Jules Verne, among others.

Often, perhaps too often (some deemed such predisposition a "malignancy") I'd turn to Kafka, the conjurer, Kafka, "the supreme fabulist of modern man's cosmic predicament," for booster shots of spleen and cynicism, the serum that inures dreamers against groundless hope, idealists against pointless fancies. I meandered casually and without haste in his miasmic labyrinths, ready to lose my way, to become ensnared in his inscrutable plots, to merge into them. Kafka would bequeath a lifelong reflex and a healthy lack of forbearance for the meanness, the absurdity, the despotism of officialdom, the odious banality of bureaucracy, the effrontery and intolerance of the ignorant, the shallow intellect and miserly preoccupations of the petty bourgeois, the boorishness and vulgarity of the rabble, the sham majesty of the privileged.

Hardened by experience and an ebbing regard for all authority, this amalgam of aversions would be reinforced by Nietzsche's warnings against mindless dictates. What I chose to distill from his florid orations is that I was now obligated to dismember the tentacles of stupidity, dogma and prejudice (Maimonides called them "degenerate practices and senseless beliefs"). Oh, how I struggled with Nietzsche. But I read on and reread *Ecce Homo* and *Twilight of the Gods* and I dissected and agonized over every word, every twist of phrase, every last convoluted paragraph until his awesome genius erupted and lit up some heretofore dormant synapse inside my brain.

From Spinoza, my father's favorite philosopher (Henri Bergson came in a close second) I learned to reject doctrines that don't make room for speculation or doubt, to call a lie any truth that owes its sole existence to blind faith. Shackled to unbending creeds, afflicted with intellectual villainy, his contemporaries shunned and rebuked him. Excommunicated by Jews, vilified by Christians, he was a heretic and a rebel. His was an enviable malediction, I mused, and I remember vowing to emulate him in some way. It would take a more mature perusal of his work to recognize that I lacked both his formidable intellect and his couth. I would have to settle for a Spinozan willingness to invite hostility.

__Men struggle and fight. They're so busy fooling themselves so they might endure what is unbearable that they'd rather live with lies than truth. In attempting to rationalize mirages, they dupe others along the way.__

Voltaire, the freethinker whose moral code hinged on tolerance and generosity was also required reading at school. Hostile to all metaphysics, Voltaire warns against the perils of immoderation and groundless idealism with sardonic ferocity. A believer in natural religion, he condemns the social effects of "revealed" doctrine, calling it "pernicious," thus earning him the unwavering hostility of the Church. There can be no higher endorsement of one's relevance in a world of staggering hypocrisy, I thought, than to attract such antipathy. Convinced that it is more useful to be hated than ignored, I fantasized that my writings would one day be listed, along those of other irreligious libertines, in some Index of prohibited reading. Reserved for higher intellects than mine, such distinction would elude me. I would take comfort in the knowledge that a tight-lipped but all-knowing Big Brother was keeping me in its sights.

Orwell's view of freedom -- "the right to tell people what they *don't* want to know" appealed to me intuitively. But it was the stirring humanism of Hugo and Zola, their attention to the unlearned lessons of history, that steeled my resolve to "tell people," to startle the smug and the compliant, to challenge the established order, to prophesy chaos and decay as a hedge against their inevitability. Hugo and Zola, more than any others I knew, celebrated the enormous power of passionate, hard-hitting reporting, the poetry of polemic, the elegance of words honed to sing and sting and move men to great deeds, and occasionally drive them to infamy, shame and remorse. He whose only loyalty is to the truth, I would eventually learn, has very few friends. I would long revel in the vainglorious illusion that being friendless is a small price to pay for defending the truth -- smaller yet for exposing it. Alienation, jobs lost or denied, opportunities forfeited and, later, threats from some very irate readers, did little to tame the inner rage.

These hindrances only taught me to modulate the rhetoric, not to suppress it. As for "truth," I would quickly learn that it is the strongest and most persuasive of two conflicting doctrines, and that the urge by some to exhume it is habitually frustrated by the reflex of others to keep it entombed.

•

All my mentors were there at my beck and call, lovingly shelved in alphabetical order, ready to impart fresh insights, to titillate, amuse and exhort, astound and stir at every turn of the page. They kept me company when homework was done or postponed, or as I waited for the girls to climb to my old drafty garret. It was in the sagacity of books, in their wit and nonconformity that I trusted most. And it was in their company that I withdrew long after the girls had gone home and lust, for now appeased, yielded to more cerebral cravings and to the greater dividends of sleep, alone at last, in my very narrow bed.

•

I'd rearranged the room, pushing the bed against the skylight so I could look at my beautiful Paris, like from an aerie, while I made love to maidens with violet-scented lips, sprigs of *muguet* -- lily of the valley -- adorning their tangled tresses, as antimony clouds sailed across lavender skies.

Freckle-faced and deliciously depraved, sixteen-year-old Ginette, the concierge's daughter, had taught me things only a freshly deflowered nymphet will dare. Free of shame or pretense, spurred by precocious carnality, she'd granted me every vice, indulged every caprice. We'd performed elaborate acrobatics to the accompaniment of Ravel's *Daphnis et Chloe*, contriving to climax simultaneously as the Bacchanale's joyous tumult rose to a rapturous crescendo. Blissfully exhausted, we'd then settle back against a large down pillow and read from Apollinaire's erotic novellas, *The Adventures of a Young Rakehell* and *The Debauched Hospodar*, parodies of the sizzling French novels circulated in secret in Victorian England. I'd borrowed the books from my godfather, Ernö, a distinguished anesthesiologist who routinely entertained fellow surgeons with his readings of kinky sex during major surgery. Ginette was particularly fond of the well-endowed

Romanian nobleman, Prince Mony Vibescu, whose insatiable urges had taken him from the Paris bordellos to the bath-houses of the Orient in a never-ending quest for the supreme orgasm. Aroused, we would start all over again.

Once a month or so, with Ginette gone for weekend visits to her *mémée* in Auvergne, it was a fellow student, Isabelle -- "la belle" -- blue-blooded and demure, the niece of a high-ranking member of the Chambre des Députés, who looked in on me. Refined, exuding a breeding found only in old money tirelessly replenished, Isabelle had deemed Ravel's ballet too long and so we'd settled for Debussy's ten-minute transcendental *Prélude à l'Après-Midi d'un Faune.* Ten minutes was all Isabelle could grant me anyway. My recitations of the most grotesque passages of De Sade's *Justine* and *Juliette,* followed by the gyrations and undulations I exacted as she rode astride me at the edge of the bed, often made her nauseous. She once vomited all over me. I never quite felt the same about her patrician little *derrière* after that. I continued to see her now and then because she came all the way from courtly Le Vésinet to the plebeian escarpments of Montmartre just to get laid, and such servility in a highborn, I felt, could only be rewarded with vile, crude fornication. Years later, driven by a similar incentive -- the promise (or the illusion) of great sex -- I found myself crossing the Mediterranean, the Atlantic and the breadth of the United States. It was then that I remembered Isabelle and that I mentally sought atonement for my cruelty. Inevitably, I also understood that the cost of such expeditions far, far exceeds the returns.

Sex gives us angel wings. Then it dumps us back to earth where, thank heaven, we can take a shower.

I eventually lost both Ginette and Isabelle, the result of an indiscretion with a third *p'tite amie,* Elyse, whom I'd picked up at a kiosk on Place Blanche as I rummaged for my favorite old comics, *Les Pieds Nickelés* and *Bibi Fricotin.*

Love creates and destroys liaisons by vocation and breaks hearts by whimsy.

Elyse liked the accordion. I did too, but over fish and chips and cold fermented cider in a cozy bistro at dusk on the banks of the Marne, not as an attendant to fucking. So we had each other in silence, lulled by the gentle rains and the cooing doves perched atop the gargoyles. Of humble birth, uninhibited like Ginette, Elyse gave her all, anytime, anywhere without the slightest affectation. She giggled a lot. I'd read Rimbaud and Verlaine, and she'd nestle her head on my shoulder like a kitten and she'd stray, her eyes fixed upon my moving lips, a moistened finger buried between her thighs, her thoughts drifting on the wings of the poets' magic incantations.

> *Elle jouait avec sa chatte*
> *Et c'était merveille de voir*
> *La main blanche et la blanche patte*
> *S'ébattre dans l'ombre du soir....*

> She played with her cat [pussy]
> And it was marvelous to see
> A white hand and a paw of white
> Frolic in twilight's shadows....

There'd been others. Nothing was left of them now but the dim memory of their existence and, coalescing with New York harbor's fetid emanations, a paramnesiac whiff of *muguet* up my nose.

•

The ship came to rest in its Hudson River slip. I heard metal groaning against the pilings as the vessel tightened its moorings. In its emerging actuality, New York towered overhead, the vague manifestation of childish musings, baseless fantasies, two-dimensional Hollywood renderings of America and, from hereon in, the junction of a lifelong exile in a realm as strange and ill-fitting as an oversized garment into which I sensed I could never fully grow.

A flight of hungry gulls, their air-worthiness challenged by invisible gusts, swooped across the stern and disappeared. I looked at the behemoth metropolis spread out before me and I asked myself what in hell was I doing here. My first impulse was to remain on board, to run down to the lowest deck, to hide in the bilges if need be, and sail back across the Atlantic straight into my parents' arms. I was cold and confused. I remember shivering long and hard as if seized by high fever. For the first time, I thought of suicide. I was eighteen.

●

Two years earlier. "Ladies and gentlemen," the chancellor of the Paris School of Journalism had intoned with studied self-importance. "We're here to teach you many things. Journalism isn't one of them. Instead...."

I remember staring absent-mindedly at the vaulted ceiling imagining smiling bare-buttocked cherubs hovering over an outdoor feast attended by corpulent dryads as virile centaurs, cupidity burning in their eyes, hid behind the thicket. I'd felt the first stirrings of an erection but the solemnity of the occasion and tight-fitting pants had quickly humbled my ardor.

Across the street, in the golden luster of early fall, marked by time and history, the 11th century Eglise Saint-Germain-des-Prés stood proud in its austere architectural simplicity. On the sidewalk, jugglers, balladeers and poets, quick-sketch artists and musicians, sought in the goodwill of passersby a chance for recognition, perhaps fame. Around the corner, patrons at Les Deux Magots sipped hot fragrant espressos in thimble-sized cups and cool pale white wines in fluted glasses. In their chairs had once sat Ernest Hemingway and Pablo Picasso, Samuel Becket and F. Scott Fitzgerald, Aldous Huxley and James Baldwin, Jean-Paul Sartre and Simone de Beauvoir, to name a few. Paris had beckoned, seduced them all.

The chancellor's booming voice put an end to my reverie.

"... Instead, you'll dissect history, chew on political science, ruminate on sociology, and choke on economics. You'll learn how to conduct interviews, wrest information from recalcitrant witnesses, resist subjectivity, suppress personal biases and dominate sentences by luxuriating in as few words as possible. We'll send you on assignments -- the *Grands Boulevards,* the narrow alleys, museums and theaters, marketplaces, railway terminals, brothels, jails and morgues. If you lack basic writing skills, you're in the wrong building. Nor can we stoke let alone ignite that sacred pyre that must consume you from within. Make no mistake: journalism is no less a calling than soldiering, doctoring or the priesthood. If the Muses beckon, we can help you seduce them. We can't sell you inspiration, at any price. Nor can we instill the greatest of all virtues -- an unyielding respect for truth and the dogged determination to unearth it wherever it may hide. The truth is a loathsome and elusive beast. Like a scorpion, it burrows and flattens itself under a rock. Your job will be to lift that rock and expose the hideous creature. Speaking of which, the Bursar's office is on your left at the end of the hall. Look for Proudhon's bust. For those of you who never heard of Proudhon, he was one of the principal socialist theoreticians of the nineteenth century. It is he who declared, *'ownership is theft.'* Good luck and good day."

There was no applause. We all sat motionless, struck by the chancellor's acerbic reception, a vague uneasiness slowly scaling up the collective spine of a dozen bright-eyed adolescents dreaming of clever scoops, scorching exposés and poignant editorials.

•

My father, a physician, had hoped I'd follow in his footsteps but shameful grades in math, physics and chemistry had mercifully and decisively dashed these paternal designs. My maternal uncle, a well-to-do criminal lawyer who defended men he knew deserved to be drawn-and-quartered, had urged me to pursue a legal career. His courtroom theatrics, the flourish of his sleeve work, the ostentation of his blackjack arguments against blameless plaintiffs -- his very assertion that the worst scoundrels are entitled to due process -- had seemed incongruous at the time and given me all the ammunition I needed to reject his counsel -- and profession. Years later he lovingly chided me and claimed that mine was the only "case" he'd ever lost.

"What sort of victory would you have wrested had I ignored my instincts, disobeyed my conscience and yielded to coercion," I asked. He smiled with avuncular pride and shook his head. "Like I said, you'd have made one helluva lawyer."

Standing numb and speechless in the atrium of the Paris School of

Journalism that balmy September morning, I found myself summoned before a hurriedly convened court of self-inquiry. The evidence was slim, the exhibits trivial. Fiery high school prose had earned me a number of prizes -- a book of poems by Alfred de Vigny; a selection from the Letters of Madame de Sévigné -- and the cautious admiration of my teachers. I'd excelled in literature, history and geography, but I'd flunked everything else. Stirred by charity, the principal had written impassioned letters of recommendation, but the School of Journalism had acted with circumspection and agreed to enroll me provisionally.

I paused for dramatic effect and shrugged my shoulders. "It's either that or grave digger," as my uncle had often warned. To my uncle, who had never defended a single honest, hard-working client in his entire career, and who feared death until it claimed him, being a grave digger was a ghoulish and contemptible occupation. Having one in the family would be calamitous. I would later concede that I'd grossly misjudged my uncle's metaphorical admonitions. Being a brilliant attorney and an intellectual did not prevent him from holding manual labor in the highest regard. But the oft-repeated warning had had the desired effect. I flipped a mental coin in the air. "Heads, journalism; tails...." What an odd piece, I remarked. No tails.

"So journalism it is. It'll be a living," I reasoned with greater incertitude than conviction.

A living? Barely. Journeymen reporters earn subsistence wages. They survive on raw energy, frayed nerves, half-digested fare of dubious origin, they spend sleepless nights and torpid days separating rumor from reality, insinuation from fact and they live, as two-time Pulitzer Prize winner Russell Baker once put it,

> "...in a world where time is forever running out. On their inner clock it's always two minutes to midnight and the work is only half done, maybe not even started yet, and they absolutely must have it ready for the printer before the bell tolls, whether they have anything to write or not. It's not a work that suits everybody. High blood pressure goes with the territory, alcohol is an occupational hazard, and anyone too proud to confess cheerfully to a steady

flow of errors and bad judgments will not be happy at it. When you're playing to a large public and there is no time for second thought you may as well get used to looking foolish. Error and misjudgment are your destiny."

Baker also shrewdly observed that *"reporters thrive on the world's misfortune. For this reason they often take an indecent pleasure in events that dismay the rest of humanity."*

I was hooked.

THE OTHER PARIS

Memory deceives; souvenirs betray: They repeat everything we tell them. Reminiscing is what sets the time machine in motion. And so the past burst through the floodgates of memory, begging to be stilled by the moving pen. Buried recollections, those that sloth or scruples might fossilize, are exhumed from a vast and untidy ossuary. The others, the ones that reside just beyond the threshold of awareness -- compromising overtones, erotic fantasies, old resentments, remorse and broken dreams -- are slowly being coaxed free. They are in tatters, so I pick them gingerly between thumb and forefinger the better to resurrect and survey ancient sounds and smells and images and feelings so subtle and so fleetingly perceived that they might be silhouetted but never fleshed out. Many are of doubtful authenticity, the bastardized offspring of fantasy, wishful thinking, transference. The rest are irretrievably lost or in hiding, cloistered in the company of useless mementos and unutterable confessions. The temptation to tell all is tempered by the wisdom to say nothing.... *My memory of tomorrow escapes me.* Everything is past. In its roots percolates the sap that feeds the future.

Some memories canter on wooden clogs, others amble on rubber soles. Memory is often threadbare, short and mulish. It's almost always deformed.

•

There once was another Paris, a microcosm from which radiated a larger universe beyond. The address: 2, rue du Pont Neuf. A large, cheerful apartment doubling as my father's medical office, with fin-de-siècle windows facing the Louvre on one side in the distance, in full view of the Palais de Justice, La Sainte Chapelle and Notre Dame's sublime profile on the other. Across the street, the festooned façade of La Samaritaine, the department store where, my parents often told me, I'd been purchased "at a rummage sale."

My birth, infinitely more prosaic, took place in a private clinic of the 16th *arrondissement* where chic ladies had their babies -- or aborted them -- depending on their whim. My godfather, Ernö, the anesthesiologist, and my father -- his cousin -- were both there to witness a delivery that elicited not a single joke. The procedure nearly killed my mother. A sickly, diminutive woman, she lived on to endure with quiet dignity the agonies of war, the sorrows of a discordant marriage and the affronts of chronic ill health. I would not have survived the trauma of parturition had it not been for the frantic thrashing I received at the hands of the attending obstetrician. It would be my first and last spanking.

A difficult pregnancy and a near-fatal delivery convinced my parents not to try again, at least for the time being. Discretion became the better part of valor when France, which had been cowering under the threat of war, finally fell to the German hordes. Ensuing events would vindicate my parents' decision.

●

On June 3, 1940, the Germans bombarded Paris, killing nearly 300 people and injuring more than 600. Two days earlier, the Wehrmacht had launched a lightning three-pronged attack; three Panzer divisions, 1,000 tanks each, headed for the cities of Amiens, Rouen and Dijon. On June 7, fearing another bombardment, French General Vuillemin ordered the evacuation of Paris. General Weygand, a hero of the First World War and supreme commander of the French armed forces, directed that children 16 and younger also be evacuated. The next day, ignoring the children, Weygand chose instead to remove the entire government, *"except for members of the cabinet, whose presence may be necessary."* This decree would later be likened to the cowardice of Roman senators as they groveled before the Barbarians and laid down their arms.

The mass migration began on the night of June 9 amid incredible confusion. The air ministry requisitioned 600 trucks to carry its staff, their families, furniture and personal belongings, whereas impassioned appeals for vehicles to transport the wounded away from the front fell on deaf ears and fleeing archivists let tons of documents fall into enemy hands. Thousands of retreating French infantrymen were booted out of Paris and rerouted toward the south, *on foot*. Signaling the imminent capture of the capital, over 25,000 soldiers were quickly taken prisoner by the Germans north of Paris.

Since May 10 an endless stream of refugees had cascaded into Paris from Belgium and northern France, both overrun by the Germans. The inextricable tangle of civilians and soldiers became an easy target of German planes. The French military had tried to stanch the unending flow and quell the panic but nothing worked against a bewildered populace distracted by the occupation and terrorized by government claims that a "fifth column," invisible but omnipresent, had infiltrated and was now subverting France.

In the early days of June, tens of thousands of Parisians fled the capital by car and on foot. Trains headed south were packed. Thousands more camped in railway stations. The stragglers nervously watched the sky darken in the distance.

"We were struck," wrote a journalist who took part in the exodus, "by an eerie gloom that spread out before us at the horizon and which, as if in the throes of some gigantic seizure, turned the sky from lead to coal black. All of us who witnessed it saw in this phenomenon an omen of cosmic dimension, the presage of untold misfortunes to come." What this ten-million-strong ribbon of humanity beheld as it unfurled on the open road, were the oil tanks of the port city of Le Havre burning out of control.

South of Paris, the rout created enormous bottlenecks. German planes strafed bridges and fields, leaving hundreds of bodies carbonized beyond recognition in smoldering, bullet-riddled cars or slumped in the shallow ditches lining the road. The survivors, men and women on bicycles, others pushing wheelbarrows filled with luggage or hauling horseless carts carrying infants, cripples and old folks, kept going, their backs arched against dead weight, their eyes scanning past the blackened clouds for signs of an impending assault from the air. Half-crazed with terror and grief, some of the women wrung their hands or beat their kerchief-covered heads repeatedly. Others shuttled among the dazed, the exhausted, the downhearted, offering hope, sharing food and water. Children cried unremittingly in long, mournful, almost perfunctory wails. Men, many of them patriarchs, cursed and shook their fists at their tormentors. *"Ah, les sales boches.* They'll pay for this...." Deliverance and payback were still five years away.

On June 14, 1940, the Germans crossed the ancient city gates. Huge flags -- a red swastika on a field of black and white -- were hoisted over palaces and ministerial buildings, replacing the French tricolor. Some German soldiers were seen buffing their boots with it, arousing laughter among the troops.

Paris crumbled. A ghastly silence seemed to hover over the once bustling boulevards, plazas and age-old streets. Public buildings were empty. It was as if the city had lost its soul. On Place Pigalle, on the Champs Elysées, in the open vastness of the Place de la Concorde, everywhere it seemed, small groups of Parisians greeted and feted the invaders. Many volunteered their services. Others offered their bodies for bread or wine or money to expiate France's fervid capitulation in a symbolic act of self-immolation.

I saw Parisians standing motionless, weeping openly, a quiet rage burning in their eyes while Germans soldiers -- the reincarnated Sons of Darkness -- strutted freely in the magnificent and now cowed City of Light. I would never forget their tears. I remember taking my father's hand and huddling next to him for warmth and comfort. Sensing disquiet, he'd picked me up and held me in his arms. He'd smiled reassuringly and pressed me closer to him and I saw sadness in his face, sadness and fear.

I was three.

•

Revisionists, at best, have short memories. Most are either cretins or hate-mongers. Sixty years after the fact, they continue to suggest that France's "fifth column," a term first used during the Spanish Civil War, was a myth. Less frivolous, but equally misguided, apologists claim that its cast of spies and counterspies -- propagandists, aspiring and also-ran politicians, anti-communist noblemen, wealthy industrialists, clerics, pacifists and *agents provocateurs* spirited across the border or parachuted under the cover of darkness in remote rural areas -- was grossly exaggerated.

If the magnitude and influence of a fifth column was overstated (as was the prowess and effectiveness of the Résistance) -- a "hysterical caricature exploited by the communists," as some insist, "to heighten the perception that reactionaries were orchestrating France's demise" -- it was far from being a myth. Enfeebled by previous wars, France had fallen long before the German onslaught, not for lack of military assets but for want of pluck and endurance. A susceptibility to, or a curious fascination for, Germany's hegemonic designs -- deftly marketed by its huge propaganda machine -- hastened the decrepitude and led to the intellectual and moral disintegration of the French ruling classes.

Weakened by the 1914-1918 war, France had disintegrated long before 1940. It's not that the military establishment was substandard; its general staff lacked initiative, grit. Corruption was rampant. Historians still ask whether France was asthenic or whether it had been hoodwinked by Germany's propaganda machine, which had so deftly marketed Hitler's hallucinatory world vision. This would help speed up the intellectual and moral decrepitude of the French ruling classes, not to mention a large number of actors, artists, writers and journalists.

Elements of the French army would be contaminated by the Führer's fanfare. German cinematographer Leni Riefensthal's *Triumph of the Will*, a film exalting the Nazi Party rally that became a central motif of Hitler's dictatorship, won a major award in Paris in 1937. Scores of high-ranking French officers, stirred by the fervor the film conveyed, aroused by the gigantic billowing banners and the upturned faces of Hitler's cohorts goose-stepping passed his podium, openly endorsed the spread of Nazi ideology "in countries well behind in the application of such lofty human principles."

This infatuation was zealously shared by the Catholic Church, whose age-old anti-Semitism harmonized with Germany's aims, and whose cooperation was to exceed the occupier's demands. A defeat of Germany, the Vatican had argued, would bring down the autarchic systems that form the first line of defense against Bolshevism and help repulse the immediate communization of Europe. On the other hand, the Holy See had insisted, a victory by France would lead straight to

France's demise and the end of civilization. This was an objective to which, the Church asserted, the Jews were committed. This grotesque assessment was turned to profit not only by racketeers, defeatists and common traitors, but by rich entrepreneurs who had everything to gain from an alliance with Hitler and the Pope -- the arch-enemies of Bolshevism.

It's not enough to grasp history. One must become habituated to it.

•

We lie, we cheat, we steal by telling ourselves that men deserve to be betrayed, deceived and robbed.

The argument that the world's destiny is in the hands of bankers and industrialists is never as aptly demonstrated as in wartime. The lords of capital and the cannon merchants thrive on the menace of conflict and the conduct of war. They prosper when the first shots ring out. Uncovering threats and arousing fear grants them the right to pillage national coffers. Created as special constabularies -- "shock troops" -- against popular uprisings, Nazism and Fascism overstepped the role their mentors had intended. They boiled over and set the world afire. European and American capitalists who, by their generous subsidies, hastened the triumph of German and Italian National Socialism, lived to regret their benevolence. But their contrition rang hollow; they'd bet on the wrong horse. They would eventually recover and engineer other bloody conflicts in the name of free enterprise.

•

Among those taking part in the sellout of France were business magnates who believed that the hour of a "white" *Internationale* had come and that only a pact with Hitler and Mussolini could protect against the Red menace. One of them, multimillionaire perfume tycoon, François Coty, in an arrogant 1934 ghost-written column entitled "France first! Join Hitler against Bolshevism!" denounced [the]

"... shortsighted, misguided, biased politicians and the malevolent anti-French sect that serves the socio-financial Internationale and perfidiously ascribe to both Hitler and Mussolini a redoubtable belligerence against France...."

Ostensibly, the "malevolent anti-French sect" Coty referred to was the Jews. Most would pay dearly for this characterization in France and elsewhere in Europe.

●

So France fell. The French resisted with reckless bravery, or collaborated with the enemy, or survived, shielding themselves with indifference against everything that wasn't steak, fries, wine and tobacco. Everyone hatched his own strategy, devised his own survival tactic, all according to their wits or cravings.

"I welcome our downfall," said journalist Alain Laubreaux. "Victory would have brought our nation great misfortune."

Those who weren't squirming at such spineless rhetoric were applauding it. Others saw in defeat a kind of divine retribution, cruel but salutary, against a people and a regime that, since 1936, had favored pleasure and ease over duty and accountability. Few Frenchmen advocated open resistance. Many, including some of France's most revered writers, artists and entertainers, chose to weather the occupation, some in opulence and splendor, and, if necessary, to hobnob with the enemy. All later found the words to justify an intimacy with the Germans that, given their celebrity, they had no need to cultivate. Between these two extremes, France bobbed and vacillated and struggled against chaos and incoherence.

"The country was anesthetized, rendered stupid," said author Gilles Ragache. In six weeks, more than 100,000 French troops had died on the battlefield. Twice as many were wounded. While most of the five million conscripts never fired a shot or saw a single German, half a million endured the full weight of war. Their sacrifice enabled the most irresolute civilians and military alike to flee toward the south in one tragic, throbbing exodus.

Inevitably, "national security" -- the catchphrase and clarion call of the diehard elite -- prompted powerful right-wing politicians to issue daily amendments that amounted to drastic amputations on democracy, notably against an independent press that openly espoused liberal causes and which were increasingly seen as willing tools of communism. Many of these measures were directed against Jews.

Enacted on October 3, 1940, a law barred Jews from political office. The next day, an addendum authorized the internment of foreign Jews. In March 1941, Xavier Vallat, a monarchist named to head a commission on "Jewish matters" [the "aryanization" of France] declared with the sinister aplomb of a psychopath that his anti-Semitism "is as moderate as it is enlightened." He explained:

"There is a Jewish problem everywhere there are too many Jews. Now, Jews are perfectly tolerable in homeopathic doses. But after a while, these interlopers become dangerous, first because they are iconoclasts who resist assimilation, secondly because they scorn those who offer them sanctuary and wind up imposing their will upon them."

(In 1947, Vallat, an unrepentant anti-Semite received a ten-year prison sentence for his role in the persecution of Jews. Released in 1949, he was granted amnesty in 1954. From 1962 to 1966 he edited the extreme right-wing newspaper, *Aspects de la France*).

To forgive is to grant amnesty, not grace.

In June 1941, two new edicts denied Jews access to law and medical schools. Jewish dentists, pharmacists and midwives had their licenses revoked.

In May 1942, Jews six years and older were required under penalty of imprisonment to sew a yellow Star of David, bearing in black letters the word *Juif*, on their outer-garments.

In July, Jews were barred from restaurants, cafés, theaters, movie houses, concert-halls, food markets, swimming pools, beaches, museums, libraries and sporting venues. In December, a new decree ordered Jews to have their identification and food cards stamped with the word *Juif*.

•

France's debacle and political backsliding produced a vacuum and fed a cynicism readily exploited by flops, opportunists and small-time crooks who had nothing to lose by espousing the enemy's cause. One of them, Henri Lafont, would play a brief if tragic role in occupied Paris. Driven by gratitude, or stirred by some inner compulsion to atone for his crimes with a single act of daring and compassion, he would save my father's life and, without a doubt, my mother's as well as mine. Postwar France would not be as generous, choosing to look at the events surrounding my father's release from a French Gestapo prison -- and despite his selfless service in the *Résistance* -- with suspicion and resentment.

93, RUE LAURISTON

The will to exterminate the Jews through mass deportations to the East was absent -- or as yet unarticulated -- in the first days of the occupation of France. Jews were still defined as members of a religious sect, not a race. But by August 1940 the Germans called for the "expulsion" of all Jews and the expropriation of their assets. Two months later, Jewish heads of corporations were fired and replaced by "Aryan surrogates." Ninety percent of the proceeds from Jewish businesses were seized.

The French were anxious to placate the conqueror. They formed social, commercial and romantic connections. They opened exclusive restaurants and elegant bordellos. They created pro-Nazi, anti-Jewish militias and recruited bullies who were only too willing to do the Germans' dirty work. The government's zeal to please the Germans and the enthusiasm with which average citizens espoused Hitler's mission in exchange for tutelage and protection, made for a remarkable degree of compliance and accommodation. It also created big breaks for the quick-witted, the shrewd and the dissolute.

•

Political change gladdens those who think they have something to gain until they realize that they've lost everything.

Henri Chamberlain "Lafont" was 45 and suffering from advanced syphilis when he first came to see my father. Considered "handsome" by some (he looked more like a punch-drunk boxer), Lafont was a charismatic con man and part-time pimp. He'd been referred by a mutual acquaintance, Aristide Babin -- "Titi" to his friends -- a gendarme assigned to police headquarters, where Lafont's sister held a food concession. My father, an intern at the time, earned extra cash and gained practical experience by giving cops checkups and doing basic urine and blood work.

Orphaned at 11, abandoned by his mother shortly after his father's death, Lafont spends his childhood in misery. He supports himself through shoplifting and other petty crimes. Caught, he is sent to reform school where he refines his skills. He later joins the army and serves without incident. Returned to civilian life, he steals, goes back to prison, is sentenced to hard labor at the penal colony in Cayenne, from which he escapes. Convicted on multiple counts of theft and racketeering, declared persona non grata, he opens a prosperous business under an alias and, overnight, becomes a patron of the Paris police. Exposed, he is arrested in 1940 and soon released as Paris falls. He goes to work for the Germans first as an informer, then as a "foreman." He opens an office on Rue Lauriston and organizes a cartel made up of mobsters and pimps his friends in the police helped spring out of jail. In 1941 he teams up with inspector Pierre Bonny, a trusted confidant of the Gestapo and once hailed as the "best policeman in France." The Bonny-Lafont clique, whose crimes are recorded on a plaque at 93 Rue Lauriston, surrounds itself with a strange assortment of perverts, lunatics and whores. Their specialty: black marketeering and the traffic of gold and jewels stolen from Jews.

Working closely with the Gestapo, Lafont and Bonny convert their headquarters on Rue Lauriston and Place des Etats Unis into torture chambers. Their acolytes commit murder and hunt for members of the *Résistance*. Jacques Delarue (*Histoire de la Gestapo,* Fayard, 1962) wrote:

> *"These criminals used torture and exploited the immunity that their Gestapo badges and pistol permits conferred to commit innumerable crimes."*

Pascal Ory (*Les collaborateurs,* Le Seuil, 1976) wrote that at the summit of his career --

> *"Monsieur Henri rode in a Bentley, surrounded himself with orchids and countesses and, in his final days, was haunted by blatant megalomaniac fantasies."*

Playing on people's baser instincts, earning their confidence by showering them with gifts and favors, the two accomplices gained the support of people in high places. Many cozy up to Bonny and Lafont to obtain the release of imprisoned friends and relations. The thugs occasionally set aside their murderous activities to help someone from whom they can later extract favors or support.

•

Lafont's condition was serious. Massive doses of sulfa, popular at that time, and homeopathic treatments of dubious integrity or efficacy had done nothing to prevent a primary skin lesion, now healed, from storming the bloodstream and hastening the advance of a secondary and potentially fatal infection. A rented microscope had confirmed the presence of the slender and deadly spirochetes in Lafont's blood and my father knew it was only a matter of time before they invaded the brain and caused catastrophic damage. It took a great leap of faith on my father's part -- and several million units of penicillin into Lafont's rear-end once a week for several weeks -- to cure Lafont. Penicillin had only been discovered in 1928, barely seven years before my father graduated from medical school, and mercury and arsenic were still the treatment of choice. From all accounts, Flemming's wonder drug had not been widely used in Europe at the time and my father felt that he had taken great risks with a remedy still deemed exotic.

"I'll never forget what you did for me," Lafont told my father on his last visit. "He was bawling like a child," my father recalled. "We embraced for a moment or so. I then begged him to be more careful and resist shoving his dick in just any old thing without some form of protection. Lafont laughed heartily, gave me a bear hug and said, 'I'll always be there for you if you need me, Doc.' I was touched but quickly dismissed his exuberance as that of man who had just been granted a reprieve. Neither one of us could have imagined, as we parted, how it would all end for him. I had saved him from one executioner and, in so doing, delivered him to another."

My father saw Lafont on two separate occasions after that. Lafont invited him to his apartment to celebrate Babin's birthday. "The place was crawling with gorgeous whores, neatly attired hoodlums and all the cops money could buy," my father recalled. "We didn't meet again until five years later. His wife and his brother came to my office a couple of times with some minor health problems. It was through Babin that I would learn of his new vocation."

•

Men who are for sale but find no buyers are the first to accuse of treason those who have buyers but do not sell themselves.

•

With Paris crushed and the Germans firmly in control, opportunities abound for mercenaries, collaborators and soldiers of fortune. Doubling as black market and money-laundering networks, "auxiliary Gestapo" cells recruit hoodlums, crooked cops and spies. Convicted murderers are smuggled out of prisons to act as "enforcers." Drawn by the prospect of easy money, a number of Jews, among them former scrap dealers and future multi-millionaires Josef Joanovici and Michel Szkolnikoff (the latter was assassinated in Spain after the liberation), joined Otto Brandel, an agent of Admiral Franz Wilhelm Canaris, head of German Intelligence, in schemes that generated over 40 billion Francs. Canaris was later executed for plotting against Hitler.

The marriage between commerce and espionage was so profitable that dozens of "bureaus" popped up in some of the city's finest districts. In a statement published after the war, Belgian spy Georges Delfanne, also known as Masuy, confessed at his trial that,

> *"the idea of getting rich by exploiting the situation did not come to mind right away. I was drawn in gradually as enticing offers came my way."*

Soon, all sorts of merchants, bankers and middlemen came knocking at his door, filling his waiting room from early morning until late in the afternoon. The manager of the Claridge Hotel offered Masuy a deal involving the distribution of ten tons of stolen green coffee beans.

General Karl Heinrich von Stülpnagel ordered Masuy to crush budding clandestine units of French freedom fighters. Over two thousand people were interrogated in his office on stylish avenue Henri-Martin. Interrogation was accompanied by a form of torture invented by a Russian physician and known as the ordeal of the bathtub.

> *"Used by the Russians [the bathtub] is a crude and barbaric device. In my care, it's psychology at its finest. You have no idea how fear of torture makes torture superfluous...."*

The infamous ordeal, better known as *waterboarding,* would be resurrected in American torture chambers.

> *"Waterboarding induces panic and suffering by forcing a person to inhale water into the sinuses, pharynx, larynx, and trachea. The head is tilted back and water is poured into the upturned mouth or nose. Eventually the subject cannot exhale more air or cough out more water, the lungs are collapsed, and the sinuses and trachea are filled with water. The subject is drowned from the inside, filling with water from the head down. The chest and lungs are kept higher than the head so that coughing draws water up and into the lungs while avoiding total suffocation. His sufferings must be that of a man who is drowning, but cannot drown."*

Thanks to Masuy's intelligence the Germans were able to confiscate 54 radio transmitters and over 20 tons of weapons. Informers also helped destroy at least seven French insurgency networks, many of them, to the delight of Marshal Phillipe Pétain, Freemasons. "A Jew is not responsible for his birth," Pétain had declared, "a Freemason is: he makes a conscious choice." The seizures and arrests dealt a severe blow to France and the Allies.

●

Masuy was dubbed "the most implacable foe of the Résistance" but it was Lafont's band of killers that spread terror. Described by the postwar French press as a "picturesque gangster," Lafont had escaped from prison with a number of German agents and petty criminals recruited by the Abwehr during their incarceration. At his request, the Germans released twenty-two former inmates from Fresnes Prison, outside

Paris. Now headquartered on fashionable rue Lauriston, and sporting the silver braiding of an SS captain, Lafont specialized in kidnappings, torture and, when necessary, murder.

Lafont's crew was credited with the disabling of an important French underground network and, later, with the arrest of Geneviève De Gaulle, niece of the French general. A fellow student had betrayed her for 100,000 Francs.

Accompanied by his most trusted disciples, among them the noted soccer player, Villaplane, and backed by a detail of Algerian killers-for-hire, Lafont also took part in daring raids against the *Maquis*. Named after the expanses of dense underbrush where its members took cover, the network of French saboteurs *(maquisards)* eventually recruited my father as a field physician.

Shortly after the liberation of Paris in 1945, Lafont was handed to the police by his trusted colleague, Joanovici. Joanovici, plea-bargained his way to freedom and lived to enjoy -- temporarily -- the fruits of his rackets.

Many of the "fanatic imbeciles" who had bloodied their hands during the German occupation were lined up against a wall and shot for having followed orders. Henri Lafont was executed for issuing them. He refused to be blindfolded. He is said to have ordered the firing squad to "let the sun shine upon my face until the end. Please aim well. Deal me death if you must but make it swift and painless."

"Even scoundrels can die like heroes," a witness remarked.

Men can negotiate everything but their past.

KABBALAH AND BOILED POTATOES

Nothing turns common folk into polyglots like war, annexation, colonization, deportation, expatriation. Born in the northern Transylvanian town of Sighet, a province claimed and reclaimed as shifting fortunes redrew Austro-Hungary's map, my father had mastered Romanian and Hungarian by the age of six -- not counting Yiddish, spoken at home since birth. He also spoke Hebrew, practiced daily in *heder* and during prayers, and German, taught in public school and widely spoken by an elite minority who deemed the other local idioms to be lacking in refinement.

> *A gift for languages is the tribute vanquished people pay.*

Though he later conquered French and English, it was Yiddish, with its rich blend of Hebrew and medieval German, its earthy sonority, inflections and colorful imagery with which he felt most at ease.
"Yiddish is the language of folk tales told and retold by my father. In it I hear the gentle lullabies sung by my mother as she rocked the children to sleep, the heated arguments, shrewd observations, snappy repartees, the sardonic asides and words of love murmured with such tenderness and grace as to melt every trace of rancor, dry every tear."
Yiddish has a sound, an aroma, a taste, a feel like no other language. It's a tongue full of familiar tunes. Every note in its inexhaustible register is a melody. Now spoken by fewer and fewer Jews, Yiddish has a taste for nimble blasphemy:

> *May your wish come true when you can no longer enjoy it.*

Or for bitter reproof:

> *When one must at all cost sully something, one can sully even God.*

If nostalgia tinted many of my father's memories, he was careful not to wax rhapsodic about his childhood. His father -- my grandfather -- was seldom gainfully employed.

"He had no real trade. He kept a small candle-making business but he was too proud to work. He spent much of his time at the synagogue or immersed in his precious books -- the Torah, the Talmud, the Kabbalah -- or strolling up and down Sighet's main artery, deep in thought and attired in fine three-piece suits bought on credit and rarely fully paid for. He also kept my mother endlessly pregnant. We were nine in a three-room house -- two adults and seven young hungry mouths to feed, seven growing bodies to clothe, seven pairs of feet constantly in need of shoes, ribbons and petticoats and combs for the girls -- Helen, Malku, Lilli -- new knickers and frocks and prayer shawls for the boys -- Yosi, Leibi, Favish and me.

"We ate lots of potatoes; potato soup for breakfast, potato pancakes, salted or daubed with thin layers of homemade plum preserves at lunch, and we often dined on boiled potatoes, sautéed onions dressed in melted chicken fat and moldy crusts of black bread. Meat was a rare and welcome treat. I don't remember ever feeling full at the end of a meal. It was a miserable existence."

Lost in inscrutable mystical abstractions, sustained by rigid Orthodox discipline and endless devotions, my father's father seemed indifferent to his family's plight. My grandmother withstood multiple pregnancies, penury and privations with a stoicism and self-effacement that often made my father weep with anger.

"How can you take it, mama," he asked, grabbing her by the shoulders and shaking her.

"*Shh,* it's alright, son, that's life, you know. We must accept our lot. We're in God's hands. But things will be better, you'll see," she'd whisper. "Study hard and maybe you can leave all this behind one day."

It was shortly after his Bar Mitzvah that my father, in a fit of youthful rebellion, cut off his *peyot,* the curly ear locks that had adorned his temples since childhood, repudiated his mother's fatalism, rejected predestination, renounced God and began to defy the nearly insurmountable obstacles of youth, indigence and anti-Semitism. It was also at that time that he decided to become a doctor, "to treat humankind's tangible afflictions and to snatch my family from the clutches of poverty." My father would later claim that it was not at all a question of indebtedness -- "Children don't really owe their parents anything, they don't ask to be born" -- but a rage against life's Sisyphean absurdity and an acute sensitivity toward the suffering of others. Engaged and combative, incorruptible and iron-willed, he would spend the rest of his life fighting intolerance, denouncing hypocrisy, speaking for the voiceless and defending the weak. These contests would keep him in a perpetual state of frustration. He understood the futility of his principles and often voiced bitter disappointment at the shortcomings of those in whom he had placed his trust. When he died in 1987 at the age of 83, widowed for over fourteen years, he'd become a misanthropic recluse.

•

One day, on his way home from an errand, my father saw a high school senior set upon a small boy, pinning him against the ground, beating him about the face and pulling at his ear locks with such force that the boy shrieked in pain. Taking pleasure in the pain he caused, the bigger boy pulled harder, battering his quarry's head against the cobblestones and spitting at him.

"Filthy little Jew. Kike. Hooknosed piece of shit. That'll teach you to tread on my sidewalk. I ought to rub your face in a pig's ass. You and your foul race should be exterminated."

"I saw red," my father remembered. "Red and blue and purple, and then I saw nothing as the tears blinded me, and I felt my blood coursing through my body like acid and, even though he was much taller and stronger, I let him have it with a flurry of fists and elbows and feet that stretched him out cold in a pool of his own blood in the gutter near a pile of horse manure."

"What happened," my father asked the little boy. "He was eight or nine and shaking like a leaf. I dusted him off and wiped his face with my handkerchief."

"'I was hurrying home from *heder* and going over a difficult passage that Rebe Yanku wants me to memorize. I didn't see *domnu* ("*sir*") and I knocked into him by mistake.'"

"Well, *domnu* is out of commission for a while. I don't think he'll ever bother you again."

"You think so," asked the boy, looking at my father with awe then glancing at his persecutor with a remnant of terror.

"I *know* so. Now run along. By the way, what's the passage you're supposed to learn?"

"Habakkuk, chapter one, verses eight and nine."

"Their horses also are swifter than the leopards and are more fierce than the evening wolves: and their horsemen shall spread themselves, and their horsemen shall come from far; they shall fly as the eagle that hasteth to eat. They shall come all for violence: their faces shall sup up as the east wind, and they shall gather the captivity as the sand."

"I never forgot the incident or the prophecy," my father told me, "but it took another fifteen years or so to grasp its oracular surrealism, its apocalyptic significance."

The next day, the high school principal summoned my father.

"You nearly killed him, Ari."

"He asked for it."

"That's not the point. Meanwhile he's in the hospital with a broken nose, a dislocated jaw, a busted eardrum and a pair of very swollen balls."

"So what."

"It so happens he's the son of Colonel Petrescu, the military governor. He…."

"Fuck him."

"… He claims you attacked his son without provocation. He wants you expelled. I've no choice. He's a powerful man. Please understand I'm doing this with great reluctance and sadness. You're one of my best students. I've arranged a transfer to the high school in Cluj. Petrescu would have my head if he knew. You'll do fine there, that is, if you learn to manage your temper and stop playing paladins."

"But, sir, you don't understand…."

Able to convey tenderness and forbearance, my father's pale blue eyes could also ignite with exasperation. Lies did that to him. Lies or absurd rationalizations, and I knew that few people could withstand his disarming gaze. He would have made a lousy politician. The principal, a decent man, a kind man, according to my father, would not be out-stared.

"No, Ari. Nothing you say will change my mind. I'm sorry. Vindicating a wrong has a way of creating a fresh injustice. Sometimes, it never ends. It's better to let go. For your own good. Maybe someday we can both look back at this and laugh. Good luck."

They shook hands.

When my father got home and told his mother what had happened, "she pounded her breast and threw her hands up in the air and looked pleadingly at the ceiling where God can be found when tragedy strikes."

"Cluj? Cluj," she lamented, "it's a world away."

"A very small world measured in mere kilometers," my father replied. "Now, look *mamale*, it's not a big deal. I'll come to visit once a month or so, you'll see. Everything will be fine."

"But how will you live, *where* will you live? We don't know anyone in Cluj. Where will you eat? Who will press your shirts?"

"The principal said there's a small room in the school's attic and I can have it in exchange for doing chores and tutoring slow students. Supper is included."

"What will *Tatale* think?"

Tatale, it seems, took the matter with pious fatalism, my father would later claim without a hint of bitterness. "He must have felt relieved to learn that he'd have one fewer mouth to feed."

If God allows men to deny his existence he's either an atheist or a myth.

●

Two years later, my father graduated from high school with honors and passed the baccalaureate. He applied and was admitted to Prague's prestigious School of Medicine. As he had done in high school to support himself, he worked to pay for tuition, books, a closet-like windowless maid's room that stank of bedbugs, and two skimpy meals a day. The evening collation was generally taken in bed while studying and waiting for sleep to subdue nagging hunger pangs.

A year later, ill at ease with the school's curriculum -- taught in German to foreign students -- he obtained a transfer to the Faculty of Medicine in Paris and came home to Sighet for the summer.

"In the fall, as I boarded the bus for the train station, *tatale* offered me a new pair of phylacteries, a skullcap and a fresh prayer shawl. 'It's not good to start the day without first calling upon the Lord,' he said, patting my bare head, an air of studied mortification and pity animating his blue eyes. My mother gave me a bag stuffed with sandwiches, cake and fruit. We hugged. She whispered, 'it's not good to pray on an empty stomach....'"

Atheists live in certainty; believers in doubt.

OYSTERLISH YIDEN (WEIRD JEWS)

The postcard Paris that my father had fancied as a boy spread open before him like a pair of luscious thighs, baring treasures of rare beauty and promising unimagined delights. Prague had given him a foretaste of big city life, but Prague was grim by comparison, exquisite to look at but Germanic in temperament, stripped of frivolity, incapable of self-parody. Sublime and profane, sophisticated, palpitating with carnality, Paris quickly seduced him. The allure, the love affair -- lustful in his youth, sustained by memory and nostalgia in old age -- lasted a lifetime. He would die "in exile in Babylon," -- New York -- a city he likened to "a dynamo too engrossed in its own circuitry to foster feelings of quietude or intimacy. It's a great place if you're twenty, with acid coursing through your veins and transistors in place of nerves."

Pleasure delayed, pleasure enhanced.

In its implied eroticism, coined by my father, this aphorism also warned against the pitfalls of romanticism. Paris was an irresistible seductress but her siren call, for the good of his medical studies, needed to be temporarily stilled. Having to work to pay for tuition further reduced my father's leisure time, much of which he devoted to doing odd jobs and earning a few extra francs to send home to his parents. Twice a week he ran the night elevator of a posh 16th *arrondissement* hotel. In the morning he washed dishes in the hotel kitchen in exchange for breakfast and a hot bath. Once a month or so, he sold his blood. Between classes, he tutored dunces, unloaded trucks at *Les Halles*, the now-defunct sprawling city-center produce and meat market, and sparred with third-rate pugilists in a gym that reeked of beer, urine and sweat and where youthful dreams of glory were repaid with defeat, disfigurement and early dementia, and turned men into broken souls.

Answering a call for extras, he was also cast in a period film in which he wore a "soiled costume and a powdered wig so old, mangy and foul-smelling that it may well have belonged to the Sun King himself.

"I had no speaking part but I was given multiple roles in several action scenes. One of them had me sitting at attention on a horse in a line of cavalrymen being passed in review. My mount was an incontinent, bow-legged mule that took pleasure nipping at my shins and finally managed to throw me off. I landed in a pile of shit and promptly asked to be transferred to the infantry. In one of many battle-scene close-ups, I had to put a wounded Hessian soldier out of his misery with a thrust of my dagger. The collapsible blade mechanism failed and I would have skewered the poor bugger had it not been for the metal-studded leather sash he wore across his chest. In another scene, mortally wounded by a musket shot, I had to clutch my heart and fall to the ground, backwards. The director found my mimicry of death quite unconvincing so he made me die again and again. I was sore for days after that. I never got to see the picture. Who knows what they left in and what wound up on the cutting-room floor."

I never forgot this last remark. Uttered by my father without pretense or forethought, I later found it metaphorically rich: Is life but a mere scenario? Why are some plots granted form and substance while others are unceremoniously scrapped? What if a fiction character could seek damages from the author? Imagine if a creation could litigate against its maker, if it could sue for frivolous, unsolicited conception, flawed workmanship, pain and suffering, invasion of privacy, the burden of unattainable potentials and cruel disdain for the absurdity of existence? Oh, what a fabulous class-action suit we could file. And what a thrill to see the miscreants brought to justice at last.

I never shared these thoughts with my father. Although he valued abstract reasoning and often engaged in philosophical inquiry, he considered such mental pirouettes pointless unless they led to some verifiable, useful truth.

"You need exercise," he once offered an acquaintance that had pestered him with some circuitous suppositions -- *"suppositories"* as my father called them. "I suggest you use your feet. Walk from *l'Etoile* to Place de la Concorde and back. You'll behold superb architecture, cross paths with lovely women and revel in pure symmetry. Symmetry is everything. It calms. It gladdens. It redeems."

My father didn't mind antagonizing people if he thought it would do them good. It often did. But, more often than not, the penalty for such solicitude was resentment, followed by alienation. I inherited much of my father's irreverence and paid the price. Candor and spontaneity, in lieu of hypocrisy and circumspection have proved catastrophic. Speaking my mind has cost me friendships, family ties and prospects for professional growth. In a couple of cases, it damn nearly cost me my life.

•

On May 13, 1936, earning high praise from his professors and from the Sorbonne University School of Medicine jury for his thesis, *Contributions to the Study of Breast Cancer in Men,* my father, Armin Gutman, the 33-year-old elder son of an impecunious Sighet candle maker, became Dr. Armin Gutman.

Armed with his hard-earned diploma, he went home to Romania a few weeks later. On a visit to Bucharest he was introduced to my mother, a petite hazel-eyed brunette with art deco features and a gentle disposition, fourteen years his junior. They were married in September and left for Paris soon after the wedding. I was born a year later.

•

If my father had long since abandoned all pretense of religion -- a process hastened by Paris' irresistible embrace and consummated in the ashes of the Holocaust -- he would never regard himself as anything but a Jew. This self-image, a vestige of atavism and the consequence of an indelible Orthodox Jewish upbringing, was, however, altogether secular and devoid of mysticism or sentimentality. He accepted himself the way one accepts having green eyes or flat feet. Asked if he was proud to be a Jew he replied: "I take pride only in my accomplishments; I feel shame only at my failings. I concede all else, including the right to be asked idiotic questions." In truth, my father found dignity in his Jewishness. He was fond of quoting Peter Ustinov:

"I believe that the Jews have made a contribution to the human condition out of all proportion to their numbers: I believe them to be an immense people. Not only have they supplied the world with two leaders of the stature of Jesus Christ and Karl Marx, but they have even indulged in the luxury of following neither one nor the other."

Free as he was from doctrinal tyranny, disdainful of absurd beliefs and zealotry, my father found my mother's synthetic Jewish milieu bizarre, if not grotesque. Cosmopolitan, sophisticated, an enclave of Latin culture in a region suffused with German, Hungarian, Slav and Turkish influences, Bucharest stood worlds apart from provincial Sighet. Unlike Sighet, where Jews formed a monolithic and homogeneous core, Bucharest Jews were stratified, dissimilar and unequal, separated by religious attitudes and conventions, education, professional status and wealth, with the most pious, hence the most recognizable element generally occupying the bottom tiers. Learned, urbane and successful -- my mother's father was a noted engineer, jurist and poet; her brother was a promising young lawyer; the family my father married into was light years removed from his own. Divested of all discernible Jewish accouterments, perhaps as a hedge against anti-Semitism -- widespread at all levels of Romanian society -- perhaps because conformity and upward mobility took precedence over ethnic identity and survival, they stood in sharp contrast to the unassuming, outspoken Transylvanian Jew that my father would never cease to be.

It's only by comparing ourselves to others that we discover who we really are.

●

Assimilation had begun early in my mother's family. Both my grandmother -- born into an upper-middle-class household in the genteel Moldovan capital of Iasi -- and my mother were educated by the Sisters of Notre Dame, a German teaching order known for its demanding curriculum and the severity of its disciplinary system.

"They were mean," my mother recalled. "They took pleasure in hitting the back of our hands with the edge of a metal ruler at the slightest infraction. Failure to sit erect at our desks elicited a barrage of insults. Crossing our legs or inadvertently exposing a bare ankle drew swift penance, on our knees, in the courtyard, gravel eating at our flesh, in full view of the other pupils. 'Ill-mannered and unladylike', sneezing was forbidden." This injunction was so viciously enforced that my mother, to her dying day, could barely emit a sound.

•

Despite its air of civility, Iasi endured a long history of anti-Semitism. Jews had always been a special target of popular hostility. They were suspected of factionalism and disloyalty; they were loathed for their erudition, envied for their affluence and resented for occupying prominent positions in what was then the second largest center of Christianity in Romania. Wounded national pride and economic woes found relief in mortifying Jews, first through calumny and vilification, then by resorting to wholesale violence. The university of Iasi (Romania's oldest) and, by osmosis, all educational institutions under its superintendence, were vigorous promoters of that tradition. One of its most notorious alumni was "Captain" Corneliu Codreanu, the self-anointed *"savior of Romania from the Jewish scourge"* and founder of the Legion of the Archangel Michael, later re-named the Iron Guard. Encouraged by the success of Fascism in the 1920s and 30s, and later, infuriated by the loss of territories resulting from the Russo-German treaty of 1939, Codreanu, and his followers took "love of country" to new heights of anti-Jewish fervor.

In July 1940 Romanian soldiers went on a rampage in Dorohoi, north of Iasi, murdering more than 50 Jews, including five children. Six months later, in January 1941, Iron Guards murdered 125 Jews in Bucharest, impaling some of the victims on meat hooks.

Small wonder that many Romanian Jews, my mother's family included, eschewed the obvious emblems of their faith and adopted, without necessarily espousing them, the outward trappings of Christianity.

•

What my mother's family lacked in spiritual fervor was more than offset by a curious amalgam of idolatry, parodies of Christian liturgy, corruption of Jewish protocols, and clandestine excursions into necromancy, palmistry and divination. They crossed themselves in church, which they visited regularly "for inspiration," (they never set foot in a synagogue) put up Christmas trees, and hosted Easter Sunday dinner parties at which daintily decorated hard-boiled eggs were cracked, dipped in salt water and nibbled on to the accompaniment of rousing "Christ has risen!" cheers.

"*A leur manière,*" my father recounted, "*ces drôles de juifs*" ("these weird Jews") abstained from solid food on Yom Kippur but consumed large quantities of Turkish coffee, chain-smoked aromatic oval cigarettes and read the Tarot. Come Passover, they gingerly took part in Seders at which both bread and matzoth were served, presumably to help ease pork medallions and lobster tails onto their forks.

Just in case, prominently displayed under an ivory crucifix, and sharing honors with an ancient Russian Orthodox icon, a bisque statuette of St. Anthony sat on the mantelpiece ready to hasten the recovery of lost treasures. Locating common objects -- so long as they were misplaced on the premises -- was entrusted to a crystal glass turned upside-down and set atop a lace-trimmed handkerchief.

When they dare to confront the devil, men burn witches; when they fear him, they turn to occultism.

Superstition, it seemed, regulated every facet of their existence. Countless canons warned of impending calamities. Occult formulas, spells and incantations shielded against them. Compliance with strict taboos secured the blessings of a hundred unseen spirits: Knock on wood before engaging in self-praise. Spit three times when admiring a beautiful and healthy child lest he fall prey to the "evil eye." Defiance or carelessness could unleash unimaginable evil: Break a mirror and you'll suffer seven years of sorrow. Never offer a gift of soap. Never pass a sharp object -- a needle, fork or cutting tool -- from hand to hand; place it first on a neutral surface. Biting one's tongue was evidence of a lie unuttered. If your left ear tingled, someone was talking about you. If the right one did, you could expect news from afar. If your nose itched you were on the verge of a quarrel. An itchy left palm portended a windfall.

"And if your rectum itches," my father would add not without annoyance, "you have hemorrhoids or worms, both of which are far easier to cure than your *meshugene* superstitions."

Everyone laughed heartily but when the laughter subsided, my grandmother or my uncle would icily chide my father for mocking forces and conventions beyond his comprehension. His use of Yiddish colloquialisms also drew mortified expressions from my grandmother who deemed the language "dissonant and vulgar." He was often counseled not to speak Yiddish *"en société,"* (in company) and advised against listening to cantorial music, which he enjoyed the way a child delights in a nursery rhyme or a lullaby. He obeyed these contemptible injunctions out of love for my mother, but he resented them and he never forgot. The Holocaust, and the birth of Israel from its ashes, would infuse my mother's family with a fresh sense of Jewish self-awareness that prevailed, to their immense credit -- along with a few unconquerable superstitions -- for the rest of their lives.

UNDER THE OCCUPATION

Spurn Messalina's advances and she'll have your head. Sleep with her and Claudius will chop it off. Its conscience subverted, its soul disfigured, trapped in a paradox of its own making, Paris fell with a speed resembling haste. Capitulation led to compliance and collaboration. Accommodation invited opportunism. Parisians rushed headlong into the foe's embrace, some with grudging resignation, many displaying unmasked, if heretofore dormant veneration for the conqueror. Energies and resources that might have been pooled to undermine the occupation and bedevil the occupiers, at least for a while, were eagerly expended to reap profit from catastrophe and secure comfort from the enemy. Cynics have suggested that if the French had truly believed in, or acted in conformance with, the image of daring and invincibility their history books so tenaciously promoted, they would have either repelled the Germans or drowned them in a sea of French blood. Defeat, instead, exposed the myth and bared a dispirited and faint-hearted France.

•

"If you want solidarity," Aldous Huxley wrote in *Ape and Essence*, "you've got to have an external enemy or an oppressed minority." The external enemy was now inside, aided and abetted by domestic turncoats and profiteers. Heretofore unmolested -- though often the casualty of subtle forms of intimidation -- the minority quickly became the focus of an evil fellowship dedicated to its extinction. Said Joachim von Ribbentrop at the Nuremberg Trials:

> *"You know, I was never an anti-Semite. I disagreed vehemently with Hitler and had a terrible argument with him on the subject. I told him that it was a mistake to pit world Jewry against us. It was as if we had a fourth world power to contend with: England, France, Russia and the Jews."*

It began with a series of assaults against synagogues and Jewish study centers. At first, the Germans blamed the Jews, accusing them of seeking publicity by burning and pillaging their own houses of worship. But German intelligence soon confirmed that the attacks had been the handiwork of French provocateurs, albeit with Berlin's knowledge and blessings.

Two Jewish traitors brought from Berlin -- Israelovitch and Biberstein -- both working for a special German detail charged with "solving the Jewish problem" persuaded independent Jewish organizations in the occupied sector to consolidate and centralize their operations and resources, ostensibly to facilitate "discourse and interaction" with the German military administration. Simultaneously, Israelovitch and Biberstein helped the French police create a Jewish "membership roster" meticulously compiled alphabetically, by address, profession and nationality.

A French decree had also ordered a census of Jews living in the free southern zone but a happy coincidence of sabotage, confusion and bureaucratic ineptitude prevented the inventories from ever getting into German hands. The list turned up under a pile of scrap metal in a garage after the war.

Nevertheless, the Paris "roster" proved invaluable in three major operations. Ordered by the SS, the raids netted large numbers of Jews. Soon, a mandate signed by Adolf Eichmann, the man responsible for the liquidation of at least four million Jews, called for the deportation of Jews living in France. Logistics and a shortage of transports delayed the convoy's departure.

The SS then demanded the arrest, at the hands of French police, of 28,000 Jews aged between 16 and 50. Spreading over two nights, the raids brought in only about 12,000 people -- 3,000 men, 5,800 women and 3,500 children. The German report, from which these numbers were gleaned, observes laconically,

> *"The persons apprehended constitute, for the most part, the dregs of Jewish society. Creditable sources reveal that a number of influential stateless Jews had gotten wind of the raids and managed to slip through the net. We suspect that*

members of the French police may have warned, in exchange for tribute, the very individuals they were supposed to arrest...."

Similar raids took place in the unoccupied sector. At first only stateless or foreign Jews, such as my parents, were targeted. But the Germans made it clear that these dragnets were aimed at eliminating *all* Jews, including French nationals -- which meant me as well. By 1942, the number of Jews deported reached 27,000. A year later the number exceeded 49,000.

•

Life in Paris under the occupation was hard and perilous. But it was not without play or diversion, both ventured at great risk and with reckless disregard for curfews, raids and other intrusions on personal freedom. Now *"Verboten* to Jews," the Casino de Paris reopened weeks after the occupation. So did the city's temple of earthly delights, the Folies-Bergère, dozens of nightclubs and at least a hundred watering holes where high society, celebrities, performers, writers and philosophers toasted life and liberty with the enemy. A number of classy whorehouses, now the exclusive turf of high-ranking German officers, offered "membership" to a select French clientele less in need of sex than business connections and protection from their ever-obliging German hosts.

My father's medical practice, which had flourished until the war, waned to a trickle then dissolved. Money nearly ran out. He borrowed from friends and repaid them by selling clothes, furniture, jewelry, bric-a-brac. It was around that time that the Résistance recruited him as a medic. At first, he was also entrusted with delivering coded messages. Much of this commerce took place in public, mostly in city parks. I remember tagging along on two or three occasions. There was plenty for me to do as I waited for my father to complete these risky missions. I would keep him in sight from the corner of my eye while I took in puppet shows or launched paper boats in the *Tuileries* garden basins. Or I'd romp in the sandboxes of the *Jardin du Luxembourg*, feed the ducks in the *Parc de Vincennes* lake, or tarry by the monkey cages at the zoo.

•

In three-quarter time, like the waltz, memory picks and chooses, records and erases.

My memory of these troubled times is opaque, fragmented at best. Episodes I manage to recall with some clarity, like vivid snippets from an otherwise impenetrable dream, are frayed, out of context, out of sequence. All that's left is a peripheral vision of early childhood, mangled, colorless, two-dimensional insights, mere moments that stand out, disjointed and surreal against the blackness of oblivion. Permeating each recollection, when summoned, is deep sadness.

•

I remember going to the cinema, at night, and scrambling out of our seats during an air raid. It's raining. I see crowds milling outside the theater, gazing skyward in anxious anticipation. At first, I hear whispers then shouts. French and German blend in a tempest of monosyllabic commands, impassioned pleas and protestations. But I can't make out the words. I see fear in my parent's faces. I smell it on their breaths. I recognize the scent of cold sweat. I hold my breath against the sulfurous emanations of matches being struck and swirls of black tobacco smoke rising toward the darkened sky. The air raid is a ruse concocted by the Gestapo to create panic and lure known insurgents into its web. My father takes me in his arms. He and my mother run in the dark. Panting, they take shelter in a doorway. In the distance, the dreaded shriek of a police whistle pierces the night. I can feel my father's heart pounding against my chest. The sound of cleated shoes grows faint then subsides. We step out of the shadows onto the sidewalk. Our own footsteps, now measured and steady, echo with an eerie resonance in the deserted street. Our shadows stretch then contract as we pass under the pallid light of a gas lamp.

•

I'm sitting wearing short pants on hard wood benches in cold, narrow parlors, waiting for my parents to emerge from offices -- or were they living rooms? I see anguish and exhaustion on their faces as we run down the stairs and race along gray, gloomy streets, our heads down, our coat collars upturned under hats that raise suspicion instead of conferring anonymity.

●

I also remember being taken on endless *Métro* rides, often on the spur of the moment, but I can't say where to or why. I only recall counting the stops on the overhead chart and calling out and repeating the names of the stations on the vaulted tiled walls with a hypnotic cadence born of ennui.

Châtelet
   Réaumur-Sébastopol
     Strasbourg St.-Denis
       Gare de l'Est
         Gare du Nord
           Barbès Rochechouart
             Marcadet-Poissoniers
               Porte de Clignancourt

The names evoke images and sensations even now as I write them and utter them out loud, one by one, but I can't decipher the meager clues they offer. In one of the stations, a large poster attracts my attention: Marianne, France's voluptuous effigy, is being devoured by a large black bird, a vulture with bulging eyes, a hooked beak, a skullcap atop its head, corkscrew tresses dangling from its ears. I behold the silent manifesto, uncomprehending.

"Look, papa, look at the funny bird. Why is he eating the lady?"

"He's not eating her," my father retorts with studied impertinence. "She's forcing herself down his throat and he's gagging, so he's spitting her out. She tastes foul, like liver or tongue." He makes a face. He knows that the mere mention of liver can make me retch. Experience would at once arouse and sustain a loathing for other organ meats and, eventually, for all meat.

"Is the lady made of liver [*foie,* in French]?"

"Non, elle n'est pas de foi." No, she is not of [good] faith. The wordplay is lost on me.

"Does it hurt the lady to be spit out?"

"She doesn't feel a thing. Even her pride is unscathed." A sardonic grin illuminates my father's face. Recklessly, he looks around, seeking approbation (or a hint of rancor) from the other riders. Stone-faced, they stare at a protective void of their own creation. Revolted, my father lets out a string of expletives that draw sidelong glances of discomfiture, fear and moralistic anger.

To seize an opportunity is more difficult than to avert bad luck.

•

One day, at an intersection, I kick a German soldier in the shin and call him a "*sale Boche!*" -- dirty Kraut. The look of horror on my mother's face is indelibly etched on my conscience. I often replay her words in my mind.

"Please forgive him, *Monsieur*, he's only a child. He didn't mean it. He's only four. Please sir, please don't...."

And I relive the unimaginable, the sheer incongruity, as the soldier picks me up in his arms and says, "You know, I have a little boy just like you at home and I love him very much. I hope to see him soon again. You mustn't say what you said. It will make somebody very angry." My mother's expression changes from terror to awe, to incredulity, to gratitude as the soldier sets me gently back down on my feet.

•

In time of war, acts of kindness by the enemy are rare and difficult to measure against a background of wholesale barbarism. When peace returns, pain, bitterness and the urge to settle old scores all conspire to enshrine the evil that men do. Memory and hatred feed upon each other in a self-perpetuating symbiosis of spite and retribution.

"Yes, but this was an anomaly, an oddity, a random act, an eccentricity, as inexplicable as it was fortuitous," someone quibbles.

"The very circumstances under which this random act of compassion took place render it all the more commendable," I fire back.

"You're eulogizing an exception, a chance event, because you lived to recount it."

"It would still have ranked as an extraordinary show of mercy even if I'd later died at the hands of another."

Die and you'll be mourned; survive and you'll be resented.

The debate goes on. I won't prevail.

Breast-beating does the clenched fist more good than it does the heart.

Summoned every time a hint of prejudice threatens to spawn glib and bigoted generalizations, this incident has taught me to challenge slogans and clichés, to reject stubborn beliefs and beware of unyielding convictions. Convictions, Nietzsche warns, are more dangerous enemies of truth than lies. In the worst of all possible worlds, let tolerance be your guide.

When in doubt, celebrate the exception, not the rule.

Such high-mindedness would be put to the test several years later when, traveling on assignment in Germany, I discovered that many Germans still regret having lost the war.

●

Altruism, in any form, is in short supply between 1941 and 1945. At the urging of the Gestapo, over 11,000 Jewish children are picked up by the all-too-cooperative French police. They are roused from their sleep, yanked out of their beds in the middle of the night, seized in the streets, snatched from their parents' arms and taken to Drancy, outside Paris, a detention center staffed by French police. Following triage, the children are carted away in cattle wagons. Their three-day journey ends in death camps in the East where, like so much waste, they are exterminated and reduced to ashes.

Only 300 children survive: the oldest, the strongest, the luckiest.

•

"Inexperience and lack of focus made for a very shaky start. We had little more than purpose and will," my father said about the Résistance. "None of us had the slightest notion how a secret service works, and insights drawn from pulp fiction and *films noirs* proved faulty and dangerous. Much time was spent on organizational details. A number of operations had to be postponed or scrubbed as a result of miscommunication and confusion. In defiance of a cardinal rule of espionage which called for agents to be identified by their initials, we were each given the name of a Paris *Métro* station. I was known as St. Paul -- a neat trick for a Jew -- because I met my handlers a block away, on *Rue des Rosiers* (then and now a predominantly Jewish neighborhood). Early successes, more a function of hazard than aim, confounded the enemy. For a while, the amateurs' gamble paid off."

At first, the Résistance took on a political rather than military character. Great pains were taken to gather information and spread rumors crafted to keep the Germans in a perpetual state of alert and distraction. Teachers, lawyers, writers joined in the creation and dissemination of clandestine publications. One of them, *Résistance*, launched its first edition on December 15, 1940. A month later, acting on a tip, the German police raided a small warehouse, destroyed the presses and executed seven men. Three female employees were later deported and never seen again. Other tracts fared better, some miraculously evading the ever-narrowing German police nets for the duration of the war. One of them, the socialist *Libération Nord*, edited in the basement of a print shop specializing in religious pamphlets, circulated 50,000 copies a week through August 1944.

In 1941, the Résistance, its ranks augmented by unemployed military officers, soldiers of fortune and leading intellectuals -- among them communist and Christian men of letters -- at last turned to guerrilla warfare.

That year, Stalin had proclaimed:

"In all regions occupied by the enemy must be created detachments of irregulars, on foot or horseback, charged with

blowing up bridges, rendering roads unusable, downing power lines, crippling telephone communications, burning railroads, attacking convoys. It is the struggle for our nation's liberty that will fuse with that of Europe and America to bring independence and democratic freedoms."

Delivered for Russian consumption, and heard by communists everywhere, the challenge was not lost on the Résistance.

"We were in urgent need of weapons," my father recounted. "Our arsenal was derisory: clubs, truncheons, meat cleavers, pocketknives, axes, picks, rusty revolvers, ante-bellum shotguns. In extremis, and not without perceptible enjoyment, some of our men used their bare hands. We gained considerably more fire power with the addition of explosives, incendiary devices, and a number of small-caliber machine guns, some pilfered from the men we killed, others procured in England and parachuted behind enemy lines.

"Our orders were to engage the enemy in desperate and unavoidable situations only, and to 'disperse like mercury' which, when clasped, scatters into tiny droplets that are impossible to seize."

Orders were often ignored and lone wolves or splinter groups carried out several daring attacks. The assassination of two of Hitler's point men in France, General Schaumburg and Dr. Ritter, was the handiwork of a Jewish phalanx led by 19-year-old Marcel Rayman. Rayman was executed in 1944 by the French collaborationist *Brigades Spéciales*. Meanwhile, weapons remained in short supply and minor successes were often offset by disastrous failures. Alarmed that elements of the Résistance were joining forces and creating a "red army" on French soil, London held back additional arms shipments, thus preventing modest, isolated strikes from achieving greater tactical success. Although a document circulated by the Communist Party's Central Committee in 1944 added some weight to London's suspicions, such concern had no legitimacy. The presence of British and American troops in France was to have a decidedly inhibiting effect and the communists succeeded only in securing a voice, often strident and disruptive but never dominant, in France's otherwise habitually chaotic political life.

•

Much has been written about the *Résistance*. Opinions and facts heretofore withheld or yet to be exhumed will provide grist for future mills. The final verdict will depend on how one beholds history -- with selective amnesia or preclusive memory. Judgment will also be influenced by the role an ever-shrinking number of WWII veterans may have played in the Résistance. Whether it engages in homage or apologia, exaltation or calumny, a final chapter must justly conclude that France's liberation apparatus was neither monolithic nor homogeneous. In fact, it lacked congruence; it was crippled by discord, given to dissimulation and often compromised by paranoia. Some of its members demonstrated extraordinary daring and sublime selflessness. Others, succumbing to cowardice or greed, betrayed their comrades-in-arms and delivered their compatriots into the enemy's jaws.

"These were humans, not angels," my father would remark; "men at war." Indeed, many served the *Résistance* with honor and distinction. Others used it, fed on it. Here was a microcosm of society: misfits, intellectuals, desperadoes, liberal clergymen, Socialists and Marxists, idealists and opportunists, patriots and survivalists, deserters, decorated line officers and madmen in search of a cause. Circumstance and moral fiber -- not rank or class -- set them apart. Common men died like heroes; blue bloods broke rank, defected. Stranger gave his life to save another's; friend betrayed friend to save his own. In the death camps – Auschwitz-Birkenau, Buchenwald, Dachau, to name a few -- starving prisoners offered their last piece of bread to feed a dying child. Others smothered their bunkmates to steal their rations. Some slept with German officers for an extra bowl of soup. A few became ruthless trustees who could be counted on to beat, torture and kill other Jews.

"*C'est comme ça,*" my father would conclude. That's how it is "Don't try to figure this out. There's no explanation."

To explain evil is to trivialize it.

BETRAYAL, FLIGHT

It is how men exercise freewill under duress that earns them reverence or ignominy. The *"Brigades Spéciales,"* thugs and drifters hired by the French Police to do its dirty work, would earn, in four years, a reputation for perversion and cruelty second only to the Holy Inquisition. The methods they used to wrest confessions were so gruesome that, at his trial, a former Brigade member expressed shock at "the sadism of his compatriots." His was a desperate if futile defense. It was also disingenuous in that it glossed over French history, past and contemporary. Frenchmen had long been at each-others' throats -- quite literally during the 1789 Revolution. They would also bloody their hands during the Dreyfus "affair," a scandal that inflamed political and religious passions, and very nearly brought France to the brink of civil war. Fifty years later, exploiting the chaos and jubilation of *La Libération*, Frenchmen killed again. Some settled old political scores; others slaughtered known collaborators. Compromised, their days numbered, those who had led double lives tracked down witnesses and eliminated potential turncoats. Over 9,000 collaborators were executed at war's end; 1,500 were put to death following summary trials; 40,000 were sentenced to prison.

> *If hatred was an exploitable form of energy the world would drown in an ocean of fuel.*

•

In the "confessionals" of the *Brigades Spéciales*, an old man is denied food and drink for nine days. He expires on the tenth. A patriot's hands are tied for hours to the metal surface of a freezer, then ripped free. Another is burned over ninety percent of his body with cigarettes. A wire is connected to a *Résistant's* handcuffs; another is inserted into his rectum; the ends are plugged into a live socket. In another cell a suspected communist is stripped naked and hanged by his thumbs as heavy weights are tied to his toes. A young priest accused of hiding insurgents in his church loses his penis, and his life, to sulfuric acid. A student is repeatedly sodomized then forced to drink his tormentors' urine. The exotic is often followed by the prosaic: captives have their hair torn from their scalp. They are kicked, punched, whipped, slashed with carving knives. Bones are broken. Eyes are gouged. Ears are severed. Tongues are ripped out and, to stimulate memory or loosen recalcitrant ones, boiled and served to fellow prisoners. Hundreds of Frenchmen succumb to untold agonies at the hands of their *concitoyens*.

Victims of ill treatment can, if they have the courage -- or the folly -- file a complaint and appear before hastily convened kangaroo courts presided by three anonymous judges (the judges "deliberate" behind closed doors!). Denied attorneys, the plaintiffs plead their own cases. They can never win and their tormentors are never brought to justice. Deaf ears and impure hearts further debase the pretense of free speech and equality under law. It's unadulterated Kafka.

> « *The police are such that the Turks would rather suffer pestilence and the English deal with thieves.*
> -- **Nicholas-Sébastien Roch de Chamfort, 1741-94.**

●

The *Brigades Spéciales* also had a distinct aversion for the *youpins*, the *yids*, the Jews. Aversion turned to dementia if their quarries worked for the *Résistance*. Many were apprehended and liquidated. I remember my father sharing the bad news with my mother as they sat side by side on the settee in semi-darkness. I knew the news was bad because my father whispered and his brow was furrowed and my mother's eyes shut tight and she bit her lower lip and cried silently.

"They caught Jacques. He wouldn't talk. They shot him. Pierre is in Drancy. He's being shipped out tomorrow on the first train."

My mother would shake her head and peer intently into my father's eyes. She'd then look at me with a mixture of love and terror.

"What will become of us? We're next. I feel it."

"Nah." My father would dismiss my mother's fears with a wave of his hand. "We're fine, don't worry," he'd say, trying to comfort her.

But his words rang hollow and his reassurances lacked vigor or conviction. Exhausted, clearly overtaken by the situation, he would turn his head and stare out the window. My mother would sigh long, doleful sighs. And I would continue to push a toy truck across the floor, averting their gaze, careful not to communicate my own disquiet.

Many fell. Fellow physician and childhood friend, Samu Moldovan, was yanked out of bed in the middle of the night, hauled to the *Préfecture*, tortured and shot by French police. Another colleague and former schoolmate, Dr. Salzberger, was deported to Buchenwald where he later died. Others, inexplicably, continued to prosper during the occupation. Among them my father's cousin, Ernö Wertheimer, the anesthesiologist, who bought and managed a hospital after the war in the fashionable 16th *arrondissement*; and an old friend, Jean Klein, an internist whose practice, in a posh duplex on Place de la Nation, thrived until his death in the early 1970s. Childless, Klein and his wife, Simone, had taken more than just casual interest in me and had often jokingly offered to take care of me "in these uncertain times." They pressed the point once too often. Troubled by their "sinister jesting," and vexed by their pretense to be Christians, my father distanced himself from his old friend and colleague. We didn't see the Klein again until well after the war.

"Why do you think they made it when so many others didn't," I'd ask my father over the years.

"I won't speculate. I can't risk sullying anyone's memory."

"Surely, someone betrayed you, turned you in."

"Yes."

"Do you know who?"

"I'm not sure."

"Do you suspect anyone?"

"Maybe."

"Friend or acquaintance?"

"Acquaintances rarely double-cross each other. They have nothing to gain."

"Then who?"

"Drop it."

I did but I never stopped wondering.

Suspicion weighs more heavily on the distrustful than on the object of their mistrust.

•

Late one afternoon there's a loud rap at our front door. I'm in my room. The door is ajar but I'm engrossed in play and I hear nothing at first. My father is having coffee in the kitchen.

My mother walks to the door, her heart pounding, she recalls.

"Who is it," she asks, her prophecy unfolding.

"Police. Open up!" The command is followed by another urgent staccato.

My mother fumbles the key in the keyhole, pulls the latch and opens the door.

"Yes? What is it?"

"Let us in."

My mother complies. Two large men in black leather trench coats and wide-brimmed black hats, their hands buried deep inside their pockets, step into the vestibule. Once inside, they pull out their pistols. Lugers, I'm certain. Lugers have a devilish countenance, an air of utter self-possession, arrogance and deadly efficiency that one never forgets.

"What is it? What do you want?"

"Dr. Gutman. Where is he?"

The sound of strange voices draws me out of my room. I pass by the kitchen. My father's face is ashen. He looks dazed. His hands are shaking. Coffee splatters on the floor.

"There must be some mistake. My husband is away. Out of town. He should be back in a few days. Come back then, won't you? I'll tell him you came by."

"That's not true, *maman*. Papa's in the kitchen. I think he needs you. He spilled coffee. Come look."

The two men in the black trench coats exchange glances. A cruel smile twists their lips. They run to the kitchen. Lugers at the ready, they find my father as I'd left him, paralyzed with fear, his trembling hand still clasping the cup.

"Put the cup down," one of the men orders.

My father obeys. As he does, the other thug punches him in the face, breaking his nose. Blood red mixes with coffee brown on the white tile kitchen floor.

My mother sobs uncontrollably. She tries to intervene but one of the men pushes away.

"Papa, papa."

My father looks at me with tenderness and immense pity. He manages a smile through his tears as they drag him down the stairs and shove him in a black Citroen.

I was four, or so. I'd been taught to tell the truth.

We never learned why my mother and I had not shared my father's fate that day. My father would never mention the incident but it is with inconsolable sorrow, shame and everlasting remorse that I will remember this guileless disloyalty for as long as I live.

•

"Henri Lafont. Let me speak to Henri Lafont. This is an emergency." My mother had spent half the night and all morning trying to reach Lafont, one of my father's former patients and now chief of the French Gestapo.

Telephone lines are overloaded. She's put on hold, transferred, disconnected, directed to redial other numbers, urged to call later, tomorrow, next week.

"*Mon Dieu,* he's our last hope," my mother thinks out loud as she nervously wraps and uncoils the telephone cord around her wrist and fingers. "Please, it's a matter of grave urgency. I'm sure he'll take my call if he knows what this is about. Hurry up, please." A few minutes elapse. Suddenly, a look of relief brightens her face. She has exhausted all her tears.

"Allo, Monsieur Lafont?"

"Yes?"

"This is Madame Gutman. Do you remember me?"

"*Oui Madame*, of course. What can I do for you?"

"They took Ari." My mother breaks down.

"*Merde!* Where are you? How can I reach you?"

"At home, 2, rue du Pont Neuf."

"I had nothing to do with this, I swear. Hang tight. Let me find out what happened. I'll call you right back."

Fifteen minutes later, the phone rings. It's Lafont.

"He was taken to Fresnes. They haven't shipped him out yet. There's nothing to worry about. I'll handle this. We'll get him out, I promise. Don't move a muscle, I'll be right there."

•

Picture two Jews in occupied France riding in a German armored car in the company of a French turncoat -- now an officer of the Third Reich -- on our way to rescue a *Résistant* from the clutches of the collaborationist French police. Farfetched. Preposterous. Yet here we were, my mother and I, being waved through one heavily guarded checkpoint after another as we sped toward Fresnes, France's second largest prison located about ten kilometers northeast of Paris. This would not be the last implausible episode in a string of chance events that brought us ever closer to catastrophe. An even more bizarre odyssey awaited us about two years later when we crossed warn-torn Europe by train under Red Cross escort.

•

We arrive at Fresnes. A guard lifts the heavy wood barrier. Lafont gets off and disappears into the sentry box. Impeccably attired in his finely tailored uniform and shiny black leather boots, he oozes confidence and authority. He can be heard placing a call to the office inside the compound.

"This is Capitaine Lafont. Dr. Gutman was picked up yesterday. Yes, 2, rue du Pont Neuf. Release him."

There is a brief pause.

"Don't argue I tell you. I have the papers. Let him go. We're waiting. We're at the gate. Hurry up."

Escorted by two guards, a human figure emerges from a building at the far end of a gloomy courtyard and heads our way. We get out of the car.

"Where's papa," I ask.

"Look," Lafont replies, smiling. "That's him right there. He points at the human figure with a gloved finger.

I look but all I see is a shadow of a man, disheveled and haggard, his clothes in disarray, his lips cut open and bleeding, his eyes nearly shut, limping toward us. My mother runs toward him.

"Ari, Ari, what have they done."

Incredulous, bewildered, uncomprehending, my father spreads his arms and weeps. We rush to embrace him. He kisses my mother then drops to his knees and hugs me. He has received a horrific beating, his face is swollen, two front teeth are missing, but it's him, my beloved father, my papa.

"*Docteur*," says Lafont, "you're free. Let's go. You must leave Paris right away. There's no time to waste."

"I appreciate what you're doing, Henri, but two other men were picked up yesterday by the *Brigades*. They're being shipped to the east tonight. Arrange their release and I'll leave."

Lafont is livid. "You can't be serious."

My mother tugs at my father's sleeve. "Ari, don't...."

"Henri, I rode with these men in the paddy wagon. I don't know who they are but I know and *feel* their faces. They look just like me. See what bare fists and a mean heart can do. After the beatings we were all thrown into the same cell. We cried. We cursed. We threw up. We pissed in long fitful spasms from the blows to our kidneys and bladders. Tears and blood and vomit and urine coalesced on the bare floor in one ugly, agonized mass of mortal matter. Look at me, Henri. I *am* them and they are me. But by some providence, I'm here, alive and offered freedom -- as you were when I treated you, remember? They're still locked up, wallowing in slime, desperate, overcome with fear and about to take their last journey, in a cattle car, to one of the Fuhrer's slaughterhouses. I beg you. Two lives, two miserable souls. Surely, they can't amount to very much in the scheme of things. Why not let them live? Free them Henri. You can do it."

"Gutman, you're crazy. I know I owe you my life but what you're asking is insane. They'll have my neck. And they'll have yours too if you don't get the fuck out of here."

"Henri, you owe me nothing. It's what you owe yourself. Do you think this horror will last forever? What will happen to you when this is over?"

Lafont pushes back the visor of his cap and wipes his brow.

"What do you mean? I'm now up to my neck. What more do you want?"

People never ask for advice without hoping for moral support.

My father had learned early in life that while fresh, hope is full of promise. He could let it wilt. He gently grabs Lafont by the shoulders and draws him close, close enough to smell fear on his breath.

"Do it, Henri. Life is short but memories linger. The war will end one day. Be practical if you can't be noble. Buy yourself some 'soul' insurance. Perhaps history will take note of your magnanimity."

He who walks backwards risks tripping on his future.

•

So Lafont pulled it off. He ordered the two men released in his custody on some pretext. My father asked that they be taken back to Paris but Lafont refused. Instead, he let them loose in the Enghien forest. He would claim they'd contrived to break free.

"Then?"

"Then he drove us back home, pressed us to pack and 'decamp.' He gave us a *laissez-passer* to Lyon. We never saw him again."

•

Lafont had told my father:

"You drive a hard bargain, Gutman."

"Yes, but you were man enough not to dicker in the end. I don't know how this will all pan out but maybe posterity will concede that a sin does not a sinner make if he has shown some decency along the way."

Lafont said nothing. He shook his head, shrugged, smiled pensively and drove away.

Posterity concedes nothing that contradicts the useful or the opportune.

Lafont found it useful and opportune, as many Frenchmen did, to embrace the enemy, to merrily goose-step to its Teutonic leitmotif. It was useful and opportune for the French -- some of whom had danced with him cheek-to-cheek -- to execute Lafont at war's end as it was for Hitler's Germany to massacre millions in its lunatic drive toward world domination.

It would be useful and opportune for the evil that men do to be interred with their bones. But evil, like matter, cannot be destroyed. It is reborn, its face transformed, its essence unchanged and immutable.

Some people find all sorts of excuses to avoid doing the right thing. It's as if they're ashamed to be clean.

IN THE MAQUIS

We arrived in Lyon in the evening, worn out and destitute, save for a few clothes hastily bundled in two small cardboard suitcases, my father's medical satchel, and trinkets my parents hoped to sell for much needed cash along the way.

Abandoning the apartment on Rue du Pont Neuf was especially hard on my mother. She'd grown fond of it, felt at home. She'd described it as "cheerful and charming, a nest with windows on the most beautiful city in the world." I have only a dim recollection of the place.

My father, who had viewed the war as an unsustainable aberration, thought that "revulsion and sheer exhaustion" would soon wear the antagonists down, bring them to their senses and put an end to the madness.

"No sane man can possibly countenance war. No sane man wants to die," he argued. "Surely, when a man finds himself in the thick of battle, when the trenches fill with blood and the air resonates with the screams of the wounded and the dying, it will become apparent that he was put there by other men who will never shed a drop of their own blood, never lose their lives for the causes they espouse."

He reconciled the incongruity of his own involvement in the war by viewing his role in the *Résistance* as a means of hastening the enemy's demise. What he'd wanted most was to resume his medical practice, to heal, to alleviate suffering. His friends' assassination, the unraveling of his underground network, his own arrest, the vicious beating he'd endured, and his narrow escape from certain death in some camp in Germany, Poland or the Ukraine, tempered his optimism, shook his faith in happy endings and altered his concept of sanity.

•

We lost the apartment when we fled Paris. Under a law enacted in 1941, the pro-Nazi Vichy regime set as its objective the elimination of "all Jewish influence in the national economy." The seizure of property belonging to French Jews followed. Of the 330,000 Jews living in France in 1941, about 75,000 were deported to Nazi death camps. Only 2,500 deportees returned. Lies and official trickery would long obscure the precise role France played in the deportation of Jews and the plundering of their assets during the war. We would never set foot in our apartment again. Half-hearted attempts to regain possession after the war failed. Despite sworn statements by several fellow-*Maquisards*, among them members of the *Armagnac Bataillon*, a snarled, hostile bureaucracy and a severe housing shortage dampened all hope of restitution.

•

Lyon was a crucial center of the *Résistance* during the occupation and my father lost no time contacting Jean-Pierre Lévy. Founder of *Franc-Tireur* (Sniper), a successful clandestine publication dedicated to Socialist and radical causes, Lévy found us a small room above a barbershop for the night. We left Lyon before dawn on the first leg of a circuitous journey that would take us west to Clermont-Ferrand, southeast to Le Puy, southwest to Rodez and Montauban, south to Toulouse and west again to Auch and Vic-Fézensac, in the heart of Gascony. Coded instructions signed by the people in Lyon and addressed to a Monsieur Lagorce, owner of a café in Vic-Fézensac, earned my father immediate conscription into the Maquis. He was given a new name -- Docteur Guillemin, a *nom de guerre* by which he would be widely known and remembered in the region well after the war.

•

It was at that time that I, too, assumed a new identity. My father's miraculous escape from Fresnes Prison and our nighttime flight from Paris coincided with a scheme to erase in me any conscious sense of Jewish selfhood. This did not prove difficult; I'd never received any religious instruction. All I'd learned is that being Jewish can be detrimental to one's health. The opportunity to playact, a pastime for which I seemed well suited at an early age (I was told I used to parody Hitler and Mussolini, and imitate Maurice Chevalier and Charlie

Chaplin) added to the allure. Outlandish as it was inventive, the biography my parents concocted for me -- just in case they were intercepted and we became separated -- would have made Baron Munchausen blush with envy. We rehearsed, often and extemporaneously. My father would assume a heavy German accent, mimicking the overbearing manner of an SS interrogator.

"Vat is your name?"
"Wilhelm Guillaume."
"Vere vere you born?"
"I was born in Surabaya, Java."
"Vat vere you doink in Java?"
"My father was a career diplomat before the war."
"Vat is your religion?"
"Lutheran."

I also learned to cross myself and could recite by heart from Matthew, Mark, Luke and John. Owing an absence of any discernible stereotypical Semitic features, I managed to pass for the perfect little *goy*. This role would be further refined in a monastery where I was given refuge during a particularly perilous mission in which my mother took part. I tenaciously clung to this fiction until the end of the war.

The war, with all its dangers, uncertainties and twists and turns also taught me stealth, alacrity and patience. At an age when children are incapable of modulating their voices, when curiosity or exuberance yields an incessant flow of questions, when fun sparks laughter or a scraped knee elicits earsplitting shrieks, I learned to whisper, to hold my breath, to tiptoe, to make myself small, to sit still behind a bolted door as the cadence of German boots faded in the distance. I also learned how to wait, sick with worry at the edge of a forest clearing, for my father to emerge from the shadows in the middle of the night at the head of a dozen other men. I understood the uncompromising urgency to love him without uttering a single word and to see him vanish back in the woods with no guarantee that I'd ever see him again.

Patience is a form of self-respect.

•

It was in late 1942 that groups of insurgents joined forces and began to operate from mountain retreats, forest hideaways, swamps and caves. Efforts to finance the *Maquis* with public support bore little fruit. Everybody applauded it; few dared support it.

"Weapons were in short supply in the beginning," my father told me. "Cells in the area took turns manning a lone submachine gun. Fortunately, the Germans had no idea how poorly equipped we were and they ventured into our turf with extreme circumspection."

Several French Army officers eventually joined the *Maquis*. Pierre Dalloz, organizer of the Vercors, wrote:

"They had their idiosyncrasies, their apartments, their families in the big cities. They helped train us as best they could but when a risky operation was planned we had to act alone."

Jean Galtier-Boissière, the editor of the satirical magazine *Crapouillot* and author of *l'Histoire de la Guerre 1939-1945* (History of the War 1939-1945) wrote:

"Large sums were soon collected from raids on public funds. With the complicity of its director, one hundred million francs were withdrawn from a bank and parceled out to the families of the Maquisards -- 800 francs per wife, 500 francs per child."

Despite their vigilance, the Germans did not take the *Maquis* seriously at first. German propaganda chief, Joseph Goebbels, called it a "revolution of the lazy to defend their tendency to do nothing." This assessment was both premature and groundless. A few months later, the Abwehr and the S.D. (SS Intelligence Service) would denounce the "dastardly acts of the terrorists" against its troops and conduct punitive raids in which dozens of innocent civilians were lined up against a wall and shot.

The importance and exploits of the *Maquis* are still being contested. Many believe that its successes were rare and limited, and were offset by suffering and an unacceptably high loss of life. If the *Maquis* had not existed, some argue, France would have been retaken a month or two later, whereas German reprisals could have been avoided, as would have been the fratricidal bloodbath that followed the liberation of France.

Writing in the January 30, 1948 edition of the *Liverpool Daily Post*, Sir Basil Henry Liddell Hart (1895-1970), the British military scientist, agreed:

"The Résistance no doubt exerted considerable pressure on the Germans. The Maquis interfered with their ability to thwart the Allied advance. In analyzing these operations, however, it would appear that their efficacy was narrowly dependent on a sustained degree of coordination with regular military actions against the enemy. Thus, [the Maquis] rarely became more than an inconvenience. On the whole, its exploits proved less effective than passive resistance. Worse, they invited immediate and cruel retribution far out of proportion with the losses they might have inflicted on the Germans, and brought on enormous suffering on their compatriots."

Liddell Hart was also skeptical of some of the *Maquisards*' integrity:

"The Résistance attracted many undesirables and gave them the opportunity to indulge their evil instincts and to vent their hostilities under the cover of patriotism, thereby adding new meaning to Dr. [Samuel] Johnson's historic remark that 'patriotism is the last refuge of scoundrels.'"

Whereas German Generals Warlimont, Blaskowitz and von Wittersheim, of the 2nd Panzer Division, conceded that their troops had suffered "grave losses from the heroic actions of the *Maquis*."

Americans, likewise, lavished praise on the *"fifis"* and acknowledged their invaluable role in assisting two Allied landings. Writing in *Ultra Secret,* war correspondent Robert Ingersoll acknowledges:

> *"We were amazed to discover that the Résistance was in fact so effective that six enemy divisions failed to paralyze it -- six divisions that we otherwise would have had to face alone. The most blasé among us quickly rallied when German officers confessed that they had lived in terror in France's open country and had lost total control in many regions well before our arrival. It is likely that the Maquis achieved the work of twenty divisions."*

General Dwight D. Eisenhower concurred, though his assessment was more conservative:

> *"G.H.Q. estimated that, at times, the help lent by the Free French forces to our campaign represented the equivalent of fifteen divisions. Their support considerably enhanced the speed of our advance through France."*

•

I remember little from that period. The names of three small towns in southwestern France -- Barbotan, Cazaubon and Estang -- evoke images of frequent and hurried treks between them, by car, bicycle, on foot, in the middle of the night as a huge yellow moon cast a ghostly pallor upon my parents' faces. What stands out in this hodgepodge of mangled memories is the name of an old chateau: Bégué. In his book, Chronicles of the War Years, 1939-1945, author and Résistance veteran, Pierre Cames, describes its role in the war years as *epic*:

> *"[Bégué] was, for the Jews, an island of humanity in an ocean of barbarism. Like hunted beasts, most of the men and women who took refuge in this precarious haven had clawed their way out of a pit of human bestiality. They had eluded frightening manhunts and the implacable cruelty of Nazi madness; they could now catch their breath."*

Turning the chateau into a shelter for fugitive Jews was the brainchild of Father Elie -- Alexandre Glasberg -- the Polish-born Jew who converted to Catholicism in the early 1930s and served the Résistance with uncommon valor. Father Elie had overstepped his authority and taken uncommon risks by defying the predominantly anti-Semitic and collaborationist Catholic hierarchy. He is remembered as a hero of the Résistance and was recognized by the State of Israel as Righteous among the Nations.

The little I remember of the Chateau de Bégué is faded, gossamer, and threadbare, like fragments of a dissolving dream: A large common dining room swarming with loud, restive throngs; a place throbbing with anticipation and anxiety, hope and foreboding; a shelter where broken spirits could mend and, if they were up to the task, train for the long fight the Résistance aimed to bring to the enemy. My parents and I spent some time there. Days? Weeks? I couldn't say.

•

Recollected with near perfect clarity, two incidents would remain forever etched in my memory. I vouch for their authenticity; I can't assign them a specific place or time. Nor can I reconstruct with any degree of accuracy, the events that preceded or followed. They loom from the depths of my memory, isolated and visible like the tip of an iceberg in an otherwise empty sea.

Food was scarce during the occupation but members of the *Maquis* and their families seldom wanted. Farmers gave generously and my father accepted potatoes, leeks, onions, eggs and an occasional wedge of cheese in lieu of honorarium whenever he delivered a baby or tended to sick or wounded comrades. Fresh meat was more difficult to obtain due in part to a shortage of livestock. Hunting was discouraged because shooting guns invariably drew the Germans' attention.

Despite these restrictions, we could count on our weekly allotment, about five hundred grams of beef, horsemeat or lamb. My mother would remove the meat from the coarse brown paper wrappings, assess freshness by color and smell and cook it immediately. One day, the deliveryman brought a piece of meat that was unlike any other my mother had ever seen. Pinkish rather than red, the flesh had an unfamiliar consistency and appearance. Worse, it emitted an indescribable pungency and was adorned on one side with a patch of soft, short flaxen hair. Suspicious, my mother asked the man to wait while she summoned my father.

"Ari, look at this. What is it?"

My father exploded. "It's not *what* but *who*!" He retched. My mother ran out of the house screaming.

The deliveryman turned white and nearly fainted. "What do you mean, *who*," he asked, his eyes big with outrage and disbelief.

"This is part of a human thigh," my father bellowed. "Where did you get it?"

The man mentioned a name.

"Find out where it came from. I demand an answer next time I see you, you understand? Take this monstrosity with you and bury it."

The story, as I can best reconstruct it, is that a poacher had shot and killed a German soldier, cut up usable parts of his body, and distributed them through the underground food network. It is likely that some less enlightened -- or less finicky -- end-users dined on their gruesome ration that week.

My father later told me that he would have "beaten the poacher unconscious" had he run into him.

Something my old friend Max said thirty years later gave this incident fresh metaphorical poignancy. Max kept large land crabs in a cistern in the lush garden behind his house in Barbados. He used them for bait and fed them scraps of fish he'd caught earlier in the day.

"It gives the crabs a chance to get even -- in advance," Max had remarked without a trace of sarcasm.

•

Attacks on German soldiers were swiftly countered with public executions. Staged to set an example and deter further aggression against the occupier, these grisly pageants also palliated the enemy's frustration while satisfying their need for vengeance. One morning, I recall, ten men, eight of them veterans of the First World War, were dragged to the village square, lined up against the church wall and shot to avenge the murder of a German officer who'd been screwing the baker's daughter. I saw them crumple, lifeless, on the cobbled sidewalk. Their duty done, ten pink-faced young men barely out of their teens placed their rifles on their shoulders, spun on their heels and marched away, single file, expressionless, robot-like in their mustard-brown uniforms. I remember staring at the pitiful assemblage of inert, scrunched bodies, blood oozing from their open mouths, their eyes staring in the void, like the eyes of a doll. I also remember telling myself over and over that I'd been treated to a grotesque but otherwise harmless spectacle, a dramatization of unimaginable realism, mere cinema. It began to rain and a steady downpour washed away the blood as onlookers scattered and dissolved in a gray sulfur-laden mist.

The baker's daughter survived the war only to have her head shaved in a public orgy of bestiality and later beaten to death by exultant "freedom fighters," many of whom had screwed France to the bone when nobody looked.

•

Responding to German bombardments, Allied air forces began attacking German cities. The first raid on Lübeck in March 1942 gave the enemy a foretaste of the infernos that would engulf Berlin, Dresden, Hamburg, Frankfurt and Munich during the next two years. Wave after wave, thousands of planes dropped their deadly cargo in "saturation bombing" runs that flattened most of Germany's urban centers. American planes released nearly one million tons of bombs over Europe. The British dropped well over a quarter of a million tons of high explosives.

In France, the first major Allied raid killed 600 and wounded 1,500 civilians in and around the Renault factory. A second expedition in 1943 over Longchamps killed 400 and wounded 500. Allied planes then attacked seaports and industrial centers. The bombardment of Nantes, an important harbor on the Atlantic, killed 1,200 civilians when several bombs struck, "by mistake," an entire neighborhood. In Toulon, on the Mediterranean, 450 civilians were killed. Preceding and accompanying the Allied landings, American raids on Lyon, Marseille and the Paris region claimed an additional 2,000 lives.

French reaction to the bombings was a function of political conviction and varied, depending on the damage the bombs inflicted. Reassurances and impassioned exhortations by armchair stoics did little to comfort the victims. For the parents and children of the thousands pulverized by direct hits or reduced to pulp under tons of stone and concrete, knowing that the bombs came from the "liberators" was of very little consolation.

Resentment against the raids was not limited to collaborators, Nazi sympathizers or communists. Expressing consternation and bitterness to his handlers in London, a key *Résistance* chieftain, characterized as "moronic and criminal" bombardments that "exterminated Frenchmen by the hundreds but failed to meet the Allies' military objectives." Years later, this characterization would come to mind, justifiably, when U.S. forces shelled Vietnam, Baghdad (twice in a decade), Belgrade, Afghanistan and Pakistan.

The depraved indifference, with which the Allies -- Americans in particular -- leveled off scores of French towns and killed their inhabitants, continued after the victory in Normandy. Le Havre, which bled during the German invasion and sustained four years of "strategic" bombardments, was subsequently razed.

But the bombardments also drove a wedge in the Axis alliance. I'd learned to manipulate the radio and could fine-tune the short-wave bands and lock on the BBC for the latest news of the war. (The first four notes of Beethoven's Fifth Symphony always preceded the broadcasts. I owe a passion for classical music and a special reverence for Beethoven to these four portentous notes). The broadcasts offered up-to-the-minute reports on the latest campaigns. If the broadcasts from London were to be believed, things were looking up.

The winds of war also pushed open a window of opportunity my parents promptly exploited with a naiveté, recklessness and blind optimism that would characterize many of our undertakings.

Hard luck is more tenacious than good fortune -- and more dependable.

One trusts chance more than probability.

A fool is a brave man who won't listen to reason.

ROMANIA, ROMANIA

In June 1944, as the battle of Normandy raged on, the formidable Russian armies launched a lightning two-pronged offensive. On the Baltic, demoralized, short on supplies, large German battle groups were surrounded and captured. For the first time, entire German garrisons were surrendering *en masse*.

On the southern front, the Soviets entered and seized Iasi, the capital of Moldavia where my mother and grandmother were born. Long persecuted as "Christ-killers," hated for their affluence and scholarship, the Jews of Iasi were now accused of "communist leanings" and abetting the Russian invasion. Goaded by such suspicions, the pro-Axis government of Marshall Ion Antonescu had moved against the city's Jewish community and prominent Jews, among them journalists, were arrested and imprisoned in Tîrgu Jiu.

Soviet bombers first strafed Iasi on June 24. The attack caused relatively little damage. The second bombardment, two days later, killed over 100 people. That same day, Police Chief Kirilovich summoned Jewish leaders to his office. He accused them of covertly communicating with Soviet pilots and threatened to kill 100 Jews for every German or Romanian casualty. In the evening, looking for evidence of complicity -- flags, flashlights, radio transmitters and "communist literature" -- 800 military and civil guards fanned out in a massive raid on Jewish homes. Many were severely beaten and robbed. Over 300 people were arrested. On June 27, Romanian soldiers evacuated more than 300 Jews from the Bessarabian town of Sculeni, forcing them across the Prut River to the Moldavian side. There, they were first forced to dig trenches then robbed, massacred and hastily buried.

In a monograph published in 1988 by the International Journal of Romanian Studies, history Professor Henry Eaton, of the University of North Texas at Denton, recalls:

> "Iasi, that day, was a terrifying contrast of emptiness and violence -- silent houses and deserted streets suddenly alive with gangs of thugs, shots and screams. Towards evening, there were hurried visits to the synagogues. Five Jews were arrested and sent to the rail yard of the 13th Infantry Regiment to mark unexploded bombs and their locations. They were chosen for the dangerous work because Jews were alleged to have directed the Russian bombs onto the military compound. The five were then murdered and their bodies were dumped on the city's outskirts."

The following morning, Prof. Eaton recounts, thirty Romanian soldiers began looting Jewish residences on the pretext that they were looking for radio transmitters. That night, a plane dropped a white flare over Iasi, setting off sirens, triggering a barrage of small arms and automatic fire, and signaling the wholesale arrest, plunder and murder of Jews. German and Romanian military patrols, sometimes accompanied by civilian "trainees," broke into Jewish homes, dragged residents out into the street, beating and killing those who resisted, robbing them, and hauling them off in convoys, hands over their heads, to various police precincts. About 2,000 were rounded up by daybreak. Groups of civilians, including members of the Iron Guard, joined in the lynching, roaming Jewish neighborhoods and beating people, sometimes with nail-studded clubs or lead-weighted truncheons.

> "The new day brought more intense violence. Convoys of Jews, viciously abused, arrived at the Central Station and were forced, single file, through the gates into the courtyard, between rows of German soldiers swinging crowbars and clubs. Some of the prisoners were killed on the spot."

That afternoon, another alarm sounded and automatic weapons, including machine guns placed around the police station's courtyard, were aimed at the prisoners and fired.

> *"... The firing went on intermittently until about six. Perhaps 4,000 or more were killed and many of the survivors were wounded. A few managed to climb the stone wall and escape. Those who were not killed and others, rounded up during and after the massacre, were cruelly herded to the railway station and crammed into suffocating boxcars whose doors and vents had been sealed shut. Nearly 1,200 died in the cars of one train that meandered for six days south to Călărași. In the weeks that followed the Iasi pogrom, Romanian soldiers killed thousands of innocent people in Bessarabia. In October they slaughtered tens of thousands of Jews in Odessa."*

•

Egged on by Romanian government bulletins promising Romanian expatriates safe-conduct back home, inferring -- foolishly -- from news from the front that the war was coming to an end, and feeling increasingly unsafe as the German occupation widened across France, my parents decided to leave France. We spent three days and nights switching from crowded Pullman coaches to dilapidated wagon trains and passing through countless military checkpoints. Three days and nights spent averting the probing gaze of railroad police, internal security officers, and border-crossing constabulary. Three days and nights to reach Bucharest, convinced that peace was at hand and just in time to grasp the awful truth, that it would take yet another year, more air raids, bloodshed and madness before war gasped its last.

"We took an incalculable risk," my father would later reflect. "It was sheer folly. I don't know how we ever pulled it off."

On August 24 the Luftwaffe bombarded Bucharest. Romania seceded from the Axis, declared war on Germany and, joined by Russian forces, attacked the Wehrmacht.

Six days later, the Red Army reached the Ploiesti oil fields and entered Bucharest. On September 6, King Michael declared war on Hungary which, with Hitler's blessings, had expropriated Transylvania.

On September 12, the young monarch signed an armistice treaty with the Russians and ordered the Romanian army, heretofore an instrument of the Germans, to turn their weapons against them. In a final round -- Field Marshal Montgomery called it "a sensational knock-out punch" -- the combined U.S. and British air forces pursued the retreating Germans, severed their supply routes and proceeded to carpet bomb Bucharest.

•

I can still hear the furious dissonance of war. My mind's ear swells with the ghoulish wail of sirens as we dash frantically to reach damp, cold underground air-raid shelters. The long, low-pitched hum of a hundred flying fortresses cruising overhead in formation still reverberates inside my chest. The sounds, the images are all there to be retrieved when acts of human folly awaken childhood memories: the shrill whine of bombs diving earthward, the muffled detonations, the sickening groan of buildings splitting apart and collapsing like sandcastles, the smell of gunpowder, the odor of death.

•

One air raid lasted five days. I'd come down with the measles. Induced by high fever and aggravated by fear, hallucinations kept me in a constant state of agitation that alarmed my parents and lent a surreal aura to an atmosphere thick with desolation and fear. There was little to eat or drink. Braver men in the shelter, my father among them, periodically looted food stores and pharmacies as incendiary devices and concussion bombs peppered the city. Some of the men never made it back.

On the fifth day, when the all-clear signaled the end of the raid, my father wrapped me in a blanket and carried me out. Acclimated to darkness, my eyes refused at first to register the apocalyptic sight to which they were being treated. What I beheld was a scene straight out of Hieronymus Bosch's *Last Judgment*. The city was ablaze. Standing amid the smoldering rubble, skeletal fragments of retaining walls rose against the sky like accusing fingers. Swirling smoke and dust fused into a gritty alloy that brought on fits of violent coughing. The streets were littered with debris. Lampposts were bent out of shape or sheared clean off their base. Automobiles, buses, tramways lay on their sides, pitted, blistered and gutted, tongues of fire still devouring combustible scrap. Sewer lines had burst and craters filled with brackish water percolated spasmodically, stirred by some subterranean convulsion. Contorted and disfigured, men, women, and children lay pell-mell amid twisted, fuming wreckage. Some had been ripped apart by the sheer force of the blasts. Others were draped around tree trunks or impaled on fence posts. Frozen in time and space by death's hideous choreography, others yet hung limp over parapets and railings like disembodied marionettes. Eviscerated, blood oozing from their nostrils, horses stared into an emptiness that their eyes could no longer see. For them all, the poetry, the music, the cadence, the absurdity of life, had been cut short.

Cradled in my father's arms, witness to this unfathomable landscape, haunted by the countenance of death, frightened by its irreducible totality, I remember feeling great sadness and, beneath the sadness, a powerless, childlike rage.

"Why? papa, why?"

My father tightened his embrace, placed his forehead upon mine and smiled softly.

"Don't worry, son, don't worry. Everything will be fine. You must believe that."

I looked at the others as they scattered in search of survivors.

I remember closing my eyes, hoping in vain that this vision of hell would vanish somehow. Yesterday's visions, I would learn, are what tomorrow's nightmares are made of.

"Why, papa, why?" I kept asking, as I fell asleep in his arms. Only my own death, I understood with precocious insight, would one day put an end to the question. My father was right. There is no explanation.

When faced with the unanswerable, only questions remain.

•

On April 24, 1945, the armies of Koniev and Zukhov joined at Potsdam. The siege of Berlin began: 610 pieces of artillery rained 25,000 tons of explosives on the capital. Engaging in wholesale looting, rape and slaughter, Russian soldiers then took the city house by house, block by block.

On April 30, Hitler, Eva Braun, the Goebbels and Wehmacht Chief of Staff, General Krebs, committed suicide. Two days later, the Germans hoisted the white flag. On May 4, after blowing up the dikes of the Zuyderzee and flooding the country, German troops in Holland capitulated.

Himmler tried in vain to negotiate a deal with Swedish Count Bernadotte while Goering surrendered to an American general who promptly invited him to lunch.

At 02:41 on May 7, in Reims, the armies of the Third Reich surrendered unconditionally. Signed by General Jodl, the document was countersigned the next day in Berlin by Generals Keitel for Germany, Zukhov for the USSR, Tedder for the U.K. and Eisenhower for the U.S.

In Europe, the Second World War had ended.

I was seven.

In the frenetic few weeks that followed the liberation of Paris, court-ordered executions, military purges, political power plays and personal feuds claimed about 100,000 French lives, among them those who collaborated passively, to survive, others who had sold themselves with enthusiasm.

In his engrossing and richly detailed account, *And the Show Went On: Cultural Life in Nazi-Occupied Paris* [Knopf, 2010], Alan Riding writes,

> *"Even as Parisians finally slept without fearing a knock on their front door, a purge of the past began. No one doubted that it was necessary. France had been betrayed, dreadful crimes had been committed and now, as part of the rite of passage from occupation to liberation, the rule of law should be seen to prevail. But before an appropriate legal structure could be put in place, vengeance erupted spontaneously. As towns and villages were liberated, perhaps as many as 9,000 miliciens, collaborators and black marketers were summarily executed, both by furious individual citizens and by the resistance, now, at least theoretically, under the single banner of the Forces Françaises de l'Intérieur, or FFI."*

Condemned to death following a short trial, Henri Chamberlain Lafont, the traitor who saved my father's life, and his accomplice Bonny, were executed. Many others were among the casualties of the *"épuration sauvage"* -- the "savage purge" that swept France after the liberation.

One can be a patriot and a scoundrel. The two work well together.

The Americans had fewer scruples. They helped war criminals escape, resettling some in the U.S., others in Latin America. The Cold War had begun and former enemies could be put to work to fight new conflicts.

•

With the end of the hostilities, life in Bucharest assumed a semblance of normalcy that was as deceptive as it was brief. The next four years would bring abrupt political change, repression and, finally, a reign of terror every bit as evil and ruinous as the Fascist pogroms that preceded the communist takeover. Predictably, the staunchest backers of Nazi sympathizer, Marshall Ion Antonescu, executed in 1944, became -- overnight -- the most ardent Stalinists. The very same rabble that had strutted in green shirts, black boots and leather straps, that had spewed Nazi slogans and beat up Jews, promptly donned red scarves, learned to hum the *Internationale*, declared their everlasting loyalty to the working class -- and beat up Jews. Rarely the fruits of conviction, such metamorphoses occur in the blink of an eye and are always accompanied by both vigorous denunciations of one's previous allegiance and pledges of fidelity to the new cause. To defect is human.

•

According to Schopenhauer, all truths go through three stages: They are first ridiculed, then bitterly contested and finally, if grudgingly, endorsed. What Schopenhauer did not say is that a shift in popular convictions, both simulated and short-lived, occurs between the second and third stages. Men are less impressed by the indisputability of an argument than by the ardor with which it is promoted.

Bill Clinton would later write, "The road to tyranny begins with the annihilation of truth," a tactic that the fans of "law and order" adopt when "chaos" risks to upend their opportunistic version of discipline and public well-being. Much evil will be done in the name of "order," "justice" and a one-sided, one-size-fits-all brand of morality.

It is in the name of "solidarity" that nations commit their most heinous crimes: they demand that victims of oppression forgive their tormentors who, in the name of "national reconciliation," go scot free.

Order replaces disorder, and when order constricts and oppresses as it is wont to do, rebels and despots trade places until it's impossible to tell them apart. The world will continue to produce would-be redeemers bent on saving us -- or else. They will preach altruism and peace and practice neither for fear that doing so might cost them their power. The spider will spin her web, the sun will rise, the cockerel will proclaim the birth of a new day, and we will spurt out of our mothers' bellies, wet and cold, only to thrash about for a time on battlefields and assembly lines, while the tax collector.... "Order" is an imaginary state contrived by the political authority of the moment. Only brute will and the survival instinct animate man. All the calamities that befell the world can be traced to the relentlessness of those who believe themselves sole masters of the truth.

Treachery is the province of man.

●

Bons-vivants, gregarious, anxious to put the war behind them, my uncle and my grandmother with whom we shared an apartment in the elegant Wilson Building, on Boulevard Brátiano, began to entertain again. These gatherings -- they called them *"soirées"* -- were elaborate affairs, and my mother and grandmother would often spend the day in the kitchen, creating delicacies designed to please the palate and sculpted to charm the eye. Twice a week or so, a plump young peasant woman, a bright scarf partly covering her ruddy cheeks, would run up the back stairs and deliver some key ingredients: baskets of freshly laid eggs, sour cream, several types of cheeses, red currants, boysenberries. My grandmother would candle the eggs and reject questionable ones. The woman would also bring corn meal, pork loins, rolls of Sibiu salami and live chickens. Retiring to the rear terrace, she'd slit the birds' necks with a deft slash of a small curved knife that she kept in the folds of her multi-layered, ankle-long frock. The blood would collect in a shallow pan and I remember watching, mesmerized and horrified all at once, the desperate thrashings of the now headless birds. Squatting on her heels, her white underwear accentuating the fullness of her pink thighs, the young woman would bare a semi-toothless grin in which I discerned both reassurance and mockery. Her posture, suggestive and vaguely enticing, telegraphed more than I understood at the time. I would soon discover the tantalizing secrets that lay hidden beneath all that finery, with her help, in the maids' quarters.

•

My grandmother's "soirées" drew the cream of Bucharest society. Actors, artists, poets, architects, lawyers came together for an evening of fine cuisine and very small talk. Sometimes they split up into groups of four and played Bridge, a game that transforms the very best of friends into raving maniacs. High on strong, aromatic Turkish coffee, munching on halvah, pistachios and *rahat lukhum*, a sickeningly sweet marshmallow-like comfit sprinkled with scented powdered sugar, the players would often stay through the early morning hours. Tables had been set up in each of the bedrooms, effectively preventing reluctant kibitzers -- my mother, my father and me -- from going to bed. My mother was livid; she enjoyed company, up to a point, and on own her terms, but she favored a good book, her crossword puzzles, a game or two of solitaire and a good night's sleep to pouring coffee and emptying ashtrays. She would yawn and make frequent trips to the bathroom. Deterred by a game in which *partners* call each other "imbecile and schmuck," and bored with idle chatter, my father would retire to the terrace or go out for long walks. I would invariably be put to sleep on the settee in the smoke-filled parlor, only to be awakened when company parted amid interminable good-byes, obsequious praise for the cuisine and wordy pledges to do it again real soon.

Some of the regulars sported a stately bearing but seemed to have no clear means of support. Nobility titles, bought, granted or finagled, and friendly ties with King Michael's father, Carol of Hohenzollern, had earned them a very special ranking in Romania's class-conscious society. Status, useless unless it can be flaunted several degrees beneath one's own, compelled these people to circulate among commoners -- intellectuals, people in the liberal trades and big merchants. Despite the decorum, this was an incestuous commerce that cleared the way for endless solicitations, deals and favors. A decadent vestige of Ottoman customs suitably corrupted by Western artifice and cunning, wheeling and dealing permeated these get-togethers, as they did all strata of Romanian society.

The best deal? Buy men at their face value and resell them at the inflated price they think they're worth.

The fundamental premise of the social contract, my uncle often declared with a pragmatism that suffused all of his relationships, "is to create mutual indebtedness. A gift is an investment. The more obligations one discharges, the more tribute one can exact." It is no wonder that his law practice, dedicated to the proposition that clients who cannot be turned into long-term assets are not worth defending, thrived as it did. He also carried these principles into his love life -- but with considerably less success. He had married a ravishing but headstrong and unschooled young woman who would neither be tamed nor educated, and who, in appreciation for his efforts to civilize her, engaged in brazen affairs whenever his back was turned. The marriage lasted about a year. He never remarried, arguing that women are by nature intractable and despotic.

Incurably romantic, my uncle returned to bachelorhood, this time for good. He forgave his ex-wife's indiscretions. They remained good friends. "To love an unfaithful woman," he would assert, "is to perversely love the competition." One must suppose that infidelity absolved is the echo of an exhausted relationship.

> *One ties the knot with an infusion of courage. One remains a bachelor by scaring oneself silly. Once contracted, bachelorhood is a malady one rarely wishes to treat.*

> *Women are fond of romantic men but marry realists -- whom they proceed to cuckold with romantics.*

> *Sharing the same likes is not enough to ensure harmony in a marriage. Couples must especially hate the same things. Some eventually discover that they hate each other.*

> *Every marriage reaches a point when partners ask themselves: Should I stay or leave? Should I suffer or pack my bags?*

•

Twenty years later or so, I would emulate my uncle. I married a beautiful, stubborn and uncultured woman who resisted acculturation the way a dog recoils from perfume.

> *Every man is a Pygmalion but not all marble will produce a Galatea.*

Culminating in contentious divorce, this relationship would evoke increasingly uncharitable commentaries on love, women and matrimony.

> *There is only one thing worse than a stupid and mean woman: A stupid, mean and sexy woman.*

> *Romantic love is a perfume lacking a fixative.*

> *So long as love is aflame one can't feel the burns.*

Men are unfaithful not to "find better," but to know something else or to confirm that they can still get an erection.

•

My maternal grandparents had both purveyed and been the recipients of favors and accommodations in their day. My grandfather (he died the day I was born) was a veteran engineer with Siemens. But he was better known as a jurist, a poet and a newspaper columnist who had killed another journalist in a duel following a protracted war of words waged on the front pages of their respective publications. The incident caused a sensation. My grandfather had never owned a weapon, let alone fired one; his challenger was a marksman and a seasoned duelist. Reluctantly heard by a sympathetic magistrate (his rival was unpopular) the case earned my grandfather a six-month jail sentence. He spent thirty days in a comfortable studio, next to the warden's office, where he continued to write, entertained family and friends, and ate catered gourmet meals. The remainder of his sentence was reduced to time served and he was released for good behavior. In his day, as in this, men of means and distinction, however reprehensible their offenses, rarely faced long prison terms.

Milked for months by the press, the affair had piqued King Carol's interest and earned my grandparents entry to the court. This privilege would provide an inexhaustible supply of anecdotal material with which my grandmother, a witty storyteller, regaled her audiences. Her renderings, astute and caustic, offered a glimpse of court life and keen insights into Romanian society at the turn of the century.

King Carol's life and reign were riddled with scandal. He divorced his first wife to marry Princess Helen of Greece. He stepped down in favor of his son, Michael, in 1940. He then maintained an open liaison with Magda Lupescu, whom he eventually married in 1947. He died in Spain in 1953, the year I graduated from high school.

•

"I was pleasantly surprised to discover that their majesties were human," my grandmother remarked many years later. "Were it not for heredity and dynastic fortunes, they would have passed for the most ordinary of commoners. It's amazing how lineage, blue eyes and a crown enhance a person's stature. Mind you, I caught Carol picking his nose once or twice with a great insouciance that was as sickening as it was regal. I also remember him laughing heartily as high-ranking Prussian officers gathered around him after dinner and took turns farting with an effrontery bordering on premeditation. I coughed and cleared my throat and raised my voice in vain hopes of drowning out the contemptible cannonade. For all I know, his majesty himself may have taken part in this odious contest. You have no idea how embarrassed I was." The story goes that when the king apologized on behalf of his guests by saying, "what can you do, they're only men," my grandmother retorted, "What can you do, God created woman; *she* must have fashioned man with the scraps."

One of the officers, "Baron-von-something-or-other, a red-faced, sweaty little man wearing a uniform three sizes too small, liked young boys" -- a vice also imputed to the king but which, to my grandmother's knowledge, was never established. Anyway, the baron's tastes were an open secret, and it was widely rumored that country youths were habitually smuggled into the palace, to be enjoyed by courtiers of both sexes, with "Baron-von-something-or-other" presiding over the saturnalia.

It was also alleged that one of Queen Helen's attendants, a highly educated woman with an otherwise flawless pedigree, regularly free-lanced in one of Bucharest's vilest whorehouses. A latter-day Messalina, she would sneak out of the palace late at night, hail a carriage and drive to *Crucea de Piatrá* [the *Stone Cross*] a neighborhood on the outskirts of Bucharest known for its bordellos, and take on a dozen men -- the more lowbred and repulsive, the better. She would sneak back into the palace just before dawn and tend to the queen as if nothing had happened. Some said that Helen herself was being romanced during her attendant's nocturnal escapades by the court's spiritual advisor, a young, handsome, Rasputin-like Orthodox priest with a florid black beard, drooping eyelids and an enigmatic smile.

Gossip was rife at the court; but so was calumny. Jealousy, resentment, envy, mistrust -- all fed a rumor mill of vilification. In this Machiavellian setting, it was difficult to tell truth from innuendo, hearsay from malicious lie. But King Carol was no Borgia. He was weak, tainted by scandal and surrounded by sycophants whose presence he tolerated, depending on their rank and title, with a mixture of condescension and forbearance.

"It was quite a performance," my grandmother would quip.

•

Another spectacle would soon unfold. At first, in deference to the Red Army now occupying Romania, communists were included in -- but did not yet dominate -- the two immediate post-1944 regimes. In 1945, however, the communists engineered a ministerial crisis. The Soviets forced King Michael to agree to a government led by wealthy bourgeois Petru Groza and dominated by the Marxists. Traditional parties were then disbanded. Humiliation turned to desecration when the young monarch was ordered to abdicate, forcibly removed from the palace by thugs freshly converted to communism, and exiled. With the war out of the way, the *"Securitate,"* a rag-tag collection of misfits, street toughs and outlaws who had terrorized Romania under the Germans, were now paid to terrorize Romanians in the name of communism. *The more things change....*

Born of dissent, revolution feeds on discord, which it then hastens to suppress.

•

Across a narrow hallway lit by pink art deco wall lamps, lived Peter, a boy about my age. I was not allowed in his apartment -- I would later learn why -- so we often played in my room after school. With memories of the war still vivid, it was natural for young, impressionable minds to turn back the clock and recreate, with equal doses of innocence and imagination, the very epoch we had both lived through. We'd play at soldiering and Peter invariably insisted on being a German storm trooper or a Luftwaffe pilot, choices I did not begin to question until much later. I would take on the role of a French *Résistance* fighter, or that of a British Tommy, or I'd waddle like a cigar-chomping, gum-chewing Yank slashing his way through some dense Pacific island jungle. With much less enthusiasm, I'd gallop like a Cossack cavalryman caught in a snowstorm in the steppes of Central Asia. (I was already fond of composer Borodin's sensual exoticism). I hated winter even as a child and had inherited from my mother a fear and sensitivity to cold so intense that I'd get chills just pretending. With uncommon cunning in one so young, Peter would exploit this debility and capture me or, if unwilling to take prisoners -- as was often the case – finish me off. I'd pretend that the bullet had pierced my heart. I'd clutch my left breast and look over my shoulder as I spun around and fell, first on one knee, then an elbow, just to make sure that dying didn't hurt too much.

"We win!" Peter would intone jubilantly as he placed his boot on my chest. "*We*," meant the Germans.

Bored with ground warfare, we'd move to aerial combat, Peter piloting a Stuka or a Messerschmitt. I flew Spitfires, Corsairs and flying fortresses. We assembled our fighting machines by turning chairs upside down, with the four legs forming the struts of a snug open cockpit. A seat cushion served as the roof. Fleece caps with earflaps were converted into helmets, old wire-rimmed glasses into goggles. Once strapped into our seats -- my mother had donated a couple of old belts to the war effort -- we would rev up our engines, taxi onto the active runway, ram the throttle and take off in an ear-splitting roar of engines simulated by radio static at maximum volume. Dogfights, high-altitude bombardments, strafing runs were fierce and exacted commensurate losses. Peter, who seemed to be clueless about actual events -- or pretended not to know -- made up battles and granted the Germans imaginary victories. I went along, out of friendship. My claims that Dresden and Frankfurt had been razed to the ground, that Hitler was dead, that Mussolini had been executed then hanged upside down and bled like a porker at a village feast, that Japan's rising sun had set in an atomic twilight, all that fell on deaf ears. Peter neither admitted nor accepted the reality of Germany's defeat. He seemed so grieved, so bewildered by my assertions that the Third Reich had been crushed, that I granted him his own version of history. It didn't matter. Children can be made to believe in fairies and ogres, in God, the devil and Santa Claus. I believed in none but found Peter's convictions no impediment to our camaraderie. In retrospect, his defiant rejections of verifiable events should have aroused suspicion, but I ignored them. We shared other interests and engaged in other pastimes, one of them so intimate, that I readily indulged his chimeras once initiation turned to habit.

I'd long known the magic, felt the joyous conceit brought on by an erection -- my own -- but had no basis for comparison other than the awe-inspiring sight of my father's organ as he urinated, legs spread wide apart, in a public *pissoir* or at home in the toilet. It was both a relief and an inspiration to discover that Peter's pecker was no bigger than my own, though his sported an ugly cowl of wrinkled skin at its tip, whereas the head of my penis had the more esthetic bearing of a smooth mushroom cap.

It was during one of our war games -- the Battle of Britain, the assault on the Rhine, or the taking of Guadalcanal -- I can't quite remember -- that I felt the first stirrings of an oncoming erection. Buoyed by tight-fitting pants, the tumescence caused such discomfort that I pulled my pants down and liberated a hard, throbbing little cock.

"Heil Hitler," I exclaimed, snapping at attention. Peter was not amused but he accepted the challenge.

"I can do that," he rallied, vexation giving way to bravado. "Watch this!" Peter pulled his pants down, flicked his dick and twiddled his balls. I watched in wonder as the foreskin slowly rolled down the shaft like a turtleneck, revealing a slender, pinkish knob that rose and came to rest against his belly.

"En garde!" I grabbed my penis and hurled myself at my friend. Peter parried, clutched his weapon and lunged at me. Our penises collided and we dueled in a flesh-to-flesh contest that soon turned from sham hostility to gentle mutual indulgence. We continued to spar lustily for a moment or two, then, overcome by sensations that were as strange as they were intense, we disengaged. We stared at each other briefly, eyed our defiant little tools in mute reverence, pulled our pants up, and went back to war.

However modest or fleeting, pleasure tasted is pleasure remembered; pleasure anticipated is pleasure pursued. We would often "joust" after that, with variations on the theme -- I would take control of his penis and he would manipulate mine or, dealing a double death blow we would thrust our penises between each-other's thighs and tarry for a while, our hearts thumping through our chests, unuttered emotions coursing through our minds. The enjoyment I felt was intense. But I could not imagine the indescribable rapture I would experience five years later when, to my amazement and horror, I ejaculated for the first time and nearly fainted.

Once, as we prepared to rattle our sabers, Peter pulled down his pants. His underwear was soiled. Worse, he smelled of shit. I lost my erection instantly and was so overcome with disgust that I made up some excuse and sent him home. I remember being troubled by this act of cruelty. The snub put an end to our former intimacies. Once or twice after that, assailed by remorse -- or lust -- I made half-hearted attempts to resurrect the sex play. Peter blithely went along, but it was no use. His stench lingered in my mind's nostrils. I was cursed with an unforgiving nose, an aversion toward bodily odors, including my own, and an acute olfactory memory. Peter and I kept our pants up from that day forward.

•

One day, I heard a great commotion next door. New people had moved into Peter's apartment: a big, burly Russian colonel and his wife, a pretty major with a round face, almond-shaped eyes, red cheeks, a lively rump and a healthy pair of calves peering out of fur-lined military boots.

"Where is Peter," I asked my uncle.
"He left," he replied, looking elsewhere.
"What do you mean?"
"He and his parents went away."
"Where to?"
"Far."
"Where is far?"
"Far, far."
"Why?"

My uncle was a talkative man by nature. He had a reputation for tying up the courts, bamboozling judges, stunning juries into submission, reducing to stupor captive audiences with lengthy and convoluted narratives. He could also be close-mouthed when he wanted to be, and equally exasperating.

"It's a long story."

"Tell me."

"Not now."

"When?"

He raised his eyebrows and shrugged his shoulders.

"Some other time. Now run along."

It took thirty years to learn the story. Even so, evading direct and probing questions, my uncle fed me an eyedropper account so lacking in specifics as to make little or no sense. The pieces just didn't fit. Upon closer scrutiny, adding my own insights and drawing inferences from the scant few details my uncle granted me later under pressure, I was able to reconstruct an extraordinary scenario.

Peter's parents were first-generation Romanians, born in the German-speaking province of Bukovina. Unwavering disciples of the Führer, they'd been recruited by Germany's vast and spreading spy network. Their mission: To assess Romania's loyalty to the Axis, and to identify and monitor insurgents. (Germany had nothing to fear. Partially landlocked, politically fickle and timid, Romania had a long tradition of flip-flopping and fealty to various itinerant bullies -- Romans, Goths, Huns, Avars, Slavs, Tatars, Turks, Greeks, Germans, Magyars and Russians. Romanians served them all with equal fervor). They'd also been charged with analyzing socio-economic indicators in large urban centers such as Bucharest, aiding the war effort by reporting their findings and conducting carefully scripted disinformation campaigns. This was done through official German diplomatic channels in the early days of the war and later, as the war began to unravel and Romania joined the Allies, by radio. The radio transmitter was located in their apartment -- across from ours. This might explain why I was never allowed to set foot in Peter's apartment and why attempts to invite myself over were invariably thwarted. It is likely that while Peter and I fondled each other's cocks, his father was sending coded dispatches to Berlin. I always found an amusing irony in the juxtaposition of these two goings-on.

His parents' political leanings could also account for Peter's anguished and confused allegiance to Germany. He was no doubt convinced, as his parents must have been, that Hitler's millennium was at hand. What I can't reconcile -- and what my uncle refused to discuss -- is to what extent he knew of his neighbors' activities. More troubling yet is that he and my grandmother weathered, unscathed, the German occupation, whereas nine-tenths of my father's family perished in Hitler's gas chambers, and that they were spared the daily horrors meted out by Romania's brown-shirted Fascist thugs. Some sixty years after the fact, still lacking essential details, I accept full responsibility for the conclusions my speculations might invite.

What happened next is unclear. My best guess is that Peter and his parents were spirited out of Romania by Nazi confederates, and taken to Spain. They must have left in a great hurry. I inherited several of Peter's toys and many of his illustrated books, including the antics of *Max und Moritz*. My uncle acknowledged having been in touch with them "sporadically" after the war. I remember asking for Peter's address.

"What for? You're both grown men and you live far apart. What could you possibly have to say to each other?"

I never found out.

Time blunts curiosity. It dampens the urge to know.

MY FATHER'S TOWN

In his 1994 bestseller, *All Rivers Run to the Sea*, Elie Wiesel had mused:

> *"Why is it that my town still enchants me so? Is it because in my memory [Sighet] is entangled with my childhood? In all my novels it serves as background and vantage point. In my fantasy I still see myself in it."*

Scenes from his childhood, I could tell, danced in my father's head as we entered Sighet. As if to reconcile past and present, his eyes darted in restless syncopation from place to place, surveying the church steeple up the road, the graceful fountain in the center of the square, the shops and small eateries, the whitewashed row houses now bathed in a late afternoon amber glow. Memories quickly coalesced with the reality of the moment. It was not what had been lost or transformed that caught my father's eye but what had never changed.

The village idiot had aged but he was still a pathetic buffoon who caught and ate invisible flies and exposed himself in public. His contorted, drooling smile, his roving, unfocused, rueful gaze, his uneven stride and childish antics were no more amusing now than they'd been years earlier. The smell of poverty and madness and heedless despair still clung to his pores.

Old couples ambled arm in arm through the common, their gait tentative, their eyes fixed upon the ground. Peasants, hardship and chagrin carving deep furrows upon their weathered faces, still led teams of steer to market or drove rickety horse-drawn carriages brimming with onions and potatoes and cabbage. Children sat on porches or peered out of windows, eyeing vacantly a spectacle of tranquil desolation. Outwardly given to its usual routines, the town, my father would later recollect, seemed exhausted. But it was he who was worn out -- eviscerated by the war, baffled by the nature of immutability, stunned by the steadfastness of change. The Sighet of *his* childhood stood before him, surreal, like a movie set, a parody of a macrocosm he had once taken for granted, a mere village whose heartbeat was now out of sync with his own.

Memories are like tears; they burn or they evaporate.

●

In 1962, on a pilgrimage that set the mood for his bittersweet, *The Town Beyond The Wall,* Elie Wiesel would rummage through an ossuary of buried emotions. What he unearthed would leave him refreshed, mystically self-renewed. He would reconcile with his childhood, put it in storage, so to speak, the way one consigns cherished but cumbersome antiques to some unused antechamber.

Hopelessly pragmatic, an odium for sentimentality concealing a lacerated soul, my father found no telltale spirituality in the experience, only emptiness.

"It was as if I'd blinked and been transported to an improbable now," he sighed.

Whereas Wiesel would draw inspiration from Sighet's denizens, my father found in the broken souls that crossed his path that afternoon an echo of his own demonic inner struggles. He refused to look at the beggars and the cripples and the mad as mythic beings or wandering sages or instruments of divine strategy but as pathetic and pitiable creatures affronted by God. He found no lyricism in their disfigurements, gained no inspiration from their tragic uniqueness. He would not elegize poverty and suffering, or poeticize ugliness; instead, he deemed them an emblem of blasphemy, an insult by nature against innocence and vulnerability, an unwanted offering flung at a reluctant recipient by a scornful giver. He took care not to elevate *"the lost, the forgotten and the hopeless"* to allegorical dimensions for fear that he might learn to condone their agony. And when he visited the old Vizhnitzer Klaus synagogue and chanced upon wizened patriarchs sitting in near darkness wrapped in their prayer shawls, he wept, stirred by ancient voices tugging at his soul and mourning the ideological chasm that now separated him from them.

If men only knew how much God hates go-betweens, they'd insist on direct communications.

•

Why had we come to Sighet? Was it whim, nostalgia or master plan? An uncertain future would help shelve a tormenting past, at least for a while, in favor of attendant preoccupations, like paying rent, buying groceries, reconnecting with the minutiae of existence, this time in a small town that reeked of bad memories and seemed bereft of dreams.

"I can't find my place," my father blurted out one evening as we sat around the dinner table. We looked at each other. No one said a word for fear of uttering platitudes. We'd settled in a sprawling split-level furnished duplex in the center of town. Was it on Mihaly Street? The upper level had been transformed into a medical office. We occupied the lower level with my father's three sisters -- Ellen, the eldest, Malku (Aunt Mary to me) and Lilli, a vivacious freckle-faced redhead, the youngest. All three had miraculously survived internment and been freed by the Russians. Their parents and two brothers had perished in one of Hitler's death camps.

I remember a large kitchen lined with copper pots and pans, and the aroma of homemade plum and apricot preserves. The kitchen gave onto a narrow courtyard in which strutted a pair of jittery peacocks. I tormented the poor birds by imitating their mating call. Bright and cheerful, the den-like living room where we retreated after dinner smelled of old books and boasted a grand piano on which I would attempt to play, by ear, Beethoven's Moonlight Sonata. Impressed, a kindly neighbor offered to teach me the rudiments of piano playing. I gave up after three or four lessons, bored with finger exercises, scales and one-handed renditions of *Frère Jacques* and *Twinkle, Twinkle Little Star*. I never learned how to read music but continued to play extemporaneously, for my own diversion, painfully reminded every time I attempted to improvise, in the key of C or F, that a keen ear is meaningless without nimble fingers and years of back-breaking practice.

What my father had alluded to at the dinner table (and would echo for years to come) was not a *place* at all but a mindset -- serenity --

freedom from inner-conflict. To my chagrin, I never found the right words. How do you extend condolences to a man who grieves over his own inner death? How do you offer hope without trivializing the hopelessness? I would invariably change the subject. Too smart and too principled to insist, my father would take the bait and help clear the air. We'd then play chess, a game whose greatest virtue is the contemplative silence it imposes. I never won a single game but we were both spared the tedium of small talk.

Time flies but not always in the same direction.

As I grew up and older, I would inherit my father's anxieties and spend my life in a nearly constant state of controlled inquietude. A friend, a psychoanalyst, casually urged me to go on a popular psychotropic drug. I declined. Nor would I commit to years on the couch trying to remember life in the womb. I would overcome the incubus within, I assured him, by sheer force of will. I would harness it; use it as a gateway to inspiration and creativity. I still suffer from occasional bouts of depression -- winter and sunless days bring them on. I manage. Melancholy adds substance to form.

●

My recollections of Sighet are tenuous. From an otherwise impenetrable limbo, bits and pieces emerge but their clarity is questionable. They seem so distant and yet so real. I've resurrected a few snippets because, in their triviality, they are so telling of how memory works. They also offer a glimpse of the boy I was and the realities that permeated my boyhood.

I remember my mother watching me in silent terror as I rode a bicycle at breakneck speed in the middle of Sighet's main street, hands off the handlebars. I took pleasure in her unease and zoomed past her, back and forth, giggling.

I revisit the variety show I attended one night at the local theater. I'd snuck up on stage during intermission, parted the curtain and told the audience how the magician had done one of his tricks. I was elated at the laughter and applause this act of daring earned me. My parents had front-row seats. They were in stitches. I'd acquired a precocious taste for exposing fakes. Applause is a siren call and leading roles in high school plays would later grant me the sweet rapture of public praise. My mother's fondest wish, to her dying day, was to see me on stage, on screen. She'd been especially fond of my Danny Kaye impersonations. (I toyed briefly with show business when I lived in Hollywood in the late 1950s. Genetically disinclined to chase after money for its own sake, repelled by the celluloid world and the plastic denizens I got to know, and secure in the notion that living my life was already a command performance, I never chased after my mother's dream).

I also remember a friendly bat performing dizzying aerobatics in the living room then disappearing through a small hole in the corner of the ceiling. My mother was terrified of bats and wore a kerchief on her head for the remainder of our stay. I delighted in the little winged animal's antics and looked forward to its nightly visits.

Fékété, the cat that came with the house, caught mice in the yard and brought them indoors, a "look-what-I've-found" expression on his face. He toyed with them then feasted on his frolicsome playmates. Every night, one of the mice -- my mother swore it was the same one -- ventured cautiously toward the center of the carpet, sat upright on its hindquarters, studied us for a moment or two, then scurried out of sight.

I must have enjoyed many untroubled hours in the midst of general boredom. Melancholy and unease, percolating at the fringes of consciousness, usually faded away at the first hint of a crisis or unusual event. These would prove to be more frequent and emotionally taxing than I could have foreseen.

One day I spotted Russian soldiers swimming the Tisza River. Some were stark naked. I learned new words: spirit alcohol, drunkenness, looting, rape.

Then came a phone call in the middle of the night. It was the mayor. He wanted my father to examine the decomposed remains of a German officer found face down near an embankment outside of town. I begged my father to take me with him. He refused at first then relented.

The stench, as we neared the body, was overpowering. Mesmerized and horrified, I managed not to throw up. Almost blanched, a few tufts of hair still clinging to scraps of blackened and desiccated skin, the right side of the skull was cracked like an eggshell. Near the body rested a leather military map-holder, a pair of wire-rim spectacles and a camera, a Zeiss. The officer had died from a massive gunshot wound to the head. The film inside the camera was developed. The negative and prints would later be turned over to Israeli intelligence.

From the depths of time I also reconstruct an odd conversation: A border guard complained to my father that smuggling (once a lucrative commerce among Sighet Jews) had declined and that he was no longer getting the great "commissions" he used to earn. My father reassured the man that, "one day soon, a great favor" would earn him more than all the bribes he'd ever collected. Less than a year later, my father would escape from Romania on foot with the help of the very same border guard.

•

I try to imagine or reenact what a fading power of recall prevents me from reconstructing with any degree of precision. Sometimes, inadvertently, I succeed. I relive scenes of family life that may or may not have occurred in the time frame I placed them, or in the same setting, or with the same cast. They remind me of one-act plays or scenes from the theater of the absurd.

•

It's bad enough to be lied to. It's humiliating when the liar makes no effort to render his lie believable.

I would later learn that myth and family resentments are more likely to be remembered -- and circulated -- than truth. My much maligned great-great-grandfather Abraham, it turns out, had suffered in silence. Only Fabian knew the sadness that devoured his father. He could see it in his eyes. He could hear it as Abraham sobbed quietly in the middle of the night. He was sole witness to the daily squabbles, Sarah's petulance and spitefulness, the sleepless nights, the moments of despair, so deep and trying that Abraham stopped eating and nearly died. Yes, Abraham had had affairs. His mistresses were youthful, vivacious, attentive and full of tenderness. In their arms he could be young again and find unused reserves of love he needed to lavish and share.

"To be safe, call it fatalism or scruples, an adulterous man often stays married to his wife the way a car owner keeps a spare tire. I'd long since stopped loving Sarah...."

Often, impotence is merely the echo of indifference or disgust. Love ceases to be a joy when it becomes a burden. Sex ceases to be fun when it becomes an obligation.

His new wife Rivka had made him happy. Fabian did all he could to destroy their relationship. He criticized her cooking, mocked her gaiety and enthusiasm, and ridiculed her coquettish and loving nature. The family could not openly admit that it was not in Fabian's nature to be kind. He was jealous and vindictive. His mother had died and his father now catered to an intruder who favored spicy Hungarian dishes over the fatty and calorific Polish fare of his parents. Nor did Fabien have any affection for his mother. He resented her tyrannical nature and detested his father for submitting to Sarah's arrogance and daily taunts.

"I will never forget the day," Abraham confided in his diary, "when, enraged by Sarah, Fabian charged at his mother, grabbed her by the throat and pinned her against the kitchen wall. I thought he was going to kill her. Stunned, I felt a sudden rush of euphoria and anticipation coursing through my veins." A myocardial infarct would yank Abraham from Sarah's clutches a few months later.

Had Fabian really been forced to sleep in the attic? One of the Guzmán-Gutman who'd managed to evade the Burgos Grand Inquisitor -- a *converso* who'd mistreated Jews more relentlessly than the Christians -- declared:

"Repeated often and with enough conviction a lie becomes the truth." The axiom would not be lost on future generations of miscreants.

Three centuries later, Abraham wrote "[Fabian] could have slept in his room and snuggled under the eider down comforter. Sleeping in the attic sharpened his sense of martyrdom. In winter, with the wood stove on all night in the family room, the attic is quite warm. In summer, nights are cool and refreshing."

Had Fabian been served leftovers?

"In his dreams! Absurd. He refused to join us at the table. Rivka put his plate in the ice box and he stuffed himself late at night when everyone was asleep."

Was Fabian "exiled" miles away from Sighet?

"Not exactly. We were running out of options. Fabian was aggressive, vicious. He poisoned our life. So I asked an old friend who ran a small soap and candle factory less than two hours away to hire him and teach him a trade. Fabien had little aptitude for anything. He was lazy, undisciplined. My friend fired him twice; I had to beg him to take him back, which he did grudgingly one last time. This put an end to our friendship."

Fabian grew up. Morose, quarrelsome and unmotivated, he would blame the world for his shortcomings and take refuge from imaginary wrongs in confrontation.

The apple never falls very far from the tree. Fabian's son Yudel, my paternal grandfather, inherited the soap and candle business. My father told me that Yudel spent his days at the synagogue or immersed in his holy books -- the Torah, the Talmud, the Zohar -- or strolling attired in three-piece suits bought on credit and rarely paid in full. He and his wife, Pepi Weisz, would produce six children. Three would survive the Third Reich's slaughter houses. Yudel, Pepi, Leibi and Favish were exterminated in Auschwitz. The fat from their sizzling corpses were turned into soap and their skins into lampshades.

•

Then, early one morning, we packed our bags, hugged Malku and Helen and hitched a ride back to Bucharest. Lilli had been killed in a grotesque, gangland-style drive-by shooting. A phone call in the middle of the night had summoned my father to the scene of the crime. He had no idea who the victim was until he saw his sister's bullet-riddled body. She'd been machine-gunned, along with three friends, as they drove to a neighboring town for a wedding. The killers, Russian soldiers on a drunken joy ride, were never apprehended. Lilli had just turned twenty.

YOUR WATCH, YOUR COAT

Those who demand and seize don't know how to offer or let go.

It was curiosity, fed by restlessness -- not nostalgia -- that had drawn my father back to Sighet. He needed to know. Knowledge brought disappointment and sorrow. Resurrected in a flash of surreal lucidity, his childhood, adolescence, the years of toil, dashed hopes and tragedy suddenly compressed into a single moment of hideous irony. The house in which he grew up had been seized by the state and given to a minor Communist Party official in recompense for his zeal. (Five years earlier, that same official, a police informant, had worked with equal zeal on behalf of the Fascist Iron Guard). *Tatale* and *Mamale* were gone. So were two younger brothers. Their ashes now fattened some pasture in Germany, Poland or the Ukraine. Diminished by overwhelming losses, Sighet's Jewish community had first gone into shock. It was now in utter disarray. Frenzied anti-religious ferment and shifting political alliances threatened to extinguish its very soul.

Distraught, anxious to find his "place" in the frigid post-war sun, prodded by survivors, my father had taken a half-hearted stab at local politics and accepted appointment as president of Sighet's nearly decimated Jewish community. His Quixotic affinity for social causes would soon abate. The "people's" struggle, he quickly learned, was led by a gang of avaricious thugs intent on getting as fat as the *boyars* they were committed to oust and dispossess. The communist utopia, he observed, fostered anti-Semitism; it nourished an idiosyncratic blue-collar contempt for erudition and intellectualism; it condoned terror, advocated expropriations, built gulags and took part in disappearances, tortures and summary executions. To his immense chagrin, my father also discovered that many members of the Jewish community had since joined the "Party" and groveled at the feet of the Russian military authorities and their Romanian vassals. Disgust turned to rage when his baby sister, Lilli, the beautiful, lively copper-haired Lilli, freed by the Soviets from the horrors of concentration camp, died on some rural road, murdered by drunken Russian soldiers. He'd protested noisily and threatened to bring the thugs to justice. He'd been betrayed in Paris. He was setting himself up for betrayal in Sighet. It was time to shake the sand out of his shoes and cast a final farewell to the little town that had never really been his. He would never go back.

•

It's because the term fails to convey the concept it purports to encapsulate that I often get the urge to write "communism" in quotation marks, to read it thus circumscribed in the works of others, as if to accentuate an incongruity. The word is a paragon of vagueness. Overuse, misuse and abuse will do that to words. "Progressives," "loyalists," "conservatives," "liberals" and "independents" know what I mean. It's not surprising that Marxist doctrinaires, atheists, human rights crusaders, freethinkers, pacifists and people who wear red socks have all been labeled "communists." In McCarthyist America, artistic non-conformity and a penchant for social justice were unmistakable symptoms of "communism." Predictably, the latter was considered a far more heinous crime and is still looked with askance by right-wing demagogues. Popular liberation movements aimed at shaking the colonial yoke would be similarly imputed. Opposition to U.S. military intervention in these conflicts, when not spurred by laissez-faire isolationists, was also denounced as "communist-inspired." John Lennon's stirring pleas for peace at a time of war were reflexively ascribed to "communist leanings." Had they lived today, Thomas Payne and Henry David Thoreau would be branded communists. In Russia's new market-oriented economy, a communist is better known as a "loyalist." A hundred years ago, a loyalist was a czarist. Fifty years ago, a "progressive" was described as a crypto-communist. In capitalist circles, aggressive and daring investment strategies are referred to as "progressive." Both the Nazis and the communists persecuted Freemasons. The former regarded them as communists; the latter deemed the ancient brotherhood a tool of western imperialism.

So much for semantics.

There's another problem. What passes as communism has perverted the ideals it alleges to represent. It has also betrayed the goals to which it is theoretically committed. In assuming power -- by force -- communists, in true Fascist style, granted themselves rights that they promptly took away from the rank and file. Instead of tending to urgent social issues, such as poverty, hunger, and illiteracy, their crusade quickly became mired in proselytism-by-terror.

Ultimately, the narrow canons at the core of communism's wider philosophical tenets, like those of monotheistic religions, are simply unenforceable. Driven by disciplines and proscriptions that denounce egotism, intolerance and greed -- traits found in abundance in Homo sapiens and indispensable in the preservation of self (and the perpetuation of capitalism) -- communism is hopelessly incompatible with human nature. What the world has witnessed since Marxist theories were first propounded is a travesty wrapped in parody. Under the brutal stewardship of its disciples, communism has failed. History may yet rank this failure (as is the failure of religion to root out evil) as one of the greatest tragedies to befall the family of man.

Given a choice between ideals, and status and self-interest, men will invariably opt for the latter. This is what makes them ungovernable.

•

Growing up in Israel, and later as a journalism student in Paris, I too would toy with communism. Mine was a youthful, romantic longing for social harmony and justice, a paradigm anchored in the naïve belief that collective distribution of goods produced collectively would not only bring the world happiness but also rid it of its torments. I was rebelling against all power and authority like any self-respecting young French secular Jew who'd read the *philosophes* -- Hobbes, Locke and Saint-Simon. The amassing of personal wealth and the acquisition of corporate fortunes, I agreed then (and still believe today), are achieved through exploitation and lead to an anarchical control of assets that are never evenly shared with the exploited. By the time I became sufficiently acquainted with it, the popular 19th century Saint-Simonean movement had long since degenerated into a quasi-religious sect. It would soon break apart and be promptly consigned to history's bottom drawer as an eccentricity -- which is perhaps what attracted me to it in the first place. As time passed, bloodied countless times in the ceaseless crossfire between ideal and ideology, I would then explore the more utilitarian goals of "Socialism." I had concluded that communism did not and could not work, except on a small controlled scale, in the disciplined confines of some ancient Essene community or in a modern and self-sufficient monastery. I still recognized in Marxism's muddled stoicism and stridency an unambiguous morality that was hard to dismiss. I would continue to be drawn to the spirit long after the letter, to my immense chagrin, was shredded beyond recognition. I also understood that freedom is achievable -- in very brief spurts -- only after the dissolution of the status quo, but I was not prepared to accept the chaos and the injustices that revolutions leave in their wake. With nowhere to go, I would concede that political power is intrinsically oppressive, whether wielded by the right or the left, by a mercenary elite or a covetous proletariat. To escape pigeonholing, I resolved that conscience would be the fulcrum of my convictions. Mid-course corrections are best made from the middle of the road. I would often stray off the beaten path just to see what lay beyond my field of vision.

•

In Europe in the mid-1950s, I observed post-war communism at work in France and Italy. Neither the petulant Italians nor the irascible French ever fully championed the Kremlin's mandates. Theirs was a homespun version of Marxism, sometimes irreverent, often defiant of their puppeteers in Moscow. Party loyalty was largely contingent on how much tobacco was available, how much bread and red wine was on the table, and whether members could afford small vacation cottages in Brittany or on the Amalfi coast. Enjoyed by the leaders, such perks were largely inaccessible to the rank-and-file. Support for the cause endured so long as the practice of communism was neither ideologically taxing nor an impediment to self-indulgence, a propensity shared with equal gluttony by their "fat-pig" capitalist counterparts.

I would later witness the last gasps of nearly 80 years of communism in the Soviet Union and the evisceration of the Russian spirit. Russians were afflicted with what I characterized, for lack of a better hyperbole, as cancer of the soul. Misconstrued, contaminated and falsified by nearly four generations of hoodlums, goons and charlatans, communism remains everywhere the balm of dreamers and chronic malcontents. In Russia, where there is much to bewail, it still festers with a naïveté bordering on irrationality.

"Things were tough under Stalin and Beria [Stalin's sinister secret police chief]," said an old-timer bearing a mouthful of gold teeth. "But at least we all had jobs, a roof over our heads, food on the table. There was order. Now we have nothing, except disorder."

No. What the man endured was the consequence of a collective state of confusion. What he lacked was the courage of his convictions.

It's difficult to separate a man from his convictions; it's impossible to impart any if he has none.

•

I always found it a delicious paradox that the well to do, quintessentially upper-middle-class Karl Marx, an unrepentant philanderer and a man not known for high standards of personal hygiene, loathed and disparaged the masses. I also find it a cruel irony that ideals calling for emancipation, egalitarianism and the comradeship of men were transformed on the morrow of the October Revolution into an all-powerful and merciless doctrine of discrimination and repression. Now and then, I also wonder whether another Jew, perhaps an exalted figure such as Jesus -- had he lived today -- could have led mankind to salvation with his own brand of collectivism. I follow such musings to their natural conclusion and rule that the Vatican would have branded him a heretic and excommunicated him, and that CIA-sponsored death-squads, for reasons of "national security," would have silenced him, as the Romans did two thousand years ago.

***Struggling to rub out the indelible, man has invented the eraser.
If one can't tolerate reality one might as well abjure it.***

•

Back in Bucharest, and despite my protestations, I was returned to *La Maison des Français,* the French school I'd attended, on and off, since we'd arrived in Romania in 1944. I recognized some of the children's faces, but I knew none of the teachers. Madame Alice, a kind and sensible woman who'd endured with saintly patience many of my pranks, was gone. She'd interceded on my behalf when a little girl and I were found, stark naked, studying each other's anatomical differences in a huge wicker basket at the end of a corridor. Gone also were Monsieur Antoine, the rotund and jovial arts-and-crafts instructor, Mademoiselle Sylvie, a tall, lanky spinster who taught piano and *solfège,* and Mademoiselle Dina, the friendly principal. All had been removed, I would later learn, for teaching what the state called a "reactionary" curriculum, and replaced by a younger cadre of Romanian teachers eager -- or coerced by circumstance -- to toe the Party line.

I remember taking my seat and glancing briefly around me. Pictures of the Eiffel tower and the Arch of Triumph still adorned the walls. Posters of Notre Dame Cathedral, the Sacré Coeur basilica and Mont Saint Michel abbey had been replaced by austere representations of brawny peasants tilling the earth, sooty-faced laborers operating monstrous smoke-belching machines and burly construction workers perched at dizzying heights atop gleaming iron beams. Everywhere, large reproductions showed stylized male and female titans wielding hammers, sickles, picks, shovels and scythes, their steely gaze focused on some distant point above the horizon, no doubt where the workers' paradise can be found. Framed inspirational messages called for "HONOR TO THE FATHERLAND," "SERVICE TO THE PEOPLE," "DUTY TO THE PARTY." (Ten years earlier, Picasso had been deemed "decadent" by the Nazis, whose aims were better served by realism and figurative art. Works by Braque, Chagall, Matisse and Van Gogh were also hastily removed from German museums. Some were sold, others destroyed).

"Take this red kerchief and wear it proudly around your neck," said the teacher in heavy-accented French. "You're a pioneer now. Class, join me in welcoming your *camarade* back to his old school."

The children rose to their feet in a sea of red kerchiefs (the girls also wore large white taffeta bows in their hair), snapped at attention and applauded in measured syncopation like little automatons. Then they dropped back into their seats with military-drill precision and folded their arms upon their desks.

"Now, boys and girls, what are the badges of good citizenship?"

All hands went up except mine.

"Obedience," said one of the little robots.

"Loyalty," offered another.

"Honesty," declared a third.

"Vigilance," pitched a fourth.

"*Très bien*," cheered the teacher. "A good citizen is obedient, dedicated, honest and alert. Good citizenship begins at home and is perfected in school with the help of examples from the past and lessons for the future. When you go home tonight and join your families at the supper table, make sure you listen very carefully -- with vigilance, *n'est-ce-pas* -- to what everyone is saying. Much can be learned from what grownups tell each other. Tomorrow, in class, we'll all take turns discussing -- with honesty -- what we heard, won't we? We must all remember comrade Paul and the valiant example he set for us all.

"Yes, teacher," the children rallied in perfect unison, pledging devotion and validating their willingness to submit.

"What has Comrade Paul taught us, children?"

"Study hard, love the fatherland, unmask the enemies and expose traitors."

"Good!" said the teacher with noticeable pride.

I kept quiet. I had nothing to say. I was terribly unhappy to be back in school. The civics exercises bored me. I wasn't in the least interested in my classmates' tales and would have just as well kept mine to myself. Coping with my own inner demons, I would rather have whittled the hours away daydreaming or drawing unforgiving caricatures of the teachers.

I also resented having to wear the red kerchief just because twenty other children wore one as well. By the age of nine, I'd already acquired a healthy aversion for uniforms -- and uniformity. Looking like twenty other kids made me feel stupid, unexceptional. Worse, it robbed me of character and individuality. I was determined I would not be reduced to carbon-copy status. Claiming I'd forgotten it at home or lost it, I often challenged the teachers and taxed their patience by failing to wear the kerchief. I'd also resolved to contribute nothing of value during these morning inquests, which I intuitively deemed intrusive and potentially calamitous. After all, "Comrade Paul" was a rat, the Romanian transmutation of a Russian symbol -- *Tovarich Pavlik* -- and the newest icon in the pantheon of Communist idols.

Paul's story was an allegory and it was told with the pathos owed the cult status to which he'd been elevated. Once upon a time, it said, a young boy scoured the forest for berries. He was a kind-hearted, honest boy who knew right from wrong. When someone in his family erred, Paul told his teachers (who then told the commissar....) No one in class challenged the accuracy -- or morality -- of Paul's denunciations. In Romania, like in the rest of communist Eastern Europe, fiction was fact. This idolatry would eventually feed a culture of compliant informants, the lifeblood of a police state, and Comrade Paul's story became a favorite tool of Romania's brainwashing apparatus. What the teachers were careful not to say is that Pavlik/Paul was killed by his father and that several members of his family were in turn tried and executed for depriving the fatherland of a snitch.

A few of the kids -- some of them coached no doubt by alert parents, others having heard nothing that could compromise them -- brought to school harmless renderings of banal family chatter. Others picked on their parents' conversations the way iron filings cling to magnets.

"Dad said that the commies are vulgar thieves."

"Mom said this country was better off under the king."

"My uncle said Petru Groza can't be trusted."

"My aunt said...."

Such candor would have tragic consequences on many families. Dissidents were arrested, fined, dispossessed and imprisoned. Many died from exposure, starvation and exhaustion in hard labor camps. Many more were extra-judicially executed.

I was ready when my turn came. My candor had nearly cost my father his life and I'd since learned the strategic value of a good lie. Acting -- the art of pretense and the science of deceit -- had also become second nature. I enjoyed putting on airs, making up stories; for effect, mainly. I was already enjoying the discomfiture these yarns caused or, better yet, the utter credulity with which they were received.

"What have you for us today?"

I scratched my head, shrugged my shoulders and raised my arms in sham mystification.

"My father spoke about medical things -- vaginas, ovaries, fallopian tubes, ectopic pregnancies. I didn't understand a word. After that he read the paper and listened to music -- Tchaikovski's violin concerto. My mother did crossword puzzles and played solitaire. *Memmée* studied the future in the coffee grounds at the bottom of her cup. I finished my homework and went to bed. What's a vagina?"

The teacher blushed and squirmed with unease, and quickly changed the subject. I remember being very proud of my performance. A gadfly-in-training, I had drawn my first blood. A predisposition for iconoclasm and incitement would later become manifest in my high-school compositions. The urge to de-mythify, agitate and abash would dominate the bulk of my journalistic output.

This charade went on for a while then stopped. For want of witches, the school suspended the witch-hunt. Elsewhere, Romania's communist inquisition was now in full swing.

•

One day, *La Maison des Français* caught fire and went up in smoke. We were all hurriedly escorted down the long marble stairwell and onto the street. The firemen fought valiantly but their efforts were for naught. When the smoke lifted, little remained of the building save its ornate 19th century façade. I never found out what caused the fire but I remember feeling elated. For days, I could be heard singing a French ditty that ended with, *"... we'll burn our books and throw the teachers in the middle of the pyre."* I remember dreaming that it was I who'd set the fire. Remorseful, I would help put it out in my sleep by peeing in bed.

My education resumed at home, this time in the custody of *"précepteurs,"* all of whom quit after a few days. Deemed "incorrigible" and "uneducable," I would bounce from one private tutor to another until I left Romania in 1948.

●

It was the plump young peasant woman who delivered dairy and other foodstuffs to our door every week who taught me that a vagina is not merely the absence of a penis, as I had thought, but a basic component of female anatomy. I had long yearned to know what precious treasure women have beneath their dresses and why they so frantically try to conceal it. I'd soon find out. The maid, who lived next-door in a small studio off the rear terrace, would often invite her friend in for a chat and refreshments. This gave "Mrs. Sour Cream" – I'd given her that moniker -- a chance to rest before heading back to her village.

I was idling on the rear terrace one afternoon when I heard muffled laughter and sighs coming from the maid's room. I grabbed a hold of the windowsill and chinned myself up for a better view. The window was shut and the shades were drawn but a small crease near the bottom edge created an opening through which I saw Mrs. Sour Cream and the maid, both stark naked, kissing, taking turns sucking each other's tits and fondling the bushy nubs between their legs.

I thought of Peter and remember finding it odd that women would do what we did, especially since there was nothing to hold on to and play with. I still had much to learn. I also remember feeling a strange sensation in the pit of my stomach and getting a hard-on. As I let myself down, my feet scraped the wall noisily. The laughter and sighing ceased. A pudgy hand lifted a small corner of the shades and half a face, flushed and glistening with perspiration, came into view. It was the maid. Urging me to be quiet, she put a finger against her lips and waved me in. I hesitated. My heart raced; my legs felt like cotton. Spellbound and petrified, I went in, shut the door behind me and stood with my back against it, gaping in utter disbelief.

Mrs. Sour Cream was now stretched out on the bed. My eyes were riveted on her nakedness. Where the lower part of her belly met her thighs, I saw a peculiar elevation in the form of a fleshy triangular mound, coifed with a reddish mane. Where the thighs intersected I noticed a protuberance cleft by an enormous fissure on either side of which rested two oyster-like lips. The upper part of the crevice was crowned with a small rosy appendage half the length of my pinkie, which Mrs. Sour Cream kneaded between her thumb and forefinger. She smiled languidly, baring several missing teeth, and beckoned me closer.

"Sit, my little one, sit and watch."

"I'll stand."

"Suit yourself."

The maid pulled out what looked like an enormous rubber sausage from her night stand, kneeled at the foot of the bed and plunged it in Mrs. Sour Cream's crevice where it nearly disappeared. She then proceeded to shuttle the contraption back and forth, slowly at first, soon with a cadenced fury that arched Sour Cream's back off the bed and culminated in a paroxysm of tremors and convulsions.

"Oh, Mary, fucking Mother of God, it's coming, oh, oh...." Mrs. Sour Cream bit her lower lip. She clenched her fists. Her feet cambered, her toes curled inward. She then fell back on the bed as though she'd fainted. The maid pulled out the sausage from Mrs. Sour Cream's crack, eliciting one last rapturous shudder. The sausage was covered with slime. Some of it oozed between her buttocks and stained the sheets. I was scared, nauseated and mesmerized all at once. I'd suddenly made the connection but it would take a few more years before apprenticeship-by-observation turned to in-vivo initiation.

Mrs. Sour Cream got up, slid a chamber pot from under the bed, squatted and urinated in fitful spurts that chimed against the vessel's metal walls. The two women begged me not to breathe a word to anyone about "our little secret." The entertainment, the education, the vicarious thrill I experienced, the fantasies to which I would hence treat myself, were well worth my silence. I swore never to tell anyone. Until now. The maid and Mrs. Sour Cream kissed me on the mouth, fondled my crotch, giggled and ushered me out.

I now eat sausage with the greatest reticence.

•

Taking meals, as a child, was a chore; feeding me was a harrowing ordeal for my parents. Nauseated by certain odors, sickened by the texture and consistency of certain foods in my mouth -- I used to *chew* soup -- I would often run from the dinner table retching. The smell of boiled or fried organ meats, sickened me, and no amount of coaxing, gentle or stern, could persuade me partake of liver, giblets, kidney, tongue or brain, all of which were occasionally served and savored by the grownups. I also had an aversion to milk and butter, and I rejected most vegetables, except potatoes, raw onions and some leafy greens. My poor mother would wring her hands with worry. My appetite was severely depressed. I was underweight and calcium-deficient, and my father would often give me painful B12 injections.

This was also a period of protracted illness for me. In a span of a year or so, I came down with diphtheria, whooping cough, dry pleurisy, rubella and scarlet fever. I caught the mumps -- twice. I contracted other ailments, many of which baffled the "specialists" who were summoned to my bedside, and from which I recovered without their intervention. My father's minimalist approach to medicine (he believed in the body's own restorative powers) was often challenged by my grandmother and uncle who, despite a conspicuous lack of knowledge of anatomy, physiology and every other science associated with medicine, considered him too young and inexperienced to make valid diagnoses. My father's exceptional skills as a diagnostician had in fact earned him early praise in medical school but my uncle and grandmother would not yield. They placed greater credence in *professeurs,* old bearded men wearing vests and pocket watches, and prone to oracular speculation.

Faith in the erudition and competence of tenured experts notwithstanding, and all else failing, my uncle and grandmother did not hesitate to prescribe their own therapies. A favorite weapon against both disease and the evil eye -- the latter often blamed for the former -- was a thin piece of red ribbon sewn on the inside of my clothes. Another all-purpose amulet consisted of a small linen pouch filled with either camphor balls or a couple of cloves of garlic which I was enjoined to wear around my neck at certain times of the month, especially during a full moon. In league with my father, who despised superstition and knew that garlic was infinitely more useful in my stomach than around my neck, I would remove the cloves from the pouch and eat them raw. I would then pretend that they'd miraculously disappeared. My father would back me up, raising his arms skyward, closing his eyes and declaring with the trance-like bearing of a mystic, "Heaven works in such mysterious ways." His irreverence drew vexed glances from my uncle who tolerated no blasphemy in his presence. My father would smile impishly and shrug his shoulders. Anything that contradicted his brother-in-law's sensitivities or challenged his beliefs was blasphemy. Of course, my breath gave me away and so the bags were refilled with fresh supplies of garlic. This is how I began to develop a taste -- now a passion -- for raw garlic. I continue to have garlic "orgies," a ritual my wife tolerates with a selfless grace only love can sustain.

•

My mother was not as superstitious as her mother or brother. What she lacked in irrational beliefs or self-limiting fixations, she more than made up in intuitive power. Akin to clairvoyance, but devoid of pretense or theatricality, it was a faculty -- she called it a curse -- that would sharpen with age.

One afternoon, deep in thought in a game of solitaire -- I was sitting on the floor engrossed in the wicked pranks of *Max und Moritz* -- my mother looked up and surveyed her surroundings as if stirred by an unfamiliar presence. She placed the rest of the deck on the table, rose and walked toward one of the living room windows. I sensed unease in her gait and stood up.

"Stay where you are," she whispered.

"What is it?"

"I don't know. Just stay put."

At first, I felt a slight flutter. The floor quivered under me, as if roused by the vibrations of a distant jackhammer. The air pressure changed, clouding my hearing. I had to swallow hard to make my ears pop. The trembling ceased momentarily then resumed, accompanied by a low-pitched hum. The pane on the balcony door began to undulate. A second later it buckled and cracked, shattering inward. A small glass fragment struck my mother on the forehead, drawing blood. Soon, the whole building began to shake from side to side.

"It's an earthquake! Don't move," she ordered

Pictures flapped against the walls and came unhooked. The massive oak dining room table slid off center and knocked down several chairs. The sofa on which my mother had been resting spun on its axis. Lifted by an invisible hand, several vases came crashing to the floor.

Still standing by the terrace door, dazed and bleeding, my mother suddenly brought her hands to her face. Her eyes widened, ablaze with horror. She then pointed at the unfolding scene before her and cried out.

"Mon Dieu!"

Less than fifty meters across the street, an apartment building not unlike our own was collapsing like a house of cards. Rushing to my mother's side, I managed to glimpse the fatal seizure that split the building from roof to ground. It looked as if a giant cleaver had sheared it straight down the middle. In slow motion at first, then, drawn by its own momentum, the building disintegrated in a furious downward and outward rush that raised a thick cloud of dust and hurled tons of bricks and twisted metal in all directions. I heard muffled screams, frantic, hopeless screams. As if from a dream, I saw my mother wipe the blood off her face. She would be all right. It was just a superficial flesh wound.

Smaller aftershocks grumbled briefly underfoot then ceased. An eerie stillness filled the air. I'd broken into a cold sweat and I could hear my heart pounding inside my chest. My head was on fire. I also felt a warm liquid trickling down my leg. I'd pissed in my pants.

•

I must close my eyes and silence all extraneous voices to resurrect even a fleeting likeness of Bucharest. I was seven when I arrived; eleven when I left. I can describe it only in the vaguest of terms. I remember an attractive capital with wide esplanades at its center and crowded districts at its peripheries where occidental traditions and Slav and Levantine influences had fused. Whereas Romania's spirituality had long since been consigned to the opulence and intoxicating mysticism of the Orthodox Church, its stomach was indulged in the earthy conviviality of small taverns redolent with Middle-Eastern viands, spices and confections. Even as a child, I favored these lively haunts to the glitter and ostentation of big-name restaurants where Bucharest's elite congregated just to be seen. I sat in mute fascination of the bouzouki, balalaika, pan flute and tambura players, as I gorged on halvah, marzipan, comfits and "sherbet," a fragrant taffy of exquisite sweetness served on a spoon inside a glass of rose water. The colorful costumes the musicians wore, the strange harmonies, dizzying quarter-notes, trills and ornamentations their instruments emitted, awakened what would become a lifelong infatuation with the exotic, the faraway. I could feel myself traveling, as I listened, through a kaleidoscope of fairy tale images that filled me with wonderment and introspection. I would later roam the uncharted and forever twisting paths to melancholy, as I surrendered to Borodin and Bartok, Rachmaninoff and Ravel, Schoenberg and Stravinsky. Tactile and transcendent, music would become both a conveyance and an asylum.

Despite the geography, its dappled countenance notwithstanding, Bucharest was a Latin metropolis, a throwback to its early origins as one of Rome's easternmost outposts. If its heartstrings and stomach betrayed strong Balkan and eastern influences, its eyes were turned and its ears tuned to France. Everyone spoke French at the time, at least everyone I knew. Nearly all considered Paris their cultural homeland. Others dreamed of Paris the way Jews long for Jerusalem and Muslims yearn for Mecca.

•

It was at the *Athénée Palace* that I attended my first live classical concert. I remember little of the theater itself but I will never forget the artists or the program. On tour in Eastern Europe from Paris where he now lived, George Enesco, the eminent Romanian composer and conductor, was at the podium. On stage, by his side, was his pupil and child prodigy, violinist Yehudi Menuhin. Their names meant nothing to me at the time. Nor could I grasp the prodigious talent their combined presence embodied. I was in the company of genius, but it wasn't until mentor and disciple joined to perform Mendelsohn's violin concerto, that I understood the meaning of genius. I felt transported, no, enraptured by the orchestra's enfolding resonance, by the dialogue between soloist and orchestra, and I was stirred even as a ten-year old by Menuhin's virtuosity, by the brilliance of his style, the eloquence and amazing fluidity of his bow.

The program also included one of Enesco's earliest works, his *Poem for Orchestra*, written when he was 15, a composition redolent of his homeland, sensual and brooding in parts, teeming with lively folk cadences in others. Vestiges of Romanian atavistic selfhood resurface whenever I listen to Enesco. My mother would later proudly tell everyone that I'd refused to get out of my seat when the curtain came down.

"He asked for more," she'd say -- more music and, I was unable to explain it then, more of music's otherworldly power on a young boy hungry for new sensations. Music would teach me to manipulate my emotions, from exhilaration to dizzying spirals of gloom. Music must not only delight my ear, it has to touch me, tear at my heartstrings and carry me to unknown and endlessly renewable states of exaltation. Debussy, Fauré, Vaugn Williams, Mahler, among others, arouse in me a longing for some unattainable, wholly indefinable secret realm of my own and into which, in the composers' custody, I finally gain entry. Mozart comforts me. Beethoven reduces me to insignificance. I often weep, from euphoria or emotional exhaustion whenever I hear his Ninth Symphony. Genius does that to me; genius and minor chords. There is joy in depression. I often cloister myself in its lair where no one will find me.

•

Now and then, my mother would take me to see my uncle *sur scène* -- literally "on stage." It was in the Appellate Court, where his most contentious cases were often heard, that he shone brightest. Self-assured, confident that the prosecution could be easily defeated, he would invite family and friends to hear his summations. He called them "a class act." In reality, it was skill, cunning and an otherwise encyclopedic knowledge of Romania's legal codes -- many drafted by his father -- that ensured his stunning courtroom victories. A consummate tactician, he had also long made it a practice to curry favor with certain judges by praising their decisions in legal columns that he contributed to Bucharest's major daily newspaper.

My uncle's summations (a peculiar term for the convoluted filibusters he delivered) were jewels of ambiguity designed, I'm certain, to drive the court to insensitivity. He would often use these very stratagems to force an opinion -- his own -- on a less discerning audience, or to win an argument against a weaker opponent. What these harangues lacked in brevity, they more than made up in flamboyance and showmanship. Tall and trim, magnificent in his freshly pressed black robe, a white ruffled bib conferring an air of sacramental authority, a kind of truncated black miter cockily angled on his head, he looked more like a rakish exorcist than an attorney. His arguments would often begin in a studied whisper, his gaze fixed on a distant point in space, an incredulous forefinger pressed against his lips. His voice would then build to sepulchral intensity as he tore down the opposing counsel's case and dared the judges to overturn a lower court's decree. He would often pause in mid-sentence, his head tilted at an unnatural angle, his arms extended skyward, his eyes riveted on the stern-faced, ermine-clad men perched on the high bench. These orations would invariably end in applause from the spectators' gallery, a display the judges were careful not to censure. Attorney and clients would then hug and kiss and we would all be invited to celebrate yet another courthouse triumph. We'd pile up in my uncle's chauffeur-driven Adler and burn rubber all the way to some popular restaurant where the cream of Romanian society gorged itself on *canard à l'orange*, suckling pig and truffles, rack of lamb, pheasant and quail.

I remember seeing a patron vomit on the sidewalk as gypsies with babies at their naked breasts begged for a morsel of food.

•

Widespread and heretofore immune from scrutiny or liability, these

courtroom capers would eventually help bring down the praetorian Romanian justice system. They would also lead to the creation of equally corrupt and far more sinister French Revolutionary-style "people's courts." Judges, public defenders, bailiffs, juries, prison wardens and amateur executioners would be drawn, as they'd been during the 1792-94 reign of terror, from the dregs of society. Among those who'd been spared by a flighty and collusive judiciary, many would in time be indicted and punished by the very people they had betrayed or swindled. It was the rabble's turn to repay the elite and they would do it with ravenous zest. Justifiable rancor soon turned to vile orgies of indiscriminate violence against the titled, the wealthy and the learned, whether they had done anything to deserve it or not.
Stern, fixated and meticulous, the process-oriented Germans had chased after their dream of world domination with punctilious precision. Surely, many must have reveled in the lunacy of their grandiose crusade. Most just followed orders, zombie-like, the sap of unconditional compliance coursing through their Teutonic veins.

In contrast, the Russians -- and their all-too-willing Romanian vassals -- were less interested in perfection than in giving free reign to their resentment and perversity. They refined torture and raised humiliation to fresh inquisitorial heights. Bestial, committed to creating a classless society, they inaugurated a reign of terror and anti-intellectualism unknown in Paris during the German occupation. Romania, submissive if not slavish, crumbled and rotted under the grubby thumb of its Kremlin puppet masters. This dizzying descent into hades, later hastened by Nicolae Ceaucescu and his band of thugs, lasted for many years unchecked. As it did elsewhere, communism paralyzed and emasculated a once sybarite Romania. Fortunes, political might and privilege changed hands but life for the vast majority of Romanians did not change a whit. Weakened by political scandals, regime collapses, mounting debts, inflation, higher taxes and crippling austerity measures, Romanians traded one form of serfdom for another. Now, in the name of market reform, they have since elevated rigor, privation, humiliation and hopelessness to new pinnacles. Justice, the most serious casualty in such contests, remains in critical condition and is not expected to survive.

•

The history of dictatorship is convoluted and so is that of communism. Its birth in central and southeast Europe was hailed with massive popular support. This phenomenon is narrowly linked to both the hopes and aspirations awakened following the overthrow of the Nazis, and to the unerring skill of communist leaders to rhapsodize their creed, foment unreasoned zeal and arouse latent hatreds, especially among the young, the restive and the maladjusted.

The elements of terror were in place in Romania well before the advent of communist regimes. Violence had long been an integral component of its social and psychological reality and Romanians were ill-prepared to defend against yet another wave of barbarism. The instruments of violence, this time, were the so-called communists. Unwavering disciples of Bolshevism, a doctrine further "enriched and fortified" in Stalin's Soviet Union, its leaders' first order of business was to obliterate both their ideological adversaries and their competitors. They did so by swiftly banning all other political parties. The second implement in their panoply of repression was the piecemeal destruction of civil society. It is in the prisons and concentration camps built earlier by the Fascists that this process took its most innovative form. Romania is rightfully credited with reinventing the science of repression in Eastern Europe. Indeed, it was the first nation to introduce on the continent the persuasive "reeducation" methods and "brainwashing" techniques long in vogue throughout Asia. Encouraging inmates to betray and abuse each other was the culmination of a collection of monstrous physical and psychological ordeals the Romanians would hone to an art. It was in the prison of Pitesti, a stygian house of detention outside Bucharest, that these outrages would find their most fiendish expression. What took place at Pitesti between 1949 and 1952 deserves a special spot in the ghoulish repertoire of horrors. In his book, *Pitesti: Detention Laboratory*, Romanian journalist Virgil Ierunca focuses on the methodical use of torture of inmates upon other inmates and puts on display one of the most appalling examples of dehumanization our era has ever known.

"Some inmates had to swallow a bowl full of excrement. When they vomited they were force-fed their regurgitations. Others were 'baptized' every morning head first in a basin filled with urine and fecal matter while the other inmates mockingly recited the baptismal prayer. To avoid drowning, the victim's head was lifted briefly out of the basin then re-immersed in the loathsome concoction. One of the 'anointed' who had been repeatedly tortured in that manner acquired a tragic automatism that lasted two months: Every morning, to the delight of his re-educators, he would reflexively dunk his head in the basin..."

"Reconditioning" was achieved at the end of four stages. First the prisoner had to prove his loyalty by confessing that he had deliberately withheld vital information during the inquest, including an exact accounting of his relationship with family members, associates and acquaintances. He then had to denounce anyone who might have acted kindly or offered him assistance during his incarceration. The third phase called on the prisoner to repudiate everything he held sacred -- parents, wife, husband, children, God. The fourth and final phase was essential if the candidate for "rehabilitation" ever hoped to "graduate;" he had to "re-educate" another inmate, usually a trusted friend, by torturing him repeatedly. Exhausted, stripped of their dignity, hardened by suffering and lacking the capacity to commiserate, many of the surviving Pitesti alumni -- thousands perished in captivity -- took their own lives or ended in mental institutions. Others gleefully joined the ranks of Romania's swelling hordes of inquisitors.

•

In 1948, shielded by my French citizenship, and under diplomatic protection from the French Embassy in Bucharest which interceded on our behalf, my mother and I were among the dwindling few who exited Romania legally, by plane. Freedom came at the price of one last indignity.

"Your watch. Your coat too," barked a uniformed Amazon before letting us aboard. We complied. I will never forget the smugness of her smile as we stripped in the name of the "Popular Republic." My mother had to surrender her rings, a necklace and a bracelet. I was forced to part with a pair of gold cufflinks and a small but valuable stamp collection that I'd inherited from my grandfather. We climbed a foul-smelling and noisy DC-3 that shook, rattled and rolled during the two-hour flight to Oradea, in northwestern Romania. There, we changed planes and flew to Prague in a similarly malodorous and clattering tin can. Two days later we boarded a sleek, white Air France four-engine Lockheed Constellation alive with cheerful blue-clad hostesses who filled my pockets with candy. We arrived in Paris later that afternoon with the shirts on our backs.

    I was eleven.

APRIL IN PARIS

In the final months of the German occupation, as young people serenely unconcerned by the rising chaos around them basked in the sun on the banks of the Seine, Paris succumbed, once more, to fratricide. For many Frenchmen the ultimate act of defiance against the Germans had been to die: on the battlefield; in detention; in daring urban raids or -- betrayed and trapped -- at their own hands. Busy tracking Jews, communists and Freemasons, remnants of the militias ignored, with characteristic imbecility, the rapid Allied advance. They went about their ghoulish task convinced that Hitler's One Thousand-Year Reich was at hand.

An ebbing war, a looming insurrection and daring forays by the *Résistance* did not dampen the resolve of theater owners to keep the stages lit and the curtains up. Nor did frequent blackouts and sporadic street violence stop crowds from flocking to the latest film, play, or girlie show. As fighting intensified in the marshes of Normandy, Edith Piaf and other entertainers filled the Paris music halls. Falsely accused (by Life Magazine, among others) of consorting with the German high command while in captivity during the first World War, Maurice Chevalier, who had negotiated the release of several French fellow inmates, was rehabilitated and returned to his adoring fans.

Journalists, novelists, poets and pamphleteers wrote feverishly, some vying for eminence or political clout, others desperately in need of cash. With the end in sight, many celebrities hastily deserted Paris. Crippled by fear or old age, unwilling to risk flight, others sought refuge in the very bowels of the capital. Meanwhile, clandestine anti-German publications and official pro-collaborationist papers raised the volume of dissent and sharpened the rhetoric. Doctrinal and procedural disagreements polarized the leadership on both sides. Infighting caused rifts that further diluted their reach. The *Résistance* was largely indifferent to these conflicts. Emboldened, it hunted down collaborators, shooting some on sight, arresting and imprisoning others. Over 10,000 collaborators were executed, 800 following summary trial. The rest were liquidated extemporaneously throughout France.

Nor were men of letters and media icons spared. Scores of writers and journalists were rounded up and charged with treason. Eighteen were sentenced to death. Five were executed by firing squad. Four were slaughtered in cold blood as they ventured into the streets. Targeted for assassination, trapped in their lairs or consumed with shame and remorse, several committed suicide. The rest died in exile or at home, disgraced, destitute, trivialized.

Sixty some years have since passed. The theorists and commentators of that epoch are long gone but their writings echo with unsettling obstinacy, inciting Frenchmen to hazard, again, through the quicksand of history, to challenge its inferences and conclusions. All have left a rich harvest of ideas and persuasions, some noted for their decadence, others reviled for the evil they inspired, a few enshrined for their wisdom and refinement. Masterworks of agonized introspection, they are the testament of weaklings and heroes, martyrs and villains cowed, debauched or ennobled by the monstrosity of war. Their manifestos have kept the embers of dissension smoldering beneath a heap of ashes. Unlike the sanguine Americans, who catalogue their past and move on -- perhaps out of shame or utter lack of remorse -- the skeptical and disputatious French cling to outmoded rationalizations. Beating a dead horse is one way of keeping ugly memories and uglier passions alive.

•

France never readily accepted responsibility for the crimes committed in its name, not just by collaborators like Henri Chamberlin Lafont or traitors like Marshall Philippe Pétain, who died in prison, or Prime Minister Pierre Laval, who was executed, but by thousands of anonymous civil servants who stayed at their posts, some too scared to look, others pretending not to see what was happening around them. Many did terrible things that were later whitewashed by a nation all too eager to forget. Nihilist anti-Semitism fed the furnaces, but so did indifference and cowardice.

W. E. Gutman

Obfuscation and official sophistry continued to shroud the precise role France played in the deportation of Jews and the plunder of their properties long after the end of World War II. Seeking to draw a distinction between the puppet Vichy regime and the "loyalist" French state, post-war France doggedly shielded the forest from the trees. It took more than half a century of selective amnesia for the French to come to grudging terms with their past.

Among the many miscreants long protected in the name of "national reconciliation," was Maurice Papon. To please his German mentors, Papon, a high-ranking police official, rounded up hundreds of foreign-born Jews and sent them to Drancy. Tried on charges of complicity in Nazi crimes against humanity by ordering the deportation of 1,560 Jews, including 223 minors, he later served as Budget Minister in Paris until his past came to light in 1981. He was directly involved in quelling a demonstration called by the Algerian National Liberation Front on October 17, 1961, in the seventh year of a bloody war to overthrow French colonialist rule. Violence erupted on the streets of Paris. Demonstrators were fired upon. At least 200 Algerians were slain. Others "disappeared" after being arrested. For weeks, bodies were fished out of the Seine and Paris canals.

"We went to the upper floors of buildings and fired at anything that moved," said a policeman who participated in the carnage.

First indicted in 1983 then again a year later, Papon was released on "technical grounds" in 1987. In 1997, a second investigation paved the way for a trial. Papon steadfastly denied any wrongdoing and invoked "extenuating circumstances" in defense of the crimes committed under his watch. In April 1998, then 87, Papon was sentenced to 10 years in prison. He served fewer than three and died at his family home in 2007.

René Bousquet, national police chief under the occupation, directed the deportation of 194 Jewish children. Although his criminal past was a matter of public record, he held a number of high government posts long after the war. He was killed in 1993 before he could be brought to trial.

Paul Touvier, militia chief in Lyon, was protected by the Catholic Church for 17 years. Finally convicted of ordering a number of summary executions, he died in prison in 1996.

There were others.

Dutch writer Abel Herzberg, who survived the Bergen-Belsen extermination camp, said that six million Jews were not killed but rather that one Jew was killed, and then another, and another, and that the process was repeated six million times. France, to its shame, added to this mathematics of death.

Self-hatred is the beginning of a long love affair.

•

We landed at Le Bourget Airfield, my mother and I, in a dense, slanting rain that washed away all color and turned the surrounding countryside to a streaky blur. I remember alighting from the plane in a steaming, all-encompassing grayness. I did not immediately make out the dim figure standing on the apron by the arched hangar doorway. But the figure recognized us and ran in our direction, arms outstretched, tears streaming down his face.

"Papa, papa."

The rain turned to mist then stopped. The sun tore through as we sped away from the airport in a bus belching black, acrid smoke. By the time we entered Paris the city had shed its gray mantle. Like a butterfly emerging from the chrysalis, it had unfurled its magnificent wings in fitting self-glorification.

•

My father had fled Romania six months earlier. Traveling mostly on foot, at night, his journey had been slow and fraught with perils. He'd crossed into Hungary, then Czechoslovakia and Austria, reaching France through Italy and hitching his way north to Paris in lorries, hay carts and private cars. The overland trek had taken nearly three months. Penniless and jobless, he'd borrowed money to pay the first few months' rent on a small furnished apartment near the Denfert-Rochereau *Métro* station, in an attractive middle-class district boasting terraced cafés, shops, outdoor food stalls and neatly landscaped public parks. This latest leg in a seemingly endless quest for stability and peace would keep us in Paris for only a year. From the Land of Canaan to Babylon and the sands of Egypt, from Worms to Burgos and back, from the Occident to the portals of the Levant, the Guzmán-Gutman tribe, it suddenly dawned on me, was destined to roam. Any attempt to secure a tranquil existence would inevitably be scuttled by adversity or the irrepressible urge to move on. For a long time, wanderlust ablaze inside me, I took comfort in the notion that I could pick up and go if I really wanted to. It's not that I had a specific destination in mind. It was the illusive belief that I could escape the status quo that kept me in its grip. It was the possible loss of such freedom that often sent me on the wildest goose chase.

●

Three years had passed since the end of hostilities, a mere ten since Paris reveled in the gentle radiance of hedonism and insouciance. Shell-shocked and enfeebled, France was slowly stirring from a postwar gloom that would continue to suffuse its soul long after the flesh wounds had healed. Traumatized, dazed, the French would surrender to a world of make-believe that hearkened to a time long gone, enjoying in childish evasion what they could not yet accept as stark reality.

"Nous faisons semblant" -- we pretend -- some would confess with touching candor. They pretended that the war had never taken place; that native thrift, not penury, now shepherded the economy; that indolence, not impotence, impeded national reconstruction; that rationing and power outages and wildcat strikes and the successive rise and fall of inept, erratic and visionless governments could be wished away by ignoring their very existence and the harm they'd caused.

The rekindling of France's élan vital -- much of it contingent on *biftek* and *pommes frites*, bread, wine and tobacco -- entailed privations and sacrifices that the testy French endured with alternating doses of fatalism and irascibility. In short supply in the best of times, civism and solidarity had now been reduced to final fits of vindictiveness and retribution against anyone perceived to have abetted or benefited from the German occupation. My father's petitions to be granted French citizenship were denied. Affidavits, stirring letters of recommendation and pleas from former Resistance colleagues attesting to his bravery, selflessness and loyalty fell on deaf ears.

A document signed on October 10, 1939 by the commander of the French Foreign Legion Recruitment Center in Paris, declared my father "fit for service."

On February 29, 1944, as the Gestapo net tightened around us, the French Ministry of the Interior issued us a "Safe-Conduct to Romania valid on buses and railroads." The document was signed by Adjudant Lins, chief of police in Vic-Fezensac where my father had last served in the Maquis.

Dated 9 November 1946, a sworn statement signed by Lieutenant G. Luino, former commander of the Armagnac Battalion of the 158th Infantry Regiment, and countersigned by the mayor of La Chapelle de la Tour, read:

"I declare, on my honor, that Dr. A. Gutman, a Résistant known as Dr. Guillemain, has always demonstrated in word and deed feelings and ideals of typical French character. Forced to flee Paris to escape the Gestapo in 1943, he joined our ranks for which he performed invaluable services. Having left France for Romania in 1944, he is remembered with fondness and admiration. Nothing in his demeanor, selfless devotion and extraordinary bravery could possibly cast doubt on his loyalty."

On September 5, 1947, as he readied to leave Romania, my father was issued an Allied Forces Permit authorizing him to enter the "Zone of the Allied Forces in Austria en route to Italy." The permit is signed by Lawrence G. Leisersohn, Captain A. C. Adjudant, United States Military Representation.

On January 15, 1948, shortly after his arrival in Paris, my father received the following testimonial from the president of the French community in Bucharest:

"... Dr. A Gutman, now residing on the rue des Rosiers in Paris, has treated generously and at no charge members of the

French colony, especially during bombardments by the Allied air forces from May to August 1944. In September of 1944, and under especially difficult circumstances, he escorted our sick and wounded back to the capital [Bucharest]."

And on April 26, 1948, the mayor of Cazaubon, a small town near Vic-Fezensac issued what would be the last of a series of tributes and accolades the post-war French government would ignominiously ignore. It reads:

"I, the undersigned mayor of Cazaubon, hereby certify that Dr. A Gutman, aka Dr. Guillemain in the Résistance movement, doctor in medicine, presently residing in Paris, has always manifested sentiments representing French ideals. As soon as he arrived [in Cazaubon] he placed himself at the disposal of the Résistance and took care of resisters and Maquisards in the area."

"After all," French authorities concluded, "Dr. Gutman's life was saved by a traitor -- the infamous Henri Lafont -- and he fled France in 1944, at a pivotal moment in France's struggle against the enemy, ostensibly to shield himself and his family from harm."

My father and a number of former Maquis comrades tried to challenge the obtuse logic of that argument, without success. Attempts to repossess the apartment we had hastily abandoned five years earlier would be met with equal hostility, presumably for the same reasons. My father would harbor a lifelong resentment against the authorities that had denied him the privilege he believed he'd earned. But he never stopped loving France.

•

Spared deportation and the Nazi death camps, delivered from the communist yoke, we were now held hostage by uncertainty and creeping indigence. I was a Frenchman by birth and, as a minor, I was legally entitled to the guardianship of my parents in France. Stateless -- one of them spurned by the country he had served -- my parents were vested with no more than the perfunctory and provisional privileges accorded political refugees. The future, deferred by endless frustrations, looked bleak.

It was my education, interrupted and seriously compromised during the previous four years, which took center stage in my parents' life -- or so it looked from my vantage point. Restless and vaguely apprehensive, too busy absorbing and digesting the newness of our present circumstance, I was in no mood to be returned to school. I dreaded discipline, resented authority and begrudged the studied remoteness of teachers (later of military superiors, bosses and petty bureaucrats). Worse, I feared the scorn of children, pint-sized predators-in-training who would see right through this morose, confused and agitated boy's very thin mask of poise and cockiness.

Two of Paris' most prestigious schools, *Lycée Lakanal* and *Lycée Henri IV* denied me a seat, perhaps judging me unworthy of their high academic standards. Moved by my father's pleas, a third school -- its name escapes me -- enrolled me provisionally. I did poorly, especially in math and sciences, and I was soon politely sacked. I remember being mocked by a teacher for drawing a map of France bounded by an Atlantic Ocean and a Mediterranean Sea so implausibly blue – I'd painted these bodies of water a deep shade of purple -- that "no marine life could possibly survive in them...." Eager to curry favor with the teacher, a thin, grim-faced man with an acerbic tongue, and animated by their own cruelty, my classmates roared with laughter. I survived the affront with feigned stoicism and withheld tears of rage until I got home.

Located in the Paris suburb of St.-Cloud, *Lycée Maimonides*, a non-sectarian Jewish boarding school, agreed to take me in, unconditionally and, as my mother, quoting the director, would later relate, "mindful of this young boy's tribulations."

I have no recollection of life in the classroom. While I can still see the face and bearing of the scornful pedagogue who had ridiculed me a month earlier, I can't conjure up the features of a single *Maimonides* schoolteacher. Nor can I say how well or how poorly I did scholastically. The absence of clear reminiscences suggests that I must have coasted along with habitual mediocrity, and that no one had taken issue with my performance, not the teachers or my parents.

What I remember is a handsome château-like structure with a baroque façade and a sprawling, tree-lined courtyard where pupils played during recess and where I often hid to avoid gym class, relay races and ball games. It was not exercise that I shunned. I ran and gamboled and climbed trees and scaled fences and ascended atop roofs and executed double somersaults with the greatest of ease. It was the formality and protocols of compulsory communal activity, the chronometer, the tedious circularity, the intrinsic competitiveness of team play that I abhorred. I might have found some allure in games had they not been ruled by rivalry or constrained by score keeping.

"Winning is the incentive of champions," the gym teacher preached.

"Poets need no incentive. I feel no urge to triumph over anyone but myself. "

"Only losers feel that way."

"I concede that there can be no *winner* without a *loser* -- assuming that contests have any relevance whatsoever and that anything of exceptional worth is to be gained by engaging in them in the first place."

I would remain mildly interested in the dynamics of play, not in trophies. This attitude, sharpened over the years, would baffle people. In America, where sports assume idolatrous dimensions, it would often elicit scornful pity, the kind granted village idiots.

I also vividly recall a feeling of estrangement and degradation at having to sleep with twenty or thirty other boys in a large, drafty dormitory, at sharing tasteless meals in the company of rowdy kids, of queuing up for a seat on the toilet, a shower head, a bathroom sink. I would feel the same way, some eight years later, when, common sense be damned, I joined the U.S. Navy "to see the world." Life at sea, painted by the likes of Herman Melville, Robert Louis Stevenson and James Michener -- some of its grubbiest aspects conveniently disregarded -- had beckoned since childhood with growing lust and fury. But the fickle siren call landed me on a very small wooden ship -- a minesweeper -- that never ventured far from shore. I would note as I grew older that the same providence that paid heed to my wildest dreams took fiendish delight in granting them -- with a twist.

Lacking even a speck of lyricism, boarding schools are apt to transform poets into misanthropes. So does life in the close proximity of conscripts.

●

The strong friendship I would form at home with a rare and like-minded loner made up for the alienation my reclusive nature had invited in the school's impersonal setting. A good-natured boy my age, Marcel, the janitor's son, lived next door, on *Square Henri-Delormel*, a cul-de-sac fronted by a U-shaped block of townhouses where my parents and I had taken up residence. Peering from behind a thick set of lenses, Marcel's myopic eyes conveyed kindness and forbearance, virtues missing or unrevealed among my classmates. Ours was the kind of camaraderie that blossoms quickly and eagerly, honed by the discovery of common tastes and shared aversions. We hated liver and fish and school and the biting chill of winter and the haughty, dismissive attitude of adults. We loved escargots and pasta and maps and the strange-sounding names of faraway places, and we'd often invent exotic domains -- lush islands, jungle citadels, desert retreats -- and fashion cryptic languages in which we conversed for hours with great solemnity. On weekends and holidays, when I came home from St. Cloud, we spun our tops, played marbles and kicked a soccer ball in the sunless oval courtyard. On rainy days, we sat side by side engrossed in the *Adventures of Tintin,* the madcap exploits of *Astérix* and his band of zany Gauls, the daft escapades of *Bibi Fricotin* and the reckless pranks of *Les Pieds Nickelés*.

Marcel and I also enjoyed swimming, a pastime we likened to "flying through liquid butter." This analogy elicited countless puns in Parisian *argot* -- slang -- none translatable into English. It was at the pool, built below ground and reserved for tenants, that we perfected underwater stunts (including the "butter-fly") which amused the grownups, stupefied other kids and thrilled Françoise, Marcel's sister. Françoise, I soon discovered, had become infatuated with me. I could tell by the look in her eyes, maternal and seductive, by her habit, tiresome at first then soon strangely alluring, of wedging herself between me and her brother on the narrow settee, gently pressing herself against me, fussing with my hair and brushing off nonexistent dust flecks off my pants. It was also at the pool that Françoise, pigtailed, freckle-faced Françoise, whose dreamy gaze no longer escaped my attention, explored the fullness of her awakening sensuality with the uncommon grace, candor and tenderness of a loving child.

One day, as I headed back to the dressing rooms, I found Françoise skulking in the cubicle where I'd stowed my clothes. Surprise gave way to an odd thrill that coursed through my body, first raising goose bumps then flooding it with a warmth so intense that I felt it in my loins. Françoise put her hand on my mouth.

"Shhh."

"What?" I whispered.

"Nothing," she murmured. She shrugged her shoulders. Her eyebrows arched with mischief. She smiled.

We stood there motionless, looking at each other under the dim dressing room lights. Françoise bid me to sit on the wooden shelf that doubled as a bench. I obeyed, enthralled by her presence, fearful that we might be found out. She gently pried my lap open, slid between my thighs and moved in close, so close that our chests and bellies converged. She put her arms around my neck and drew me to her. Our foreheads met and our lips touched, softly. My arms encircled her waist. I can't describe the exhilaration I felt. I closed my eyes. My heart raced and I became aware that an erection, ignited by some primal craving and fueled by the wonderful warmth Françoise's body radiated, now distended my bathing suit.

My hands slid downward, cupping her buttocks. I felt a rush, an exquisite longing in the pit of my stomach and I began to rub myself against Françoise in slow, ascending undulations that flooded my being with ecstasy.

I did not climax. I would not experience the rapture of a full-blown orgasm for another two years or so. Instead, bliss turned to panic as I heard Marcel calling for his sister. The icy hand of fear squeezed the nape of my neck and my mighty hard-on collapsed as rapidly as it had risen.

Françoise and I quickly unfastened our embrace. I chinned myself up and over the partition. The coast was clear. We tiptoed out of the cubicle and dashed in opposite directions. I caught up with Marcel halfway down the corridor.

"Where were you?" I asked with an informality that scarcely concealed my unease. "I was looking for you everywhere."

Effrontery gives lies legitimacy.

Rounding the other corner, Françoise, her cheeks a crimson red, ambled toward us in her calico two-piece bathing suit, an icon of poise and girlish innocence.

•

Back in school the next day, I replayed the extraordinary happenstance in my head a thousand times or more. I was in love. Or so it seemed. Only love, I surmised, could bring on such hitherto unknown euphoria. But while I credited Françoise for helping unleash the powerful sensations I'd savored during our brief romp, I quickly realized that she was -- as were many of the women I would later court -- an agent of gratification, not an object of love. In a vain quest for epic romance, I would -- at times naively, often out of exasperation -- confuse love and sex, seeking one in relentless pursuit of the other. Soon, I found myself sauntering from bed to bed, adrift in muck on a rudderless vessel of debauchery that ran aground on the shoals of matrimony.

To love is to be all at once oneself and the object of one's desires.

•

I would marry young; I was twenty-four, naïve, reckless. Wise beyond her years and as shrewd as a fox in a hen house, my wife was four years my junior, a slim, pretty brunette with a boyish haircut and the self-assured stride of a model surfing a chic Paris runway. We'd met at an uptown New York coffee shop where stale poetry, competing with the jangle of china and the strumming of badly tuned guitars, elegized maladjusted youth and ill-defined utopias. Three months later, confident that a marriage certificate would mitigate the penance of pleasure postponed (she'd steadfastly spurned my advances, insisting that a wedding band must firmly encircle her ring finger before she would "lavish the treasures of her femininity," I did the unthinkable and took her to the altar.

It was shortly after the honeymoon, an awkward, week-long tedium during which I learned the sad art of pretense (it's all right, she'd faked virginity with equal poise) that I apprehended the folly of my deed. It was also at that time that my wife began to show signs of disquiet. Baffled by my priorities -- Beethoven and Mahler could make me weep but a leaky faucet, a creaky hinge or a loose roof tile wouldn't elicit a tear -- and nonplused by the waning ardor in my loins, she'd hinted that it just might become necessary to "reconstruct" me for my own good. In the beginning, her playful admonitions, followed by fleeting, crude frolics in bed where she validated my virility and gauged the constancy of my passion, suggested little more than the pitiable if clumsy stirrings of a woman struggling to be loved. In time, flirtation and coquetry dissolved, turning to rancor, spite and hostility, I'd since forced myself to become the dutiful husband the world expected but I never learned to love her no matter how hard I tried. The Promethean man she yearned -- part-father, tireless lover, servile flatterer -- existed only in her mind, the mangled resurrection of childhood fantasies fed by pulp fiction, buttressed by weak, coddling parents and invigorated by a large and all-consuming ego. She proceeded to destroy what she could not reconstruct and spent the next twenty years punishing me for failing to match a single blueprint in her aberrant grand design.

Skimming the edges of psychosis in an ever-tightening spiral toward deliverance, I'd resolved to surrender to madness in exchange for peace, or to die in a final bid for freedom. I took refuge in silence at first, caulking my mind's battered ears against the martial clangor of her footsteps as she stalked me around the house ready to chasten me for some petty infraction, against the drunken wails, the incessant scolding, the ugly threats. It was at some ineffable distance, far away from her corrosive presence, that I could find myself, glimpse the man I once was.

Oh, melancholy, I'd scribbled in my notebook, *take me in your arms, wrap your icy fingers around my burning nape. Your embrace heightens the wellness of being. Without you I am but a stone unturned.*

My wife had branded such musings "radical and offensive," a twinned label she would often pin on propositions that eluded her or threatened her sense of self-worth. Giving in to melancholy, she thought, was inconsiderate and disloyal.

"I should be uppermost in your thoughts," she groaned. "There should be no room for the mindless trips you take into your self-pitying void."

The bitch.

The bitch always wanted sex on stormy nights and cold winter mornings. She would stir me awake from some delicious tryst and rub herself against me in a kissless frenzy of self-arousal, denying me the courtesy of foreplay and inducing reflex erections that I managed to sustain by reentering the dreamtime for the duration. Satisfied that my virility rivaled the fullness of her passion, she would then turn around and offer me her back, her thighs tightly pressed together, a feverish finger twiddling her clitoris, and I would mount her from behind, awaiting the cataclysmic orgasms that erupted within seconds, and she would often pull away long before supreme flights of fancy or the legitimate urge to please myself could take me to the brink. On rare occasions, she would let me catch up, a privilege she extended in exchange for grateful praises of her lovemaking and pledges of undying fidelity.

I would have gladly strangled her as she crested and spasms of pleasure jolted her raw-boned, nervous body, but it was my own demise I engineered instead, fearful of man-made justice, seeking fresh scenarios and unexplored paths to freedom.

Melancholy and introspection further sharpened my sense of alienation. I felt lonely, no, sequestered, cast out, a pariah in my own house. Loneliness and alienation are merciless foes. They kill slowly, hope by hope, dream by dream, breath by mournful breath. So I took my dreams to other women, the few I knew -- my wife's friends, all of whom I fucked in dingy hotel rooms or at home when their husbands were away -- and the many I had never set eyes on but in whose imaginary company I lingered as I masturbated, for I had endowed them with empathy, wit and the capacity to dream, virtues I found in none of my wife's friends, nor sought. These escapades did little to temper the ferment that churned my insides. They had, in fact, the opposite effect, adding a measure of self-disgust to the nausea the unholy trysts had induced.

As time went on, my sorties awakened new phantasms, they unearthed fresh sepulchers, pushed open abandoned gateways that gave onto epochs long forgotten, or as yet unrecorded, all of which I dutifully shared with my notebook as I embarked on the rapturous flight to freedom.

Early one morning, seven thousand and three hundred days and nights after I'd pulverized a sacramental glass under the richly festooned dais where our union had been hallowed, I left my wife at last. I had escaped the asylum but madness still stalked me. There were too many ghosts to exorcise, too many shadows to dust off and ventilate. I'd survived but survivors, I knew, are the illegitimate children of defeat. They must bear witness to be avenged.

Deliverance would come one day in the form of a waning libido and a creeping lassitude toward sex. Mercifully, these transformations occur when one is ready to concede that sex is overrated and that love is as elusive as it is brittle.

If the vehicle of marriage was outfitted with a "front-view" mirror, the betrothed would rarely make it to city hall or to church.

•

Little did I imagine, now that Françoise occupied the totality of my puerile erotic universe, that I would spend a lifetime chasing after the same indulgences in the arms of countless women -- "decent" family girls, respectable housewives, nubile hookers and, *faute de mieux*, my future ex-wife. From the fog of time roam memories of fainting couches and canopied beds and the lumpy mattresses of Paris bordellos and the stinking rattan floor mats of remote jungle shacks. I remember Jones Beach, Pebble Beach and the secluded sandy coves of Grenada. Opportunity always favored the moment and the moment always dictated the venue: The tar-covered roof of an apartment building in New York. A darkened alley in Marseille. A Mediterranean cruise ship. The bushes in a park, at dusk, across Amsterdam's *Rijksmuseum*. The credenza in my office, in full view of the United Nations. A transatlantic flight to Frankfurt. An overnight Greyhound bus trip to Pittsburgh, with a perfect stranger. A sleeper car on a Chicago-bound train. A movie house. In broad daylight on the verandah of Reverend Johnson's Barbados estate -- with his daughter -- as he led a breakfast prayer meeting in the garden below.

•

Françoise and I tried to finagle other rendezvous but conflicting school schedules and other unforeseen hindrances conspired against us. The winds of change were blowing once again and one day the suitcases came down from the top of the armoire where they'd been stowed and onto the bed where neatly folded clothes were now piling up.

I learned that my uncle had lost his job at the paper in Bucharest, that he'd been disbarred for possessing a few dollar bills -- or so his denouncers alleged. A reign of communist terror was now raging in Romania. French authorities held fast in denying my father citizenship. Last resort or rash improvisation, we were now headed half a world away across the Mediterranean. I wept as I bid Marcel and Françoise farewell. Barely appeased, wanderlust and the lure of the unknown quickly dried the tears. I would not see my friends for the next five years.

I'd just turned twelve.

EXODUS

*They came because they were afraid or unafraid,
because they were happy or unhappy, because
they felt like pilgrims or did not feel like pilgrims.
There was a reason for each man....
They were coming with small dreams
or large dreams or none at all.*
The Martian Chronicles, Ray Bradbury

Spurned by the country he'd served and loved, it was my father's failure to find his "place," a restless discontent that would stalk him for the rest of his life -- and which I would inherit -- that prompted him to uproot anew and embark on yet another Quixotic odyssey. We were setting sail, this time, to the "Old-New" land, the recently created State of Israel. The catalyst for what would prove to be an ill-conceived decision lay in a thoughtless pretense (reckless incitement might be more accurate): I came home one day and claimed that someone had called me a dirty Jew.

"Where?" my father asked, his brow furrowed with concern.

"Oh, in the street," I replied.

"Who?"

"I don't know, somebody...."

I clearly remember alleging the incident but have no recollection of it actually taking place. Nor did the slur -- assuming it was ever uttered -- seem to cause me the outrage it warranted, perhaps because I'd lied, blurted out the kind of untruth children tell that is as impulsive as it is preposterous. This fabrication, unchallenged and uncorroborated, would have immediate and long-term consequences on our lives. To my father this meant war, war against anti-Semitism, which he knew lurks in the shadows and stalks every Jew. This was his way of intellectualizing the frustrations of the moment. He was already struggling against a host of inner demons -- pain, still raw, at the loss of his parents and siblings, horror at the murder of his youngest sister, dashed hopes, self-doubt -- all of which he faced with a gallantry and stoicism that left him emotionally exhausted.

The awful untruth I had uttered may also have provided him with a ready-made pretext to validate a nascent but utterly atypical gush of Zionism. As years went by, with hindsight as evidence, I would conclude that my father, who never ceased to be a Jew, had little feeling for the Zionist cause. The hardships and setbacks we would face in the "Land of Milk and Honey" would leave him bitter and resentful. Israel would be yet another milestone on a very bumpy and circuitous journey to nowhere.

Near the end of his life, my father reflected that old age had affixed "a coda, forcibly and cruelly, onto an unfinished symphony." Like him, I discovered a metaphorical connection between music and vagabondage. I would indulge in both when dissonance and boredom begged for unusual harmonies and unexplored horizons.

•

Nor did I believe that some obscure scruple, some scrap of reawakened piety had driven a confirmed agnostic to exclaim "next year in Jerusalem," not even in symbolic jest. Israel's rebirth had heralded the apotheosis of Jewish survival but to my father, who now viewed religion as an absurdity -- "faith by force and psychological extortion" -- and nationalism, in any form, as "a heady tonic for the dim-witted and the bellicose," Israel was little more than a historical eccentricity and it aroused only mild interest as a revived or artificial ethno-geopolitical entity. In the circumstances of the moment, however, it also afforded an opportunity to escape, yet again, a no-exit status quo.

Whereas I could not imagine, let alone fully grasp, what years of religious indoctrination had done to shape my father's psyche, I understood even less how deeply entrenched beliefs can be so effortlessly jettisoned. Heretofore introspective and atavistic, devoid of dogmatism or militancy, my father's Judaism had withered to a vestigial self-view: He was aware of the existence of a primal nexus that linked him to the very deepest part of him, but the bond was now stripped of all metaphysical accouterments.

The soul cannot remember its former lives but carries within it the regret of having forgotten them.

•

Predictably, I was never given a religious education. Nor did I ever ask for one. Instead, my father and I spent hours dissecting the major doctrines -- focusing mostly on the aberrations, paradoxes, inconsistencies and the atrocities committed in their name. We conceded that all are anchored in some sublime if unattainable ideal but found none that does not claim preeminence, none that condemns, tacitly or explicitly, the use of force -- apostolic or separatist -- to defend it. We reviewed the fury unleashed among the multiplying cults, the cleaving into "denominations," each fond of vilifying the other. We noted that ministers, instead of teaching and enlightening, are often ignorant, parochial and bigoted. Ascetics, instead of facing life's turmoil, are idle, misanthropic parasites and shameless sensualists who take masochistic delight in self-denial and pain. Rabbis, instead of being rapt in Talmudic studies, dabble in commerce and other profane pursuits. Blinded by mutual contempt, polarized by exegetic discord, Catholicism, Protestantism and Orthodox Christianity make a mockery of the Christian ethic. Hindus and Muslims are at each other's throats -- as are Jews and Arabs -- all mired in a turf war fueled by hatred and envenomed by the inflexible credos that divide them. Unchallenged by the flock, gingerly overlooked by the shepherds, such arrogance, it was obvious to us, refutes the model and invalidates the mission.

Sects and cults are like vultures that feed on the decomposing corpses of traditional religions.

My decision not to be Bar Mitzvah would be greeted with consternation, not by my parents, but by acquaintances who, like ticks, had embedded themselves in our private lives and meddled in matters of personal conscience just to assess the depth of our "Jewishness." When challenged, I retorted that I found the rituals, the perfunctory protocols, the circular stagnancy of worship tedious and meaningless. Such apostasy in one so young drew sharp criticism, most of it hurled at my father who, his critics protested, should have had the good sense to anticipate and prevent his son's defection. Rebuke would turn to vitriolic condemnation when, unable to catch up with the public school's Hebrew-language curriculum, I was enrolled in a French Catholic mission school.

My father had accepted my anti-religious rationale without editorial comment. But I felt I owed him more than flippancy or sarcasm. I needed to articulate my feelings with a candor that not only mirrored their intensity but crystallized them as well. First set on paper then memorized, like a soliloquy, I had recited the following apologia with equal doses of theatricality and conviction:

> *"It's the words, papa, words not my own, the injunctions, the admonitions, the supplications, the jeremiads, the breast-beating, the utterances of indebtedness and veneration, all repeated ad nauseam, day after day, to a God who never shows his face, never bares his heart, never weeps, never says he's sorry, a God who grants life and, with it, the fear of death. I would happily surrender to an all-comforting creed. But God upon whom we turn for succor, whose indulgence we seek for our sins and whose wrath we invoke against our enemies, turns a stone visage to human misery and a deaf ear to our most heart-rending cries."*

I would reprise the theme, less charitably, in a school essay that earned me high grades for style and a glacial two-page red-penned review by Sister Louis, of the Order of St. Joseph, in whose care my education would soon be entrusted.

Lacking spiritual guidance, I remember searching, even as a teenager, for an idiom, a concept anchored in reason, not dogmatism, a path devoid of ceremony and mimicry that would lead me to enlightenment and wisdom. When I was old enough to apprehend the enormity of the Holocaust, I found in it no telltale revelation. I discovered no occult moral, no oracular grand design in the extermination of millions of innocent people, no defensible argument buttressing the existence of a deity so impervious to human suffering that it gapes with serene unconcern at the torments it inflicts on its very own creation. My mother's death -- no, her murder by pancreatic cancer twenty-four years later -- would obliterate the last traces of cautious trust in an omnipotent, just and merciful entity. I rejected as cruel and deceitful the explanation that God *works in mysterious ways*, and proclaimed that such mythic being was unworthy of veneration.

Nature created man in an infinite variety of models; lacking nature's imagination, man created God as one of a kind.

Maturity, introspection and exposure to the works of great minds would eventually help blunt this rigidity and lead me to conclude that God, stripped of hackneyed human clichés, is simply inaccessible to human thought. In time, I would challenge this notion of inaccessibility to find that God, ineffable and inscrutable, if beheld as the essence of absolute truth -- or "endlessness" as the Kabbalists perceive it -- is a more approachable concept, one that parallels science's attempt to bring all natural phenomena under one law. I would become convinced, as I am today, that a unified theory linking the totality of cosmic reality will eventually be elaborated. I would also conclude that, at its core, such theory would contain an irreducible abstraction no less impenetrable than the very concept of God and that God, for lack of a better name, would be ruled "first cause." Elevating God to such empyrean status, however, did not prevent me from rejecting the institutions created in its name. Marketing, I have always held, somehow debases the merchandise.

Advertising is the wickedest form of deceit: it creates in people the illusion of need.

•

My father favored contrition over righteousness. He derided "the good man" as an uninspiring, spineless creature too timid to misbehave. Echoing a Lutheran perspective that was as unrehearsed as it was devoid of religious inspiration, he often spoke of the banality of goodness:

Better a sin expunged than the triteness of unerring virtue.

He also believed that sins of omission are worse than sins of commission because they are premeditated.

"One can commit a heinous crime on the spur of the moment, ignited by unbridled rage or a sudden burst of folly. One does not *abstain* from doing the right thing unless urged by intent."

It would be his lot to discover, no, to re-discover, this time in Israel, that the self-righteous abound even in Zion and that their capacity for evil -- rendered or countenanced -- far surpasses the good man's pointless innocence.

•

We set sail from Marseille in the fall of 1949 aboard the S/S Kedmah, an old tub that bobbed and wheezed as it sliced through heavy seas during the next seven days. I remember a dank, narrow cabin painted a sickly shade of green, and I can still hear the metal bulkheads groaning whenever the bow lurched into the foot of a wave and the rest of the hull struggled to right itself up over the crest. At times, the stern would lift out of the water and the propeller shrieked as it idled in the air, sending shivers through the length of the vessel. Located below the waterline, the cabin reeked of petrol. The mattresses were thin and emitted foul odors that kept my mother awake. Despondent and bereft, she wept during the entire crossing. My father was unable to console her. He spent much time on the bridge, lost in thought, or playing chess with the captain or first officer.

For me, this was yet another adventure. I'd flown on an airplane, traveled by train, explored the entire Paris subway network. Even the garishly painted wooden stallions of the old merry-go-round in the *Tuileries Gardens* or at the foot of the Sacré Coeur, had delivered the thrills of motion and emancipation. One can imagine what a voyage to the "Levant" meant to a twelve-year-old boy enamored of atlases, travel posters and stamps from faraway places. Let's see what magnificent odyssey the future yields, I murmured to myself. The thrill of living rests in the discovery of tomorrow's infinite possibilities.

But as the French coast receded in the distance, bathed in twilight's milky opalescence, a million city lights twinkling in the afterglow, I remember being overcome with sadness and disquiet. Too young to lament the loss of earthly possessions -- we had discarded anything deemed superfluous, shipped a few pieces of furniture in a large wooden crate -- I was old enough to experience and pinpoint the cause of this strange new malaise. It dawned on me that I was rootless, incomplete, truncated, a seedless weed grafted onto a sterile bough, flotsam forever adrift on the currents of fate. Separation anxiety subsided after a couple of days, replaced by moments of exhilaration, flashes of freedom and serenity, now that I was one with the sea, a slate-blue, animate expanse that stretched, heaving and shimmering, all around me. But the inner turmoil that had assailed me shortly after embarkation resurfaced when I sighted land in the distance. It grew sharper as the diamond-studded nighttime visage of Mount Carmel came into view high above the port city of Haifa. And as we disembarked, lugging our weathered cardboard valises onto the darkened pier, I was revisited with the same feelings of dislocation, uncertainty and impermanence that had ushered all of our migrations. Years of privation, false starts and setbacks would follow.

●

Home for the next four years was a large square house with three-foot stone walls and coifed with a gently sloping ivy-patched red tile roof. Located in Jerusalem's Greek Colony, a quiet, lush oasis south of the busy downtown district, the house sat at the center of an inner courtyard fenced off by a stone parapet and a forged iron gate. Lined on one side with towering eucalyptus trees, the gate ended on each side with a portico flanked by two tall columns that my father promptly nicknamed "Boaz" and "Jachin." I would have to wait nearly forty years to learn, by initiation, the cryptic symbolism these pillars conveyed.

The backyard was overgrown with a tangled expanse of wild flowers, bushes and tall grasses where lived a couple of venerable desert tortoises. I adopted them both, christening one Schmiel -- he looked "Jewish" -- the other Franz, a name befitting his decidedly "Teutonic" features -- a square jaw and a pugnacious nature. I was very fond of them. Several generations of chameleons that thrived in the garden, two stray dogs and a lame crow would become cherished pets and, when fellowships with the neighborhood kids turned mercurial, noble and fascinating companions.

It was on Boaz that my father proudly affixed a freshly painted sign. It read, in Hebrew and French: **ARMIN GUTMAN, MD, GP -- GYNECOLOGY/ OBSTETRICS**. Below, in smaller cursive letters, the sign read: *Diplomate of the Faculty of Medicine, Paris*.

Across the street, unbeknownst to him, a curtain had parted and someone had witnessed this proclamation. The sign would be defaced or vanish in the middle of the night and had to be replaced several times. Though my father was never able to prove it, suspicion fell on a fellow physician, an older man with whom relations, cool and distant at first, eventually turned glacial. Within less than a year, the small but steady clientele that my father had cultivated would be reduced to a trickle. Rumors alleged that my father was performing abortions, a procedure he vehemently opposed except in the rarest of cases, and that several of his patients had died in the process. Neither claim was true. His fellow doctor and neighbor, my father conjectured, was behind this odious smear campaign but no proof of such complicity would ever surface. Struggling to make a living, my father did not have the energy to play detective. Logic suggested, however, that at a time of great post-war economic frailty, in a community boasting only one physician, the arrival of a younger competitor on the block was bound to be seen as a threat and arouse resentment.

Such is kismet in the realm of wolves. Unlike people, wolves cannot be corrupted.

Another near-catastrophe would take place shortly after we moved in when someone set fire to the wooden container that had housed our furniture during the crossing. Awaiting removal by the trash collectors, it had been resting in the yard. When we were awakened early one morning to shouts of "Fire, Fire," the blaze had nearly consumed the crate and combustible packing material within, scorching a set of shutters and igniting a tree whose branches dangled perilously over the roof. We summoned the fire brigade and the pyre, labeled "suspicious," was quickly brought under control. I enriched my vocabulary with a new and frightening word: arson.

•

Surreal is how I remember the morning I was ushered to my desk by the headmaster of Jerusalem's prestigious Rehavia High School. Surreal and daunting. I was first introduced to my classmates, a formality greeted with indifference. I was then handed a Talmudic text and invited to demonstrate my powers of deduction by joining in on a debate involving the hypothetical death of a cow being cared for by someone other than its owner. Various scenarios, I recall, influenced the custodian's legal obligations. Had the cow been unwell? Was it being looked after on the owner's premises or elsewhere? Did it fall ill *before* or *after* leaving its owner's shed? Was it the victim of negligence or foul play? Did it die of old age? Was it gravid? Did its master own more heads of cattle or was it an only cow? Was it being raised for beef or for dairy? Had it been purchased, inherited or received as a gift?

All this must surely have had great dialectical merit but to a 13-year-old boy with uncontrollable erections and a roaming eye for the girls these cerebral contortions lacked meaning or utility. Here I was, a young irreligious French Jew, familiar with *"our ancestors, the Gaul"* but unacquainted with the Gittites, Gileadites or Gibeonites. I could describe Napoleon's seven military campaigns but I knew nothing about Nathan, Nahum or Naphtali, whose exploits I could much less read -- in Hebrew -- let alone discuss. So to my immense relief, after less than a month, I was quietly removed from that eminent institution and given a seat in Sister Louis' all-girl class at the Lycée Français St. Joseph. I resumed my studies in French under the agonized gaze of Jesus crucified dominating the facing wall and surrounded by a dozen *demoiselles de bonne famille* whose coy, sidelong glances kept me in a perpetual state of arousal which I struggled to contain with periodic fits of buffoonery.

•

Fought and won just before we arrived in 1949, the War of Independence had been a war of reaffirmation and Jewish self-assertion against the armies of four Arab countries that had pounced on the newly founded State of Israel. King Hussein had sent crack British-trained commando troops across the Jordan, occupying Judea, Samaria and the eastern half of Jerusalem, including the Old City and Temple Mount, and destroying all Jewish settlements. Egypt had seized Gaza. Syria and Iraq had attacked from the north and the east.

Israel had waged the first of its five wars with severe handicaps. Great Britain had drastically trimmed the territory granted the Jews and reduced to a trickle the number of settlers allowed to come to its shores. It then prevented the Jews from arming themselves while allowing increasingly large shipments of weapons to the Arabs of Palestine. Possessing virtually no tanks, artillery or aircraft, Israel's ragtag forces were outnumbered and outgunned. Israel's very life hung in the balance. The 20-month carnage cost the lives of 6,000 Israelis, many of them Holocaust survivors. By June, the Jews had reached a state of near-exhaustion. Yet even on the brink of disaster, they somehow held on and managed to repel the Arab onslaught. Writing *in A Place Among Nations*, Benjamin Netanyahu, whose anti-Palestinian virulence I would one day denounce, recalls that –

> *"... the Jewish state was now a fact. It had come into the world after an agonizing labor. It would have no happy childhood, either, with frequent cross-border attacks by Arab marauders and daily promises from Egypt's President Gamal Abdel Nasser and other similarly disposed neighbors that Israel would shortly be "exterminated."*

•

Having failed to destroy the newborn state in 1948, the Arabs would resort to an unremitting campaign of terror. Border villages were repeatedly shelled at night with mortar fire. Lurking in the dark, exploiting the ensuing confusion, the marauders then attacked from all sides, slaughtering old people and children in their beds.

Fierce battles must have taken place in the Greek Colony. During the next several months, I found many live bullets and spent shells in the scrub-filled vacant lots adjoining the main thoroughfare. Rummaging through the skeletal remains of houses destroyed during the conflict, or whose erection had been halted, also yielded large numbers of projectiles and spent ammunition. Boys in the neighborhood taught me how to pry the slug from the shell and set fire to the powder. We would then gather copper casings in burlap sacks and sell them to a scrap dealer.

There was such a scarcity of copper at the time that my playmates and I pilfered every bit of copper and brass we could find -- lengths of tubing, electrical wiring, fittings, faucets, flanges, lugs. When copper became scarce or no longer safe to filch, we tore loose sheets of corrugated metal roofing, gutters and spouts, and harvested tin cans, cast iron manhole covers, barbed wire, in short anything we could easily haul away. We would pool the few coins we earned from this illicit commerce to buy cigarettes and gain entry at the *Semadar,* the local movie house where Flash Gordon, Abbott and Costello, Charlie Chaplin, Tarzan and Laurel and Hardy were standard fare.

●

Tsena -- "modesty" in Hebrew -- is the word Israelis coined to describe, with a lyrical restraint characteristic of heroes, the long and difficult period of penury that lingered after the war. Reminiscent of the privations we'd endured in France, *Tsena* was ubiquitous and all pervading. Gasoline, engine parts and specialized tools were in short supply, putting a strain on public transit and delaying the movement of vital goods between cities. Construction projects were on hold for lack of bricks and mortar. Every able-bodied man 45 and under was in the reserves, on 24-hour call, and often summoned to leave family and job for "parts unknown." This exigency, in the face of continuing border skirmishes and sporadic terrorist assaults, impeded the timely erection and repair of infrastructures vital for the absorption of new immigrants who were now "ascending" to Israel from all corners of the globe.

Sharing in the collective hardships and anxieties of the newly founded state, life in Zion assumed for us the characteristics of a Passover Seder preamble -- bitter herbs, salty tears and the memory of choices not fully explored. Uprooted, disheartened, daunted by the challenges and uncertainties facing the infant nation, intolerant of the climate and unable or unwilling to learn Hebrew, my mother buried herself in domestic chores. She kept the house immaculately clean and fed a family that, within a year of our arrival, would be augmented by her mother, who, owing her age, had been granted exit from Romania.

Preparing meals, an all-day affair, was as much a labor of love as a feat of wizardry. Basic staples, including eggs, butter and meat, were rationed. The icebox -- we had no refrigerator -- was often empty, save for oranges and a few desiccated vegetables kept questionably fresh by a large block of ice purchased daily from a vendor who led a horse-drawn carriage and rang a loud bell. Indifferent to food -- I spent hours on end reading or listening to the radio -- I don't recall being inconvenienced by the scarcities we endured.

Owing its thick stone walls, our house was cool in the summer but winters were chilly and damp and kerosene heaters were strategically placed to keep it warm. The kerosene dealer, a wizened bearded old man who sharpened knives and resoled shoes, also steered a horse-drawn cart with wobbly wheels that shrieked dolefully at every turn. He too rang a bell but its timbre was more high-pitched than the iceman's.

•

Between 1948 and 1952 nearly one million Jews were expelled from Arab countries. Most went to Israel. A large number came from French-speaking Morocco, Algeria and Tunisia. Others crossed the Tigris and the Euphrates fleeing Iraq and Kurdistan. There was little about the latter that matched my perception of Jews. Dress, manner and speech -- the men wore loose-fitting pantaloons, vests and turbans, blew their noses through their fingers, chain-smoked, snorted and spat copiously and communicated loudly in an alien and dissonant tongue

-- betrayed strange influences to which I was unaccustomed. It would take a generation of assimilative processes to turn coarse desert Jews into modern Israelis.

Overnight, a group of Kurdish Jews commandeered our semi-attached garage and turned it overnight into a synagogue and community center. Several times a year, they would convene outside the temple at about midnight and conduct prayers dedicated to the moon. Their loud and lugubrious wails woke us up but religion would prevail. When my father complained, the Ministry of Religious Affairs replied tersely -- I'm paraphrasing -- that being unoccupied, and with space at a premium, the garage had been declared eminent domain and "donated." The letter also obliquely alluded to my attending a Catholic mission school and advised against entertaining future grievances against "pious Jewish brethren."

Circuitous and irresolute at first, the community's resentment against my parents for sending me to a Catholic school reached a furious pitch when I befriended a Palestinian girl my age. Leila, the daughter of a local tribal chieftain, was beautiful, smart and proud. My parents took an instant liking to her and did nothing to discourage what was my first teen romance. One day, a delegation of about half a dozen persons headed by a rabbi came to our house unannounced. The rabbi addressed my father in Yiddish. He scolded him for sending me to the *Lycée St. Joseph* and directed him to discourage me from "fraternizing with the enemy." He meant Leila. My father, never to be trifled with, especially by bigoted busybodies, stood his ground. He was magnificent. I don't remember his words and won't attempt to reconstruct them for fear of diluting what must surely have been a knockout riposte. What I vividly recall is that he then opened the door and invited the "delegation" to get the fuck out of our house.

Predictably, my father's attitude did not help mend fences in the Greek Colony. Acrimony and ugly rhetoric festered for the duration of our stay in Jerusalem.

Leila ceased to visit. I looked for her. Her father told me she was no longer allowed to see me. "It's best." There was sadness in his voice. I was heartbroken.

•

One day, "Cousin" Suzanne came to visit from Tel Aviv for a weekend.
"Guess what I brought you."
"What?"
"Chocolate." My mouth watered at the thought. "Thank you."
"Well, the thing is, you see, it's like this. I got so hungry on the bus that I ate the whole bar. Will you forgive me? I promise to bring you some next time I come."
The imbecile.
"Why did you tell me you brought me chocolate?"
Confused, Suzanne, a family friend who earned a living as a pedicurist, grimaced awkwardly. Her large, round bovine eyes filled with tears. There had been no malice in her faux pas. She just wasn't very bright.

Stupidity is no impediment to lechery and Suzanne, in her early twenties, was as horny as she was dim-witted. Sharing my narrow bed that Saturday night -- my parents had gone to sleep and were occupying the only other bed in the house -- Suzanne unceremoniously placed a hand on my penis, stroking it gently, and guided mine toward her pubic area. Her caresses brought on a fierce erection and the urge to thrust myself, I knew not exactly where or how, into this squirming, sighing protoplasmic mass that now covered my face with kisses and sought my mouth with hers.

Suzanne spread her legs to receive me. As she did, my hand chanced upon a slimy shaft of such mammoth proportions that I mistook it for a penis. I later learned, perusing one of my father's gynecological atlases, that the colossal appendage was a prolapsed uterus that Suzanne could push back in at will through her vagina. The poor girl tried as best she could to conceal her discomfiture and secrete the grotesque infirmity while attempting to revive, to no avail, my deflated libido. Repulsed by the incongruity, I turned my back and eventually fell asleep. I remember dreaming that I was slithering on my belly through a dark, steep, viscous tunnel of unimaginable length. Then, an explosion of ecstasy ripped at my loins and I awoke to find that Suzanne had me in her mouth. I surrendered to the last vestiges of pleasure, feigning sleep at first then dozing off mercifully at last.

When I arose in the morning, Suzanne was up and about, helping my mother with some chores. We glanced at each other when no one looked. She smiled softly. I returned the smile. Suzanne took the bus back to Tel Aviv that afternoon. I never saw her again. All I thought about was chocolate.

A DISSOLUTE LITTLE BRAIN

Sister Louis and her younger colleague and substitute, Sister Clémence, a diminutive nun armed with a razor-sharp intellect and a tongue to match, were strict disciplinarians, founts of erudition and skilled teachers. They would struggle, for the next two years, to educate me or, as they put it, "to deposit something of value inside this untidy, dissolute little brain of yours!"

The broad knowledge the Sisters of St. Joseph possessed -- they were licensed to teach everything from algebra to zoology -- was often overshadowed by an appalling lack of objectivity. It was their very scholarship that enabled them, wherever they could, to skew history or to rewrite it by opining unabashedly about people long dead or editorializing about events exhaustively chronicled in the otherwise unembellished secular French government curriculum they were required to follow. Royalists, as are all devout French Catholics, they steadfastly extenuated the arrogance and cruelty of French monarchs by insisting that they were, after all, "good Catholics." It is true that many of them spent much time genuflecting in their private gilded chapels on ermine stoles and rich brocades while their vassals lived in squalor, starved and died of the plague. Distant abstractions, the Crusades and the Inquisition elicited a kind of nostalgic admiration stripped of all compunction for the horrific crimes committed in their name.

I remember learning about the events that took place on the night of August 23, 1572, better known as the Saint-Bartholomew massacre, during which 3,000 Protestants were slaughtered in the streets of Paris on orders of Catherine de Medici. Reviewing the incident did not seem to evoke in my teachers any discernible unease. (News of the slaughter had been cheered by Spain's Philip II, himself busy purging Spain of Protestants, Jews and Moors, and Pope Gregory XIII who, for lack of better things to do, reformed the calendar.)

It was at that time that began germinating in me the notion that the

Inquisition, as an ethos and instrument of statecraft, did not expire in the bonfires of the Dark Ages but endured. It would mutate into the ghoulish instrument of colonization, racism, slavery, segregation, wars of imperialism (territorial and political) and the curtailment of civil rights in times of internal strife. Future events, some of which I would write about, among them the murder of Central American street children by police, and the state-sponsored persecution of indigenous minorities, would help crystallize this insight. I would later discover that historian Jacques Barzun, writing in *From Dawn to Decadence*, had far more eloquently reached the same conclusion:

"The many dictatorships of the 20th century have relied on [the Inquisition] *and in free countries it thrives ad hoc -- hunting down German sympathizers during the First World War, interning Japanese-Americans during the second, and pursuing Communist fellow-travelers during the Cold War. In the United States at the present time the workings of 'political correctness' in universities and the speech police that punishes persons and corporations for words on certain topics quaintly called 'sensitive' are manifestations of the permanent spirit of inquisition."*

The climate of fear and suspicion that befell America following the tragic events of September 11, 2001 would lend credence to the notion that the inquisitorial spirit, dormant in times of tranquility, will be speedily aroused in times of turmoil. To its immense credit, America, while vigilant, did not succumb to wholesale paranoia -- or at least did not openly admit to doing so as it secretly began to snoop into the lives of private citizens and launched undeclared, illegal, immoral and unwinnable wars.

Half a century earlier, injecting personal bias into their instructions, the sisters of Saint Joseph presided over their own kangaroo court. They scorned the Huguenot Henri of Navarre, but lavished him with praise when, crowned Henri IV and fearful for his neck, he converted to Catholicism. *"Paris vaut bien une messe!"* ("Paris is well worth a mass.") Praise turned to condemnation when the king, now firmly enthroned, issued the Edict of Nantes, a decree restoring religious and political rights to French Protestants. A few chapters forward, my teachers applauded the Edict's revocation, 87 years later, by the "Sun King," Louis XIV, the archetype warmongering despot whose conceit was eclipsed only by his thirst for ostentation. Unaware of, or utterly indifferent to the immense suffering of their subjects, Louis XVI, who spent his reign tinkering with clocks, and his wife Marie-Antoinette, who plundered the nation's coffers to keep the court royally entertained, elicited pity and sympathy.

"*Ils étaient très pieux et se recueillaient en prière plusieurs fois par jour,*" they intoned, exculpating crooks because "they were very pious and joined in prayer several times a day." As these enormities were being casually spouted, I would retrieve from the depths of memory images of priests sprinkling holy water on tanks and canons and the fuselage of dive bombers so that Christians of one nation could wreak death and destruction upon Christians of another nation with the full blessings of the "Almighty God."

My impious orations, smack dab in the middle of history class, would elicit stern, if florid, reminders of God's irrefutability:

"Between God and us rises a tall glass partition, transparent for Him, opaque for us," Sister Louis would sermonize.

To which Sister Clémence would add, "God does not reveal Himself; we wouldn't recognize Him anyway. To be found, He must be discovered.

"Discovered? Discovered?" I would retort. "Logic suggests that what doesn't exist can't be *discovered.* If God -- invented by man -- really existed, wouldn't he by now have been discovered, validated?"

To which Sister Louis haughtily replied, "God grants us some of his spirit but will never reveal his logic." (Or, as my uncle often asserted with self-justifying bravado, "I believe in God, *therefore* he is....")

What I would learn from these debates and artful equivocations is that God might only be a hypothesis but that to many people he's indispensable. Troubled by the subconscious fear that reason might dim his existence they struggle to rationalize it.

Knowledge demystifies myths; faith enshrines them.

•

The French Revolution, my teachers insisted, was "an outrage masterminded by Jewish financiers, Freemasons, degenerate philosophers and other irreligious libertines." This characterization was nowhere to be found in the history text I'd been issued. It's interesting to note that, in reading selected works by Diderot, Montesquieu, Rousseau and Voltaire (the chief "degenerate" French philosophers) we were encouraged to analyze and emulate their elegant literary style but enjoined from embracing their "amoral teachings." The reign of terror that followed the fall of the Bastille on July 14, 1789 was summarily blasted as a "grotesque act of barbarism against Christian values." Yes, many innocent heads rolled during the two–year frenzy. But Sister Louis and Sister Clémence could not bring themselves to view the insurrection as the cathartic articulation of centuries of misery and oppression or as the impetus that would help rid France, for the first time in its history, from the yoke of feudalism, theocratic control and absolute monarchy. The assassination, in his bathtub, of Jean-Paul Marat, a populist physician, lawyer, journalist and legislator in 1793, would be flippantly dismissed as *the "elimination of a scoundrel by a brave Catholic young woman* [Charlotte Corday]." Corday, of noble birth, would die on the guillotine. In contrast, the beheading of two royal idlers who bankrupted France while they wined, dined, gambled, gathered in prayer and unleashed their dogs on helpless foxes, they insisted, was murder. Nor did my teachers seem to understand that revolution is a process, not an incident. History manuals tend to think of the French Revolution as a single event rather than a trend. The burgeoning concepts of human rights, equality, suffrage and the abolition of monarchy actually took root 100 years before the storming of the Bastille.

In a letter to his king, Louis XIV, François Fénelon, a French theologian and writer and the king's almoner, had warned:

"Sire: For thirty years your ministers have violated all the

> *ancient laws in the state so as to enhance your power. They have increased your revenue and your expenditures to the infinite and impoverished all of France for the sake of your luxury at court. They have made your name odious. For twenty years they have made the French nation intolerable to its neighbors by bloody wars. We have no allies because we only wanted slaves. Meanwhile, your people are starving. Sedition is spreading and you are reduced to either letting it spread unpunished or resorting to massacring the people that you have driven to desperation."*

A sharp critic of the monarchy, the very politically incorrect Fénelon was fired by the Sun King for uttering truths the king did not want to hear. Less than 100 years later, the long simmering embers of misery and discontent ignited the Revolution. Two centuries later, George Orwell would define freedom as the right to tell people what they don't want to know.

When the truth is ignored, history has a habit of repeating itself.

•

The French Revolution was an extraordinarily complicated affair rooted in centuries of mismanagement, extravagance and war, and ignited by the rising friction between the three Estates -- a bloated nobility, a corrupt and dissolute clergy and a crushing mass of dirt-poor, illiterate and downtrodden people.

Unlike the American Revolution, which has been likened to an act of defiance by a prodigal son against his mother -- and much like the Russian Revolution, which had already begun to simmer -- the French Revolution was a genuine insurrection against small, all-powerful, ruthless elites. In 1789 France was a nation of 26 million. Society was made up of three distinct and unequal groups. The nobility of the sword (some 500,000 people or about 2 percent of the total population, among them the high aristocracy -- 4,000 families close to the throne, hangers-on and sycophants; the petty nobility, composed of provincial gentlemen of lesser means but matching greed; and the nouveaux-riche, the parvenus, those who bought nobility titles and who, despite their wealth, were scorned by the traditional bluebloods for their miserly origins.

Next was the clergy -- 120,000 strong, among them 139 bishops, and also divided between high clergy (members of the aristocracy) and the common clergy, all corrupt, depraved and decadent.

Last was the Third Estate, the vast majority of the people -- 98 percent -- representing day workers, farmers, peasants, craftsmen, and the bourgeoisie -- bankers, lawyers and trades people.

The king's power was absolute, limitless and issued from none other than God. The king hired and fired his cabinet at will. All authority was centralized in Paris and, as the Revolution simmered, in the hands of Louis XVI, a meek and irresolute monarch who would have rather flown kites and repaired locks than governed. Injustice, ineptitude and corruption were rampant. Louis would have liked to redress these problems; instead, he tightened his authority and the kingdom surrendered to the kind of despotism in vogue in Russia, Austria and Prussia at the time. Louis hid behind his neurotic piety (and a bad case of phimosis -- a condition in which the foreskin of the penis of an uncircumcised male cannot be fully retracted, thus causing pain, especially during an erection). He neglected his wife in favor of hunting dogs, locks and clocks. He was drawn neither by royal duty, love, sex, politics, or war, which he entrusted to pompous and inept generals. Deaf to facts, unwilling to heed advice, incapable of making a decision on his own, he took solace in his wife's opinion of him, *"Pauvre homme, il est bon"* -- "poor man, he is good." Goodness in 1789 was apparently not enough.

For her part, Marie-Antoinette wielded little influence on her husband. A spendthrift with a colossal disregard for the well-being of her people, her reputation further sullied by the famous Necklace Affair and allegations of infidelity, she had become not only unpopular but loathed. Apparently, neither Louis nor Marie-Antoinette had read *The Prince,* or they had both ignored Machiavelli's counsel to avoid being hated and mocked by one's subjects.

●

Since 1777, with Lafayette and his volunteers, then in 1779 with Rochambeau and the French Royal Expeditionary Corps, France fought alongside the Americans against the British, culminating in the 1781 victory at Yorktown and the surrender of General Cornwallis. This little adventure cost France two billion gold pounds.

This was the twilight of the 18th century, the era of Enlightenment, and France was tired of the ancient and traditional monarchical order in which the king is commander in chief, judge, jury and executioner, and wary of a system that calls for the nobility to defend the nation with the sword, the clergy to pray for victory and the rabble to work and pay taxes until they drop. But King Louis was an inept military strategist; his officers had lapsed into mediocrity and the Church, fat and corrupt, made a mockery of religion. The clergy paid no taxes but charged tolls on behalf of the crown, and sold indulgences and first-class passage to paradise, with much of the monies collected diverted and adding to the personal fortunes of dozens of "princes of the Church." The commoners -- peasants and bourgeois alike, crushed by unfair and exorbitant taxes and levies, were fuming. Soon, they'd open the shutters wide, lean out their windows and shout, *"We're mad as hell and we won't take it anymore...."*

My teachers should have known all that. They probably did but they never allowed fact to interfere with their faith. As Nietzsche wrote, *"Faith" means not wanting to know what is true."*

A revolution is less an act of insubordination against despotism than a rebellion against inequality and discrimination. It's a social, not a political movement. Social movements rarely prevail.

•

Conceding that Napoleon was brilliant, ruthless, lofty, utopian and flawed, Sister Louis glossed over his triumphs, the idealism of his reforms, his contributions to the arts, science, education and jurisprudence, but ranted about his "impiety and vanity, sins even a great man can never expiate." She was referring to an incident during his coronation as emperor of France, when Bonaparte *"shamelessly and sacrilegiously yanked the crown from the Pope's hands"* and placed it on his own head. There was something offensive about the vilification of a man universally acclaimed for his genius, if not always for the wisdom of his geopolitical objectives. For my part, taking a secular view, I lamented his strategic blunders and stunning military defeats on the frozen plains of Russia and at Waterloo but found myself in no position to criticize his vast and peerless intellect.

Prevalent during history class, this form of propagandizing was absent in geography and science courses. After all, rivers are not readily diverted from their beds and mountain ranges cannot be pulled out by their rocky roots and relocated. Nor are the laws of mathematics prone to falsification, except by a dunce like me who, enjoined from turning in "blank test papers," filled them with nonsensical algebraic equations -- and flunked. I'm certain that if the Sisters could have put a papist spin on these subjects they would have readily done so.

Outspoken, my teachers' antipathy toward their fellow Christians -- they scorned Protestants, sneered at Greek and Russian Orthodoxy, mocked the "lesser faiths" of Copts and Maronites -- assumed subtler hues when it came to Jews. Their brand of anti-Semitism was abstruse and furtive, tempered no doubt by persuasive political realities: The convent and school were now seated in Israel, not "Palestine," as it had been two years earlier, and they were licensed by the State and four-fifths of the pupils were Jewish. I did not feel in any way threatened. Wary of beliefs that defy verifiable fact, intuitively aware that the role of a school is to ossify young minds – I'd already been exposed to the crude encoding methods of Communist pedagogy in Romania -- I didn't take these digressions too seriously. Instead, I learned to beware of opinions -- hand-me-down convictions usually impossible to temper and often adopted in defiance of manifest fact. Besides, I had enough trouble keeping up with schoolwork, and whatever reflex contempt the nuns had for "Christ's killers," did not seem to be directed at any of us personally. Sisters Louis and Clémence were in fact quite fond of their students. I would be less than honest if I did not acknowledge a measure of esteem for their patience and forbearance, and gratitude for every snippet of knowledge they managed to instill, including, inadvertently, the art of skepticism. Esteem did not prevent me from challenging them on occasion and standing my ground until they relented or changed the subject.

Learning about -- in my case reexamining -- the Dreyfus Affair, gave rise to such occasion. I was ready. I'd read a great deal about it and my father, who had studied the case in depth, had helped sort out documented fact from hearsay and put in perspective minutiae and nuances I'd failed to grasp. The Dreyfus Affair aroused passions and prejudices that divided France and very nearly triggered a civil war. An epic of treachery, intimidation, fraud, and injustice, it revived and widened the philosophical rifts that polarize the French in times of unrest and discontent: the right against the left, the aristocracy against the proletariat, the clerical elite against the secular masses, anti-Semites against liberals and freethinkers. The same antithetical ideologies that polarized the French during the 1789 Revolution, the German occupation and the wars of Algeria and Indochina, would lead to the alarming ascent in the late 20th century of ultra-conservative, xenophobic parties in Western Europe.

•

The Dreyfus Affair begins as a banal case of espionage. On September 26, 1894, the Office of Statistics learns of a memorandum purloined from the German Embassy attesting to the presence of a traitor in France's military high command. Suspicions focus on a young officer, Captain Alfred Dreyfus, whose "race" -- he is Jewish -- offers a military establishment more noted for its anti-Semitism than its prowess on the battlefield the pretext it sought. Two weeks later, on very flimsy evidence, Dreyfus is arrested. French War Minister Mercier, chiefs of staff and high-ranking political figures, aware of the plot against Dreyfus, press on for a trial. Dreyfus is found guilty, condemned to deportation and life imprisonment in a "fortified compound," a sinister euphemism for the hell hole that Guyana's Devil's Island would prove to be. On January 5, 1895, Dreyfus is publicly stripped of his rank; his saber is broken in half as crowds demand "Death to Jews! Death to the traitor! Death to Judas!" Having barely survived five years of incarceration in one of the most infamous penal colonies, Captain Dreyfus is pardoned in 1899, reinstated by the Supreme Court in 1902 and promoted in 1906 largely thanks to the tireless efforts of Emile Zola and others.

The government had first offered Dreyfus a plea deal -- a pardon (rather than an exoneration), which he could accept and go free, thus effectively admitting guilt, or face a re-trial in which he was sure to be convicted again. Although he was clearly not guilty, he chose to accept the pardon. Zola died in Paris in 1902 of carbon monoxide poisoning caused by a stopped chimney. He was 62. There is circumstantial evidence that he may have been murdered by political enemies.

Dreyfus, who attended Zola's entombment at the Pantheon, was shot and slightly wounded by a man who, despite witness accounts, was cleared in court. Unmoved by a growing wave of revulsion sweeping France, most politicians continued to insinuate that Dreyfus was guilty or aligned themselves with factions opposed to his rehabilitation in the court of public opinion. Fresh rumors were circulated to perpetuate and legitimize ill will toward the officer's defenders.

"Yes," Sister Louis orated, "the Freemasons engineered his release and he was returned to France. *But his innocence was never proven and....*"

This was pure fabrication. What Sister Louis had no way of knowing -- or may have deliberately overlooked -- is that Masonic lodges, not quite ready to open their doors to Jews, had conveniently retreated behind their statutory shield during the "Affair." The Anderson Constitution, the founding principles and catechism of Freemasonry, declares that Masons are law-abiding citizens who do not meddle in the affairs of state. Sympathizing with Dreyfus, let alone negotiating on his behalf, would have violated Masonic protocols and redirected the Church's historic anti-Semitism against the fraternal order. Thus, the "fraternity" not only could not intervene, it responded with cowardice and irresolution in the face of gross injustice; and the Widow's Son was immolated, once again, at the altar of political expediency.

"What about the forgeries by the French chiefs of staff?" I interjected. "What about Count Esterhazy," -- a name absent from history books at the time. "What about his jailhouse confession, his suicide note?"

Sister Louis smiled with unease. "Well, that proves nothing"

"What about the 'lion'? The mighty Clémenceau had roared with outrage. The great Zola had thundered and exhorted France to look at itself. And the entire French military high command had been accused of conspiring to pin an act of high treason on an innocent man -- a Jewish officer. None of this is spelled out in here," I cried out, tapping excitedly on the history book with my forefinger. "But aren't these the facts?"

I don't remember ever getting a straight answer.

•

I was nearly 50, now living in America, when in tribute to my father who'd recently passed away, I knocked three distinct times at the door of Freemasonry, seeking initiation. It took no time at all to discover that, unlike Europe, where Masons had long since established a reputation for discreet but effective social activism, scholarship and enlightenment, American Freemasonry was little more than a refuge for the geriatric set. Having once drawn mavericks (George Washington, Benjamin Franklin, John Hancock, Paul Revere, among others) and celebrated gadflies (most of the "Indians" who dumped tea in Boston's Harbor were Freemasons), the fellowship had since lapsed into irrelevance and become an anachronism. It ceased to be an instrument for reform. It had turned inwardly and evolved into a bastion of religious and political ultra-conservatism; it remains an anemic, insular, closed-circuit, self-serving institution that will limp along but cannot thrive. The democratization, no, the vulgarization of Freemasonry in America has resulted in the adulteration of its original concepts and aims. It has abdicated its traditional role and lost its efficacy as an emissary of universalism. It can never recruit the likes of Bolivar, Garibaldi, Goethe, Kipling, Lafayette, Mozart and Swift, some of the great men who kneeled at the altar and asked to receive a part of the arts and secrets of the Craft -- men of action, shakers, movers, thinkers, creative geniuses and revolutionaries. One is either an agent of change or a victim of inaction.

Those who believe that the revolution is over are doomed to inspire it.

•

It is difficult for schoolchildren to extricate fact from fancy. Teachers, venerated professionals when I grew up, can add to the confusion. Depending on our knowledge and common sense, we see them as champions of Solomonic wisdom or purveyors of deception. We marvel at their erudition or dismiss their asides as the views of demagogues intent on scuttling the truth. It is when these agents of persuasion resort to calumny, when they trivialize or repudiate verifiable fact with outlandish allegations, devious logic and grotesque beliefs, that the truth drowns.

•

Is reality merely what the self perceives? Or is there an immutable reality that transcends deeply held convictions? What emerges from the doctrinal struggles that cleave society is a frenzied tug-of-war between conflicting ideas. The truth is often trampled in the process.

Everybody has opinions. Much of our mental constructs are erected on a vast scaffolding of doctrines -- generally someone else's. Keen on cramming dormant brain cells, we adopt them, cling to them, claim they are the offspring of our own cogitations because they encourage us not to think, because they shield us from what we fear most: the truth. This explains why there are more opinions than facts and why we are so enamored of them. After all, opinions can blithely ignore, defy and, if need be, corrupt the truth. Tainted fruits of ignorance and self-delusion (or planted seeds of malice) opinions conveniently overlook faulty data or peddle arguments riddled with ideological monstrosities. In the mouths of tub-thumpers, opinions assume dangerous dimensions: They are no longer what can be borne out by experience but what opinion-mongers themselves can get away with. Regurgitated by imbeciles, they are promptly espoused by other imbeciles.

Voicing an opinion, especially when unsolicited, is an incorrigible human reflex. Every time we inhale a wisp of fact, we exhale a gust of inferences. This compulsion has been elevated to sacred entitlement in free nations. Which is why, exploiting the rights that democracy grants them – or flouting them -- advocates of extreme political and religious dogma are particularly adept at blurring the truth to advance their own agendas. The greater their zeal in promoting these causes, the more tempting it becomes for them to suggest that freethinkers are not merely factually wrong but actually engaged in blocking verities they would otherwise have to embrace. In practice, this assumption has led to brainwashing, as ancient and modern witch-hunts have shown.

Only those willing to question the validity of entrenched convention ever get closer to the truth. Fallacious reasoning and arrogant convictions, licit as they might be, are more dangerous enemies of truth than outright lies. They are the prisons in which we lock ourselves to feign a clear conscience. As someone once remarked, a clear conscience is usually the sign of a very bad memory. It is this willful myopia that helps defile the truth.

Troublesome facts, computed by rational minds, are more useful than myths peddled by uninformed crusaders. When flock mentality is at play, it is the latter, alas, that captures the imagination of the majority. Inflexible convictions render men blind, arrogant and, carried to the extreme, insane.

•

Many years later, I would ask in a published commentary:

> *"...What if history was drawn not from verifiable facts and scrupulously recorded events, but from the opinion pages of newspapers? What if the sum total of human knowledge was distilled from unsigned editorials, bylined manifestos, letters to the editor and the blogosphere -- that soap box legions of bottom-feeders so impetuously ascend to orate, often with shameless fatuity?"*

To my great disappointment, the questions, provocative as they were meant to be, elicited no response. In time, it dawned on me that this rhetorical decoy contained within it the seeds of its own definition. I had asked the obvious.

W. E. Gutman

Silence is often a form of self-incrimination.
●

The good Sisters must have known that I would be a handful when they accepted me in their school. Endless pranks, habitual insubordination and a barrage of firebrand compositions, I'm sure, propelled them toward early sainthood. What they did not anticipate is that raging hormones and the premature onset of puberty will transform a brat into an *enfant terrible* and that harmless antics are apt to mutate into socially unacceptable mischief.

One day during recess, as a sudden downpour forced students under the convent's vaulted ambulatory, I took a seat on one of the stone benches and invited a girl, whose budding curves I had eyed with lustful interest, to join me for a chat. As she was about to roost, I slipped a hand under her, an inquisitive middle finger poised for the occasion. Buttocks made contact with covetous hand. Startled, the girl sprang up like a jack-in-the-box, giggling. Sister Louis, who'd witnessed the scene from afar, was not amused. Red-faced and fuming, she flew toward me like some stygian specter, buoyed it seemed by the fullness of her black robes and veil. Before I had a chance to react, I felt the searing impact of her open hand upon my cheek.

She'd slapped me with such force that I nearly fell backward. The sting subsided soon enough but I was mortified. The girl glanced at me sheepishly before returning to class. She would later console me by letting herself be fingered in one of the school's utility closets. Such encounters, during which I harvested an array of strangely enticing aromas, were followed by furious mutual masturbation. I would then carry her scent back home on my fingers, lock myself in the bathroom and masturbate some more, often to exhaustion.

Not long after that incident, my parents received a letter from Mother Superior, Marie Jeanne-d'Arc, informing them that I was now too old to continue my studies in an all-girls school and that I'd have to transfer to the all-boys *Collège des Frères* in Jaffa. Tucked away, memories of boarding school life, drafty dormitories and rank, institutional food came back to haunt me. I spent the last few sleepless nights in a state of emotional disarray that vanished soon after I boarded the bus for the two-hour dizzying descent from the hills of Judea to the coastal plains of Sharon. Every unexpected turn in the road, every counterpoint in a life otherwise marked by inconstancy and turmoil, I'd reasoned, teaches lessons begging to be learned: A lesson about the cunning savagery of life, about the absurdity of the best-laid plans, about the frivolity of presumption. A lesson about the duty to resist, to fight back. Such concepts, I also learned, are easy to intellectualize, hard to implement.

•

On the eve of my departure, I spent the better part of the afternoon perched in my sylvan "lookout," the highest branch of a towering, densely foliated eucalyptus tree. This is where I often retreated when I felt dispirited or in need of solitude. There was something about climbing up that tree that set my mind at ease. I was far from prying eyes, wagging tongues, inquisitive ears. I could survey things from a loftier perspective, much as I did in a recurring dream that allowed me to leap up high in the air and levitate over the rooftops without the slightest exertion. I felt enveloped, no, embraced by nature, swaying in the wind, intoxicated by the peppery odor the leaves exuded. I could gaze at the purple afternoon sky or take in, alone and unmolested, the night spectacle of an imponderable, cosmos. I was a solitary mariner aboard a ghostly Flying Dutchman and the tree was my crow's nest. As I smoked dried eucalyptus leaves rolled in newsprint, I imagined the ground undulating beneath me like a vast and bottomless sea. Oblivious to my mother's insistent calls to dinner, hearing nothing but the whisper of the trade winds and the lament of the albatross, I set sail for distant lands glimpsed only in my dreams.

THE FEAR OF ALL SUMS

History may be a long march but life is a short stroll on a very narrow footpath. The road from Jerusalem to Tel Aviv was littered with the mementos of war: A charred, overturned bus; a mutilated armored troop carrier resting on its side atop a desolate bluff; a tank, its turret gaping like an open wound, its tracks severed and caked with mud, its formidable cannon truncated, its flanks now etched with graffiti -- anonymous initials, cryptic verses, arrowed hearts, words of love and sorrow and peace and hope for fallen heroes and an infant nation bleeding as it took its first breath. I would travel this road many times as I went home to Jerusalem on precious few weekends and holidays. The spectacle would bring back memories of wartime Paris and Bucharest. It would also inspire lasting views on the folly of war, the fragility of life and the lunatic ambivalence of the human spirit.

•

I arrived at the *Collège des Frères* late in the afternoon. It had rained but the clouds had dispersed and the setting sun cast a golden glow on the old minarets. The Mediterranean spread before me, flanked on one side by the ancient port city of Jaffa, its fortress-like stone visage seemingly untouched by time, and Tel Aviv's airy perspective of seaside hotels and modern apartment buildings on the other. Behind me, facing the sea, stood the high-walled cloister-like mission school where I would spend the next two years.

I rang the bell. The groundskeeper, a surly old man with huge hairy arms, opened the massive wooden door and let me in. I told him my name. He pointed to the main building across the courtyard and clambered back to his lodgings without uttering a word. The Brother Procurator (I would never learn his name) a tall, gaunt cleric with an angular face and a weasel-like expression, peered over his glasses, sized me up and extended a long, bony arm. We shook hands.

"*Alors, Gutman, c'est vous?* So, you're Gutman?" There was more smirk than smile in his greeting. His teeth were small, pointy -- all canines -- blackened by years of chain-smoking.

"Sisters Louis and Clémence told us about you. They called you a 'rough, stubborn diamond encrusted in granite.' That's a mighty daring assessment, wouldn't you say?"

I said nothing.

"Well, never mind. Let's see what we can do to extract and polish this precious stone," he said with palpable sarcasm.

"Let's hope you don't break your pickax in the process," I replied, looking him straight in the eyes. The shark smile faded from his lips. He stood up from behind his desk and bid me to follow. I complied, carrying the small valise in which lay, neatly folded, an assortment of clothes that my mother had monogrammed, as instructed by the school, with my initials. We climbed the stairs to the second floor. He showed me my classroom and the back row desk, near a window, to which I'd been assigned. He then took me across the hall and into the dormitory. He pointed to a bed, a sagging metal cot on which lay a lumpy mattress and a thin, coarse blanket that reeked of insecticide. In place of a closet, five rusty nails protruded from the wall over the bed.

"All yours," he declared, probing the depths of my discomfiture.

"You're too kind."

"The others are having supper in the refectory. Might as well join them."

"I'm not hungry."

"Suit yourself." He spun around on his heels and exited the dorm.

We would never speak again. In due time, Brother Procurator, who also taught algebra, geometry, trigonometry and calculus -- subjects that put me in a cataleptic trance -- would conclude that whatever buried gift I possessed was too deeply embedded and not worth mining. Having sized me up in math class, he was quite willing to let me spend the next two years looking out the window, daydreaming, doodling and writing poetry as he droned on about algorithms, quadratic equations and vertical asymptotes. It would take me thirty years to discover the poetry and magic of mathematics. By then, my reputation as a mathematically challenged individual had become legend. I would make no attempt to alter this perception. I can still be seen using my fingers to make simple computations, but I'm also exploring the hypnotic realm of quantum physics and discovering mind-boggling treasures along the way. I could not possibly have imagined that such transformation was possible as I plodded through the school's barren math curriculum. Intimidated by its cold, cryptic character, stumped by its glacial logic, I would be slowly drowning in a viscous sea of incomprehension and self-doubt that very nearly caused me to drop out of school.

●

Tired, confused, annoyed, I lay down. I'd been consigned, yet again, to involuntary captivity in a boarding school, this most alien, most hostile setting for a child. In the process, I'd lost the little privacy my former life afforded. Worse, as a social-animal-in-training, wary of hasty friendships, indifferent to my dorm-mates, I now had to learn to adjust to the practicalities of mutual forbearance.

Cruising on the ceiling was an enormous cockroach. I flung a shoe at it but missed. I closed my eyes and let the thoughts submerge me. I was 15, gushing with energy, brimming with mythical visions of life on the loose. But here I was, confined against my will, forced to labor for snippets of knowledge that would open up a near-lifetime of low-paying jobs.

●

My two years at the *Collège des Frères* in Jaffa are a near blur, broken here and there by vivid if disjointed still images that have somehow survived the depredations of time. What emerges from the fog is a medley of memories. Among them are the haunting reminders of inner turmoil, wretched grades and relations with teachers and students marked by dissonance and rancor.

Agitation best describes my state of being at the time, a restlessness augmented by resentment and feelings of uncertainty about the future. I stood at the edge of a chasm looking down, aware that the distance between equilibrium and the dizzying void was less than a breath's length away and mindful that every step taken retreating from the brink only brought it closer. I fought back angst and foreboding the only way I knew, by weaving fantastical scenarios involving journeys to faraway places. I made sketches of schooners and brigantines aboard which these expeditions would take place. I also drew maps, plotted convoluted itineraries across the oceans and kept a detailed log of distances covered and ports-of-call yet to be espied from the safety of an anchorage at the center of a shallow blue lagoon. Everywhere, graceful, doe-eyed maidens with long black tresses and easy virtue awaited my return. And we would feast late into the night, under a full moon, to the beat of the tom-tom. And when morning came, I would weigh anchor, unfurl the mainsail and the mizzenmast jib, catch the wind and point the bowsprit straight at the open sea.

I'd seen too many Errol Flynn and Douglas Fairbanks, Jr. epics at the *Semadar* Cinema. Emboldened by Brother Procurator's utter lack of interest in my person, an attitude further evidenced by his contemptuous demeanor, I embarked on these imaginary peregrinations during math classes. I owe them my sanity.

Determined to rescue whatever small nugget of genius Sisters Louis and Clémence might have seen in me, I had the good sense or the prudence to apply myself in Frère Jean's French and social studies classes. Frère Jean was a good-natured man with a broad, projecting lower jaw, a huge aquiline nose, splayed ears, an easy smile and a weakness for metaphors. He enjoyed teaching and, as school librarian, he encouraged his students to read a book a month. Book reports and surprise written quizzes were his stock-in-trade. I did generally well, an achievement I owed as much to his amiability as to my natural skills, and which prevented abysmal math and science grades from scuttling my scholastic average.

While Brother Procurator's disdain was non-verbal -- an occasional glance in my direction sufficed to telegraph it -- the scorn evinced by two boys, both excellent in math, mediocre in everything else, was blunt and relentless.

"X plus five equals ten. What's the value of X? I dare you," Kabile would grimace.

"Don't rush him," Chapat would intervene. "He hasn't yet learned to count to ten. How many fingers do you have, Gutman?" We were encouraged to call each other by our patronymics.

"Enough to shove one up your smelly ass, you cocksucker."

"Brother Procurator, Brother Procurator, Gutman spoke dirty."

Indifferent to the origins of this confrontation, more so to justice, Brother Procurator would show me the door and I'd spend the rest of the period in the hallway, plotting my revenge or sailing the South Seas.

Kabile, a Greek Jew from Salonika had pink cheeks, hairless legs and an effeminate stride that drew conspicuous glances from the priests and the older boys. Chapat, a Bulgarian Jew from Plovdiv, was short, stocky and hirsute. He had beady eyes that peered from behind thick round glasses and conveyed a look of mocking suspicion. They would take turns, conspiring to cause embarrassment or bring discredit upon me from teacher and class alike.

I may have been a dunce in math but my tormentors' compositions were badly written and prosaic. They spoke fractured and heavily accented French, and their knowledge of world geography -- my best subject -- was rudimentary at best. Though I would have gladly throttled them, I got even instead by writing a caustic parody that mimicked Theophrastus' style of social satire. Much of it is untranslatable in English: full of double entendres and lewd puns that only make sense in French; something about *"the Pasha taking pleasure entering Kabul from the city's rear gate...."* Frère Jean never caught on, or pretended not to, and Kabile and Chapat, loath to draw attention by claiming to be the butt of my unsparing lampoons, kept their mouths shut from then on.

The only other schoolmate I remember, this time with lingering remorse, was a shy, gentle, obese boy everyone called *Mammouth*. Tactlessness and stupidity, rather than malice -- I addressed him that way too -- blinded me to the pain and humiliation this despicable sobriquet must have caused him. It was when some boys got physical with him one day, pushing and shoving and pinching and tripping him as he wept softly pleading for mercy that I intervened. I sent an older boy to the hospital with a broken jaw and fractured my right fist in the process. Many years later I learned from a girl I began dating while in school, that *Mammouth*, now in his early twenties and in a final parry against the insensitivity of man, had shoved the barrel of a rifle in his mouth and pulled the trigger.

•

As I pored over Frère Jean's history assignments, trying to decipher the past and filtering from it not even a telltale hint of tomorrow, my father was decanting the bitter dregs of a present that seemed without future. His clientele had dwindled to a handful of loyal but destitute patients. Most were North African immigrants who seemed in greater need of kind-hearted counsel in French than medical care. At the dinner table, talk focused on the gravity of our circumstance. Money was running out. But penury was not the only bondage my parents feared. They were also suffocating with boredom in a vacuum of social and cultural alienation. Governed by tyrannical theocrats, administered by pseudo-religious sycophants, Jerusalem was a den of intolerance in which religion regulated life's every cadence and breath. Sabbath rules were rigorously enforced. Stores, cafés and movie houses were closed, vehicular traffic prohibited. Even innocent activities such as picking flowers from one's own garden, riding a bicycle or washing windows came under hostile scrutiny. Everyone in the neighborhood took a dim view of our impious, worldly ways. In a newborn nation whose very existence hinged on uncritical compliance with elemental canons of solidarity, we were perceived as meddlesome outsiders ill-tuned to the prevailing ethos. It was time to leave the holy city and exhale its vitiated air. Hoping to revive his practice, my father moved us to Ramat-Gan, on the outskirts of modern, secular Tel Aviv. I could now sleep in my own bed and ride my bike to school every day. But the winds of change were blowing once again. Summoned by the Israeli government, my father accepted a number of delicate missions that would set the stage for yet another detour in our lives. One such mission, masterminded by Israeli intelligence and coordinated at first by a network of Freemasons, took him to Tunisia. His efforts would help kick off and hasten the massive emigration -- via France -- of most North African Jews to Israel.

•

Colette Avital (née Abramovich) was my age, a Romanian dark-eyed honey blonde with ripening curves and the gait of a girl eager to reach womanhood. The mischief in her smile and the coquetry of her body language concealed a subtle mind overshadowed only by an all-consuming ego. These traits, undergirded by the knowledge that men with a hard-on can be useful, would serve her well in the pursuit of a brilliant political career. They would prove worthless in bed where she laid bare a disconcerting lack of enthusiasm for sex. I would not be surprised to learn that her dalliances with a bevy of newsmen, high-ranking military officers, parliamentarians and diplomats were short-lived.

I met Colette, a future ambassador and member of the *Knesset* (Israel's Parliament) at one of the rare functions sponsored by the Brothers and Sisters of St. Joseph -- Jaffa campus -- during which boys and girls could mingle on school property. Like me, she'd been sent to a French Catholic school for a quality education. That did not prevent Colette, a brilliant student and teachers' pet from spreading irreverent rumors. Our respective playgrounds were separated by a high wall breached by an ivied forged iron door through which, Colette insisted, priests and nuns met on dark moonless nights for bacchanalia of unholy communion. Apocryphal and told with sham solemnity, her story had made me laugh. I would in turn regale her with my own spurious fabrications of priestly buggering, all heavily inspired by the Marquis De Sade and French student songs dripping with anticlerical irreverence. We soon began dating. It wasn't long before I tried to take her to bed. At home in her in parents' Tel Aviv apartment, stripped down to her panties, she lay limp and lifeless like an alabaster statue on her satin sheets, her eyes wide open, amusement etched on her lips and showing not the slightest trace of arousal. I tried again on other occasions, each time with less enthusiasm. It would take another twenty years or so before I tried again -- she was by then Consul of Israel in Montreal, an attractive, ripened but sexless woman who found it opportune to tell me that *Mammouth* had blown his brains out as I retreated from her passionless embrace. I would try yet again several years later -- she'd by then served as first consul in Boston and been elevated to a higher post at Israel's Embassy in Paris. Her meteoric ascent in the arcane and elitist world of diplomacy had done nothing to enliven a hopelessly torpid sexuality. A dozen years or so later, now

Consul General in New York, she would offer me a job in the press office. The svelte, sprightly Colette of my youth had turned into a corpulent, cantankerous despot. She would make life so unpleasant that I quit after less than two years of employment.

In 2000, I received a note on *Knesset* stationery. It read: "I made it." I replied on the back of my business card, saying: "Better watch out. If you're not careful you run the risk of becoming Prime Minister."

Buoyed by colossal *chutzpah*, Colette would have the effrontery (or loutishness) to run for the office of President of Israel. Predictably, she lost.

I would not hear from her again.

•

In 1954, armed with a letter of recommendation from Sister Louis and Frère Jean to the School of Journalism in Paris, I left Israel, my parents and a host of tattered memories. Five years had passed since I'd first glimpsed Haifa's tawny shores. Gazing at the open sea, I was now headed on a one-way journey to early manhood. I never looked back.

ON MY OWN

There are no surprises in life, only latent events we subliminally nurture to fruition. Everything we do is undertaken in pursuit of a distant but manifest objective. As I stood at the window of my Montmartre garret, transfixed by the beautiful city that lay before me, I kept telling myself that being back in Paris was no happenstance but an epiphany willed from the depths of my subconscious. Fate had played no part in this latest transmigration. It was the culmination of an immeasurable hankering stubbornly chased and at last apprehended. These abstractions helped dispel the haunting suspicion, as I scanned my hometown with wonderment and elation, that the runaway train I'd been riding since birth, the tracks on which it thundered, the junctions, the country depots and drafty, smoke-filled terminals along the way, had all been pre-scripted and immutable. I needed to believe, at an age normally unclaimed by existential turmoil, that reason coincides with reality, that intent and force of will stimulate and whittle the future. I would have ample cause to revisit this thesis, to refute it in my darkest hours, only to embrace it again as a hedge against the tyranny of predestination. And as I surveyed familiar landmarks in the distance, each one evoking a special childhood memory, I knew that the same impelling force that had led me back to my roots would soon distance me from them yet again.

God created space; the devil created time.

•

Kismet or purpose attained, I was thrilled to be back in Paris. I was seventeen, free, on my own, ready to spread my wings, lusting for life, craving self-discovery in the newness of the moment.

Pallid like an anemic girl, Paris had weathered its share of storms and indignities. Nine years had passed since the end of the war, not enough to erase the stain of defeat, the agony of foreign occupation and the stigma of a lackluster victory against a hated enemy. But beneath the pallor of its sooty face, under its leaden skies and intermittent September rains, Paris sparkled and I was eager to bathe in its luminescence.

I looked up Marcel, the boy I'd befriended before moving to Israel, but it was Françoise, his sister, I'd really come to see. I'd thought about her often and fantasized about the day when we would consummate what had so fleetingly, so innocently been assayed five years earlier. I found Marcel at home. He was having lunch in the kitchen. He recognized me.

"You've grown taller but your face hasn't changed," he exclaimed.

I wish I could have said the same about him. The once spindly Marcel was now a strapping young man, apprenticed to the neighborhood butcher shop. Barrel-chested, he wore a thick turtleneck sweater, sleeves rolled up to his elbows. A blood-splattered white apron encircled his corpulent girth. His shoes were caked with scraps of viscera and organ meat. His cheeks were ruddy; his fingers red and bloated like sausages. He smelled of freshly slaughtered venison. Peering through thick lenses, his gentle, myopic eyes hardened when I asked about Françoise.

"Elle est à la campagne." She's in the country, he said evasively.

"Where?"

"A la campagne!" he repeated, a hint of impatience hardening his voice. I didn't insist. I paid Marcel a couple of visits after that; we went to the cinema once or twice, then I stopped calling on him. His sister had not come back from the country and he'd reacted to my ceaseless inquiries with petulance.

"Enough!" he exploded, grabbing me by the lapels and shoving his face against mine. "How many times have I told you? Enough about Françoise, you hear me!"

Carnivores have lousy dispositions.

Startled, left to ponder the fleeting essence of friendship, I concluded that Marcel and I had little in common save one year or so of trivial puerile pursuits when we were twelve. Five years had passed. We'd evolved in mutually exclusive ways. There was no camaraderie in our relationship, no enduring intimacy that might help bridge or attenuate the differences in our temperaments. I was nauseated by his occupation, repelled by the rawness of his temperament. He did not share my love of books, music and theater; my informality and bohemian ways vexed him; culture wearied him, erudition made him feel uncomfortable. I was reading Bazin, Camus and de Montherlant; he'd never heard of them. He obsessed on food; I ate sparingly. I still hated liver; he was pawing it, selling it all day long, devouring it fried in lard and onions.

Many years later, while visiting Paris, I learned that Marcel had married an English girl and moved to London. Had it not been for a fortuitous encounter with his sister shortly after Marcel and I parted company, I would have never known the dark, painful secret he had so valiantly tried to conceal.

•

When I was not in school or toiling as a low-level clerk at the U. S. Embassy three days a week, I spent endless hours exploring and getting re-acquainted with my hometown. These serpentine perambulations always began on *Rue du Pont Neuf,* the epicenter of Paris's 2,000-year history and the focal point of my own origins. Driven by instinct or nostalgia, I invariably turned my gaze upward and beheld with indescribable melancholy the building in which I'd spent the first three or four years of my life. There was little I remembered about the apartment, its configuration, the furnishings that adorned it. What drew me there time after time was an intuitive connection to a tangible beginning, to an anchor that had once secured me in time and space. Replaying my father's arrest by the Gestapo and our subsequent flight from Paris, I always wondered who might be living there now. Did new generations of tenants have any inkling of the drama that unfolded in the apartment they now occupied? Once or twice, I felt the urge to take the elevator, knock at the massive carved wooden door with the polished brass knob and inform whoever might open it, "You know, I used to live here when I was four." The urge remained just that, a whim wisely held in check.

Senseless nostalgia set aside for now, I crossed the Seine over *the Pont d'Arcole*, lingering a while to watch the river's slate-colored waters flow beneath, then surveying the splendor that stretched before me. To my left stood Notre Dame Cathedral, the jewel, the very soul of Paris. Overtaken with awe, electrified by the purity of its form, conscious of its antiquity, daunted by its timelessness, I just stood there, gawking at the sublime edifice. Sometimes I closed my eyes, eclipsing the throngs of tourists and idlers, and I embarked on the wings of fantasy, weaving implausible but engaging scenarios. From the depths of an overactive imagination and vague evocations of Hugo's masterpiece, I conjured the fiery Esmeralda and asked her to dance for me. She offered me a rose, lifted her skirts and, flaunting golden legs, pirouetted on the age-worn esplanade to the accompaniment of flutes, lutes and drums. Lurking high above the gargoyles, clambering about in the bell tower's tangle of crossbeams and alcoves, Quasimodo strained against the weight of the ropes as the seraphic Angelus chimed in the noonday tumult.

Amid the din and boisterous cadence that was medieval Paris, I became François Villon, the morose 15th century poet whose impudence, drunken brawls and petty thievery earned him several stints in prison and banishment -- and nearly cost him his head. There, where once stood the very gallows he had narrowly managed to escape, I caught myself reciting a quatrain from a ballad I'd learned by heart. Drawn from his *Testament,* a collection of satirical poems in which he ponders the brevity and absurdity of life, his verses, chiseled in the archaic French of the time, warned potentate and bard alike:

> *Princes à mort sont destinez*
> *Et tous autres qui sont vivans;*
> *S'ils en sont courciez n'ataynez,*
> *Autant en emporte le vens.*

> *Princes are destined to die*
> *As are all those who live;*
> *If this vexes them by the bye,*
> *That too shall be gone with the wind.*

Enfant terrible, minstrel, scholar and agitator, Villon epitomizes the vitality and charm of eccentricity and iconoclasm in an age of anxiety, intolerance, religiosity and superstition. A master of the allegorical and moralistic literature of the "Dark Ages," he nimbly decomposes real persons and reconstructs from their parts semi-fictitious characters who are free to expose the emotions, instincts, fears and contradictions that haunt the human soul. An early champion of free speech, he remains one of my favorite poets.

Alighting from these flights of fancy, I then strolled on *Quai de Montebello* and *Quai de Tournelle,* leafing through old books, foraging for comics and 3-D erotic postcards in the *bouquinistes'* stalls. *Rue Lemoine* took me past *Lycée Henri IV,* one of the prestigious schools that had denied me a seat five years earlier. Skirting the Panthéon, where the mortal remains of Voltaire, Hugo and Dumas, among others, are laid to rest, I went up boulevard St. Michel, past the Sorbonne and the Faculty of Medicine, my father's alma mater, and I ambled on into the heart of the Latin Quarter. The School of Journalism, where I was enrolled, stood across the *Eglise Saint-Germain-des-Prés*, the 11th century Romanesque basilica in whose cool shadows I often retreated on warm days. The school has long since been relocated and the ornate, *fin de siècle* building in which it was housed was taken over by a welfare agency.

It was at that juncture in my perambulations that I took time out to sip a fragrant cup of espresso at the terrace of the *Café Les Deux Magots*. I was not interested in clever conversation, nor did I seek inspiration, as Hemingway, Becket, Fitzgerald, Baldwin, and Sartre are said to have done long before me. It was not to be seen by an endless parade of faces that I immersed myself in a sea of humanity, but to watch the faces drift past me in a lulling cadence of form, color and motion.

Rue Bonaparte is a narrow street lined with quaint boutiques, antique shops and art galleries; it leads to the banks of the Seine. It is there that I re-crossed the river, taking *Pont Royal* and making a beeline for the *Tuileries Gardens.* Walking its entire length, from the Louvre to Place de la Concorde, I remember ogling young lovers as they exchanged tender kisses, oblivious to the world around. Further on, a new generation of young sea captains navigated their galleons in the same boat basins where I'd played as a toddler. Soon, I reached the final leg of my marathon excursion -- the ascent up the Champs Elysées to the Arch of Triumph. Exhausted yet strangely energized, I then took the Metro to Place Pigalle and walked the rest of the way up to the network of narrow streets and flowered escarpments of Montmartre which I called home.

Later undertaken to appease what would become a lifetime longing for Paris, future pilgrimages, however brief, held the promise of a hike that rarely veered from its inaugural course. I have since added other tributaries, other neighborhoods to these ritual outings. They always begin on Rue du Pont Neuf.

•

And then I discovered night. And night bared a reverse image that transmutes the City of Light into a city of shadows, of wan, angular glows that bathe half a building while the other half is swallowed in Stygian blackness, of stealthy denizens who come out and prowl its darkened streets as the gentry sleeps. I was drawn by the cold phosphorescence of neon lights shimmering on rain-slick sidewalks, the bluish halos encircling streetlights when fog rolled in, the sound of my own footsteps echoing in the distance.

It was inevitable that among the picturesque bestiary that Paris becomes by night I would seek out its *filles de joie*, the "joy maidens" I'd often noticed from afar as a boy, the tawdry women who loitered aimlessly and drew condescending glances from the squeamish and the hypocrites.

"Papa," I remember asking as a tot, "the ladies seem to be waiting for someone."

"Yes, son, they're waiting for someone. Don't worry. *Someone* will show up real soon."

It took an amateurish solicitation on my part -- and a curt and disdainful send off -- to learn that the girls who cruised around the Opéra, the Champs Elysées and other patrician neighborhoods were well beyond my means. I settled instead for the plebeian and incomparably more libertarian bordellos of Pigalle, Clichy, the

Châtelet district, Rue St. Denis and Rue Blondel. Staged as a prelude to wholesale copulation, these nocturnal romps also took on an aesthetic dimension, one that helped define and shape my taste in women. I chose them carefully, discarding the corpulent, the raw-boned, the wilted, the overly made-up, the frumpish. My *putes,* were I to enjoy their services, had to be graced with charm, not classic beauty, with that indefinable *something* -- the piquancy of spice, not sweetness, tang not Grecian profiles. This may explain an early and lingering penchant for African and Asian women. Above all, they had to be pleasing to look at, especially when I climaxed. Looking into their eyes as I crested then came, heightened the rapture. It also added an element of intimacy to an otherwise hasty and perfunctory act. I would seek a sign of pleasure withheld, a hint of impeding surrender to the forces that kept us fused in carnal embrace. But there would be none. I'd startled several of the girls, asking that they look straight into my eyes as I felt myself coming. I would try to kiss them on the mouth, an indiscretion they gently but firmly rebuked. Their bodies were for sale; their lips, which they deftly used to invigorate a sluggish erection, were off limits. Instead, they stared at the ceiling or sideways, anticipating the premonitory spasms, bracing themselves against the paroxysm that ensued with nary a sign of vicarious emotion. Most of them, no doubt exhausted by the tedium of their profession, were cold and lifeless as dead fish.

I would eventually learn to shut my eyes when fantasy and anticipation exceeded reality, as it often does.

It was near Place Blanche that, to my great astonishment, I spotted Françoise one night. Spring had sprung and the air was filled with the scent of lilac. She'd been pacing the pavement back and forth with one of her "colleagues" in front of a small, drab hotel that rents rooms by the hour, "a fresh towel included." I walked up to her and stood in mute amazement, checking her out from head to toe. She wore a tight, short Kelly green skirt, a black bolero from which beamed a luscious cleavage. Stiletto-heeled open-toe shoes enhanced the curvature of her long supple legs. She did not recognize me at first. Or she pretended not to.

"Françoise? It's me. We used to be neighbors. Marcel, you and I…. The pool…," I ventured.

She blushed and let out a nervous laugh. She turned to the other girl.

"I'll catch up with you in a minute. It's a friend. I'll fill you in later." She then spun around and looked at me, not with the starry-eyed fondness she'd shown when she was a little girl, but with the studied poise, listlessness and self-possession of a seasoned streetwalker.

"So, what brings you to Paris?"

"School."

She nodded and looked elsewhere.

"That's good," she replied without a shred of conviction in her voice.

I gazed at Françoise. The precocious little girl who'd made my heart flutter was now a shapely young woman. I was about to ask what calamity had landed her on the Paris sidewalks but I remembered my father's counsel:

"Don't ask a whore for her 'story.' You'll never get a straight answer."

Prostitutes have a "story," a tale, a yarn that varies from place to place, a recurring leitmotif concocted to hide the truth or help endure it in Paris and Paramaribo, Cayenne and Calcutta, Marseille and Montevideo, Amsterdam and Ankara:

"I'm helping put my boyfriend through medical school."

"My little girl is attending the conservatory."

"My husband lost his job. We were destitute."

"My boyfriend (father, uncle or perfect stranger) got me pregnant and left me to fend for myself and the baby. I had to earn a living."

What whores won't say is that they were the neighborhood slut at the age of twelve, horny little fucking machines bent on seducing every male who crossed their path (perhaps to get even with their father, uncle or perfect stranger), that they hate men, would rather sleep with women, are hopelessly hooked on drugs and regard the prospect of honest work -- something that would bankrupt their pimp -- an affront to their dignity.

So I didn't ask. Nor was I particularly interested in Françoise's story, however bizarre or improbable. I just wanted to get laid. We looked at each other in awkward silence for a moment or two. I cleared my throat.

"Alors, on monte?" So, shall we go up?" I ventured.

She studied me, frowned and shook her head.

"No," she replied.

"Uh, why not?"

Françoise crinkled her freckled nose, brushed aside a rebellious lock of copper hair from her eyes and grinned.

"Listen, it's like this. We're old chums. I couldn't take your money. Please understand, I work by the hour and I don't bare my ass for nothing. So you see...."

Her "colleagues" had no such scruples and Françoise cheerfully recommended those she thought I would enjoy. She warned me about the others.

"Jackie's a nice girl. She'll show you a great time," she said. "Helene is beautiful but self-absorbed and impatient. She's all business. If you don't come fast enough, she'll fidget and gripe then she'll just get up, wash up and leave. Mireille gives fabulous blow jobs but she fucks too many Arabs and skips her doctor's appointments. I'd keep away if I were you. Denise, there, the second from left by the doorway, the one with the gold lamé mini and the cute buns, she's ...well, she's a he."

•

And so, I settled into a steady regimen of school, work and nightly excursions into a sulfurous underworld of darkened alleys, smoky cabarets and dingy hotels. I surrendered to what the French call *"le goût de la fange,"* literally "a taste for muck." This expression implies a sudden and inexplicable forfeiture of all civility and refinement during which many men, and certainly some women, plunge headfirst into a pit of lewdness and depravity, of boozing binges and wild and degrading sex with humankind's most repulsive down-and-outers. Think of a dipsomaniac who disappears for a day or a week, gets stinking drunk, sleeps off his hangover in some downtown flophouse then goes home, showers, shaves and return to his high-paying Madison Avenue job. I once knew such a man, an otherwise decent married man who cultivated a homosexual relationship with the art director and often called me into his office, wept and vehemently denied being either gay or a lush. He got smashed one time too many -- I remember him bouncing off the walls one morning as he came to work. He was fired. I inherited his job that same day.

●

I can never explain how during two years of heedless promiscuity in Paris I never contracted a venereal disease. I would have to wait a couple of years when a nice Jewish girl from Glens Falls, New York, contributed in a single encounter a raging syphilitic chancre that took several million units of penicillin to cure and doused, for a while, an otherwise overactive libido.

TRUTH AND CONSEQUENCES

*G**ringoire* is a comic drama by 19th century French playwright, Théodore de Banville. The play is loosely based on the life and travails of poet Pierre Gringoire, a Villon clone immortalized by Hugo in *Notre Dame de Paris*. Like Villon, Gringoire is a firebrand, pitiless annotator and critic of his time. Weak from hunger, burning with fever, hunted by the authorities, he composes verses that excoriate the king and his court, mock the clergy, ridicule the oligarchs and galvanize the proletariat. I'd played the lead role in a school production staged in a theater in Jerusalem when I was about thirteen. The press lavished generous reviews and my performance brought accolades from teachers, fellow students, the French Consul -- Monsieur de Neuville -- and the audience. I enjoyed playing Gringoire. I liked and admired the character, and found myself *being* Gringoire long after the curtain had fallen and I'd shed doublet, leotards and buskins. His exhortations and caustic commentaries, his defiance and solemn forbearance in the face of adversity kept dancing in my head for months after that. Gringoire -- as Villon did -- made a powerful and lingering impression on me. I became Gringoire for a mere two hours on stage during three performances. He would dwell within me and inspire me for years to come. No doubt, his nonconformist ideas continued to simmer on some back burner in my mind. A month or so into my first term as a journalism student, the cauldron came to a boil. Rich in acidity, the overflow inspired a composition on the vestiges of feudalism in modern society. Set in rhyming quatrain form and entitled *The Ballad of the Rolling Heads*, the essay was a stinging satire on the guillotine and the political structures that sanctioned its use. [The contraption was retired in 1981 when France abolished the death penalty.] Honed to sow consternation, my words and the imagery they conveyed shocked some members of the faculty but earned me private praise from my creative writing professor.

It was with the same testosterone-driven verve that I attacked other school projects, often with less than glowing results. I took on assignments that I liked, ignored those that I didn't or, worse, completed them with transparent scorn for the topic. Sometimes I turned in papers on themes of my own choosing, short lampoons in which I parodied teachers, students, political figures and my bosses at the U.S. Embassy where I worked on off-school days.

I did receive a special commendation for an essay on the 50th anniversary of the death of Jules Verne. The piece was "scrupulously well researched, written with obvious knowledge of and regard for the subject," as one of my professors noted in his report. This minor tribute would be obscured by repeated infractions that exasperated the faculty. I often played hooky. My papers were late or unfinished. I tried to seduce one of the professors, the voluptuous blonde sociology instructor. She resisted my advances with skill and refinement and had me promptly transferred to another class.

●

To supplement my parents' meager monthly stipends (and help subsidize my nightly outings), I worked as a foot messenger, ferrying mail and unclassified documents between the U.S. Embassy on Avenue Gabriel and the U.S. Information Service office on Rue St. Honoré. This was my first real job. I learned early on that the only way to survive the humiliation of a menial job is to take pride in it and do it with dignity and skill. There was nothing shameful about the work itself. My routine kept me mostly outdoors, which I enjoyed. It was the behavior of my superiors -- leery, often choleric third-echelon paper-pushers who'd found in civil service an obliging refuge for mediocrity -- that I resented. Hard as I tried to read them, to distill from alternating states of aloofness and irascibility some self-revealing trait, the Americans with whom I worked remained distant and impenetrable. I learned little more from them about America than I did from "Mademoiselle Vanda's" booze-induced recollections of her childhood in Steubenville and her failed marriage to a pig farmer in Topeka. I concluded that the image of fairness, high moral fiber, gallantry and altruism associated with Americans was a myth. How could a race of He-men and dragon slayers be so ... human?

•

Of America, which forswore all princes and potentates in exchange for the majesty of self-rule, I would soon distill a theocentric nation given to hero-worship and gluttonous consumerism, beguiled by its grandiose self-view and readily seduced by the idolatrous slogans it keeps coining in its own name; a nation of superlatives obsessed with bigness: Big Macs, huge SUVs, giant trucks, enormous TVs, gargantuan pizzas. Of Americans, I would deduce a sanguine, gregarious and generous people, outwardly cocksure, inwardly skittish, overindulged, overfed and oversexed -- the men high-strung, homophobic, sexually conflicted, testosterone-bursting badass action figures desperately protective of their masculinity, enamored of their weapons which they keep oiled loaded and cocked; the women prematurely pubertal, neurotic and capricious -- all in awe of status symbols, deaf or hostile to unorthodox ideas, and with whom, owing differences in temperament, tastes and attitudes, I, a hopeless cynic and restless solitarian, would never entertain long-term relationships.

Human nature denatures man. It is the chief impediment to harmony among the species.

•

Another myth, this time perpetuated by France, proclaimed that Algeria was French. Algeria was in every sense a wretched colony whose subjects, nine million strong, had been held in a crushing vise of political, economic, social and cultural inferiority by fewer than one million French for over 100 years. France had built roads, hospitals and schools. Infant mortality had dropped significantly and many endemic diseases were eventually eradicated under French rule. But the overwhelming majority of Algerians enjoyed neither the rights nor the privileges of their colonial masters.

The humiliation endured by the colonized rests less in the inequity of their circumstance than in the figurative and literal status of inferiority imposed by the colonizer. The division of colonial society into two separate and distinct realms -- the conqueror's and that of the conquered -- lasted well into the mid-20th century. By then accorded "conditional" French citizenship but denied political representation, Algerians eager to exercise their newfound rights at the polls were thwarted in their effort by a tangle of bureaucratic obstacles, including "misplaced" or fraudulent muster rolls, sudden and arbitrary change of venues, and defective or doctored ballot boxes. When rigged elections drew widespread protests, censorship, mass arrests, extra-judicial executions and disappearances followed.

In November 1954, two months after I arrived in Paris, 70 simultaneous terrorist incidents against the French in Algeria turned a smoldering struggle for independence into all-out war. Not long before, according to James Bamford in *Body of Secrets,* the French, *"driven by greed and replaced by the Americans, [who were] driven by anti-Communist hysteria"* had abandoned Indochina after a bitter and fruitless war that culminated in a stinging defeat at the hands of anti-colonial forces at Dien Bien Phu. France's debacle in its former colonies of Vietnam, Laos and Cambodia, its loss of prestige around the world, kindled an upwelling of nationalistic fervor among the French, particularly those who were born in Algeria and claimed the country to be their own. France moved the bulk of its Foreign Legion troops to Algeria. Regular army conscripts followed. Soon, anecdotal accounts and isolated eyewitness reports of gross misbehavior by the French army surfaced in France, as did carefully filtered news of high casualty rates among French soldiers. Algerian women were routinely raped, the men treated to beatings, prolonged immersion in freezing water or excrement, and electric shock. Declassified documents, including photos and a glut of press reports, books and documentaries shed a stark light on the atrocities committed by the French in Algeria. Not to be outdone, the Algerians, who fought fiercely and lost over half a million people during the eight-year conflict, showed no mercy for the French they captured. The bloody war ended with Algeria's independence and signaled the disintegration of France's colonial empire.

My parents were now living in Marseille. My father had been appointed medical director of *Camp d'Arénas,* a compound Israel had leased from France and through which North African Jews fleeing Morocco, Algeria and Tunisia, were examined and treated before being allowed to proceed to Israel.

Determined to keep me from becoming a statistic, my mother urged that I be dispatched to America. My father demurred at first. Strong-willed and persistent, happy, it seemed, only when called to rise against titanic obstacles, corporeal or transcendent, he argued that I should not be encouraged to run from risk or responsibility.

"He would have incurred the same risks in Israel had he stayed. We sent him to France to keep him out of harm's way. Who is to say that he won't face new perils in America? Is America immune from war? The world is forever teetering on the brink of catastrophe. War lurks at every turn. He's at ease in France. I think he should stay put and finish his studies."

"You don't know what you're saying, Ari. He is just a boy," my mother retorted. "He was born in France. He's subject to the draft. He's bound to be called any day now." She looked at me with tenderness and apprehension.

Gentle and conciliatory, my mother had always been a buffer between my father and me, especially on those rare occasions when hormones and youthful rebellion got in the way of tact and justifiable respect. She was the perfect arbiter. She pressed on, vividly conjuring up an array of gruesome scenarios.

"Ari, imagine: If they ship him to Algeria, he could be seriously wounded -- or worse. The idea brought tears to her eyes.

My father frowned and stroked his forehead as if brushing away monstrous thoughts.

"You're right."

The truth, the awful truth is that I would be dispatched to America not to seek my fortune but to evade the draft and near-certain service in Algeria where the French were dying like flies.

There was another reason. I was doing poorly in school.

"It's not the writing," the dean wrote in a letter to my parents. "He can write. It's the rest -- spotty attendance, unfinished assignments, a penchant for rabble-rousing and an immoderate fondness for the opposite sex. Your son has been a constant distraction since he enrolled. We showed patience and restraint. We were lenient. When leniency failed, we took stiffer action, all for naught. Your son is smart but headstrong, gifted but undisciplined. He resents authority. He is not a team player. In time, perhaps, these shortcomings will abate. Meanwhile, we regret we cannot encourage you to enroll him for the coming term."

I'd lasted two years.

All events are both cause and effect.

•

With the rest of the immigration paperwork out of the way, I was summoned to the U.S. Consulate for a final interview. The consul, a diminutive, overbearing civil servant visibly luxuriating in his American-in-Paris dream job, handed me one last document, a three-part sworn affidavit that he watched me read and fill out with depraved fascination.

I first had to pledge that I'd not engaged in "adultery, fornication or sodomy." I asked him to define each of these infractions. He complied. Probing my political convictions, the second part inquired whether I was "now or had ever been a member of the Communist Party." The third bluntly asked whether it was my intention "to overthrow the government of the United States by unconstitutional means." Having answered all of the above in the negative and so affirmed with one hand on the Bible, I was issued an immigration visa and granted entry into the Promised Land. I would soon discover that in America, the most sex-obsessed nation on earth, promiscuity thrives in the very lap of Puritanism, that organizations such as the John Birch Society, the Ku Klux Klan and Opus Dei, to name a few, are far more malignant than the atrophied and decrepit Communist party, and that the Constitution is routinely violated through the use of loopholes and feats of acrobatic legalism that encourage the privileged and the powerful to defy the rule of law.

As yet unpolluted by such insights, I bid farewell to my parents for a second time in two years. I left Paris on a cold, rainy mid-winter morning and arrived in balmy Cannes that same evening. After a sleepless night, I embarked the next day on the USS Constitution for the 10-day crossing to New York. I had fifty dollars in my pocket, which my mother had dutifully sewn shut.

Lured by the siren call of adventure, I tried to mute the voices within. This time, they spoke with troubling vehemence and clarity.

"So, you're on the road again, hey? Leaving against your will this time around," they said. "What happened to your manifest objective? You could have stood your ground, but you didn't. When will fails, fate triumphs. You must now learn to ride with the flow lest you be swept beyond your own reach."

I would have cheerfully consigned America to that special cubbyhole where phantasmagoria, myth and legends are stowed. Why couldn't America have been a vague eventuality instead of a destination?

All rivers spring from a source. All events have a cause. Every event triggers other events. The process is continuous and the permutations are endless. In a sense, all events are related. In apprehending this insight, I was taught a lesson that was both axiomatic and un-learnable.

I watched France's coastline recede in the distance and I wept.

PART TWO
MIDSTREAM

Against the current

A HANDSHAKE WILL DO

And so New York, gargantuan, gray, deep-throated, shrouded in an ashen mantle of fog and smoke, lay before me, a demonic hulk apt to pulverize anyone powerless or unwilling to keep up with its dizzying pace. The great city would remain for many years elusive, intimidating and incomprehensible. In time, she would slowly adhere to me like a spurned lover begging for affection and I would learn to love her in return with the reticence, circumspection and lust of a boy infatuated with an older woman.[*]

The old man who'd stood by my side at the railing since daybreak was gone. He'd bid me good luck and I'd seen him clamber down toward the lower decks in a state of euphoric agitation. Passengers were now disembarking, scrambling down the gangplank and spilling into the arms of loved ones massed in clumps on the windswept pier. Dawn's dank murkiness had turned into day and New York was now towering above me like a cyclopean citadel. I would have given anything to stir awake from this unbelievable dream and find myself in bed in my little Montmartre aerie, the aroma of fresh croissants rising from the bakery below.

Aunt Mary -- Malku -- who'd come to fetch me, had noticed sadness in my eyes, weariness in my voice. The curtness of my replies, in response to a thousand questions, further accentuated my discomfort and fueled my feelings of alienation. I knew I should have faked a smile, simulated a semblance of joy for this woman, my father's sister, who so generously offered me shelter during my first few months in America and kept her home and heart open to me for years to come.

---

[*] It would take the tragic events of September 11, 2001 to realize how much New York and I had coalesced in 45 years. Incinerated and pulverized, the majestic Twin Towers had snuffed out the soul of this great city, leaving us, the survivors, the real victims of the terror attack, to ponder the limits of human hatred, the banality of evil. Those who perished, all New Yorkers now understood, would have nothing more to fear. It is we, the survivors, who are being smitten, doomed to remember, sentenced to anticipate, fear gripping our hearts, the echo of our own worst nightmares.

"Won't you tell me what is troubling you," she'd asked, kindness and concern radiating from her eyes.

"Maybe some other time."

I kept my feelings to myself, determined to weather the inevitable, eager to prospect the knowledge and challenges this senseless adventure might yield. I'd spent ten days at sea. The voyage, it seemed, had just begun. I was 19. It was best that dismal thoughts of home be brushed off like desert sand from a pilgrim's sandals.

●

I heard a key turning into the lock.

"Louis' home," chimed Mary. I rushed to the door, opened it and spread my arms, ready to embrace him. Prematurely gray, a tall, lanky man with stooping shoulders stopped me gently but firmly with one hand on my chest and offered me his hand instead.

"You're in America now. A handshake will do."

Words don't hurt until they're uttered.

I would forgive the affront but I never forgot it. Accustomed to my parents' warmth, I found the snub incomprehensible, almost hostile. Spurning a hug, I thought, even from a perfect stranger, as I was to him, was cruel and boorish. I would learn in time that Louis' reserve was less the product of ill breeding than an inbred inability to demonstrate affection. His father Sam (Schmiel), my father's paternal uncle, was a sullen old man who denied relatives a glass of water but invited derelicts to his table. His wife, "Meema," was a stoned-faced, acerbic borderline schizoid woman. Her pinched lips, furtive glances and calculated irascibility betrayed meanness beyond pathology.

Meema and Sam had immigrated to the United States in the early 1900s, when Louis was just a boy. Soon after the end of World War II, Louis, at my father's behest, had invited Mary, his first cousin, to come to America and become his bride. I don't think Mary ever forgave my father for engineering the compact.

A veteran of New Guinea, the Philippines and Okinawa, Louis was intelligent but utterly lacking ambition. He earned a living pressing ties in a sweatshop in New York's garment district. He and Mary produced two daughters -- Pearlyn, who was eight, and Sherry, still incubating in her mother's belly when I landed in America. Now in her fifties, my pretty, dreamy-eyed cousin Sherry had been diagnosed with schizophrenia when she was thirty or so. I'd called it "Meema's revenge."

Soon after I arrived, Louis took me to Macy's for a complete makeover. He bought me a see-through plastic raincoat that folded into an envelope-sized pouch, a fedora that aged me but did not impart the look of respectability Louis had hoped it would lend me, and a pair of "rubbers," hideous overshoes that old men wear in the rain and snow. I never wore either.

Eager to dazzle me, Louis, who'd never been to Paris, also introduced me to the Horn & Hardart Automat, then located around the corner from Macy's West 34th Street store. At first, I considered the whole concept of mechanized dining bizarre, something out of Flash Gordon. But as time went on I found myself drawn to this immense den of anonymity gleaming with chrome-and-glass coin-operated machines, art deco mirrors, marble floors and fancy marquetry. The automats had by then became an American icon. With their uniform recipes and centralized commissary system, they were America's first major fast-food chain. Patrons composed their own meals. Hot food was always hot and tasty. The huge rectangular halls were filled with shiny, lacquered tables, and women with rubber tips on their fingers -- "nickel throwers" -- perched on high chairs in glass booths exchanged paper money for the five-cent pieces required to release food and drink. There were many advantages to this style of dining. Patrons could see the food before buying it. The glass-fronted compartments and gleaming fittings looked reassuringly clean. The coffee was probably the best in town. At a dime a cup, it was also a great buy. The last automat closed in New York City in 1991.

•

In less than a month, I found a job as a junior clerk with a shipping company, Overseas Maritime Corporation. I'd withdrawn from Aunt Mary's tutelage and moved to a furnished room on 113th Street, between Broadway and Amsterdam Avenue. My landlady, Mrs. Neumann, was a stern German Jew who laid down the law: No guests. No music after 10 p.m. No metal-cleated shoes on her shiny parquet floor. No baths allowed -- only showers. No leftovers in the refrigerator. I had no problem complying with four of her injunctions. I deemed the first -- no guests -- groundless and unjust. I'd begun courting several girls, including Priscilla, the daughter of an elder at Riverside Church, and doe-eyed Blanca, the eldest of five children of a working class couple from Puerto Rico. Barred from ushering them in through the front door, I smuggled them to my room, which gave out on the street, by lowering the iron ladder and having them climb up the fire escape. Priscilla, a picture of Protestant primness, had a volcanic libido. She erupted in multiple orgasms, some in mere anticipation of coitus. Kissing her and rubbing my penis against her nipples was enough to send her swooning. Thrusting myself in all the way to the hilt catapulted her from one pinnacle of ecstasy to another until, weak from self-exhaustion, she let out long, tremulous sighs. I often had to place a hand over her mouth to muffle her ululations.

Blanca, Catholic down to her armored underwear and unyielding bra, vowed to surrender only in exchange for an engagement ring. She steadfastly resisted my advances but agreed, perhaps hope eternal springing in the face of crass exploitation, to submit to dry sex, which, *faute de mieux*, was better than nothing. Those were the days when some girls clung to their virginity, others pretended not to have lost it. I would never get to examine Blanca's credentials.

Mrs. Neumann, it turns out, was aware of these nocturnal escapades but never said a word until, in search of greater privacy and larger quarters, I moved out of her apartment.

"I must say you were a model roomer," she declared as we parted, shaking my hand with Prussian vigor. "You paid the rent on time. You were quiet, neat and thoughtful. Of course, I didn't really expect you to obey *all* the rules. I am, however impressed by your resourcefulness and stealth, and grateful for your discretion. Good luck, young man."

CHANCRES AWAY, MY BOYS

Getting up at the crack of dawn, taking a shower, fixing breakfast, running for the subway and riding all the way downtown in a state of stupor to make it to the office by "nine sharp" proved easier said than done. I was partying all night, a routine that, after a while, impairs motor skills and blunts concentration. My job at Overseas Maritime Corporation consisted of monitoring teletype communications and entering, first in a log book, then on a huge blackboard, the flag, registration, provenance, sailing dates, movement, cargo content, and final destination of various ships plying the seven seas. Many of the entries had to be updated several times a day. Bleary-eyed and bored to tears, I soon began to make a number of faulty transcriptions. The first couple of incidents earned me the wrath of my supervisor -- I remember him cursing me in Greek. The last one got me fired.

Fatigue and boredom were not my only foes. Keeping track of ships and ports of call inevitably revived the wanderlust that lay dormant within me. I resented being cooped up in an airtight office perched at dizzying heights over a gray landscape of concrete canyons. I lusted for sunshine, fresh air and the limitless expanse of the deep. It was with a sense of relief that I tore up the pink slip and cashed my miserly severance check. The next day I took the subway to the armed services recruitment center on lower Broadway and enlisted in the United States Navy. I would regret this reckless impulse. I had traded one form of bondage for another.

•

"Can you swim?" The asshole! Of course I could swim. Couldn't everyone? I'd been swimming since I was seven, self-taught, buoyed by the brisk and chilly currents of the Tisza River in Transylvania.

"Why, don't you have ships?" I asked without a trace of sarcasm. The Navy recruiter looked at me with annoyance. He scribbled a few words on a pad. They could have read, "wise guy" or "to be watched" or "troublemaker." He then proceeded to fill out the enlistment form.

"Why are you joining the Navy?"

My answer, *"so I don't have to swim the Atlantic,"* pissed him off. "Seriously, I added in a conciliatory tone, "I'd like to shorten the naturalization process, see the world and continue my education through the G.I. Bill."

"Of course." The recruiter grinned. "Just sign here on the dotted line." I complied.

Two weeks later, shorn like a rat, riddled with painful injections in my arms, forearms and buttocks, and doused from head to toe with DDT, I learned that the recruiter had lied to me, perhaps to avenge my cheekiness, perhaps because he had his orders. It would take five years to qualify for citizenship. Automatic naturalization had been rescinded at the end of the Second World War. The G.I. bill was no longer in effect, except for Korean War veterans. As for seeing the world, the U.S. Navy, for reasons it did not explain, would station me on a wood-hulled coastal minesweeper that rarely ventured out into the open sea.

An early taste of military life at the United States Naval Training Center in Bainbridge, Maryland, long since decommissioned, would inspire resentment and the urge, later satisfied, to terminate this Neptunian charade and return to civilian life. Company 237, Second Regiment, First Battalion, to which I'd been assigned in boot camp, consisted of Bible-belt white boys with thick, unintelligible drawls who slept with the Confederate flag tucked under their pillows -- *"the South shall rise again..."* -- and ghetto and rural blacks who found in fractured grammar, tribal malapropisms and intricate handshakes a cozy refuge from a very hostile white society.

Seaman Recruit Sirotta was the only other Jew in a company of some 60 adolescents, many who had grown up believing that Jews sprout horns and feast on small children during Passover. It's no wonder that Sirotta did what he was told and kept his mouth shut. Mistaking horse sense and opportunism for good citizenship, the Navy assigned Sirotta to a cushy job on the USS Forrestal, then the newest and most formidable aircraft carrier in the fleet. Using a different set of criteria, the Navy dumped me on a rust bucket no bigger than a tugboat.

Sven "Big Swede" Svenson, a gentle giant who'd also recently immigrated to the U.S., and I were the only foreigners -- *aliens*, as the high born Navy brass referred to us. We would both endure the xenophobic remarks of our bunkmates and the haughty disdain of our commanding officers.

Belying his name, Boatswain's Mate First class, Mr. Angel, the company commander, was a merciless drill instructor whose inventiveness was overshadowed only by his cruelty. Sven and I were his choice quarries. He lavished upon us special challenges on the obstacle course -- obstructions and pitfalls from which the other recruits were exempt -- and he dispensed diabolical punishments for bogus or petty infractions. Unhappy with the way I'd folded a set of white uniforms ("regulations" demanded that they be pleated and creased a certain way) he instructed Sven to dig a hole behind the barracks, pour water and stir until the hollow thickened with bubbling slush. Mr. Angel then ordered Sven to dunk my uniforms and trample them underfoot. I spent the better part of that night restoring the uniforms to their original *Rinso Blue* bleached whiteness. Another time, "since the 'frog' and the 'boxhead' are such good friends," Mr. Angel decreed with unctuous sarcasm, "and because neither took the trouble to use a razor this morning, they will proceed to the parade grounds and dry-shave each other in full view of the visiting Inspector General and his staff." For the first time in my life I felt the urge to kill. Sven and I spent days plotting to send Mr. Angel to hell. He may well owe his life to a lack of resolve and opportunity on our part, not qualms.

When I wasn't slogging in the rain chilled to the bone, holding an M-1 rifle high above my head until my arms ached and my knees felt like cotton, learning the secrets of knot-tying, standing watch in the middle of the night, peeling potatoes, swabbing the "deck," and performing other essential naval duties, I earned extra cash composing love letters for some of the half-wits of Company 237. Homesick and quasi-illiterate, these boys, most of them from the Deep South, lapped up my syrupy missives as if they were Shakespearean sonnets. Oozing corn, they rarely veered from a standard text that contained all the buzzwords and pushed all the right buttons. Jealously protective of what they believed was tailor-made prose, none of the Romeos suspected that their Juliet was receiving the same inane message as their fellow sailors:

> "*Dearest* [Darlene, Irma, Lullubelle, Gladys, Wilma]: *"As I lie in my bunk alone with my thoughts, I can see the moon up above. Its glow, reflected by the whiteness of the paper upon which these words are committed, reminds me of your sparkling* [blue, brown, green, hazel] *eyes and the gentle breeze wafting through the half-open window feels like the wispy caress of your* {blonde, red, black] *tresses brushing across my face. My arms cry for your arms, babe, my body aches for yours, my lips thirst for your kisses. I shall hug my pillow tonight and let sleep overtake me before the pain of missing you becomes too much to bear. Until we meet again, with all my love,"* [signed] Clem, Dwayne, Elmer, Leroy, Otis, etc.

●

Homesickness and girlfriends notwithstanding, the boys of Company 237 were boys, and none demurred when, halfway through our ten-week training, we were treated to a day of R&R in neighboring Baltimore. Implicit in this sortie was the inference that we were free to seek pleasure wherever we might find it. We were each issued three condoms and reminded that they might protect us from the hideous suppurations and tumors featured in the classic military training film lavished at the time on all military recruits.

To the best of my recollection, Baltimore in 1956 was an urban eyesore, a grimy expanse of tenements, some crumbling under the weight of abuse and neglect, a tangle of garbage-strewn empty lots fronted by dingy bars and fleabag hotels around which orbited clusters of vagrants, junkies and other reprobates.

Sven and I entered one of the popular drinking holes patronized by sailors and merchant seamen. We surveyed the "merchandise," looked at each other and shook our heads. Accustomed to the appetizing *demimonde* that graces the Paris and Stockholm sidewalks, we wisely decided to pass. The women on display can only be described as shopworn whores who reeked of alcohol and tobacco, and whose physique and crude overtures were apt to nauseate all but the most feral of men.

The boys from Company 237 were not quite as picky. Several of the dolts who'd paid four bits to pledge undying love to their sweethearts were now spending ten or fifteen dollars to get laid with loathsome harlots.

"... *My arms cry for your arms, my body aches for yours, my lips thirst for your kisses,*" I whispered to one of the guys.

He looked at me through a drunken haze and whispered back, "Yeah, but meanwhile, I'll be gold-durned if I'll pass up a chance to get me'self a piece of ass."

•

Back in Bainbridge that night, inebriated and flush with remorse, several of the fellows whose Roxanne I'd dazzled with my latter-day Cyrano poetic intercessions now averted my gaze. Visibly contrite, they also seemed ridden with anxiety. None had heeded the corpsman's advice to use the condoms they'd been issued. This defiance, they feared, would surely invite a bad case of the clap.

"Listen," I said with all the gravity I could muster, "gather 'round. It's too late to cry over spilt milk. A penis is a precious asset. One should be extremely careful of the cavities in which we shove it. There is, however, a safe and foolproof method guaranteed to purge your system of any sex-borne viruses: First, vigorous masturbation. Then, a few drops of after-shave lotion down the urethra. You hear me right. If you value your manhood and your health, you'll do as I tell you. There's no time to lose. Go take a shower and beat your meat as hard as you can. When you ejaculate, the semen will dislodge and expel any germs that might have taken residence inside. Trust me. I know."

One by one, racked by misgivings and unease, and seized by the notion that they had nothing to lose, a dozen or so of the boys retreated to the showers. There, facing the wall, shrouded by clouds of billowing steam, they proceeded to jerk off, first with slow and cadenced strokes (some of them tucked their balls under their buttocks and squeezed their thighs for better traction) then at a frenzied tempo that culminated in a chorus of primal grunts. Pleasure soon turned to scorching pain when they doused their dicks with Canoe or Brut or Aqua Velva. I watched them squirm for a few seconds with all the solemnity I could muster.

"Very good," I said shaking my head approvingly. I then retreated behind the barracks to stifle the waves of laughter that welled within me.

●

About six weeks into boot camp, members of Company 237 were invited to take an Officer Candidate School exam. I asked to be allowed to take the test.

"No can do. You're not a two-generation American citizen. You've not even been naturalized and … er… you lived in a Communist country, isn't that right?"

"Yes, when I was seven years old and not responsible for the political follies of the country in which I resided at the time. I'm now nineteen, lawfully admitted to the United States and a legal resident. Won't you at least let me try? If I pass, I pass. If I fail, I fail. Surely there's not harm in that."

"Sorry."

"I was good enough to enlist, maybe to die for a cause not of my choosing, but I'm not good enough to be an officer, is that what you're saying?"

"Case closed. That's an order."

Democracy is a commodity Americans are eager to export but are loath to cultivate at home.

I would have gladly dipped my tongue in H. L. Mencken's bile at that moment. Unfortunately, I'd not yet discovered the eminent journalist. Dreamers are never short on hope but every ounce of hope is often dashed by a pound of disappointment. My next setback took place a couple of weeks later, when I opened the official envelope that contained my orders. I'd applied for journalism school at the Great Lakes Naval Base in Illinois. Instead, I was to report on the USS

Hornbill, home-based in Charleston, South Carolina, for "general sea duty." The Hornbill was a wood-hulled coastal minesweeper skippered by a lieutenant junior-grade. A paragon of ambiguity, the term "general sea duty" alludes to miscellany chores, some degrading, others hazardous, all grueling, to be performed above or below deck, in peace and wartime, at sea or in port. My world, for the next several months, would be glimpsed from the cramped and suffocating murkiness of the bilges, which it was my duty to inspect, drain and caulk. I would also minister the bottom of urinals and toilet bowls, and wield a paintbrush in a never-ending war against rust. I would eventually be entrusted with the care and sustenance of a huge coffee urn that the captain ordered "piping hot and ready to pour by no later than oh-four-hundred." It is at that time that I learned how to nap while on watch, eyes wide open but unseeing, all systems in neutral. I would later refine the technique, this time with my eyes closed, when, unable to find a seat, I had to stand during the long and jarring subway ride between Main Street, Flushing and Grand Central Station.

●

" ... One more day and I'll be home, honey,
one more day and I'll be home ba-abe,
one more day and I'll be home,
drinkin' beer and pissin' foam,
honey, oh, baaaby mine.
Go to your left your right your left, go to your left...."

●

At last, boot camp was over. Weeks of grueling physical exertion and pointless instruction earned me two seaman apprentice stripes. I returned to New York on a fourteen-day furlough. A friend offered me a bed in his Greenwich Village apartment. That same night, he introduced me to an attractive Jewish girl from Glens Falls who contributed, in addition to free sex, a raging syphilitic chancre. It took massive doses of penicillin to heal the painful lesion. The incident also helped put a new spin on the ambiguities of sex, which I impetuously forswore and promptly reclaimed when the next opportunity arose.

•

I'd read Uncle Tom's Cabin and Huck Finn as a boy, and studied the rudiments of American history in school but the scenes these works depicted and the lessons they imparted had an academic remoteness about them that denied me the privilege of first-hand experience. It's one thing to read about intolerance, quite another to see it replayed *live* in all it ugliness. It was when I landed at the Charleston airport that America put on its vilest visage. I would never forget. I was startled at first, then frightened, then outraged. I'd just alighted in a Kafkaesque realm of incomprehensible madness. Longing for a good piss after the flight, I headed to the men's room. Two signs greeted me. One read **WHITES**, the other **COLORED**. Caucasians went one way, men of color went another. Seized by a brief moment of indecision, I stood there not knowing what to do. Drinking fountains, I noted, were also segregated although, in a twist of irony lost neither on the whites nor the "colored," they were both fed by the same water supply system.

Two incidents cost me brief periods of detention, first in the city jail then, preceded by a tirade from the captain, in the ship's brig. Riding for the first time from the base to the USO in downtown Charleston, I casually proceeded to the back of the bus and sat down. Seeing me in his rear-view mirror, the driver brought the vehicle to a screeching halt. He got up, walked to the back of the bus and ordered me to move to the front.

"Why?"

"Do as I say."

"I'm quite comfortable right here, if you don't mind."

"You don't understand. *Nigras* ride in the back. White folk ride up front. It's the law."

"It's a stupid law, if you ask me. I'm not budging an inch."

Black riders around me demurred. Their expressions conveyed a mixture of hesitant esteem and alarm. I was creating a scene into which they were loath to be drawn.

"Please, just move up front. It's best that way," pleaded a black man.

"I can't. If I do that I agree to this madness. I become part of the problem."

The bus driver summoned a patrolman and had me ejected in handcuffs. I was charged with disorderly conduct and spent two hours in one of the city's lockups. I was then turned over to the Shore Patrol who escorted me back to my ship.

The second incident was more serious. I was strolling in one of the city's princely neighborhoods, admiring the handsome antebellum mansions along the way. Hobbling toward me on the narrow sidewalk was an old, portly black woman leaning on a cane. Her gait was unsteady, her stride slow. She seemed out of breath. When I realized that we could not both navigate the sidewalk, I stepped onto the curb to let her pass. I had not gone two paces when a man rushed toward me, spat in my face and barked:

"That's for letting that nigger woman pass through."

Overcome with rage, I pounced on the man, punched him several times, breaking his nose and knocking off a couple of his teeth in the process. I would have been charged with aggravated assault had I not successfully argued that I'd had been provoked, spat upon and publicly humiliated for acting with courtesy and compassion toward an elderly person. I was charged with simple battery and remanded to naval authorities. Placed on report, I spent two nights in the brig. Shore leave privileges were suspended for a month. Relieved of watch duty, I spent the next four weeks scrubbing the galley, chipping away at rust, waxing and buffing the lower decks and tending to the latrines. I would later be reminded that if basic human rights in America had been entrusted to a plebiscite, people of color would still be riding in the back of buses, schools and lunch counters would still be segregated, and lynching would still sate the racist hankerings of America's heartland.

•

For most recruits the first few days in boot camp are mortifying enough without having to justify one's origins. Being the only Frenchman in a company of small-town bumpkins, backwoods yokels and taciturn blacks from Dixie where the great American sport --

lynching -- was still in vogue, presented some elemental problems. Half of them had never heard of France; the other half gawked at me with suspicion: I was a big-city slicker, no doubt a perfidious Yankee; and I spoke better English than they. We trained and studied as a unit but I pretty much kept to myself. We all completed basic training without incident and we went our separate ways.

On board ship, challenging the young officers' stereotypical taunts -- "you French surrendered to the Germans without a fight; we had to come and bail you out;" or "you eat frogs and smelly cheese;" or "what did France ever do for us," was trickier. Enlisted men have to stand at attention, eyes-front and chin out, a bearing that makes intelligible speech problematic. Such invectives begged for a riposte. I didn't mince my words.

"First of all -- *Sir* -- if it hadn't been for France, which went bankrupt to finance *your* Revolution and help you fight *your* war of independence while its people were starving to death, you'd all be kowtowing to a monarch. The great French architect l'Enfant would have never designed Washington, DC.; and instead of Bourbon Street and great jazz and Irving Berlin and Leonard Bernstein and Aaron Copland, you'd be listening to Gilbert and Sullivan; you'd be dining on shepherd's pie and greasy fish and chips and licking the back of stamps bearing the effigy of a fucking queen. As for our culinary tastes, *Sir*, people who switch the fork from the left to the right hand and use the knife like an assault weapon while feasting on opossum, squirrel and rattlesnake are hardly qualified to niggle. Besides ...."

"Dismissed."

"But...."

"DIS-MISSED, you hear!"

I was about to credit France for the discovery of oxygen, hydrogen and radioactivity, for the invention of the oboe, manned flight, photovoltaics, still photography and moving pictures, for producing fine wines and hundreds of varieties of cheeses, for gifting the world haute couture, perfumes and cosmetics, for drafting and ratifying the Universal Declaration of the Rights of Man, for creating the first secular nation under the constitutional separation of church and state... and for devising the metric system. I could have touted the roulette and the periodic table of elements, the modern Olympic Games, beryllium and chromium; pasteurization, neon, the calculator, blood transfusions, cataract surgery, codeine and aspirin, the hypodermic needle and the stethoscope, antibiotics, the taxicab, the steamboat, the hot-air balloon, the internal combustion engine, the helicopter, the sewing machine, the optical telegraph, Braille, dry cell batteries, reinforced concrete, the aqualung, the incubator, ball bearings, the pencil and the gyroscope. But now in contempt of naval authorities and risking yet another night in the brig, I snapped to attention, saluted the officer, did an about-face and walked away muttering loud enough to be heard:

"Champagne, the bayonet, the bikini, the guillotine, the bidet."

Shore leave was suspended for a week and I was assigned to latrine and KP duty. It was then that I realized that freedom of speech comes with a price.

•

One day a flotilla of French Navy ships entered Charleston harbor during an official visit. One of the ships docked alongside my own. I was elated. I could speak French again and my compatriots delighted in the rich and vulgar Parisian argot I adopted to describe the life of a Frenchman in the U.S. Navy. I befriended several of the deck hands and one night, as I stood watch, I climbed over the railing under the cover of darkness, boarded the French ship and scurried down below. The crew could not have been more accommodating. I was treated to wine, pastries and Gauloises cigarettes whose pungent aroma reminded me of home. Touched by their hospitality and very much in the mood for mischief against my U.S. Navy tormentors, I offered to repay their kindness by escorting a small group to the nearest whorehouse. Mine was a brazen and cunning scheme fraught with risks. The logistics involved in bringing it to fruition called for a flawless strategy. A number of elements -- method, timing and stealth -- had to be fine-tuned. The Charleston red light district was out of bounds to U.S. naval personnel. I could not be seen shepherding French sailors without attracting the attention of the Shore Patrol and getting into more hot water. Also, the sortie could only take place when I was off duty. The answer was obvious. I would borrow a French uniform -- pants, jumper, white tam, blue ribbon and red pompom -- and wear it to go ashore with my companions. I requested and was granted a 24-hour pass. The operation would go without a hitch.

A day later, at dusk, I crossed over onto the French vessel, took off my work denims and put on a French uniform. I remember parading in front of a mirror and laughing like a kid on a joyride. I also liked the way I looked. Once an object of desire, the U.S. Navy livery, compared to the stylish French one, now looked like pajamas.

The French ship was tied alongside my own on its seaward flank. This required that the half-dozen French sailors and I first board my ship to get ashore. To make sure that my own shipmates didn't recognize me, we ran across the deck in tight formation, babbling in French, and scrambled down the gangplank under the amused gaze of several of my shipmates, some of whom whistled, made frog sounds and engaged in coarse humor.

Once ashore, we all piled into a cab and drove to a nightclub in a restricted black neighborhood. I could hear music and muffled sounds of laughter but the club door was locked and the windows were lined with black crepe on the inside. This reminded me of Paris during the occupation. I knocked at the door. A curtain parted, revealing a black man's face and, in the background, a smoky purple haze hanging over the dance floor. The man unlocked the door and opened it partly. I offered him my hand. He hesitated but took it.

"What can I do for you?"

"We are with the French Navy. We want to dance and have a good time," I replied in my best Charles Boyer accent.

"You can't come in."

"Why not?"

Still locked in a handshake, he pointed at the difference in skin color between our two clasped hands. "That's why," he said without hostility.

"But we're French. It doesn't matter to us."

"You're not in France. Don't insist."

"Look, we're only here for a short time. We've been at sea for over a month. My buddies and I are looking for, uh, how shall I say, a little fun."

"Sorry, I can't let you in. We'd get in trouble and so could you. But I tell you what. Go down the street, turn right at the end of the block and count five doors on your left. Ring the bell three times. Tell'em Watson sent you. I think you'll find what you're lookin' for."

What we were looking for and what we found were worlds apart. A black woman, wilted before her time and thin as a rail, let us in without uttering a word. She took us to a room, past a sitting room in which somnolent adults were sprawled on gutted, dingy sofas and small children with stupefied expressions played on the bare floor. The room was small and dimly lit by a single low-wattage pink bulb that cast a ghostly pallor on the French sailors' faces. The woman got undressed, stretched on the bed, spit in her fingers, lubricated herself and spread her spindly legs. Acting with gallantry toward my guests (or was it queasiness?) I offered to go last. One by one, lust having subdued the last vestiges of good taste, my French comrades surrendered to the woman's embrace. They fucked her fast and furious, some from behind, others exacting uncomfortable positions that exhausted her. She winced several times and moaned with visible discomfort.

The enthralling spectacle of chain sex had aroused me. I was sporting a superb erection and I had unfastened the fly in preparation for my own final assault. But when my turn came, I stood there, transfixed by the slime that oozed out of the woman's vagina. Overcome with nausea, I retched. My hard-on went into an unrecoverable nose-dive. We paid the woman for her trouble and left.

I later returned to the base, using the same stratagem I'd devised to get off, boarding the French vessel, changing into my U.S. Navy work clothes and sneaking back on my ship when no one looked.

●

Several weeks later, I was transferred to an ocean-going minesweeper. The captain, a former "white hat" who'd received his commission during World War II, invited me to the bridge and offered to train me as a quartermaster and pilot. The new assignment, a welcome relief from the drudgery of deck duty, would last less than a month. Trouble had flared up in Lebanon and looming on the horizon was the Sinai Campaign, in which the combined forces of Britain, France and Israel pounced on Egypt in retaliation for that country's blockade of the Suez Canal. My ship had been summoned and was readying to join the 6th Mediterranean Fleet. I was elated at the prospect of a long sea voyage that would take us to the Azores, Gibraltar, France, Italy, Greece, Cyprus and, possibly, Israel. That was not to be. Inexplicably, I was transferred to the USS New Orleans Parish, a decommissioned LST that had been welded to the pier and served as a floating barracks. A few days later, I learned from one of my former shipmates, a yeoman, that I'd been transferred "because the captain was uncomfortable having a foreign Jew on board during an overseas deployment." I will never know if I'd been told the truth but, at the time, this outrageous pretext seemed to make sense.

Demoralized, mortified, I went AWOL. After a week of frolic in New York, I surrendered to naval authorities and spent several days in confinement at the Brooklyn Navy Yard. I was returned to my ship "on my honor" by Greyhound bus. A summary court martial resulted in a reduction in rank to seaman recruit. I would engineer my next demotion -- to civilian life -- with a zest overshadowed only by the extreme despondency that sustained it. I began to fake nightmares, during which I would thrash about and scream or sob uncontrollably in the middle of the night. This pantomime lasted several days. Less than a week later, I was taken to the U.S. Naval Hospital's cuckoo's nest for observation and placed under the care of a Navy psychiatrist, Dr. Schwartz.

Brief interviews, during which Dr. Schwartz, a consummate Freudian, probed into my life in the womb, infancy and early childhood, were often followed by the all-telling Rorschach inkblot tests. I'd learned from my father many years earlier that a normal response was no response at all, that is, the assorted shapes one is asked to interpret are just that -- shapes, period. I remember telling my father that people who fail to see beyond the symmetry of the inkblots must be dull-witted and unimaginative.

"Isn't 'normalcy' a sign of mental sterility, of a bland intellect," I asked. My father laughed. "Highly imaginative, highly creative people tend to be regarded as deviant. There's a pathological aspect to genius absent in 'normal' individuals."

I remembered my father's words: It would serve my purpose to flaunt the richness of my imagination and feign pathology.

"I see a giant bat, wings poised for attack, swooping down on me." Or, "two bears stand upright clawing at each other as a cub cowers in fear between them." Or, "Siamese twins joined by a common penis poke each other's eyes out with their tails." Or, "This reminds me of a vagina armed with teeth ready to devour me...."And so on.

I remember Dr. Schwartz looking at me with increased amusement. His eyes seemed to say, "Who do you think you're fooling?" But he was too smart and tactful to express his skepticism so crassly. Instead, he grabbed my wrists, leaned across the desk until our faces were inches apart and whispered:

"Anyone who would go to such lengths to fake lunacy, my boy, must be ill; ill or desperate. Now think very carefully before you answer. Which are you?"

I swallowed hard. "If I can choose between the two, *'desperate'* seems a more fitting diagnosis, Doctor. I believe that, unchecked, despair will lead to illness, won't it?"

"Only in the most extreme circumstances. But you may have a point, tenuous and conjectural, but a point nonetheless."

"Please, doctor, you must help me. I've got to get out of this. I can't stand it anymore."

"Let me see what I can do."

•

There exist ill-defined forms of mental illness, so subtle, so skillfully concealed and so utterly undetectable that they elude even those trained to recognize the myriad faces behind which they hide. Is he demented who pretends to be sane? Is he who fakes madness -- mad? Is "normal" behavior evidence of sanity? Is a clown "crazy?" Would his buffoonery be sanctioned outside the circus tent? He's only play-acting, you say? What about motorists who willfully exceed the speed limit: are they clear-headed? Are citizens who, time after time rush to the polls and vote into office inept or corrupt politicians under the ludicrous pretext that they're taking part in the "democratic process"-- in full possession of their faculties? Or are they imbeciles who deserve the scoundrels they helped elect?

Is the soldier who fires at an enemy he can't see behaving rationally or, to dilute the horror (or ease his conscience), is he pretending to be shooting blanks every time he squeezes the trigger? If not, if he finds moral justification in sanctioned murder -- or derives some secret thrill from it -- is he demented, evil or a hopeless moron?

Are boxers who bash each-others' brains out -- for money -- out of their minds? Would their fights-to-the-finish seem less brutish if they didn't appear to enjoy themselves so much? Aren't the fans who salivate at the prospect of blood, of a bone-crushing knockout, equally deranged?

Are the uninvited zealots who compel aborigines to cover their genitals "for the love of God," who force-feed guileless children alien concepts and rob cultures of their identity, sane or psychopaths further unhinged by religious zeal?

What about the "prophets"? Were they merely deranged talking heads or cunning terrorists; clueless prognosticators or schemers blinded by their own fury; soothsayers and mystic diviners who spoke in riddles and esoteric babble or crafty politicians bent on sowing fear in the hearts of the masses? Were their intentions noble or did they suffer from acute megalomania, monomania and thanatomania (a consuming preoccupation with death?) Wouldn't they all have been diagnosed as certifiably insane -- or called charlatans -- had modern psychiatry not spinelessly declined to see them as superstitious crackpots pickled in gooey mysticism and predisposed to treat all inexplicable natural phenomena as the manifestation of some unknowable, invisible spirit?

Aren't the dream merchants, the demagogue-pedagogues and the healers who deconstruct reality and peddle cheap imitations of Utopia -- insufferable egomaniacs?

If men were put away for their natural tendencies, prisons and mental hospitals would be bursting at the seams. Madness is somehow less reprehensible when it festers in high places, when ruthless entrepreneurs and corporate kingpins are eulogized for their "initiative" and cunning, when my-country-right-or-wrong "patriots" brush aside lies, rationalize injustice, defend sleaze and political chicanery, when fanatical evangelism is hyped as "God's work," when fraudulent and unwinnable wars that only enrich bankers and cannon merchants are waged far from home in the name of "national security," when freedom of thought is condemned as heresy and when all moral codes are rescinded to protect the interests of the moneyed elite.

Pray tell, who are the mad, I wondered as I agonized over Dr. Schwartz's decision. A lifetime detour to America's world of make believe would help tell them apart. Meanwhile, feigning madness was the only way I knew to regain my sanity in what appeared to me as a very deranged universe.

•

Citing *"an intractable incompatibility with the exigencies and rigors of military life,"* Dr. Schwartz recommended that I be discharged, honorably and unconditionally. As the paperwork made its way through the slow and serpentine bureaucratic maze, I spent another few days at the U.S Naval Hospital in a ward filled with men who had shot and stabbed themselves, ingested razor blades and narrowly averted strangulation in exotic but unsuccessful attempts at suicide. A few thrashed about and screamed or sobbed uncontrollably in the middle of the night. These men were not faking. Fearing for my life, I got very little sleep.

On the morning of January 16, Dr. Schwartz, accompanied by an orderly, presented me with a large brown envelope. He smiled.

"You're free, Gutman. Get the fuck out of here."

I let out a scream, jumped up for joy and hugged Dr. Schwartz.

"Thank you, doctor, thank you ever so much."

"Don't thank me. I just did my job. I believe that in the long run you and the U.S. Navy will be the richer for having parted company. Good luck."

Dr. Schwartz smiled. We exchanged salutes. He spun around on his heels with military panache and resumed his rounds. I opened the envelope and pulled out a lily-white certificate. I'd been honorably discharged. My past misdeeds and subsequent hospitalization, I assume, were dutifully chronicled and may still be filed away in some Navy archive. Nothing in the discharge certificate itself, however, hints at my turbulent and foreshortened service.

The orderly helped me pack my sea bag and escorted me through a series of double-bolted iron doors to the hospital's outer gate. I waved my discharge at the sentry as if it were a victory pennant. Deliverance has a very special scent. I inhaled deeply, turned my face toward the sun, slung the sea bag over my shoulder and walked out.

I had already seen and would see far more of the world as a civilian.

UP THE FOURTH ESTATE!

To speak English is not a virtue. Not to speak it is an infirmity. And so I proceeded to conquer the strange language I'd first mastered in school, a virile idiom full of Anglo-Saxon dissonance, peculiar rhythms and intonations, an alien tongue as bizarre as the fabled domain on which I alit that bleak morning in late January 1956.

But fluency in English, I soon discovered, was not enough. In language are imprinted elements of culture peculiar to those who speak it. I found myself denied a subtler eloquence, a poise, an intuitive effortlessness granted native speakers who acquire and articulate without the slightest exertion all manner of doctrines, partialities and cultural idiosyncrasies, most of which, hitherto unknown to me, and promptly rejected, would forever deny me the rewards of total assimilation.

After fifty-six years in the United States, I still have a hard time reconciling with a host of eccentricities, anachronisms and absurdities. Among them, is the two-party system -- two parties indistinguishable one from the other except for the partisanships and antipathies they inspire in their respective camps, both tied to corporate wealth, both intent on blocking reform in the name of capitalism, both involved in immense larceny against the poor. A close second is the Electoral College, which fails to accurately reflect the national popular will and risks foisting a minority president. (I would remain conflicted about the Electoral College every time I reminded myself that, in America, a reflection of the "national popular will," would keep blacks confined to the back of the bus, going to ghettoized schools and eating at segregated lunch counters).

Transmitted from father to son, racism is an infectious disease that even self-described democratic societies do not seem able or willing to cure.

The rest includes a hodgepodge of contradictions, customs, biases and affronts: blue laws, the obscene incongruity of Thanksgiving as Indians pine away in "reservations," the worship of matinee idols, the lionizing of athletes, root beer and sarsaparilla, televangelism, Girl Scout cookies, Roe vs. Wade, the death penalty, feminism, chauvinism, negritude, white supremacy, the senior prom, baseball, Columbus Day, the Super Bowl, cheerleading, soccer moms, baby beauty contests, marshmallows, reality shows, rodeos, and hog calling contests.

•

It took more than thirty years to climb the treacherous slopes. I began at the bottom, sharpening pencils and running errands for the legendary Red Smith and other luminaries -- Earl Ubell, Judith Crist, Walter Kerr among them -- at the late great New York Herald Tribune. My skills as a pencil-sharpener and a capacity to endure with a smile the cold indifference or the daily slurs flung at me by these demi-gods of the Fourth Estate eventually earned me a promotion of sorts: I was entrusted with emptying their wastepaper baskets into a large wooden bin kept in a hallway near the service elevators.

One day I asked to be allowed to work on the obituary column, a modest and reasonable request, I thought. The request was denied without explanation. Sensing my frustration, and bending the rules, Walter Hamshar, the kindly shipping news editor, sent me to the Hudson River piers "on assignment," a euphemism for fresh air. I returned to the office empty-handed save for a bad case of wanderlust and a pocketful of demented notes in which I successfully argued all the reasons why I should sneak aboard a bauxite-laden freighter en route to Vancouver, Valparaiso and Vladivostok or hitch a ride on an old tramp steamer headed for Panama, Pago Pago and Papeete, instead of going back to work.

Every once in a while, when the Muses beckoned or when my need for acknowledgment overshadowed the wisdom of anonymity (or the reality of an inflexible pecking order), I would compose short essays on this and that and submit them to the city editor. My tracts were invariably tossed, unread, into a large metal-rimmed receptacle that flanked his desk and which it was my duty to empty several times a day. In desperation, I wrote:

"There are people who make themselves inaccessible to those who need them most, those who most depend upon their tutelage. Like quicksilver, they're never still enough to be overtaken. Agitated, choleric, bellowing here, clamoring there, they breathe fire, spit magma and piss vinegar. Bloated with self-importance, they secretly resent their superiors, pretend to tolerate their equals and openly delight in bullying the underlings. It's impossible to get near them unless, exhausted and oxidized by self-combustion, they relent and become approachable -- and useless. One must learn to shut up in their presence. Addressing them might seem like praise to them. In their case, praise is flattery corrupted. Speaking ill of them while they are alive is risky; cowardly after they are dead."

The city editor, a seasoned newsman on whose desk I'd placed my silly tract, was no fan of dark humor. He turned to the copy boy pool and pointed at me.

"Copy."

"Yes, sir?"

"Hand me my waste basket, will you, boy."

"Certainly, sir." I walked over to his desk, picked the basket off the floor and held it at arm's length.

"Paper is a precious commodity. It comes from trees and shouldn't be squandered," he said, tearing my essay into thin strips and letting them flutter one by one down the receptacle.

"Now please empty the basket." He smirked and turned his back. Undaunted, I composed another tract.

"When the mighty have an opportunity to guide the meek, they rarely have the inclination to do so. When they wish to cow them, they never lack the means. The mighty scorn the gifted whose only possession is talent. The talented despise the mighty whose only gift is power. The others pity both for being endowed with either might or special aptitudes but no other discernible virtue. What reassures and sustains me against the contempt of the mighty is the certitude that they begrudge my

gifts, not my frailty in the presence of might. They would no doubt kiss my ass if I were mightier but less talented than they."

The city editor was not smiling this time.

"Now look, I could have you fired on the spot. If you value your job, you'll stop pestering me. You hear!"

"Yes, sir."

When one is accustomed to them, kicks in the ass no longer hurt, an axiom understood by those who dole them out as well as those who endure them. It becomes a habit. Copy boys belong to the latter category. Irrelevant, expendable they are the pariahs of a newspaper's manifest caste system.

God denied animals speech to prevent them from telling humans off.

•

Across the short no-man's land that separated the city editor from the rest of his staff, sat an old man whose features seemed frozen in a perpetual grimace, his upper lip curled menacingly, his nostrils flaring as if some foul odor inhabited his space, a scowl conveying both hostility and exasperation etched upon his face. On his desk rose in a neat pile a stack of paper towels and, next to them, a tall goblet of water which he fed with maniacal regularity from a glass carafe I was in charge of refilling. An empty carafe elicited a litany of half-muttered expletives in my direction. Every ten minutes or so, he would rip a few sheets, crumple them into a ball and dunk them in the glass. He would then scrub the palm and back of his hands with a vehemence suggesting self-loathing. I called him Lady Macbeth. The skin on his hands had acquired the sickly whiteness and texture of boiled chicken. He would call out, "Boy," without a trace of a smile misspent and I'd have to run to the water fountain and fill up his carafe, or ferry a sheath of galleys to reporters, editors or headline writers huddled by the big horseshoe-shaped table. I resented these intrusions upon my time and inner-musings but survived them by engaging in smutty speculations about this strangest of compulsions. I imagined him engaged in furious masturbation and conjured scenes of maternal wrath for having "spilt his seed and fouled his hands in the presence of God." The man had a wretched temper. He invited these unkind fantasies and I found myself despising the man more than the obsessive-compulsive disorder that afflicted him.

Partly dirty is not clean. Partly clean is still filthy.

•

Then, one day, the mighty Herald Tribune expired. In a few years, in rapid succession, New York, America's media capital, went from a dozen newspapers to fewer than a handful. The war for jobs, fierce and bloody, proved beyond my capacity to wage. I was now 22, inexperienced, quixotic, trusting, naïve and ill-equipped to compete in an industry where natural selection had produced its own tiger sharks.

Survival dictated that I set aside any serious journalistic aspirations, and there began a slow, steep ascent consisting of one teetering step forward and three breakneck backward slides. I went to work for "trade" magazines in the food, beverage, plumbing, medical and aviation industries. My longest job -- I took over the reins of an environmental engineering publication when the editor could no longer hold his liquor -- lasted eight years. I attribute this extraordinary longevity to impudence, luck, necessity in the face of looming indigence and the esteem of an editorial crew in whose eyes I could do no wrong. Other jobs came and went. I was fired, demoted, laid off. Several publications died under me in rapid succession. Many more moved out of town and were never heard from again. I called myself a journalist, but paying rent and feeding a young family demanded that between frequent sorties to the unemployment office I also accept work as a dishwasher, waiter, barman, elevator operator, cab driver, night-shift cable dispatcher, shipping line clerk, messenger and security guard. I ferried books in Columbia University library's maze-like sub-basement. I then managed the *Bizarre*, a dismal Greenwich Village coffee shop specializing in unpalatable drinks and bad poetry artlessly recited by haggard bards bombed out of their skulls. Some jobs lasted less than a month, others less than a day. I would be fired for indolence, ineptitude or insubordination. Friends envy my mottled past. Why not, it's easier than living it.

I survived and kept writing feverishly, often in anger and frustration, sometimes the docile medium of inspiration, often the instrument of a dull but providential freelance project. Neither my failures nor friendly advice -- "Come to your senses boy, it's time you learned a real trade" -- diminished my resolve. I was writing and getting better, if not yet good enough, at what I did best. I believed in the dignity of my cause and the legitimacy of my aims.

•

Sometimes, in exchange for quasi-security, one is forced to give up one's freedom, swallow one's pride. The New York Academy of Sciences, where I worked as a copy editor, fostered a climate of self-denial bordering on masochism. Mrs. Miner, the director, was an ogress. Diminutive, capable of glacial stares and pinch-lipped sarcasm, she ruled by fear and intimidation. Headed by Frank Furness, a meek and unremarkable man past retirement age who trembled in her presence, the editorial staff was recruited by Mrs. Miner from a flotsam of misfits, openly gay aspiring literati and educated blacks willing to earn slave wages in exchange for a prestigious Upper East Side office address. I have no precise recollection of the type of manuscripts I edited. I remember working in a Dickensian ambiance where dress and deportment were subject to scrutiny and criticism, where chatting was forbidden, overtime obligatory, lateness and absenteeism punishable by docking and a very public lecture, compliments of Mrs. Miner, on the virtues of punctuality, loyalty and decorum.

I quit after less than six months.

We deplore failure by ignoring the problems success might have wrought.

•

My first big break came when I was 48. Years of monotony dissolved instantly in an avenging sigh of triumph. Awestruck by a career that stretched from the sublime to the ridiculous, impressed by the number of languages I spoke (some of which are useless even as a last resort) an executive at OMNI, the now-defunct futurist magazine, hired me on the spot. A previous stint as the managing editor of *Aerospace America* earned me the editorship of a newly launched publication devoted to nuclear, biological and chemical warfare. The magazine was an instant success. I traveled far and wide in search of fresh stories. Contributing editors picked from academia, national security agencies, counterespionage, think tanks and the military wrote probing features and insightful analyses. Stringers unearthed facts that not only out-scooped the major dailies but also earned us a loyal following among U.S. and foreign military, intelligence and diplomatic circles. We were the first to point fingers at Saddam Hussein, warn against the growth of international terrorism and offer a quantitative assessment of the global biochemical threat. We ran smuggled photos shot with subminiature cameras showing captured weapons, gas masks and decontamination equipment in Southeast Asia, Africa and Latin America. We were the first to report that Argentina had stockpiled large quantities of nerve gas and was readying to use them against the British during the Falklands conflict. We traveled to Iran's southern front and witnessed the horrifying aftermath of Iraq's mustard and nerve gas attacks against civilians. We uncovered and reported on efforts by Russia and North Korea to turn snake toxins, botulism, ergot, anthrax, smallpox and the castor bean into weapons of mass destruction. In short, we were the first and only magazine of its kind, anywhere in the world.

It is little wonder that Col. Anatoly Makhov, a military attaché at the Soviet Mission to the United Nations, would show such keen interest in the magazine. Printed in Birmingham, England, the magazine was first distributed in Europe, then shipped to the U.S. I'd met Makhov at a party held by the late Bob Guccione and his wife Kathy Keeton at their palatial East 67th Street Manhattan townhouse to celebrate the launching of the magazine. A former fighter pilot and a KGB agent, Makhov had made a strange request: He wanted to receive his copy *before* his counterpart in London got his. I found this curious rivalry between two associates serving the same master fascinating. Makhov had a habit of sneaking past security, first in the lobby then on the third floor where my office was located. I never found out how he managed this sleight of hand. When I asked him, he just smiled. I remember Makhov with fondness. He was a bright, cultured man who never ventured into the minefield of international politics. Instead, we chatted at length about Russian music and literature. I wonder what became of him.

After eighteen months of sluggish advertising sales, and despite a loyal and growing audience, we also became the last magazine of its kind. Publication was suspended and I was unceremoniously "terminated." Following twelve months of unemployment during which I exhausted my meager savings, OMNI called me back and refitted me with two hats. I became an in-house consultant (I never found out what I would be consulted about) and U.S. editor of Science in the USSR, the official organ of the Soviet Academy of Sciences, which OMNI published in English and marketed in Anglophone countries during its brief and turbulent existence. This new venture took me to Moscow on several occasions. It was an experience that would deeply affect me, filling me with new insights and radically altering some of my perceptions.

•

Strolling in Krasnopresnensky Park, along one of the many elbows of the Moskva River, I saw lovers kissing as they do everywhere when spring alights and lust, like sap, percolates through the veins to flush out winter's numbing grip. Pigeons cooed, pecking at the graveled walkways, geese waddled to-and-fro in search of a crumb or two. Sparrows chirped boisterously in a tongue understood by sparrows from Central Park to the Great Wall of China. Overdressed red-cheeked toddlers frolicked under the half-attentive gaze of stern-faced parents. Huddled on a bench barely wide enough for three, five furrow-faced matriarchs, their heads covered with kerchiefs, knitted furiously in unison as though guided by the hand of an invisible taskmaster.

From a humpbacked bridge, her reflection playing brightly in the pond below, a little girl with a huge white bow in her flaxen hair cast a baitless hook in the fishless water. Poised for a strike that could never be, her eyes fixed on the concentric circles radiating away from the quivering line, she waited. I took her picture from a distance. She may still be there for all I know, undaunted, Quixotically defiant, a symbol of the Russian quest for the impossible dream.

Seventy-three years after the September Revolution, I thought, dreams are especially useful. They help deflect an existence colored by yesterday's nightmares and corrupted by a national psyche that would rather bring back the Bolshevik straight jacket than savor the risks and rewards of freedom. Dreams, when carefully managed, also interrupt reality or, at worst, blunt it for a while. What cannot be prevented must be endured until the nightmares dissolve or return transformed.

Gray and gritty, dusk slowly settled on Moscow like a shroud, accentuating the surreal lifelessness of the Ukraina Hotel rising in the distance from the river's murky waters. Dusk would linger for an hour or so, swallowing shadows and jealously postponing night which -- like all my Moscow nights -- would be spent awaiting dawn. Krasnopresnensky Park was now nearly deserted and I knew that bands of marauding young thugs would soon be on the prowl.

I returned to my room at the Mezhdunarodnaya Hotel -- "Armand Hammer's Folly" -- past the unavoidable "floor lady," a matron of redoubtable girth endowed with a persistent gaze and an inquisitorial manner. I bolted the door behind me, more out of symbolism than practicality, and I settled down to thirty minutes of news on CNN, my only lucid window on the outside world.

Following the news, another slice of the Soviet dream was being dished out for all to feast on, like manna from heaven. Dr. Anatoli Kashpirovski, the alchemical man, miracle maker, healer extraordinaire and perestroika prophet, was about to bend the airwaves, as Uri Geller would a vulgar spoon.

In lifting countless taboos, perestroika, or "restructuring," had reopened the floodgates of credulity among a people noted for their mysticism. A craving for miracles, fortified by mounting social and economic problems, Kashpirovski had galvanized the Russian people, many of whom, haunted by apocalyptic visions, were willing to entrust their fate to psychic sleight of hand for the grandest dream of all -- a cure against despair and hopelessness. This time, perestroika had aimed at far more than meets the eye, the blunted eye, that is, of television viewers who, night after night, were being lulled into insensitivity by the ubiquitous drone of political speechmaking. It may in fact have sought to conquer the wounded Slav soul by seducing its weary optic nerve.

Such seems to have been the inspiration for the launching of a fortnightly prime-time program promising relief against everything from acne to senility, gout to cancer and, the architects of perestroika hoped, destined to shake off inertia and emotional paralysis.

It failed on all counts.

While reformers had quickly understood that social and political changes can help reduce the de-civilizing effects of past repression, no social restructuring, however swift and radical, can eliminate them all. Ultimately, the individual must come to terms with society by adjusting to it. Television, they thought, could act as a therapeutic go-between and foster a re-humanization process.

Positioned to follow the Sunday evening news broadcast, "Time," a mild anesthetic in the bountiful pharmacopoeia of Russian TV soporifics, the program reached 200 million viewers, all of whom anxiously focused their wistful pupils and battered psyches on the soulful eyes of the charismatic hypnotist and healer, Dr. Kashpirovski.

The rationale was deceptively simple.

"There are too many sick people in this country," Kashpirovski had told network executives. "I will speak to them, touch them. I will reshape their egos as I entertain them. What have we got to lose? Our healthcare system is so primitive."

This was an understatement. Hospitals were overcrowded, understaffed. More than two-thirds of the 4,000 rural hospitals lacked hot water and more than one-third had no sewers or indoor plumbing. Despite a thriving black market, pharmaceuticals were scarce.

But the crisis had reached the cities as well. A paucity of modern surgical equipment, including disposable hypodermic syringes and needles, inadequate post-operative facilities and an acute shortage of nurses and technicians had forced the National Institute of Orthopedic Medicine to limit the number of operations it could perform to five or six a year.

"It may take our physicians five thousand years to reach all of our sick and infirm," Kashpirovski had warned. "Only a miracle, only the unshakable belief in a wondrous and heretofore untested oracle can help. I have an antidote against all human ills and suffering, and it's as easy to administer as turning on the TV."

"Think of it as mass-market medicine," Kashpirovski had argued. "Millions of people can seek and be granted a miracle in the privacy of their own home just by looking at their television screens. For free."

In only a few weeks, Kashpirovski had insisted, devastating illnesses, some in their terminal stages, could be cured (or ousted from consciousness). Tumors, cerebral lesions would shrink and disappear. The blind would regain their eyesight. Warts, scars, migraines, insomnia -- "a mere trifle" for Kashpirovski -- would vanish. The bald were promised full heads of hair; the impotent, the libido of Siberian tigers.

Delivered against a bland musical backdrop, Kashpirovski's pronouncements were designed to conquer incredulity, thwart cynicism, overcome doubt and suppress skepticism.

"Whether your eyes are screwed onto the television screen or whether you go about your household chores," he intoned with rapt eloquence, "you are now under my spell. You are now healing yourselves."

Faith in the "mystery of miracles," Kashpirovski urged smugly, "augments my curative powers." He was now the shepherd who forgives an errant flock, a savior who absolves the unbelievers who denigrate him, a redeemer who exonerates the pitiable skeptics who scoff.

The program had none of the tawdry glitter of American televangelism. Absent were the sumptuous stage settings, the cosmic lighting displays, the ethereal vaulted spaces where the heavens themselves are born and from which are echoed the stentorian voices of the self-anointed. Such stratagems do not enhance the mystical experience. Instead, Soviet-gray proletarian-drab reality in its most elemental manifestation helped deepen the urgency of salvation.

His rotund face overflowing from the television screen, his eyes lost in an all-knowing void, exuding serenity and love, Kashpirovski had succeeded in reducing his audience to cataleptic trances and other states of exaltation resembling extreme religious fervor. This would prove to be his undoing.

On the eve of the 11th Congress of the People's Deputies, the Soviets had suddenly been offered a double ration of television therapy: hypnosis on Saturday, to mend the soul; a political sermon on Sunday, to reshape perceptions and behavior. Who knows, the architects of perestroika must have reasoned, perhaps faith in miracles can help us too.

Their benevolence -- or their credulity -- was short-lived. Whereas writers continued to mix metaphors on Sundays in the name of social equilibrium, Kashpirovski, show-biz demi-god and prime-time exorcist, was suddenly taken off the air. In the rich lexicon of Soviet euphemisms, his brand of "healing" was deemed "counterproductive." It may have been more than even perestroika could bargain for. Not unlike Mephisto, Kashpirovski had bartered the souls of his flock against the promise of an afterlife as a TV celebrity.

Born from an ideological crisis, incapable of dusting off the unraveling webs of communism and thus depriving itself of the comforts of a hereafter, perestroika failed to ensure liberty, to kindle abundance, to hasten the end of economic exploitation, to inspire and bring about social equilibrium. The new Russian classes faced an awesome problem: Perestroika, the powerful instrument of social destabilization had not yet learned to become an instrument of social conservation. Thus, miracles like hot running water or uninterrupted telephone service or fully stocked grocery shelves, would continue to be transient phenomena. After all, too much of a good thing will corrupt the national dream. And many will wonder, as the nightmare lingers on, what schism can the malcontent turn to, what shape will idealism and humanism and justice take now that communism is dead.[1]

Mankind is at its own mercy. The stomach growls whereas the heart can only murmur.

---

[1] First published in Penthouse, March 1991.

•

A year later, OMNI suspended its Russian venture. A series of internal convulsions cleared the way for the creation of a tailor-made new post on its editorial staff, that of International Editor. For the first time in more than 30 years I was now doing what I'd always wanted to do, what I knew would bring the best in me. I was traveling, managing my own assignments, writing articles about germ warfare, monasticism, UFOs, voodoo, the physics and poetry of speed, France's newly launched super train, the TGV, the rise and fall of Grenada's former and perennial candidate prime minister, the late Eric Gairy.

•

Later that year, I successfully argued at an editorial round table chaired by OMNI's founder, the late Kathy Keeton, that the future must look beyond space-age gadgets and the search for extraterrestrial intelligence; that vexing social issues such as human suffering at the hands of other humans are as likely to alter the course of history as any wondrous technology or mind-bending science fiction come true.

I remember suggesting that the future is a real place, that posterity has an inalienable right to occupy it and partake in its fruits, and I asserted that in several parts of the world this right was being abrogated by recurrent, state-sponsored orgies of violence, including murder, against society's most vulnerable outcasts -- street children.

"Where is this is happening," Keeton asked.

"In this hemisphere? Brazil and Guatemala," I replied.

"Brazil's too far," retorted the fiscally conservative Keeton. Go to Guatemala."

•

I spent the next three months immersed in research. I also sought counsel from the leading children's rights advocates. UNICEF admitted the problem existed but refused to point fingers. "We can't afford to alienate host countries," explained the Director of Communications. "A confrontational approach to human rights abuses would be counterproductive. We must maintain strict neutrality." The DoC also said something about "the exigencies of cultural relativism."

Eager to glean practical information but in no mood for doubletalk, I countered that "neutrality in the face of hideous crimes is the crassest form of indifference." The DoC said nothing. Perfunctory smile turned to blank, lifeless stare. As for cultural relativism (its leading articulator at the time was Singapore's Lee Kuan Yew, who justified the brutal repression of those who got in his way) I asked her whether this newfangled doctrine was not being foisted on the world "to extenuate, condone and exonerate aberrant behavior, degenerate traditions, rabid ethnocentrism and an orgy of human rights violations." In lieu of an answer, she handed me a large envelope, stood up and bid me farewell. I left her office with a press kit containing success stories of land reclamation, reforestation, water purification, Guinea worm eradication, salt iodination and oral rehydration, all peppered with photos of happy, smiling, well-fed Third World children. (Photos I shot of heavyhearted, starving or mutilated children, which I later offered UNICEF, were rejected on the grounds that "they're apt to traumatize our donors.") The UN's policy of accommodating warlords coddling thugs and overlooking rampant abuses, apparently, has no effect on donors.

Save The Children, which, like UNICEF, does not work with homeless minors, also conceded that street children were being habitually persecuted in Guatemala, Honduras and Mexico by vigilantes and agents of the state, but refused to share useful intelligence or offer assistance in the field.

Christian Children's' Fund declined to be interviewed and thwarted efforts to visit one of their sites on "logistical grounds." Both Save The Children and Christian Children's Fund would later be embroiled in major scandals.

Childhope, an obscure UNICEF adjunct, provided me with some data but used the opportunity to upbraid *"rogue organizations that, in pursuit of justice, interfere with the internal affairs of sovereign nations."* It was precisely such a "rogue" organization, Casa Alianza, the Latin American branch of Covenant House that would provide the unvarnished tutorial elements I needed and shepherd me through the abyss where Central American street children live and die.

Nothing could have prepared me for what I was to see and feel that first night in Guatemala City. Retold in an essay entitled, *Witch Hunt in the Land of Eternal Spring*, and published in OMNI magazine, this dizzying descent into a nether world of terror and suffering would constitute a turning point in my career. It would lead to a keen and sustained interest in Central America and a deepening involvement in human rights issues that would eventually wane and cease. Dedication to a cause must be measured against the results it produces. After twelve years in the belly of the beast, I realized that I was powerless against corruptible individuals (the politicians) and that I'd stopped fretting about people who don't fight back. It was no longer my battle. Others would step in, also brimming with idealism, until their fanciful optimism was slowly eroded by reality -- as had been mine. The "struggle" will continue I'm sure -- with the same short-term triumphs and intractable defeats. In the grander scheme of things, nothing will ever change. It's not that I didn't hear the cries or see the tears; I did. It's not that I was insensitive to injustice; I wasn't. It's that I'd exhausted my capacity to care.

When will goes to sleep, instinct keeps watch.

YES, THEY SHOOT CHILDREN

Dawn rises behind Guatemala City's 16th-century cathedral, flushing the nave with shafts of spectral radiance and suffusing the marble altar and colonnades, crystal chandeliers, richly carved gilt pulpit and solid mahogany pews with a celebration of light over the forces of darkness.

For Jorge, sunrise heralds the start of another perilous journey. He'd just spent the night in the fetid culvert that girds the cathedral's flanks, drowsing into a thin, turbulent sleep, one eye trained against the creeping shadows, his ears alert to any sound louder than his heartbeat. Normally, Jorge beds down with his friends Pedro and Felipe under a pile of filthy rags, sharing scraps of food pilfered from an outdoor market or recovered from a garbage pit. Normally, they huddle like newborn pups, seeking warmth, sharing a tin or two of cobbler's glue until the noxious fumes release them from the grips of hunger, cold and fear. But these are not normal times. Beatings, torture, rape and extrajudicial executions have been on the rise in Guatemala, and Jorge, Pedro and Felipe decided to split up for a while, to disperse, to find safety not in numbers but in seclusion and stealth, like hunted animals.

Jorge's eyes are red -- his pupils dilated, the eyelids puffy and pasty. A yellowed cigarette butt dangles from a blistered lower lip. He reeks of sweat and urine and shoe glue.

"Un quetzal, Señor, dame un quetzal por favor," he ventures. I stop and dig into my pockets, averting his eyes. He has that look that vagabonds and madmen convey that is best unheeded, unacknowledged, a liquid gaze in which float the cadavers of hope, will and purpose. I surrender all my change. It isn't much. I mumble an apology and walk away. Jorge follows me, ambling along sideways like a crab, tugging at my sleeve. He wants to shake my hand. I pat a grimy cheek, drawing a nit-infested head toward me. Jorge puts his arms around my waist. Pity renders me speechless.

Jorge dries a sea of bitter tears then bursts into joyless laughter. He blows into a small plastic bag lined with a sticky amber substance -- Resistol, a brand of cobbler's glue -- and avidly breathes in the caustic fumes. A flood of words gushes forth. I don't understand everything he says but his expression speaks volumes about the pain, the hopelessness, the cruel absurdity of life.

Jorge is eleven. Pedro and Felipe are twelve and nine, respectively. They all look half their age. Life is cheap. They may never grow up. Or old.

•

"The Reverend Billy Graham is too busy to comment on this issue." -- **The Billy Graham Evangelistic Association.**

•

Eyewitness accounts and graphic photographs shot by this writer, confirm that *niños de la calle* -- street children -- are routinely abducted, beaten, burned with cigarettes, subjected to mock executions, sexually assaulted and routinely slain by members of the national police, urban constabularies and private security guards. Some had their ears sliced off (they heard too much). Others had their tongues ripped out (they snitched). Others yet had their eyes gouged out, ostensibly because they'd witnessed things that put the cops at risk, before the merciful coup de grace was applied, generally a blow to the head or a bullet to the base of the neck. They were then heaved into the countless ravines that gird the city's shantytowns, stinking chasms littered with garbage and human waste, and haunted by feral dogs and desperadoes.

While the 1980s witnessed dramatic political changes that culminated in minor victories for human rights, violations continued to defile a world already crippled by war and disfigured by chronic poverty, misery and disease.

"Human rights have taken a back seat to trade and diplomatic concerns," Amnesty International reported in 1991, "and become the casualty of political expediency."

In Central America, a region traumatized by social and political turmoil, shaken by wild swings from dictatorship to anarchy and back, human rights violations are legion. And in Guatemala, a country kneaded by volcanic and seismic upheaval, where lush mountains and precipices and fertile escarpments join to create a lush landscape of extraordinary beauty, crimes against humanity often eclipse the excesses recorded in other parts of the world.

Congressman Jim McDermott (D., WA), whom I first met in Guatemala, described U.S. foreign policy in Central America as "a disaster. We've had a long and shameless history of picking the wrong sides, of aiding and abetting despotic regimes."

•

Promised anonymity and baited by a five-dollar bill, a Guatemala City cop told me that "crime has been spiraling out of control. There are more and more street children. They've been giving us a lot of trouble. They're bad for business, bad for tourism, bad for our national image."

"Bad enough to kill?"

"We do what we must. We have orders."

I'd heard this excuse in another time and place.

It is this bureaucratic insolence that has time and again helped block investigations into an upwelling of human rights violations, including the assassination of several prominent Guatemalan centrist politicians, lawyers, human rights activists, journalists and children's rights advocates. Anthropologist Myrna Elizabeth Mack Chang was murdered on orders from a high-ranking member of the Guatemalan Army. U.S. citizen Michael Devine was abducted, tortured and killed by a group of uniformed men.

According to a U.S. State Department source:

"...evidence indicates that Guatemalan security forces and civil patrols commit, with almost total impunity, most of the major human rights abuses. These include extra-judicial killings, torture and disappearance of, among others, human rights activists, trade unionists, indigenous people and street children.... Security forces are virtually never held accountable for these crimes. With few exceptions, the government has failed to investigate, detain and prosecute perpetrators of extrajudicial and politically motivated killings. It has also been

unwilling to investigate cases aggressively if the military were thought to be involved. It is likely that military officials also shield lower-ranking personnel involved in the killings. Approximately 400 policemen were discharged for a variety of abuses, including corruption."

The ex-policemen did not idle for very long; they were swiftly resettled as bodyguards or given various private security assignments -- and continued to carry guns supplied by the U.S. and Israel. No one protested.

The reign of terror that gripped Guatemala had also thwarted probes into the brutal abduction, torture and gang-rape by Guatemalan police of Sister Dianna Ortiz, an American nun working with children. ABC's Diane Sawyer eloquently told Ortiz's story on Prime Time Live.

•

Guatemala City is a dusty, noisy metropolis that has grown and spilled over its outer limits, physically and economically. Like a festering sore, far from the opulent *estancias* and chic town villas where the well-to-do live in splendid isolation, the city has spread, tentacle-like, into pestilential slums, along sunlit ridges and down the slopes of dank garbage-strewn canyons where barefoot children, vultures, feral cats and dogs share a precarious existence.

It was in one such slum named Limón that thirteen-year-old Angela agreed to meet me. With a price on her head, stalked by the policeman who'd raped her and threatened to kill her, Angela was moving from hovel to hovel, hiding during the day, earning a few *quetzales* at night in the arms of strangers. I found her sitting at the edge of a cot, her feet and calves pitted with insect bites and scarred by skin lesions, in a bunker with bare cement walls under a leaky sheet metal roof.

On the streets since she was eight, Angela saw her mother murdered by the woman who now lived with her father. She started drinking and sniffing glue when she was ten. A man raped her when she was eleven. She was placed in a shelter where an older girl molested her. Caught stealing trinkets from a street vendor, she was dragged by a policeman into a cul-de-sac and raped. The officer then shoved the barrel of his gun into her mouth and, smiling, threatened to kill her if she "squealed." Angela staggered into a hospital and told her story. A formal complaint was filed on her behalf and forensic evidence submitted to a local judge. The policeman, who was identified three days later, was never charged.

In one corner, under the pallid rays of a bare 40-watt bulb swarming with flies and moths, stood a table littered with rags and old newspapers and on which rested a garishly painted plaster figurine, a Madonna and child whose introspective gaze conveyed a trance-like stupor. Every now and then, almost mechanically, Angela cast a forlorn glance at the holy icon, perhaps for reassurance. But in her large brown eyes all I saw were false hopes and broken dreams.

Outside, the vultures, the ever-present vultures, had resumed their abominable vigil, gliding overhead like black-winged demons at a Witches' Sabbath, awaiting death, smelling it, tasting it. Surely I reflected, even God must find Limón a very bitter fruit.

•

For most of Guatemala's street children, the nightmare begins at conception, an act endorsed and sanctified by the Church and very soon trivialized by the postpartum experience. Life thereafter has neither meaning nor value. Aloof and ethereal, Guatemala's Catholic Church has the solid backing of some mighty friends who have demonstrated greater obedience to doctrine than ethics. Continuing to bow to interests stretching from the Vatican to powerful Christian right-wing cells with close ties to the murkiest segments of U.S. intelligence and paramilitary communities, Guatemala's Church has little time for street children. While the Church cannot be directly linked to the killings, it bears a burden of guilt by omission -- it denies women access to birth control and abortion, it censures the teaching of safe sex, forbids the use of contraceptives, and demonstrates gross indifference toward the causes and consequences of overpopulation. Because of its affinity for conservative politics and its support of the military, the Church is also guilty by association.

While a number of activist priests and nuns were executed in Guatemala and elsewhere in Latin America -- front-line soldiers are always in the line of fire -- princes of the Church had been immune to such dangers. That was to change with the 1980 assassination of Salvadoran Archbishop Oscar Romero by CIA-trained Col. Roberto d'Aubuisson during the U.S.-backed "Contra" war and, eighteen years later, with the slaying of Guatemalan Bishop Juan Gerardi, a maverick cleric who had accused the military of horrific human rights abuses. There is strong circumstantial evidence that high-ranking members of Guatemala's U.S.-trained military intelligence apparatus, and supervised by then President Alvaro Arzu, were directly implicated in the crime.

These tragic exceptions notwithstanding, the Church's actions, or lack thereof, on behalf of its flock, the company it kept, the tenacity with which it wielded control, the arrogance of its double standards, all speak louder than words and all too sadly point to what must be perceived as a depraved indifference to human life.

> *"His Eminence has asked me to inform you that he has no time to comment on the issues addressed in your article."* -- **Father Whalen, spokesman for [New York's] John Cardinal O'Connor.**

•

This callous indifference was replayed when, not to be outdone, Guatemala's first and second ladies -- both touted as ardent supporters of children's rights, both blue bloods and devout Catholics -- failed to appear for a prearranged interview with this writer. No apology or explanation was ever issued.

"There is no justice in Guatemala," a fellow journalist commented on the eve of my return to the U.S. "Kids are abandoned by their families, persecuted by the State, rejected by society. Ironically, it is those most apt to help cleanse the 'sins that cry to heaven for vengeance' -- oppression of the poor and the orphans -- whose hearts have turned to stone."

Two crossed rifles with fixed bayonets and two crossed boarding sabers flanked by two olive branches on a field of double blue and white adorn Guatemala's coat of arms. A nation of contrasts, it continues to live by the rifle. Sabers keep on rattling. Both are trained against easy targets. Inexplicably, as if guided by an irresistible urge to self-destruct, Guatemala is immolating its children. It may be depriving itself of a future as well.

•

A week after my return to New York, I learned that a shelter for children in Guatemala City had been peppered with machine-gun fire. The unidentified assailants, *"four heavily armed men driving a dark blue BMW threatened to kill the director, the staff and the children."*

Several days later, I was also informed that a seven-year-old street boy had been beaten to death by police. His head had been so severely disfigured that positive identification could not be made. That same day, a fifteen-year-old boy was dragged by police beyond city limits where he was savagely beaten and burned over 90 percent of his body, including his genitals.

I called Tom Strook, then the U.S. ambassador to Guatemala, on the phone.

"Tom, I need a statement from you, something that echoes your personal optic and mirrors U.S. policy on the subject. Make it strong, please."

"Will do. I'll fax you something first thing in the morning." The next day, Strook's offering was waiting on my desk. It read:

> *"The depraved conditions in which Guatemala's street children live are, unfortunately, too reminiscent of situations in many other parts of the world."*

I reread the anemic statement and nearly threw up. I telephoned Strook and asked him for an elaboration, anything that demonstrated a virile stand by the U.S. on a problem that was causing outrage around the world.

"That's the best I can do."

I wove Strook's masterpiece of diplomatic doublespeak into an article, verbatim, and let the chips fall where they may.

•

News of the bludgeoning death of the Financial Times correspondent in Guatemala also reached me at that time. He'd been probing local connections to the Bank of Credit and Commerce International scandal. This brought to more than 50 the number of journalists killed in the line of duty in Guatemala since 1978.

•

Ah, the press. What strange and wondrous tidings it will impart when it is not busy manufacturing the truth or manipulating events. It seems like yesterday. One morning as I rode Metro North on my way to work, I read the following headline in the Wall Street Journal:

"General Media to cut 120 jobs."

OMNI was folding, moving to Greensboro, North Carolina. Other properties in Bob Guccione's shrinking publishing empire were "restructuring," "retrenching" and "consolidating." I'd lost my job. Had I not fortuitously picked up a copy of the Wall Street Journal at the Stratford, Connecticut train station, might I still be blissfully ignorant of my fate? I often toy with *what ifs*. But being skeptical of everything I read in the papers, I waited until I reached the office to confirm that the news of my demise had not been exaggerated. My professional obituary was replayed as I crossed the threshold. I was given the rest of the day to pack up and vacate the premises. Many of those who shared my fate were in shock or in tears.

"You must try not to take this personally," said the human relations director, who didn't lose her job.

"Really? I'm pushing 50, my whole world is caving in under me, I'm losing my livelihood, possibly forever, and I'm supposed to be relieved because this castration is not 'personal'?"

"Who knows, perhaps if the economy picks up...."

Sure. Good journalists are expendable when the chips are down but, after all, we're the "schmucks with typewriters" that publishers can't quite do without.

Writers face all sorts of occupational hazards: a highly volatile work market, a fickle public -- it's publish or perish -- long nights spent facing blank sheets of paper (now a blank computer screen) merciless deadlines, heartless editors who get paid to slash and burn precious prose and low, very low pay.

We live in a society that scorns culture, resents and mocks intellectualism and abhors free thought. The joy of reading has been replaced by the rapture of catatonic stupor in front of giant TV screens. Programming is shrinking, commercials are multiplying in number and duration. The object is to ensnare more viewers, trick throngs of gullible consumers into hoarding the sponsors' products. In print journalism, photos are getting larger while text is shrinking to the bare essentials. Publications are dying left and right like cicadas in the first chill of a late summer night, their ephemeral lives cut short by declining circulation, dwindling advertising revenues and, in OMNI's case, sundry stratagems engineered to prevent owner-publishers from having to relinquish the opulent lifestyles to which they are accustomed.

And so, a thing of beauty, OMNI, the exquisitely designed and trendy futurist vehicle in which the likes of Isaac Asimov, Ray Bradbury and Carl Sagan had taken an ever wider audience to the far reaches of the cosmos, died in the spring of 1995. Older, richer, bored perhaps, Bob Guccione bled the magazine by committing it to the cold regions of cyberspace. It continued to orbit for a while, its propulsion system inert, now an aimless, lifeless, unidentifiable object that would be mourned by the generation it had transported to the frontiers of knowledge and the outer reaches of imagination.

And, once again, I found my way back to the far end of a long unemployment line.

Like happiness, misery arrives uninvited and lingers on.

OUR DAILY BREAD

In the beginning, comes inexperience. Armed with little more than snippets of lore, a zest for life and a spirit corrupted neither by worldliness or maturity, my friend's son, Eli, soon to graduate from college, was looking for work. Finding a job that harmonized with his grades, aspirations, self-view and crass earthly needs, wouldn't be easy. He lacked "experience."

"Take heart," I reassured him, cynicism and life's lessons guiding my words. Inexperience is the gateway to "under-qualification." The under-qualified always find work. They're the backbone of the labor force, the mid-level cadres, the silent and unseen legions who energize America's economic engine, the multitudes willing to be consigned to a life of mediocrity just to survive. (Employers consider "under-qualified" any 22-year-old first-time job-seeker who doesn't have a Ph.D. and at least 10 years' experience and/or anyone unwilling to start at below-subsistence wages "for the privilege" of forking a goodly percentage of their earnings to the IRS).

"Work hard," I told Eli, "and in 20 years you too can become 'over-qualified.' (Over-qualification is a common malady that afflicts 40-something job seekers. It's also a code word for "we think you're terrific but because you seem to need us more than we need you, we'll play mind games with you and offer you a salary we know is both shamefully low and inconsistent with your skills and experience.")

Mergers, consolidations, "downsizing," the ever-popular government "reductions in force" and hiring freezes are the trendiest pretexts for denying an over-qualified person a job. This artifice also allows an enterprise to accelerate production, cut down on overhead and protect that mighty profit margin. Over-qualification is a status narrowly averted by faking under-qualification and/or dyeing one's hair a shade darker. Left untreated, over-qualification leads to un-employability. An unemployable person is entitled to great reverence, but no paycheck.

As we perused the want ads, I taught Eli to decipher the buzzwords. Job descriptions are cleverly crafted paragons of equivocation draped in minimalist prose. Unlike Haiku, whose exquisite simplicity condenses an idea to its irreducible essence in a few words, want ads lack both the lyricism and the poetry of truth.

I offered a few telling examples -- suitably decoded:

Ideal candidate: Mythical creature invented by employers.

Highly organized: Boss is inept.

Bright and eager: Naive and stupid.

Creative: Willing to bend to crass conformity and forego recognition for your talents, which in no way can be allowed to eclipse those of your superiors.

Dynamic: Human dynamo; unimaginative automaton.

Aggressive: Ball-buster; martinet-in-training; middle-management recruit.

Self-starter: Swim or sink.

Team player: Self-effacing milksop ready to sacrifice personal growth for the good of an enterprise that doesn't give a shit whether you live or die.

Cheerful and hardworking: Witless beast of burden.

Flexible: Willing to be tied in knots.

Strong interpersonal skills: Shifty, manipulative brownnoser.

Must work well under pressure: Must have the constitution of a mule, the temperament of a saint.

Detail-oriented: Must not see the forest from the trees.

Personable: Meek and unassuming.

Entry level position: No-exit career.

Exciting work: Excruciatingly dull.

Bright future: Somber present.

Excellent opportunity: Risky gamble.

Comprehensive salary: Colossal exaggeration.

Generous benefits: Bottom-of-the-barrel healthcare benefits, standard legal holidays and the tedium of an obligatory annual loyalty oath disguised as a summer picnic or Christmas party.

Good opportunity for growth: If you're under 21, you can expect to grow another inch or two.

Outstanding opportunity: Stepping stone to nowhere.

Will train: Will domesticate.
Leading company: Lackluster performance.
Multinational corporation: parochial policies.
Pleasant working conditions: Cramped quarters.
Modern facility: Claustrophobic windowless cinder block bunker.
Conveniently located: Decrepit downtown dungeon.

Eli got the message. Determined to avoid the humiliation and pitfalls of job hunting, he stopped looking for work. He stayed home and insisted that his parents provide him with room and board by arguing that he didn't ask to be born in the first place.

●

It was at UNICEF, where I worked for nearly two years as a consultant, that I mastered newspeak, the language of deceit and obfuscation. I'd been hired to revamp the organization's worldwide media network and supervise a group of stringers who reported regularly on various community development projects in Africa, Asia, Latin America and the Indian subcontinent. Their dispatches, filed for later consumption by donors, were, for the most part, dull technical reports written in the "feel-good" propagandistic style that UNICEF had adopted. Hidden in terse jargon about irrigation, water purification, multiple recipes for mango soup, tsetse fly eradication campaigns, mother's milk and infant diarrhea, were keywords of hope and success designed to mollycoddle the donors, most of whom never venture far enough from the safety and comfort of their stylish existence to be splattered by the stinking foulness of truth. Photos accompanying the reports invariably focused on smiling children against backgrounds of squalor that the art department deftly airbrushed before publication. Whereas I knew from experience that vast numbers of Third World children live in extreme poverty and face a barren world of abridged opportunities, UNICEF doggedly candy-coated reality for the benefit of its sponsors who, I'd been warned, have no stomach for nauseating reality.

"Every word you write, every gesture you make in public as a UNICEF representative must be consciously honed to *extract* (sic) donor-dollars. You must accentuate the positive, soften the negative.

'Problems' are *welcome challenges*; obstacles are *valuable opportunities* that UNICEF assesses, strategizes and solves with the generous support of its benefactors. Your responsibility is to help keep the money coming. Sob stories prejudice our fund-raising efforts."

So had decreed Edgar Koh, my supervisor. Koh was a petty pen-pusher from Singapore who lavished praise on his compatriot, strongman Lee Kuan Yew, and affected his stiff, despotic stance. Koh seemed quite content to spend his life behind closed doors neatly shifting stacks of paper from one side of his desk to another, reading dull U.N. reports that cost thousands of dollars to produce and that no one read, and talking to his wife on the phone a dozen times a day or more. He knew that a formidable bureaucracy, erected on an elaborate scaffolding of arcane symbioses and mutually-profitable alliances shielded him from serious scrutiny. Though he sported a *veddy propah* British accent, his writing and editing skills, I discovered, were less than sterling. He delighted in rearranging everything I wrote, adding or deleting punctuation marks without regard to syntax and inserting fractured or irrelevant clauses. His tightly scripted corrections, made in red ink, were gratuitous and excessive but I said nothing. I understood he was justifying his existence and, in the process, bolstering his sense of self-worth. In rare moments of informality -- generally a few minutes before five in the afternoon -- he would call me into his office and recount the exploits of some noble if obscure Chinese ancestor. I countered with great solemnity that I too was a blueblood whose forefathers included King David and King Solomon. Koh greeted such disclosures with noticeable disdain.

His boss, Mehr Khan, the Pakistani Director of Communications, was tight-lipped and cranky, except among her entourage of Pakistani flunkies she'd hired and installed in various key positions to maintain a perpetual motion of paper pushing. She was disdainful of Europeans and harbored deep feelings of antipathy against Jews, a proclivity, I would quickly learn, shared by many cadres in this den of anti-Western agitation. Koh yielded to Khan in all executive decisions; Khan upheld all of Koh's verdicts, however flawed. I was earning good money, an incentive that, for a while, tempered a growing sense of frustration and subdued the rage that was welling up in me. I would not contain myself for long.

Self-confidence is a suit of armor; self-importance is a paper hat.

•

I'd just returned from Grenada, the "Spice Island," one of the jewels of the Caribbean where I'd spent two weeks, doing research and getting much-needed rest. The assignment: *"children in especially difficult circumstances"* -- another UNICEF weasel term for abject misery. The targets: neglect, physical and sexual abuse, malnutrition, primitive or nonexistent sanitation, marginal health care. The culprits: poverty, illiteracy, superstition, family violence, alcoholism, drug addiction, teen pregnancies, a rising tide of single mothers, runaway inflation, corruption and government apathy.

Such are the demons that haunt paradise, for Grenada is just that, a heavenly golden speck rising from a sparkling turquoise sea at the southern tip of an archipelago of incredible beauty, dominated by lush, mist-shrouded peaks, ringed by sandy beaches and bathed by gentle, cooling breezes. That is the Grenada most tourists know. Descending upon the island by the jet-load, they check into posh hotels armed with golf clubs, tennis rackets and scuba gear. Transfixed by the idyllic setting, lulled into semi-comatose bliss by radiant sunshine and daily transfusions of nutmeg-laced rum punches, they jet back home sporting Hollywood tans and laden with trinkets they will trash a few days later. The song of the trade winds, the feverish mid-air dance of the hummingbirds drinking from the buttercups, the symphony of colors, the heady aroma of saffron and mace, orchid and passion flower -- all but silence the anguished cries, mask the tears, fan away the stench of poverty. Paradise, I'd discovered ten years earlier as I bummed around between Grenada and Barbados, is a nice place to visit but you wouldn't want to live there if you're an unwanted child. For if you are, chances are you suffer from some form of malnutrition, mostly a deficiency in micronutrients such as iron and vitamin A. Chances are that physical and sexual abuse will forever scar your body and soul. Chances are that child labor and parental scorn toward education will shut the doors to all but the most menial jobs. Chances are that low self-esteem and a craving for love and attention denied by abusive or indifferent kinfolk will lead to unwanted pregnancies among young girls, homosexual prostitution among young boys. With any luck, a life of servitude awaits you as a domestic or day laborer. If your luck runs out, or if jobs become scarce, you may wind up combing the silver beaches of your beautiful island in search of visitors willing to buy -- out of compassion, not necessity -- coconuts, black coral, shimmering seashells, perhaps a nickel bag or two of freshly harvested marijuana. And if despair and hopelessness finally rob you of the will to live, as police reports reveal with alarming frequency, for some children suicide may be the choice exit out of childhood. Marked, stigmatized, the rest will reach adulthood, strapped with an inheritance of poverty, neglect and abuse not of their own choosing, and which they are destined to pass on to succeeding generations.

•

Mehr Khan perused my report. She was livid.
"What are you trying to do," she fumed, "scare off our donors?"
"I told the truth."
"That's not the point. How many times were you told to filter the truth and focus on the positive?"
"Trust me, I did both."
"You did not. You went out of your way to paint a canvas of filth and gore."
"I painted what my senses recorded. I could have said a lot more."
"You should have consulted with our local representative and let him fill you in."
"Your agent in St. George's is busy sailing his sloop in some blue lagoon between Carriacou and Petite Martinique. He expressed no interest in my assignment."
"That's a lie!"
"Call him. I have it on good authority that he attempted to muscle in on a local orphanage and turn into a cash cow for UNICEF. And that's the truth."
Mehr Khan stood up, cutting a formidable figure in her purple sari,

her bare midriff jiggling like Jell-O, her lips trembling, her black eyes aflame.

"Take back everything you said, you hear," she shrieked. "Now."

I turned around and walked out.

Edgar Koh, Khan's yes-man, had not yet read the piece. That did not prevent him from excoriating me publicly for going over his head and denouncing my work as a "paradigm" (another favorite in a rich lexicon of U.N. catchwords) of "defiance toward mandated rules of reporting."

"If the truth intimidates your donors, so be it. I can't stare horror in the face and remain unmoved."

"You will do as you're told." Koh was red with rage.

I laughed. "We're not in Pakistan or Singapore. I won't be treated like a coolie."

"Enough!" Koh slammed his fist on his desk.

I looked at Koh. His eyes were bulging. His face was flushed. The muscles on his neck were distended and throbbing. His lips were twisted in a menacing snarl. He reminded me of a toad. In a moment of excruciating clarity of purpose, egged on by months of exasperation, I exploded.

"You know what, take this job and shove it. And tell Mehr Khan to go fuck herself." I turned around, picked up my jacket and headed down the long corridor toward the elevator.

Koh screamed. "Come back this instant, you hear! How dare you leave."

"Try and stop me."

I kept walking, took the elevator, landed in the lobby and calmly exited the building. I breathed deeply the oxygenated air of salvation. Elation, sustained by anger and pent-up resentment, carried me through the evening. I was riding the crest of a cathartic high. With morning came reality. I was out of a job – again.

A PRAYER FOR AN INFIDEL

"*Bis du a yid?*" -- are you a Jew? -- queried a bearded, bushy-browed giant clad in black as he unfurled his prayer shawl with the bravura of a bullfighter testing a new cape. Accustomed since childhood to treat such indiscretion on a need-to-know basis, especially at 38,000 feet above sea level on a Tel Aviv-bound El Al flight from New York -- and just as I was about to surrender to sleep -- I replied:

"*Far wus fregsde?*" -- why do you ask? -- mimicking my father who always answered impertinent questions in the interrogative.

"*Kenst du daven?*" -- do you know how to pray? -- he asked, now noticeably less impressed with my potential.

"*Warum, ist der pilot krank?*" -- why, is the pilot ill? -- I shot back (still in the interrogative), having by now exhausted all my Yiddish.

A scowl of contempt twisting his patriarchal expression, the bearded giant snapped his prayer shawl and cloaked himself in it as if to abjure this arrogant infidel, this fake Jew who would rather daydream or sleep than exalt deity. Turning to face the emergency exit where great devotions take place, he began bobbling into prayer.

●

David, the gift-shop clerk at my Jerusalem hotel, insisted that God is dead, immolated by man, his creator. He had stumbled upon this epiphany by means he deemed too complex to reveal. Mystified, I egged him on. He waved me away with the back of his hand, unconcerned by the curiosity he'd elicited, an all-knowing scowl twisting his handsome face. Perhaps he didn't trust me. I'd spent all too little on the sacred objects, Jewish and Christian, he displayed side by side with casual neutrality. Or did my choice of a miniature book of Psalms (for my friend Ron, a Baptist minister) and the olive wood rosary (for Tante Esther, who believes in nothing but collects talismans representing every sect known to man) elevate David's disdain for religious pluralism to near-nausea?

"I'm Sabra," he proclaimed with a defiance characteristic of those who take pride in circumstances over which they have no control. "So was my father, grandfather, great-grandfather and great-great-grandfather," he added, drawing four lines in the air, one for each branch in his family tree.

I marveled at his self-assurance, envious of the vigor of his genealogy, I, the wandering Jew, I the son, grandson and great-grandson of nomads who traded one hostile European fiefdom for another, I, the stateless citizen of the world who lived in suitcases during the better part of my childhood, I, who learned how to deny being a Jew in half a dozen languages and narrowly missed burning at the stake for having had no say in my own heredity.

"Does being Sabra offer immunity from faith," I asked without a trace of irony.

David smiled with condescension. "You don't understand."

I offered David an opportunity to elaborate. After all, I'd asked for nothing but the privilege of buying some of his wares. He now owed me one direct, unabbreviated, unambiguous reply.

"O. K. Please explain."

But business was brisk and an American woman with magenta tresses peering over rhinestone-studded heart-shaped eyeglasses and donning a sweatshirt proclaiming, *"I bathed in the Dead Sea and lived"* entered the shop, saving David the trouble of splitting hair.

I paid for the trinkets. David dropped them both into a single paper bag. I found such promiscuity refreshing. And I retreated to the no-man's land of the hotel lounge.

•

It was time for another cup of coffee but acrid tendrils of cigarette smoke wafted in my direction, stabbing at my throat and digging deep into my sinuses. I gagged, coughed, sputtered and reflexively sought out the source of this befouling onslaught. Nostrils flaring, I turned my head every which way, craning my neck up and down like a periscope in enemy waters. Aware of my discomfiture, a kindly old man asked, "Nu, vat's de madder?" Touched by his solicitude, grateful for the opportunity to fume at the offensive exhalations and counting on his sympathy, I broadcast my predicament.

"I'm allergic to smoke...."

Grandfatherly smile turned to grimace.

"Vell, maybe you should have your coffee sent up to your room. Smokers have rights, you know."

Retrieving the reeking ordnance from under the table where he'd kept it hidden from view and bringing it up to his lips with deliberate slowness, the old man took a long, deep puff and proceeded to quote from obscure biblical sources, punctuating every maxim by shaking a saintly -- if nicotine-yellowed -- digit in my direction. Oration had turned to hectoring. He dug up precedents from a vast glossary of aphorisms and drew Talmudic parallels just for the occasion.

"It is written that...."

No cup of coffee, however tempting, was worth this lecture, so I threw the gauntlet.

"It is written that smokers prevent non-smokers from enjoying the right not to inhale their poisonous emanations," I offered, this time in the declarative, and boldly venturing into the epigrammatic by fabricating my own common law.

There was hurt and disappointment in the sage's limpid blue eyes. There was also rancor and a damning gleam characteristic of the rebuked sermonizer.

•

Rachel expressed an unflinching belief in the supremacy of the Jewish people, in their cosmic destiny among the peoples of planet Earth. Hers was not so much a theistic view of Judaism as an unflagging conviction that Jews are genetically preprogrammed for greatness. The zeal with which she articulated her views was nothing short of messianic. Her eyes gleamed with redemptory ecstasy. She barred the door of her Ben Yehuda Street souvenir emporium with her corpulence, denying me a hasty getaway and thrusting a shot glass of Kiddush wine into my protesting hand. She switched to English.

"Come, it's time to praise the Lord." A travel-worn gray beard, crumpled trousers, a cotton-kneed, jet-lagged gait and eyes red with fatigue had given me away. Or was it the camera casually slung over one shoulder?

"Why are you assuming I speak English," I replied in fluent Hebrew. You could have tried Japanese, you know. After all, this *is* a Minolta," I added, feinting annoyance and perilously mixing interrogative and declarative.

Rachel overlooked -- or failed to appreciate -- the diversity of my rhetorical skills and proceeded to cross-examine me, this time with the seriousness of a prophet in search of disciples.

"So, you're from New York, aren't you?"

"Well, I'm from Paris but I live in New York."

"What brings you to Israel?"

"I'm researching an article on the Dead Sea Scrolls."

"You don't say. Anyway, listen, when you get back to New York you must go to Brooklyn and see the *Rebbe* and seek his blessings."

"The *Rebbe*?"

Rachel mentioned a name. "Who else," she snapped with a sidelong glance of consternation and suspicion. "Surely you've heard of him, haven't you? You must go to him, he'll...."

Ah, yes, I mused, the holy man who distributes crisp dollar bills to an adoring army of *shnorrers* [spongers], the would-be Messiah who recites sententious maxims disguised as unintelligible grunts.

"He'll energize you," Rachel exhorted. "He's a pious and saintly Jew. He performs miracles."

"If he is so saintly and pious a Jew, shouldn't he be performing miracles in Israel instead of Williamsburg," I ventured, risking and ultimately earning the bile of this tenacious missionary.

"You wouldn't be a *Satmar* by any chance?" Rachel squinted with mistrust, probing my eyes for telltale Transylvanian treachery. Finding none, she focused on the small square and compasses pin adorning my lapel.

"What's that," she asked with unmasked ferocity.

"I'm a Freemason," I said curtly, in no mood for syntactic variety.

"A Freemason! *Oy gevalt!*" Rachel's eyes rolled with anger and disbelief. Her mouth arched with disgust. "Blasphemer! Irreligious libertine!" She yanked the glass of sacramental wine from my hand and threw me out of the store.

One of the symptoms of stupidity is an overabundance of preconceived notions.

•

No sooner ejected from Rachel's emporium than I was accosted by Menachem, a Philadelphia Greek Jew and self-avowed born-again Christian sent to Israel to convert Jews to a newfangled brand of Christianity that postulates the worship of Jesus through Judaism (sic). My father, who coined many a colorful simile in his time, might have likened this swindle to having one's hand down the cookie jar and one's soul up in heaven. But being a gynecologist, and with an earthiness characteristic of his peasant origins, he would have given the comparison a somewhat coarser texture.

I looked at Menachem, feeling compassion more than annoyance. Only faith in the infallibility of his own convictions, I told myself, prevented him from grasping the enormity of such ministry. But who was I to question, let alone contradict him? I'd long given up reasoning with the unreasonable, ceased debating the unarguable, vowed never to get sucked in religious diatribe. It was not easy. Gullibility and benevolence ensnare the perplexed and kindhearted alike. Often disguised as curiosity, or mistaken for self-quest, their tender traps yield fresh victims at every turn. Hadn't I once been held captive in my own home by a squad of smooth-tongued but unimaginative Jehovah's Witnesses? Didn't the Hare Krishna buttonhole me and thrust unsolicited literature in my hands? Hadn't the Moonies tried to recruit me? Wasn't I badgered into buying a volume of the Zohar by a commando team of Kabbalah proselytes operating in the main concourse at New York's Grand Central Station?

•

Back in New York, unpacked and listless, I collapsed on the sofa and closed my eyes. I'd alighted from what seemed like a dizzying trek through a storm-buffeted kaleidoscope. Jumbled scenes from that journey danced in my head like the shredded vestiges of a dream -- Jerusalem basking in a timeless golden radiance, the stone house where I'd lived forty years earlier, the eucalyptus tree I'd climbed, now dwarfed it seemed, the eerie absence of the boys and girls I'd befriended, the long, winding road to Jericho, the shimmering Dead Sea, the ghostly ruins of the Essene settlement of Qumran, the inscrutable stillness of the mountains of Moab in the distance. I remembered the pious Jew on the plane, replayed Rachel's invincible exuberance and Menachem's wacky ministry, envied David's imperturbable godlessness. I found myself wondering, in the interrogative, naturally, what it had all been about. A distant voice whispered: *"The truth is nothing but the loudest and most persuasive of two opposing arguments."* It's around that time that I began to toy with the notion that any assumption, scheme or system that is anchored in the certitude of its own infallibility and which, through skewed logic, considers all other assertions, schemes or systems to be flawed, must be invalid. But, I reasoned, in the land of the blind, the one-eyed are king.

Lost in the fog of my post-travel blues, I was suddenly reminded of the compactness of time. I'd expanded resources I could ill-afford to squander. I surveyed the copious notes I'd brought back from my trip. Meanwhile, I was still out of work and running out of options.

A PERILOUS INCOMPATIBILITY

Colette Avital, my childhood friend and once very brief object of desire, now Consul General of Israel in New York, had heard of my situation and offered me a post in her press office. A month-long investigation by the intelligence unit probed into my past, anatomized my family, dissected my work history and scrutinized my political proclivities. Declared "kosher," filled with eagerness and anticipation I went to work as a press officer. Thus began for me a dizzying descent into obscurity, an obstacle course to nowhere, a road jealously patrolled and sabotaged by petty bureaucrats sporting large egos and armed with an ambition eclipsed only by mediocrity and ineptitude. Before long, I was suffocating -- no, drowning -- in a fishbowl infested with piranhas. Abandoned as I was to a rat pack of power-hungry mandarins, all busy feeding their vanity, I surrendered and retreated to the numbing routines to which I'd been consigned. I'd been hired to work as a press secretary, publicist and media point man. Instead, I became everybody's translator, proofreader, scribe and linguistic troubleshooter. Every upstart paper-pusher who couldn't put a fucking comma in its proper place, much less write a coherent sentence, came to me for help and expected to get it at once. I complied because, in good conscience, I could not allow the tripe that was being placed before me to appear on Consulate stationery. In short, I'd been alternately unused, misused, abused and exploited. In the process, I discovered that diplomacy (politics/propaganda) and journalism are perilously incompatible -- if not mutually exclusive. I was a journalist, not a politician, less yet a diplomat. I'd acquired a fresh inventory of newspeak and, in the process, developed an increased intolerance for the genre.

Eighteen months later, I quit. Addressed to Colette and never acknowledged, my letter of resignation, here heavily redacted in the interest of discretion, read:

I should have written sooner, when the idealism and exuberance I'd brought to the job of press officer began to erode. Both have since been replaced by feelings oscillating between exasperation and insensibility. The climate in your Communications department swings precariously between lunacy and inertia, confusion, and gloom. Everything is ad-libbed and executed badly on instructions by taskmasters who are out of their element and who delegate work they themselves are utterly incapable of conceptualizing. The strictures inherent in my present circumstance have made it painfully evident that I could not ply my trade from within your bureaucracy. Most disheartening is the realization that I was unwittingly used to help promote other's people's diplomatic careers. Under the circumstances, disillusioned but confident that at the age of 56 I can still attain some measure of professional contentment, I hereby tender my resignation. I gratefully acknowledge your initial support at a difficult juncture in my life.

●

Considered an oddity by some, a loose cannon by others, I never learned how to play "the game." Incorrigible, bored by routine, undisciplined, easily disillusioned by people, I'd skirmished and burned bridges before. I would do so again, in personal relationships, when friendships turned flighty, when compelled to wonder to what extent kindness of heart makes stupidity bearable, or in employment, when shackled by inhibiting rules and strictures. The penalties for such deviance include defeat and alienation. Dreamers never win. Victory would render us superfluous. The dividends, however, often hidden from view in a moment of crisis, include an array of fresh challenges and opportunities that I would be quick to seize, often oblivious to or in defiance of the perils they entailed.

Less than a month later, determined to return to traditional journalism, I moved to San José, Costa Rica. Free-lance assignments involving the plight of Central American street children and persecuted indigenous minorities, opened new doors and served as a springboard for more lucrative employment as an independent reporter. This extraordinary odyssey, which would last twelve years, took me from the Mexican highlands to the jungles of Panama and yielded a bounty of articles and commentaries that graced the pages of various U.S. and Central American newspapers and infuriated some readers.

•

Fiscally motivated, Kathy Keeton's suggestion that I travel to Central America instead of Brazil would, in retrospect, prove auspicious. Brazil had long been synonymous with festering hillside slums and chic downtown esplanades teeming with rising tides of homeless children. It also had the dubious distinction of turning a blind eye to self-styled enforcers bent on purging these omnipresent pariahs from Brazilian society. Whereas these well publicized pogroms are reactive and spontaneous in Brazil, a nation of nearly 200 million, they seem to have escaped serious scrutiny in parts of Central America, notably in Guatemala and Honduras, with a combined population of about 15 million, and where the systematic, pro-active, state-sponsored extermination of homeless minors had reached epidemic proportions.

Central America is a region rocked by political chaos, plagued by economic decay and convulsed by horrific violence. Entrenched military plutocracies have given way to civilian puppet regimes that continue to thwart efforts at democratization by intimidating the feeble and indecisive voices of reform. Gross inequalities in wealth and status (fewer than one-tenth of the people own and control over ninety percent of national resources), unfavorable currency exchange rates and mounting trade deficits have further weakened faltering economies by increasing unemployment, freezing wages and unleashing unforgiving rates of inflation. Conservative estimates place the combined regional unemployment rate at nearly forty percent. Better than seventy-five percent of all households earn poverty-level incomes. The level of poverty for children under five has topped at eighty-five percent. The poverty level among kids aged between six and fourteen now exceeds eighty-six percent.

A steady decline in family income had led to an increase in child labor. In addition, already skimpy state-sponsored social programs for children were being stripped to the bone by recurring and increasingly harsher austerity measures. As a result, more children were being abandoned or expelled by families that obeyed the Church's mandate to multiply and populate the Earth. Regrettably, the Church, which is wont to voice concern for the unborn, does little or nothing on behalf of the living.

The 75,000 children roaming the streets of Central America are divided into two groups: runaways from households eroded by overpopulation, poverty, alcoholism and abuse; and children abandoned or cast out by families no longer able to provide for them. Viewed as "vermin," "a blight," "parasites," and "criminals," unwanted, unloved, the inheritors of dysfunctional societies, they are invariably labeled as "bad for tourism," "bad for the neighborhood," "bad for the country." Endorsed by indifferent or openly hostile governments, this perception had inspired successive waves of bloodletting against these children. Intimidation, threats, illegal detentions, vicious beatings, torture, rape and extra-judicial executions at the hands of law-enforcement agents, once sporadic, were now widespread. Corrupt and inept judicial systems turned a blind eye to such impunity and rarely arrested or convicted the culprits. Mounting evidence suggested that the executioners were "embedded" in government. And the carnage continued.

•

What began as a probe into state-sponsored killings of street children set the stage for the study of other socio-economic ills in the Isthmus, mostly in Guatemala and Honduras, all traceable to the vestiges of colonialism, government corruption, political chicanery, apathy, sloth and other signs of decadence. It would be a bumpy ride on a road strewn with hazards.

Large obstacles put us on guard; small ones whet our appetite. It's often the latter that makes us trip.

PART THREE
THE ESTUARY

Muddy waters

JOURNEY TO XIBALBA

From the mists of time, deep in the primeval Guatemalan jungles, comes a document known as the *Popol Vuh*, a fragmentary chronicle of the allegories, beliefs and attitudes of the ancient Maya. An epic poem of great lyric beauty and haunting melancholy, the *Popol Vuh* is also a record of the peregrinations of a people caught in life's struggle for survival, identity and cultural self-affirmation.

The Maya feared death more than any of life's ordeals and only exceptional individuals, they claimed, could find their way to the heavenly gates. The unworthy were hastily dispatched to *Xibalba,* the Mayan hell, the "House of Gloom," the "World of Ghosts," the "Mansion of the Damned" -- an icy abyss teeming with monsters that inflicted unspeakable torments.

If the Maya took great pains to elude the dreaded chasm -- self-mutilation and orgiastic human sacrifices, they believed, could forestall the inevitable -- they had no illusion that life "on the surface" was apt to be as hideous as in *Xibalba*'s entrails. Ego, greed, cruelty, deception, vengeance, all prevailed, acted out with an incontinence bordering on lunacy. Blood-lettings, wars, decapitations, amputations, in short, senseless carnage, were as likely to envenom their mortal existence as the "lower regions" to which their souls would eventually be consigned.

Longing for redemption, their governors engaged in an endless consecration of grandiose ideals. Fearing night, awaiting the advent of dawn but not the passage of greater events, they yearned for a spiritual reawakening that would never be. They pandered to unfeeling gods and offered sacrifices to atone inexpiable sins while the masses were fated to a life of submission and servitude in the shadow of despotic and degenerate elites. Busy erecting flamboyant pantheons, obsessed with their own place in posterity, the nihilistic demigods the people idolized were no kinder than the bloodthirsty Lords of *Xibalba*. They knew that they were false of heart, promoters of evil and tormentors of men, and that their extravagance and folly would lead to civil strife, social disintegration, economic exhaustion and, in due course, apocalypse.

Eventually, the debauchery, the drug-induced stupor, the bombastic mystique of their masters' esoteric pursuits began to wear thin in the eyes of the overburdened populace. "Of what practical value to us, illiterate peons," they pondered, "are such abstractions as systems of reckoning dates, stargazing and arcane hieroglyphics, when this knowledge is the exclusive domain of our rulers?"

Too long had the people been forced into a state of servitude; too exacting was the endless labor to erect temples, sacrificial altars and ball courts. They were tired of tending the fields of the princely castes and paying exorbitant tributes to corrupt and insensitive monarchs. For centuries the multitudes had surrendered to the ruling aristocracy and soon the sting of despotism, the ignominy of persecution would lead to open revolt.

Along with a sharp increase in the dominance of the elite and the unfettered opulence and ostentation their lifestyle demanded, the number of underlings required to cater to their whims grew to colossal proportions. This imposed additional burdens for food and other goods needed to sustain the hierarchy. It is likely that these burdens triggered ever-widening divisions and fed mounting hostilities between the lower classes and their masters.

There is evidence in the Late Classic era, the period foreshadowing the "fall," of a population explosion that led to the growth in the number and size of urban clusters. All these pressures -- overpopulation, soaring demand for goods and services, diminishing resources and widening rifts between social strata -- had a profound and everlasting impact on the Maya: It left them teetering on the brink. Mortally wounded, nudged by an irresistible momentum, the once great, the magnificent Mayan civilization quivered, froze and dipped over the edge.

The exact dynamics that led to the Maya's sudden and staggering collapse is not well understood. What is known is that famine -- brought on by deforestation, over-cultivation, climatic changes, droughts, floods, outbreaks of infectious diseases, rising infant mortality, declining life expectancy and widespread discontent with an increasingly remote and self-absorbed plutocracy -- led to chaos, fragmentation and dispersal.

Mel Gibson's haunting 2006 film, *Apocalypto,* which focuses on a few days in the dizzying tug-of-war between life and death in early 16th century Mesoamerica, hints at the sudden collapse of a once-glorious empire. Savage, hypnotic, this troubling epic telegraphs a larger message: It warns that a system of governance rigged to benefit the few eventually invites anarchy.

For the surviving full-blooded Maya -- some four million live in Belize, Guatemala, Honduras and Mexico -- only two paths of survival remain: serfdom and assimilation, or alternating states of neglect and violent repression by the interlopers who now occupy their domain. Like their tribal brothers and sisters in the region, they remain suspended between two contrasting and incongruous worlds: ancient (intimate and familiar) and modern (alien and menacing).

In Central America, where waste and want coexist in shameless intimacy, *Xibalba* is a familiar signpost on the well-traveled road to nowhere. Sadly, for indigenous communities in the Isthmus, there is no exit ramp. New dynasties of rich and powerful overlords are hell-bent on keeping them idling on the road to nowhere.

Mr. Gibson is a gifted actor and moviemaker. Will he have the moral courage to crown *Apocalypto* with a sequel that picks up where half-naked, bronze-skinned "savages" glance toward the sea, speechless, terrified and uncomprehending, as tall ships drop anchor in pristine bays, and helmeted hirsute men wielding swords and crosses steer their long boats ashore?

Could future Gibson blockbusters cast an honest cinematic eye at the horrors of the Crusades, which preceded the rape of the "New World," and the "Holy" Inquisition which was already underway? Can the internecine savagery of the ancient Maya ever be compared with the depraved barbarism of their "civilized" conquerors?

LIBERATION THEOLOGY SHACKLED

Newsmen don't live by fact alone. Fact may be the backbone of a story that can be told with the cardinal "who," "what," "where," "when" and "how." But there is a latticework of nerve and sinew and flesh -- the *"why"* or *"why not"* of an event or issue -- that begs to be dissected and bared because such autopsy helps advance the cause of truth. Bringing into focus the shadowy forces and peripheral influences that shape history, stirring the slime that percolates beneath actuality, is the duty of honest journalism. But doing so invites accusations of muckraking, rabble-rousing and radicalism, labels that the "mainstream" journalists work hard not to earn. Such timidity, driven by tacit covenants with or pressure from the government -- not scruples -- often leads to selective coverage and results in partial or hasty inferences slanted to conform to the orthodoxy of the moment. In this climate of coerced "political correctness," intemperate nationalism and religious fervor, this pusillanimity also tends to corrupt the newsman.

Working in Central America would offer me unusual opportunities to break some taboos (exposing U.S. criminal activities in the Isthmus) and defy the canons of sanctioned journalism (ignoring my editors' injunction to lay off certain subjects) -- sometimes at great peril. I'd long resolved to serve no master; I would neither pay lip service to America's propaganda, nor would I obey the conditions imposed by some of the papers for which I free-lanced. In time, emboldened by the acrimony that my renderings inspired, seduced by the effect they had on readers in Central America and the U.S., I would take on some of history's more sinister sideshows. One was the incestuous relationship between the Church and political power structures, that grotesque symbiosis during which religion and politics intersect, merge and feed on each other. The other was the destabilizing consequences of U.S. military adventurism in the region. The perfidious war waged by the Vatican against Liberation Theology and the wasteland of death and destruction left by alumni of the U.S. Army School of the Americas would provide me with additional targets.

•

In appointing arch-conservative Bishop Fernando Saenz Lacalle to succeed slain Salvadoran Archbishop Oscar Romero, Pope John Paul II, then on a whirlwind tour of El Salvador, Guatemala, Nicaragua and Venezuela, struck hard at the Theology of Liberation, the oxygen-rich doctrine that has redefined and, for the poor and voiceless, enlivened Roman Catholicism in Latin America in the past 50 years.

The roots of Liberation Theology are found in the prophetic tradition of evangelists and missionaries in early colonial Latin America -- clerics who questioned the Church's elitism and denounced the way indigenous people and the poor were being treated. Antonio de Montesinos (1480-1540), Bartolomé de las Casas (1484-1566), and Antonio Vieira (1608-1697), were some of the men who inspired the social and ecclesiastic dynamism that would later emerge in the pastoral ministry of Liberation Theology.

It was in the 1960s that a great breeze of renewal wafted through the churches. They began to take their social mission seriously. Lay persons went to work among the poor. Charismatic bishops and priests called for progress and innovation. The work of these dedicated Christians, mostly middle class, was sustained scripturally by the European theology of earthly realities, among them the integral humanism of Teilhard de Chardin (1881-1955), the progressive evolutionism of Jacques Maritain (1882-1973), and the social personalism of Emmanuel Mounier (1905-1950).

The 1970s ushered a vigorous current of reformist thought that unmasked the true cause of underdevelopment, poverty, social alienation and widespread popular discontent: The Third World was being immolated so that the First World could continue to enjoy the fruits of its overabundance. More and more theologians became pastors, militant agents of inspiration for the grassroots life of the church. They took part in epistemological discussions in learned synods and congresses then returned to their parishes among the people where they immersed themselves in matters of ministry, trade unionism and community organization. Thus, Liberation Theology spread and codified Christian faith as it applies to the needs of the poor. As these developments took place, misgivings then open opposition began to animate those who feared that faith was becoming over-politicized and others who mistook the redemptive nature of Liberation Theology for Bolshevism.

Predictably, in a region bled dry by war, devoured by economic decay, and enfeebled by harsh austerity measures, Pope John Paul II's choice came as a shock and resonated like thunder throughout Latin America, where dozens of activist bishops were being fired and replaced by pliant champions of Catholic doctrinal extremism.

According to the Rev. Joseph Mulligan, an American Jesuit I met in Nicaragua, these clerics "toe the line very carefully on issues of doctrine. They are 'yes-men' doing Rome's bidding." As a result, Mulligan said, the Church is "suffering a pulling back from the strong commitment to social justice that marked the past five decades."

Now retired, Spanish-born Archbishop Saenz was a former Vatican liaison to the Salvadoran Armed Forces and a member of Opus Dei, the ultra-right-wing lay organization dedicated to promoting and enforcing Catholic dogma. His critics have accused him of cozying up to the ruling party, the plutocracy and the military. Their claims are not without merit: Saenz accepted over one million dollars from the Salvadoran government and the country's richest families to resume erection of a cathedral left unfinished when Archbishop Romero proclaimed that it was "time to build the Church, not churches." Much to the dismay of the Vatican, Romero had also long insisted that it is blasphemy to coddle men's souls while ignoring their earthly needs.

It is easier to tolerate an idiot than a principled man.

In a plea for "compassion," and in the name of "national reconciliation," Saenz had asked the government to pardon two former national guardsmen convicted of raping and killing three American nuns, Ita Ford, Maura Clark and Dorothy Kazel, and of a social worker, Jean Donovan in 1980. The two soldiers served 19 years of their 30-year sentences. "Let us have mercy and pity for them. They have demonstrated their repentance," the archbishop remarked without a trace of pity for their victims, who had confessed to killing the women on the orders of superiors who were never prosecuted. The victims' families, who filed suit against El Salvador's former defense minister and the former director general of the National Guard, accusing them of covering up the killings, believe the women were attacked because officials suspected they sympathized with leftist guerrillas.

Short on resources and influence, but long on memory, the people of Central America were also mindful that former Salvadoran President Armando Calderon Sol was a member of the same political party that engineered Archbishop Romero's assassination and masterminded -- under the command of death squad leader, CIA stooge and U.S. Army School of the Americas alumnus, Roberto d'Aubuisson -- the 1981 massacre of 900 men, women and children in the village of El Mozote. Nor will they ever forget that the Pope paid a courtesy call on Calderon, cavorted with barrel-chested colonels and generals bristling with medals, and granted audiences to high society women sporting low-cut dresses and dripping with diamonds -- instead of kneeling at the grave of six Jesuits slain in 1989 by a Salvadoran Army death squad.

•

It was during a visit to Central America that Pope John Paul II first clashed with supporters of Liberation Theology. In Managua, Nicaragua, he publicly humiliated the Rev. Ernesto Cardenal, a noted writer, philosopher and social activist who would later be suspended from the priesthood. The Pontiff would "retire" scores of vocal Latin American liberal clerics. The headstrong or the unrepentant, among them Rev. Bertrand Aristide of Haiti and Rev. Fernando Cardenal (Ernesto's brother), would also be unceremoniously defrocked.

Hastened by papal nepotism strongly biased in favor of diehard bishops, this dilution in the ranks of progressive clergy has gained new impetus in Latin America. Tragically, in the most Catholic domain on earth, the peaceful message of Jesus has been subverted by martial attitudes that view the faithful as the very enemies of the state. Astute and opportunistic, the Church continues to tap into the reactionary power base to maintain both doctrinal monopoly and political custody over the masses.

There is a precedent -- and a disquieting parallel. Nine hundred years ago, bloodhounds of orthodoxy sniffed out heretics and the carnage began. People who held unacceptable views were thrown in dungeons. There, they were tortured with inventive cruelty, then killed. They were accused of harboring heterodox opinions. They were forced to confess that they worshipped the devil (translation: they were freethinkers); engaged in heretical pursuits (they hungered for knowledge); and conspired against the established order (they spoke out against corruption and intellectual turpitude).

The Church's obscene quest for supremacy, inspired and abetted by successive papal dynasties, was prelude to six "Crusades" during which hundreds of thousands of "infidels" -- Moslems and Jews were slaughtered. The same religious fervor later fanned nearly four centuries of inquisitorial frenzy that devoured Europe and sent another half a million innocent people to the stake while their possessions, confiscated as "evidence" fattened the Church's bulging coffers.

Like Karl Marx, who scorned the proletariat, the Church has never fully expiated its contempt for the masses, its feigned homophobia or its misogyny. It steadfastly rejects the notion that people can govern their conscience without its guidance or control. Worse, it denies them the right to manage their political destinies by consigning their existence to the same Pharisaic elite that Jesus rebuked.

Few of Christianity's rulers, however outwardly pious, have lived up to the principles of Jesus, the Jewish radical who preached compassion, pacifism and egalitarianism. Faced with a choice between Jesus' ethic and political expediency, Pope John Paul II and his successor, Benedict XVI, opted for the latter. They came to Latin America and told the poor that poverty is good. They then urged the rich to reject materialism -- they might as well have sweet-talked hyenas into giving up a simmering carcass. In Mexico, donning silk and gilded vestments, Benedict -- who had looked the other way when anecdotal reports of sexual misconduct by some of his foot soldiers soon revealed a global pattern of priestly promiscuity -- called for a return to "traditional Christian values." A day later, in Cuba, he praised democracy then flew back to his sumptuous lodgings in the Vatican, the richest and most autarchic empire on Earth. In casting out the good shepherds of Christianity from the fold, both John Paul II and his successor also surrendered the flock to the carnivores.

GOD'S "WORK"

Outside its own doctrinaire circle of followers and fans, Opus Dei, or God's Work, has a dappled reputation, mostly bad. Andrew Greeley (b. 1928), the eminent American Catholic priest, sociologist, journalist and best-selling author, has described it as

"a devious, antidemocratic, reactionary, semi-fascist institution, desperately famished for absolute dominion in the Church and quite possibly very close now to having that power."

Calling the elite group, "authoritarian and power-mad," Greeley warns that

"Opus Dei is an extremely dangerous organization because it appeals to the love of secrecy and the power lust of certain kinds of religious personalities. It may well be the most powerful group in the Church today. It is capable of doing an enormous amount of harm. It ought to be forced out of the shadows or suppressed."

Opus Dei has about one million members worldwide. At least 2,000 are ordained priests. With this international cohort of dedicated warriors, Opus Dei has successfully penetrated schools and universities, banks, publishing firms, television and radio stations, ad agencies and film companies. It has been accused of deceptive and aggressive recruitment practices, including *"love bombing"* -- the deliberate and syrupy show of affection by an individual or group as a tool of conscription or conversion -- and instructing celibate members to form friendships, attend social gatherings and submit written reports on potential converts.

The core precept of Opus Dei is *"to help shape the world in a Catholic manner." Helpers* include clergy, captains of industry, high-ranking military officers and government officials. The group *"comes surrounded by a political miasma,"* the British daily, The Guardian, noted recently. The super-stealthy organization was founded just before the Spanish Civil War and blossomed in the halcyon Catholic days of *El Caudillo*, fascist dictator Francisco Franco's "crusade" against the Republican left. When Opus Dei came to prominence in the late 1960s it was because Franco's cabinet included an inordinate number of *Opusdeistas* -- too many to be the result of coincidence.

Opus Dei, which strives for a reunification of church and state, arms its members with special and far-reaching powers driven by the God-driven longing to cleanse the world of heretics and deliver sinful, rudderless humanity, by force if necessary, into Christ's loving arms.

The 900-year-old organization was formerly known as the Sovereign Military Hospitaller Order of the Saints John of Jerusalem, Rhodes and Malta. Modeled after an ancient group of soldier-monks who massacred "infidels," (Muslims, Jews and Cathars) Knights of Malta, ceremonies and rituals *"inculcate lessons of chivalry and courage, and inspire a militant spirit in opposition to all non-Christian ideologies and powers."* With over 10,000 members in 42 countries, the Knights are influential Vatican surrogates with extensive ties to right-wing intelligence networks.

Originally trained as ruthless tactical fighters, later adopting a fiercely anti-communist stance, the Knights were instrumental in the creation of the Central Intelligence Agency. They also took part in U.S. global "black" (covert) operations. The founding fathers of the CIA, William "Wild Bill" Donovan and Allen Dulles, the longest-serving CIA director, were Knights, as were many in the CIA hierarchy, including John F. Kennedy's director, John McCone and Ronald Reagan's director, William Casey. McCone helped engineer the 1973 military coup against Chile's democratically elected president, Salvador Allende. According to journalist Carl Bernstein, Casey gave Pope John Paul II unparalleled access to CIA intelligence, including data on spy satellites and field operatives.

There is compelling evidence that the Knights of Malta were linked to the "Rat Run," the post-World War II getaway route used by Nazi top brass and death camp "scientists" from defeated Germany to the Americas. These thugs were issued new identities and special credentials that ensured escape from prosecution for crimes against humanity. One of them, Major General Reinhard Gehlen, a devout Catholic and legendary Cold War spymaster, surrendered to the U.S. Army Counter-Intelligence Corps in 1945. Because of his experience and useful contacts in the Soviet Union, he was freed, as were seven of his senior officers, in exchange for their pledge to gather intelligence for the United States. Flown to Washington, Gehlen went to work for Donovan and Dulles, then the Office of Strategic Services station chief in Switzerland. Gehlen handed over the names of several OSS officers who were members of the U.S. Communist Party.

A year later, Gehlen was flown back to Germany where he resumed his spy work, this time as a lackey of the U.S. He set up a dummy organization composed of 350 former German intelligence officers. That number eventually grew to 4,000. For many years, the "V-men," (*V-mann* or *Vertrauensmann* -- trusted man) as they were known, were the eyes and ears of the CIA in Western Europe and the Soviet Bloc during the Cold War. Recruited among men who had as little culture, common sense, objectivity or logic as possible, they were used primarily to maintain surveillance of civilian populations in Germany and occupied countries.

Overall, the Gehlen organization's performance was at best disappointing. One rare successful mission infiltrated some 5,000 anti-communists of Eastern European origin into the Soviet Union and its satellites. These agents were trained at a facility named Oberammergau, site of the yearly staging of one of Hitler's favorite diversions, the unambiguously anti-Semitic Passion Plays. The organization was severely compromised when it was infiltrated by communist moles -- as were the CIA and the British MI6. One of the double-agents was the illustrious Harold "Kim" Philby, spy-extraordinaire who served the communist cause until his death in Moscow in 1988.

Gehlen employed hundreds of "ex-Nazis," among them Alois Brunner, Adolf Eichmann's right-hand-man and commander of the Drancy internment camp near Paris. Brunner was responsible for the slaughter of 140,000 Jews. His death has never been confirmed; he was believed to be still alive in 2007. The CIA turned a blind eye and, owing the exigencies of the Cold War, even took part in some of Gehlen's operations.

Robert Wolfe, historian at the U.S. National Archives wrote:

"U.S. Army intelligence accepted Reinhard Gehlen's offer to furnish alleged expertise on the Red Army -- and was bilked by the many mass murderers he hired."

In appreciation for his work, Gehlen, Hitler's Eastern Front intelligence chief who organized and took part in atrocities against Jews, Gypsies and Slavs, was awarded the Knights of Malta's highest decoration, the Grand Cross of Merit. (In 1988, Ronald Reagan received the Knights of Malta's Grand Cross for his *"devotion to Christian principles."*) People in Central America still remember Reagan as the man who funneled millions of tax dollars to repressive regimes whose U.S.-trained death squads murdered hundreds of thousands of innocent civilians.

One of the Knights of Malta's main spheres of influence is Latin America, where fascists and escaped Nazis were given a warm welcome. The late Chilean strongman, General Augusto Pinochet, a CIA-stooge and convicted human rights violator, was a Knight. So is deposed Peruvian dictator, human rights violator and embezzler, Alberto Fujimori, America's "man in Lima" until his arrest in 2005. So was the late Argentinean president Juan Peron who, recently declassified CIA documents suggest, laundered Nazi gold through the Vatican Bank subsidiary, Banco Ambrosiano, which collapsed in 1982. The Vatican Bank is widely believed to have channeled covert U.S. funds to Poland's Solidarity trade union and transferred laundered money from the illegal sale of arms to Iran to the Contras through Banco Ambrosiano.

The scandal, "characterized by persistent duplicity and inordinate secrecy," would prompt the U.S. Congress to conclude that "a cabal of zealots" (members of Reagan's cabinet, later the Bush-1 administration) violated the Hughes-Ryan Act and the Boland Amendment by failing to inform congressional intelligence committees about its covert actions in the Middle East and Central America. *[Passed in 1974, the Hughes-Ryan Act requires the president of the United States to report all covert operations of the CIA to at least one Congressional committee. The Boland Amendment was a triad to amendments enacted between 1982 and 1984 aimed at limiting U.S. assistance to the CIA-financed Contras in Nicaragua].* There are those who wonder to this day why Ronald Reagan wasn't impeached and George H. W. Bush indicted for their approval of black missions.

"After World War II," Roman Catholic writer Penny Lernoux writes in her *People of God*,

> *"the Vatican, the OSS, elements of the SS, and various branches of the Sovereign Military Order of Malta joined ... to help Nazi war criminals escape...."*

Documents reveal that New York Cardinal Francis Spellman, head of the Knights in the U.S. from the 1940s to the 1960s was directly involved in the 1954 right-wing military coup in Guatemala during which at least 200,000 indigenous Maya were massacred and in which the CIA has acknowledged complicity. Spellman was also linked to organized crime by his long involvement with Archbishop Paul Macinkus of Chicago, former head of the Vatican Bank, and a suspect in the highly suspicious death of Pope John Paul I a month after his election.

•

The Catholic Church no longer relies on inquisitorial torture chambers and auto-da-fés. It now engages in psychological extortion by exacting unconditional obedience from its crestfallen congregants.

Growing disenchantment with the Vatican's archaic and unyielding mandates will have woeful historical consequences. Virulent opposition to reproductive rights, vicious attacks on feminism, an eagerness to coddle Jewish and Islamic hard-liners when their fanatical anti pro-choice, anti-progressive, homophobic agendas converge, and refusal to accept moral responsibility for the political crimes committed by the right-wing regimes it favors, all demonstrate how desperate and estranged the Church has strayed from reality. Worse, attempts to demonize grass-roots religion by equating it with communism has had a dispiriting effect on the faithful, especially those in Latin America who, benumbed by years of armed conflict, dislocation, oppression and privation, have tried desperately to wrest their nation's politics from the merciless clutches of a privileged few.

•

H. L. Mencken defined religion as "the illogical belief in the occurrence of the improbable." Nietzsche viewed it with greater ferocity: "Religion has been reduced to not wanting to know what is true…. It is an affair of the rabble." While conceding its fragile potential for good, I see religion as a supercilious, divisive and exclusionary artifice contrived to benefit the theocracy. Like capitalism, religion is a diseased and avaricious system driven by and dedicated to the fattening of the corporate queen at the expense of captive worker ants. Like capitalism, it is fickle, unpredictable and blind to human needs. The deep and palpable pessimism of Latin America's poor, whose faith in the hereafter exceeds their prospects in this life, can be characterized as a rational response to an inescapable kismet that religion cannot forestall. For them, such predestination includes more of the same, compliments of the hegemonic interests of a few.

Sic transit gloria mundi.

THE POLITICS OF ASSASSINATION

Getting rid of someone is easy. Destroying popular aspirations takes more effort but you can always count on someone willing to do the dirty work. For money; favors, influence; power, mostly power. When conventional methods -- elections, plebiscites, national referenda -- fail, or when the results threaten the oligarchs, the U.S. Army School of the Americas (SOA), a shadowy but formidable war factory billeted at Fort Benning, Georgia, will answer the call. Here, there are no petty bureaucrats taking up space and stealing time waiting for retirement. The SOA is a model institution. Its instructors are recruited from the cream of Latin America's military establishment. The curriculum it offers includes counterinsurgency and "irregular" combat (translation: repression), military intelligence (espionage), interrogation techniques and psychological warfare (torture), sniper fire (long-distance assassination), commando tactics (dirty fighting) and jungle operations (everything from deforestation to cooking cocaine in secret hideouts). But the students are not being trained to defend their borders against foreign aggression. They are taught, at U.S. taxpayers' expense, to make war against their own people, to subvert the truth, silence poets, domesticate unruly visionaries, muzzle activist clergy, hinder trade unionism, hush the voices of dissidence and discontent, neutralize the poor, the hungry, the dispossessed, extinguish common dreams, irrigate fields of plenty with the tears of a captive society, and transform activists and protesters into submissive vassals. Even if it kills them.

For several years, a group of U.S. legislators led by former Rep. Joseph P. Kennedy II (D-MA), the eldest son of the late Senator Robert F. Kennedy, campaigned to shut down the facility.

"Continued operation of this facility suggests that the U.S. sanctions the crimes its graduates have committed. The SOA costs the U.S. millions of dollars a year and identifies us with tyranny and oppression," Kennedy told me in a three-way conference call with Father Roy Bourgeois, the spirited founder of SOA Watch, a grassroots organization that keeps close tabs on the School.

It may not be a coincidence that the young Kennedy tried to compensate for some of his charismatic uncle's empty promises. As Howard Zinn wrote in *The Twentieth Century:*

> *"When John F. Kennedy took office, he launched the Alliance for Progress, a program of help for Latin America, emphasizing social reform to better the lives of people. But it turned out to be mostly military aid to keep in power right-wing dictatorships and enable them to stave off revolutions. From military aid, it was a short step to military intervention."*

In 1993 Joe Kennedy sponsored an amendment to the House Defense Appropriations Bill calling for an end to the training provided by the SOA. The measure was defeated. Reintroduced in 1994, the amendment was again rejected. This time the defeat was eased by a six-fold increase in the number of abstentions from the previous year. New amendments by Rep. Kennedy and other congressional backers would further erode support for the school. The SOA would eventually close and, gingerly rechristened, miraculously reopen overnight.

Founded in Panama in 1948 and relocated in 1984 to Fort Benning after Panamanian President Jorge Illueca evicted it -- he'd called it *"the biggest base for destabilization in Latin America"* -- the SOA has trained more than 100,000 Latin American and Caribbean basin soldiers and career officers. It has also produced some of the region's most despicable tyrants, murderers and crooks.

When the military go on feeding frenzies in Latin America, as they have been wont to do with unsettling regularity in other parts of the world, accusing fingers often point to Washington. That's what happened in 1989, when a Salvadoran Army patrol burst in the Central American University and murdered six Jesuit priests, their cook and her daughter. Some of the victims were executed lying face down on the ground. Human rights groups were quick to charge the U.S. with aiding and abetting El Salvador's military regime. This was not an idle allegation. Nineteen of the 27 Salvadoran officers cited in a U.S. Truth Commission report as having taken part in the massacre were SOA graduates. In fact, almost three-quarters of the Salvadoran officers implicated in seven other bloodbaths during El Salvador's civil war (including the assassination of Archbishop Oscar Romero in September 1980) were trained by the SOA. The elite institution has left its mark everywhere in Latin America. Of the 246 officers cited for various crimes in Colombia by a 1992 international human rights tribunal, more than half had been trained at the SOA.

The three highest ranking officers who supported former Guatemalan President Serrano's 1993 attempted coup trained at the SOA, including former Defense Minister Jose Domingo Garcia and the sinister presidential chief of staff, Luis Francisco Ortega Menaldo, who had taken an advanced military intelligence course. Other Guatemalan big-league SOA alumni include ex-Defense Minister, Gen. Mario Enriquez and Congress President, Gen. Jose Efrain Ríos Montt. A former president of Guatemala (1982-83), Ríos Montt is best remembered for his "beans or bullets" policy -- beans for the compliant, bullets for the restive. The current president of Guatemala (2012), Otto Perez Molina, is an SOA alumnus and former G-2 (intelligence) chief. A CIA asset, he has been implicated in the assassination of Judge Edgar Ramiro in 1994.

In Honduras, five senior officers who organized -- with U.S. complicity -- the secret death squad known as Intelligence Battallion 3-16 in the mid-80s are SOA graduates. Captain Pio Flores, whose house was used as a detention and "interrogation" center, took four courses at the SOA. Colonel Amilcar Zelaya, from whose residence muffled screams were regularly heard, also attended the School. He specialized in torture.

The three highest ranking officers convicted in February 1994 of murdering nine university students and a professor in Peru are all SOA graduates -- as is the commander of the Peruvian military who dispatched tanks to thwart the murder investigation. (Vladimiro Montesinos, exiled President Alberto Fujimori's chief of intelligence who was convicted of extortion and gross human rights violations, is an SOA alumnus.)

Also known as the School for Dictators -- or less kindly but with greater acronymic consistency, the School of Assassins -- the SOA has sired a number of miscreants deserving of historical scrutiny. They include:

• Omar Torrijos, of Panama; Guillermo Rodriguez of Ecuador; and Juan Velasco Alvarado of Peru -- all of whom overthrew constitutionally elected civilian governments.

• Leopoldo Galtieri, ex-head of Argentina's junta, defeated in the Falklands (Malvinas) "Dirty War" against the British. Galtieri helped create Honduras' death squad Battalion 3-16.

• The late Hugo Banzer Suarez, Bolivian president in the 1970s, best known for crushing dissident clerics and striking tin miners with savage zeal.

• Col. Roberto d'Aubuisson, the late Salvadoran death-squad leader who plotted the assassination of Archbishop Romero and took part in the El Mozote massacre of 900 men, women and children.

• Manuel Noriega, ex-dictator of Panama, who served a 40-year sentence in a U.S. federal penitentiary, was later extradited to France and has since returned to Panama. Arrested on trumped up drug trafficking charges, his real sins include a host of transgressions initially sanctified by the CIA, for which he worked.

• Honduran General Humberto Regalado Hernández, linked to Colombian drug cartels, and General Policarpo Paz García, who led a brutal, corrupt regime in the 1980s. Hernández was inducted into the SOA's "Hall of Fame" in 1988.

• Manuel Antonio Callejas y Callejas, Chief of Guatemalan intelligence in the late 1970s and early 1980, when thousands of political opponents were assassinated.

Less eminent but equally adept at making war, wielding in some cases formidable regional and local power, and exceeding the limits of their own authority, a number of SOA graduates have been known to take on less redoubtable foes. In Guatemala, a nation characterized by Congressman Jim McDermott (D-WA) as "a fractured society -- politically, economically, culturally and ethnically -- probably the most corrupt in Latin America," crimes against street children had long made international headlines but were never stanched. Unloved, unwanted, disposable, society's chaff, ubiquitous and growing in numbers, they continue to pay the price of civil strife and poverty, feudalism and social decay, enduring illegal detentions and beatings, often for petty crimes, including those motivated by hunger. Freshly spilled blood points to waves of mindless retribution by a constabulary gone amok. Their crimes continue to be overlooked by a judicial system disinclined to obey its own laws and disdainful of the international human rights accords to which the nation is a party.

Julio Cabelleros Seigne, SOA class of 1960, may have to answer for many of these children's lives. Head of the Guatemalan military at Nebaj, Quiché province, where some of the worst atrocities were committed against the Maya, Caballeros displaced over one million persons, many of them orphaned children, and spurred an urban migration that continues to strain the country's stagnant economy. Former head of G-2 (military intelligence), he was twice chief of the National Police (1985, 1990), a semi-militarized corps with a lengthy record of human rights abuses, many against defenseless minors. In 1993, Caballeros was named Customs chief.

In the BBC documentary, "*They Shoot Children, Don't They*," Caballeros accused human rights organizations of "demanding justice at the snap of a finger." He also rebuked them publicly for "making too much of a fuss about the death of one child." The child Caballeros referred to was 13-year-old Nahamán Carmona López, kicked to death in 1990 by four of Caballero's men. His death galvanized international attention and paved the way for a widely publicized series of legal proceedings against his executioners. Condemned to 12 years in prison during a show trial at which justice was trumped by expediency, they served less than half their sentence.

Arrogant and self-deluded, Caballeros may have underestimated the resolve of dedicated activists to take on abusive regimes. One of them, the late Bruce Harris, former director of Covenant House's Latin American Operations, eventually filed more than 200 criminal suits against 120 policemen and 30 soldiers. Arrest warrants were issued against 18 policemen. Fewer than ten were arrested. Most served token prison sentences of less than three months and were released.

A member of the extreme right-wing Revolutionary Party, Caballeros, who lost a bid for a congressional seat, favors military rule in Guatemala. It is no secret that several former administration cabinet members itching for a political comeback favor a takeover. In an open letter to his *"Querido Juan Pueblo"* (Beloved John Q. Public) in *Siglo Veintiuno*, Caballeros blamed "dirty rich politicians" for the country's problems. Given that the wealthy in Guatemala, as they are elsewhere in Latin America, have traditionally supported the military, Caballeros was being more than disingenuous. Playing on short memories and growing public discontent in order to agitate the masses -- it's called disinformation in military parlance -- he was merely putting into very effective use the lessons he'd learned at his old alma mater.

Inevitably, long-simmering rumors that the Guatemalan military was being involved in criminal activities burst like pus-filled boils when a number of high-ranking officers, among them Col. Carlos René Ochoa Ruíz, SOA Class of 1969, were charged with drug trafficking, car theft and murder. Ochoa was sought by the U.S. government in 1991 to face six drug-related charges, including the shipment of six metric tons of cocaine to Tampa, Florida. The extradition order was approved and signed by Judge Epamimondas Gonzalez Dubón. Judge Gonzalez was assassinated a week later. A few days after that, another judge revoked the extradition decision.

•

Next door in Honduras, the early 1980s witnessed political violence of a level unknown in earlier decades -- but quickly matched and exceeded in the past few years -- as the civil conflict in El Salvador and Nicaragua spilled across its borders. Many "disappeared" after their abduction or were summarily executed by death squads. Seven men, including the late Gen. Gustavo Alvárez Martinez, SOA Class of 1978, took part in the "disappearances" of scores of Hondurans. Alvárez was also charged with abuse of authority, homicide, assassination, torture and hindering due process of law. When Alvarez was shot to death in January 1989, the Associated Press described him in alternately glowing and muted terms. The AP writer called him a "passionate anti-communist" but neglected to point out that Alvarez had spent years hobnobbing with fascists and ultra-rightwing terrorists who made up the membership rosters of the World Anti-Communist League and its affiliated organization, the Latin American Anti-

Communist Confederation.

In an interview, his widow, Lillian de Alvárez, justified her husband's actions, saying he'd "fought against disloyalty and terrorist organizations."

Former armed forces intelligence chief Leonidas Torres Arias (SOA Class of 1962 and 1971), who'd copped a plea by accusing Alvárez of complicity in the "disappearances," was dishonorably discharged in 1982. In 2001, now living in El Salvador where he runs three casinos, Torres Arias put an end to persistent rumors that he'd been involved in gun-running, drug trafficking and murder by admitting to charges leveled against him by the Salvadoran daily, El Diario de Hoy.

To reports of "irregular" detention procedures and the torture of detainees during interrogation by the police, particularly at the hands of its military branch, soon was added evidence of intimidation and harassment of human rights monitors, lawyers, activist priests and nuns, trade unionists and journalists. Relations between the military and the press deteriorated when a group of journalists filmed a murder in Honduras' second largest city, San Pedro Sula. The killers were identified as members of the armed forces. The journalists were threatened. One was attacked. Another had to flee Honduras.

While there were no reported "disappearances" under the late Honduran President Carlos Roberto Reina's administration (1994-1998), serious human rights violations persisted and many of the victims were among Tegucigalpa's 1,000 to 1,500 homeless children. Investigations into charges stemming from the illegal detention, mistreatment and torture of minors were postponed "indefinitely."

A large number of SOA graduates are still "pulling strings" in Honduras and helping shape national policy.

•

Breathtaking mountain vistas, an idyllic climate, pristine rain forests, golden beaches stretching along two coasts, an exuberance of fauna and flora, Coast Rica has it all, and then some. But what makes Costa Ricans proudest of all, what they enjoy telling the world is that their small Central American nation has had no army since its abolition in

1948. Look Again.

The SOA has trained about 5,000 Costa Rican soldiers since 1949. The courses they took include military intelligence (the second most popular specialty after military police and infantry training), psychological warfare, sniper and commando tactics, airborne, combat engineering, jungle operations, mortars, "irregular warfare," counterinsurgency, "nuclear war and pedagogy," radio operation and maintenance, "special tactics," mine-sweeping, basic weapons and combat trauma medicine.

Costa Rica has also contributed instructors at the SOA. One of them, Lt. Col. Walter F. Novarro Romero, SOA Class of 1989 (psychological warfare) served as SOA base sub-commandant. Asked to comment, then SOA Public Affairs Officer Maj. Gordon Martel dismissed any inference of impropriety in the existence of a military presence in Costa Rica:

"This is a kind of police force not unlike the U.S. National Guard. Its members are trained to perform civil and rural guard duties. They also go on drug interdiction missions."

"Drug interdiction" has often been a code for counter-insurgency operations.

"So it is a militarized corps, isn't it," I asked.

"Not in the strict sense of the word."

"You're splitting hair, Major. If a man dresses like a soldier, trains like a soldier, carries weapons like a soldier and takes part in military exercises, then he *IS* a soldier, isn't he?"

Understandably, Maj. Martel demurred and recited standard SOA public relations fluff. His rationale was tenuous. In Costa Rica, as in the rest of Central America, police and army are interchangeable. Given the nature, complexity and sophistication of the courses taken by Costa Rican soldiers at an elite combat school such as the SOA, "civil and rural guard duties" are nothing but clever euphemisms crafted for public consumption. For this nation of three million, such rigorous training looks more like a state of military readiness than domestic peacekeeping or the preservation of nature's virgin beauty against human depredation. Moreover, a narcotics surveillance radar network donated and installed by the U.S. has long since fallen into disuse, allegedly the victim of cost cutbacks. Credible sources told me that the facility was shut down because it threatened to drastically diminish the flow of drug money into the private coffers of high-ranking government officials. Such action, at a time when Costa Rica has been called a "benevolent land bridge" between Colombia's cartels and North America, invalidates Maj. Martel's assertions and raises doubts about the legitimacy of Costa Rica's war on drugs. Out of 2,500 graduates, fewer than a dozen ever took the so-called "counter-narcotrafficking" course. Measured against the hundreds of students who trained in intelligence, counter-insurgency, infantry and military police, drug interdiction does not seem to have been a burning preoccupation in Costa Rica.

Costa Rica's overblown reputation as nature conservator and premier tourist attraction has obscured a less than golden human rights record. As recently as 1993, the *Cobra Commando*, a shadowy paramilitary shock unit, was keeping the narcotics pipeline open while terrorizing indigenous groups in the Talamanca jungles bordering Panama. Once a thriving and proud people, caught between the sword and the cross, Costa Rica's indigenous tribes have dwindled to a precious few and are headed toward extinction. This could explain Costa Rica's reluctance to acknowledge the very existence of an antecedent civilization.

"If we don't talk about them, they don't exist," an editor at *La Nación* admitted privately.

•

"SOA grads have seriously hindered the establishment and strengthening of democracy in Latin America," charges SOA Watch founder, Father Roy Bourgeois, a Maryknoll priest who spent two years in prison for spearheading protests against the School. A decorated Vietnam veteran, Bourgeois has long claimed that "the SOA does not screen soldiers who are assigned to it. Known perpetrators of serious war crimes come and go as they please." Indeed, a number of officers cited by the U.S. Truth Commission attended the SOA *after* they'd committed documented atrocities.

"Funded by U.S. tax dollars," Bourgeois argues, "the SOA steals from the poor. Graduates return to their countries to enrich the rich and keep the poor in their place."

Defenders of the SOA, which operates on a multi-million-dollar yearly budget (the School underwent a $30 million renovation), insist it is getting a bum rap. Rejecting all criticism, Maj. Martel told me:

"The SOA is a legitimate military institution where legitimate military skills are taught. It is not the School's fault that a fraction of graduates has engaged in reprehensible behavior."

The difference between artful equivocation and unadulterated bullshit depends on the sensitivity of one's sense of smell.

Others argued, with considerably less success, that the SOA had promoted democracy in Latin America. These are obscurantist arguments that even the Pentagon stopped short of endorsing. A senior U.S. intelligence analyst told me on condition of anonymity that the SOA "has systematically encouraged the transplantation of military structures into and facilitated the propagation of military power and objectives against legitimate civilian governments."

The future of the SOA may hinge not so much on ethical but prosaic considerations, including cutbacks in military spending. It is hard to explain why the SOA should survive when several dozen military bases in the U.S. were closed "to maintain a maximum state of readiness with existing financial resources." In what way is the SOA indispensable to a "maximum state of readiness?" What future conflicts is it preparing to thwart in Latin America when it brags -- falsely -- that it helped reestablish democracy in the region?

A healthy intolerance for the absurd should also have helped bring down the SOA. To soak up U.S. "culture" and values, SOA students are routinely treated to baseball games, excursions to Disney World and other perks, compliments of U.S. taxpayers. It is doubtful that a term or two at a school that teaches, among other useful tricks, how to filet a human being in less time than it takes to read this sentence, can imbue a Latin American hooligan with the Jeffersonian perspective.

Most of the soldiers who attend the SOA were already infused with or soon acquired America's dark view of activist priests, social workers, journalists and liberal intellectuals. To them they are all dangerous subversives. The parsimonious 12-hour "human rights" course offered guest instructors should not be expected to alter deeply rooted biases and susceptibilities. After all, this is "gringo" rhetoric and it will be swiftly discarded as a hindrance to more utilitarian objectives once they get back home.

Few as they are, what SOA supporters must grapple with now that some of its alumni's criminal history spreads like blood in bath water, is whether keeping the school open sends the wrong message, both in the U.S. and abroad. False prophets, of course, are useful. They give the truth a good name. Ultimately, they also remind the world that power struggles, particularly those engineered to take place in *other people's* backyard, sharpen plutocratic dominance, end in abuse and hasten the sacrifice of the innocent. They do not curb the bloodlust.

On January 17, 2001 the SOA was quietly renamed the Western Hemisphere Institute for Security Cooperation. The result of a Department of Defense proposal included in the Defense Authorization Bill for Fiscal 2001, the name-change measure passed when the House of Representatives defeated a bipartisan amendment to close the SOA and conduct a congressional investigation by a narrow seven-vote margin.

When doing the "right thing" threatens special interests, justice goes down the toilet.

THE RIGHT, THE CROSS AND THE CIA

In a 1992 CNN interview with Larry King, headlined *"Reagan, the Pope, Solidarity and the Fall of Communism,"* Time Magazine's Carl Bernstein made an astonishing if persuasive assertion. The Vatican, he said, had offered to help buttress Poland's ailing pro-western Solidarity Party and, later, propped up Lech Walesa's torpid presidency in exchange for a stiffening of conservative values and the establishment of the Christian Right as a viable political force in the United States.

My own research, conducted a year earlier into state-sponsored massacres of Guatemalan street children, hinted that a political "fifth column" had indeed taken root in the U.S. and simultaneously sprouted in Central America where U.S. strategic interests were at an all-time high. Other sources added convincing arguments to allegations that politicians, intelligence agencies, religious leaders, "relief" organizations and multinational corporations were engaged in a hemispheric cabal aimed at synchronizing global Christian evangelical interests with U.S. foreign policy objectives.

I wrote Bernstein, asking for details. He didn't reply. A second and a third request remained unacknowledged. And his diclosures, which should have outraged social democrats everywhere, went in one ear and out the other of a world entering the final year of the Cold War, witnessing the collapse of the Soviet Union and feeling the first stirrings, with the response by coalition forces to Saddam's invasion of Kuwait, of the unresolved conflict in Iraq and the illegal, immoral and unwinnable war in Afghanistan.

I returned to Guatemala in search of answers. Soon, fresh leads surfaced as I probed deeper into the murky world of Central American politics and the Byzantine role the U.S. plays in the Isthmus.

Guatemala had already earned a reputation for gross human rights violations that included "disappearances," tortures and wholesale murder. Although a civilian government had been in place since 1986, democracy limped along, stunted by the legacy of a brutal past and further obstructed by a corrupt and apathetic judicial system disinclined to prosecute. Gone berserk, the U.S.-trained military, the national police and urban constabularies had splattered the "Land of Eternal Spring" red with blood.

Shortly after my return to Guatemala, *Mi Casa*, an orphanage for boys founded by American John Wetterer, came under scrutiny. A peripheral figure in my investigations, Wetterer, his reputation now challenged, unwittingly exposed strange bedfellows in a tryst involving the religious right, U.S. spy services and the military, and lay bare the magnitude of their collective agenda.

Who helped bankroll *Mi Casa*? Wetterer's crumbling defenses now revealed that compassionate U.S. private donors were not the shelter's sole source of support. Benefactors included an oddball assortment of powerful confederates, among them Robert Macauley (1923-2010), founder and chairman of AmeriCares, the New Canaan, Connecticut-based relief agency, a coterie of high-level officials at the U.S. Embassy in Guatemala, and Alvaro Arzú (then foreign minister and later president of Guatemala). Most distanced themselves from Wetterer when his private life turned public; most, except Alvaro Arzú (a cousin of Roberto Alejos Arzú, whose plantation served as a CIA training facility for the ill-fated Bay of Pigs invasion) and whose interest in *Mi Casa* may have been less than altruistic.

Other high-rollers who helped replenish *Mi Casa*'s coffers included members of the Knights of Malta (the Vatican's mouthpiece, a patron of the CIA and a regular conduit into Latin America); perennial U.S. presidential hopeful, Pat Buchanan and W. R. Grace Company head, J. Peter Grace, a man associated with CIA-assisted coups and known to have tried to scuttle progressive international labor movements. Grace, who once referred to former New York Governor Mario Cuomo as "a homo" and to former New York Mayor David Dinkins as "a pinkins," also had a fondness for Nazis. In 1958, he appealed to the U.S. Ambassador in Germany to facilitate the immigration of Dr. Otto Ambros, a developer of Zyklon-B, the deadly gas used in Nazi extermination camps. Convicted at the Nuremberg trials for mass murder and for supplying slave labor to Germany's war machine, Ambros was later hired by Grace as a consultant. Other players would soon be identified, all the instruments of a strategy aimed at destabilizing left-leaning regimes and replacing them with compliant plutocratic minions willing to underwrite the Vatican's theocratic crusade.

What did the unholy dalliance between Robert Macauley, J. Peter Grace, Alvaro Arzú and the Knights of Malta have in common? They all had close ties to the CIA and professed a strong penchant for right-wing causes. AmeriCares, whose declared mission is to "offer relief worldwide regardless of race, religion or political persuasion," became active in Guatemala in the early 1980s, channeling donations to the U.S.-backed military regime. It also contributed to and took sides in U.S.-engineered armed conflicts and routinely flew its armada into ideological battlefields directly linked to U.S. strategic interests.

Macauley's long and intimate relationship with former President George H. W. Bush (they were childhood chums) and with the U.S. intelligence apparatus Bush was to manage as CIA director, is symbolic of unflinching loyalty to the former president's deftly marketed *"Thousand Points of Light"* platform which, like all ultra-conservative solutions to severe socio-economic ills, was used not to relieve misery in Central America but to further cosset the kleptocrats, at home and the Isthmus.

In 1985, Col. Oliver North got Unification Church head, the Rev. Sun Myung Moon, to fund $350,000 worth of supplies to the Contras. Three years earlier, the U.S. had withheld assistance to leftist Sandinista Nicaragua, which had been devastated by a hurricane. It couldn't get its planes in fast enough when right-winger Violetta Chamorro defeated the Sandinistas. On February 28, 1990, barely three days after the election, AmeriCares' first shipment brought in 23 tons of medical supplies *"with love, from the people of the United States to the people of Nicaragua."* Nicaraguan conservative Cardinal Miguel Obando y Bravo took possession of the first shipment and turned it over to the well-connected Knights of Malta for distribution. President Bush's son, Marvin, was aboard the next AmeriCares flight that landed days after Chamorro's inauguration. He was met by a Knights of Malta ambassador -- none other than Roberto Alejos Arzú, a man known for his long association with Guatemala's most reactionary circles, including high-ranking military officers implicated in heinous human rights violations.

The Knights of Malta, AmeriCares' acolytes around the world, is a 900-year-old organization formerly known as the Sovereign Military Hospitaller Order of the Saints John of Jerusalem, Rhodes and Malta. Modeled after an ancient order of soldier-monks who crusaded against the "infidels," and later merged into York Rite Freemasonry, Knights of Malta ceremonies and rituals *"inculcate lessons of chivalry and courage, and inspire a militant spirit in opposition to all non-Christian ideologies and powers."* With over 10,000 members in 42 countries, the Knights are powerful and influential Vatican surrogates with extensive ties to intelligence networks and, some say, to the highest echelons of organized crime.

The American branch of the Knights of Malta, which awarded Ronald Reagan the Grand Cross of Merit in 1988 "for devotion to Christian principles," counted among its members former CIA directors William Casey (1913-1987) and John McCone (1902-1991). McCone helped engineer the 1973 military coup against Chile's Salvador Allende. Others included the zealous and paranoid former CIA chief of counterintelligence, James Jesus Angleton (1917-1987); William Buckley (1928-1985); former U.S. Secretary of State, Alexander Haig (1924-2010); former Nixon-Ford treasury secretary, William Simon (1927-2000); Reagan's man at the Vatican, William Wilson (1914-2009); and U.S. Senator Jeremiah Denton (b. 1924), who sponsored a bill allowing U.S. Air Force transports to ship goods for AmeriCares, a privilege accorded no other charitable organization.

•

First indicted in the U.S. in 1990 for mail fraud and later jailed in Guatemala, John Wetterer, a.k.a. *Tio Juan*, remains under U.S. extradition orders. An Interpol arrest warrant is also outstanding.

Wetterer, a Vietnam War veteran from Massapequa, New York, collected nearly a million dollars in contributions mailed from 1984 through 1988 to help run his boy's orphanage, *Mi Casa*. Arguing that the funds were needed to give the boys a "healthy and wholesome environment," he has been repeatedly accused of molesting the wards in his care.

A 25-page deposition signed by several of Wetterer's alleged victims and a copy of the arrest warrant issued by the U.S. District Court of New York, describe in graphic details lewd acts committed on boys ranging in age from eight to 15. An affidavit signed by four Guatemalan priests charges Wetterer with showing the boys "adult films with strong sexual content."

Wetterer's arrest -- he was hastily shuffled off to jail while his good friend, Alvaro Arzú, was out of the country, then promptly released when Arzú returned -- polarized Guatemalan society (pro-*Tio Juan* demonstrations nearly turned to riot) and embarrassed the U.S. government. Faced with mounting evidence of Wetterer's misdeeds, the U.S. Embassy issued a carefully worded but ambiguous statement favoring extradition while finding words of praise for his work.

Wetterer was later re-indicted on charges he diverted $60,000 of orphanage funds to help his brother, Gary Wetterer, purchase waterfront property in Babylon, Long Island. Motions for an appeal to re-indict John Wetterer on the original charges were filed with the Justice Department in Washington but remain unheeded. Persistent rumors allege that Wetterer is being protected by powerful allies within Guatemala. A source of unimpeachable integrity told me that Alvaro Arzú and a former mayor of Guatemala City (and former president of Guatemala), Oscar Berger, were frequent guests at *Mi Casa*, where, it is alleged, they routinely "cavorted" with young boys. When *Tio Juan* was issued a restraining order ordering him to keep away from minors, Berger donated the orphanage a piece of land. He is said to have invited Wetterer and several of the kids to his home, basically snubbing the judicial order.

Requests for audiences with Alvaro Arzú and U.S. Ambassador Thomas Strook, were denied at the last minute. Arzú offered no explanation and repeated attempts to reach him were deftly stonewalled. Strook, in a telephone conversation a week or so later, told me that an "ongoing drug interdiction operation" had prevented him from seeing me. An Embassy official who agreed to a hasty, furtive encounter outside embassy walls -- "I could lose my job if I'm seen talking to you" -- put it to me succinctly. Jabbing a nervous finger into my breastbone, a mixture of anxiety and annoyance etched upon his face, he said: "I wouldn't get too close to this story if I were you." Only time will tell, I mused, whether this is a warning or just friendly advice. The next day, I found a funeral wreath propped against the door of my room at the Casa Grande Hotel, which adjoins the U.S. Embassy.

It may be years before *Tio Juan* Wetterer is brought to trial in the U.S. He is now said to be keeping "a very low profile."

•

AmeriCares, which received government funding through the U.S. Agency for International Development (AID), did more than wave the Stars and Striped in Latin America. It helped plant it on foreign soil, an act of colonial arrogance championed by the Knights of Malta and orchestrated by Gen. Richard Stillwell (1917-1991), an architect of counterinsurgency in the Philippines and, later, Ronald Reagan's Pentagon intelligence czar. Stillwell's benevolence goes back to the Vietnam War when he was a key proponent of the "Strategic Hamlet" program in which millions of villagers were evicted from their homes and herded into concentration camps to prevent contact with the nationalist Viet Cong.

This immaculate deception was later used against Guatemalan *campesinos* with brutal efficiency. In 1983, then a deputy undersecretary of defense for policy, Stillwell co-founded a super-secret Army spy unit, the Intelligence Support Activity, which operated in El Salvador, Nicaragua and parts of Africa.

In 1984, while AmeriCares flew missions to Afghanistan, the Knights of Malta distributed $14 million in "aid" to Contra-held facilities in Honduras and to Guatemalan military commandos engaged in counterinsurgency sweeps which resulted in the death or "disappearance" of tens of thousands of men, women and children in the highlands.

Since 1983, AmeriCares shipments were handled exclusively by the Knights of Malta. In El Salvador, local KoM head Gerald Coughlan, a retired FBI agent and an executive of International Harvester, donated warehouse space. Another Salvadoran Knight,

Miguel Salavarria, the manager of a large coffee plantation, befriended fundamentalist TV preacher Pat Robertson and helped launch his Latin American crusade.

The Air Commandos, a group of retired military pilots known to have had close ties with the Contras, flew large quantities of "aid" cargo. When they were not distributing ineffective or nearly expired U.S. pharmaceuticals to unwary villagers, the Air Commandos delivered shipments of Israeli weapons to the Contras. Brokered by Mike Harari (b. 1927), former Mossad station chief in Mexico, long-time friend of Panama's Omar Torrijos and Manuel Noriega, and a popular visiting professor of espionage, the Israeli arms sale took the slack left by the "official" but sham U.S. arms embargo to the region. Harari also supplied weapons to Anastasio Somoza and, later, to the Guatemalan military, the national police and anyone who could afford them. (*I later learned from a source at the Consulate General of Israel in New York, where I'd worked as a press officer, that the weapons had been purchased from Israel by the U.S. with the understanding that they would be channeled directly into Guatemala*).

Roberto Alejos Arzú, the consummate apologist politician, found this commerce neither strange nor reprehensible.

"There is nothing wrong with friends helping friends," he said. Alejos typifies the handful of Guatemalans who own close to ninety percent of all wealth -- including arable land -- while the rest of his people live below the poverty level and over eighty percent of the children in rural areas suffer from malnutrition, iodine deficiency and chronic respiratory disorders.

Jean-Marie Simon, author of the disquieting exposé, "*Guatemala: Eternal Spring, Eternal Tyranny*," describes Alejos as "a thug in a business suit." Alejos was involved in kidnappings, military coups and death squads. According to the North American Council on Latin America, "as with most of the Guatemalan elite, there is evidence linking Alejos to *La Mano Blanca*," a death squad specializing in torture, machine-gun executions and "disappearances" of political rivals. Other victims routinely included students, liberal priests, labor organizers, journalists, teachers and indigenous activists, all labeled "Marxists" because they pressed for social and economic reform. Alan

Nairn, formerly with the Council on Hemispheric Affairs and a long-time editor-at-large at *The Nation,* charged Alejos with having summarily executed workers on his plantation when they tried to strike or organize.

In Nicaragua, Sandinista officials continue to allege that AmeriCares and the Knights of Malta are CIA fronts. This allegation is not without merit. In 1984, AmeriCares attempted to fly a planeload of CIA-edited newsprint to the anti-Sandinista daily, *La Prensa*, claiming that the shipment also included medicines. That same year, the CIA used its confederates to distribute thousands of copies of a 90-page manual titled, *Psychological Operations in Guerrilla War* to CIA-backed Contra rebels. Written in Spanish and printed at CIA headquarters in Langley, Virginia, the manual urges Contra forces to kidnap Sandinista government members and to *"neutralize selected officials,"* a euphemism for assassination. The manual also advises hiring criminals to kill fellow rebels so they will be perceived as martyrs, and blackmailing Nicaraguan citizens into joining the rebel cause.

The late Senator Daniel Patrick Moynahan (1927-2003) alleged that much of the manual had been lifted word for word from protocols for guerrilla warfare training given to Green Berets during the Vietnam War. The same lesson plans were used by the U.S. Army School of the Americas to train thousands of Latin American military officers.

Although the House Intelligence Committee concluded in December 1984 that the manual violated a 1982 decoy law which forbids U.S. personnel from taking part in the overthrow of the Sandinista government, the CIA has steadfastly denied Congressional investigators and the press an opportunity to questions the author(s) of the manual.

That same year, in a vitriolic OP/ED piece rhapsodizing his supporters on the radical right and reeking of political self-predestination, then New York Post columnist Patrick J. Buchanan set the tone for eight more years of press-bashing by Ronald Reagan and George H. W. Bush, two flamboyant and insensitive presidents sinfully out of touch with their constituents and indifferent to the worsening lot of Latin America's poor. Buchanan warned that journalists, whose impartiality is apt to embarrass the administration, are the nation's "most dangerous adversaries."

Exculpation by vehement denial or the concealment of incriminating evidence is not an American invention. But the artifice has served America well in foreign affairs, in the Isthmus and elsewhere around the world.

Buchanan's penchant for right-wing causes goes back a long way and is rooted in what he describes as "the militant and uncompromising Catholicism of my youth." To the dismay of Jewish groups, he opposed the prosecution of the late "ex" Nazi and former U.N. Secretary-General, Kurt Waldheim, and fought the deportation of John Demjanjuk and Kurt Linas, two Nazi war criminals then living in the U.S.

In 1970, Buchanan, then Nixon's White House Director of Communications and a student of Ovid and Cicero, drafted a memorandum in which he outlined how "conservative philanthropic organizations" could be used to derail groups perceived as "leftist."

In recommending that "a countervailing power outside the government be created," he urged Nixon to "direct an in-house group of people -- preferably outside the Administration -- to quietly undertake a study of the top 25 U.S. foundations; to identify both their leadership and power structure; and to indicate which are friendly, which are potentially friendly; and which can be counted on to carry out the Administration's objectives."

Buchanan's memo further advocated "a policy of favoritism in all future federal grants to those institutions friendly to us [while directing] future funds away from hostile foundations [such as The Brookings Institution]." He also cautioned that some of the essential objectives of this new "countervailing power" would have to be "blurred, even buried, in all sorts of other activities managed by people who knew what was going on and agreed to it."

Among those who knew and agreed were right-wing activists, including members of the John Birch Society, the Knights of Malta and the CIA.

Men philosophize about evil, sometimes to condone it.

WHEN THE ENDS JUSTIFY THE MEANS

In a letter dated March 1998, Connecticut Senator Joseph Lieberman wrote to assure me that he wanted "the criminals identified and prosecuted." He added that "the United States should not tolerate the illegal, corrupt and despicable behavior of some graduates of the [U.S. Army] School of the Americas, and every effort should be made to investigate such behavior and prosecute offenders appropriately." His assurances proved worthless. A Republican wolf in Democrat -- later "Independent" -- sheep's clothing, Lieberman has since inched his way far up the Republican rectum and his actions and words betray a conservative, not to say reactionary perspective and agenda. It is not surprising that, ten years later, reminding him of our prior correspondence and asking him to restate his position on the SOA, Senator Lieberman responded swiftly but with characteristic evasion:

> *"Regrettably, due to the huge volume of mail that I receive, I am only able to research and address comments sent to me from Connecticut residents."*

Attempts to reach Lieberman after that proved fruitless.

Echoing the views of his colleague in a letter dated April 1998, the outwardly more even-handed Senator Christopher Dodd expressed

> *"deep concern with* [the School's] *egregious human rights violations. Time has come to determine whether it is serving our national interests and furthering our goals. It is our responsibility to closely examine the record of the SOA. I read your articles with interest, and* [they] *lend further credibility to the view that it is time to take a serious look at the program in Fort Benning."*

Requests for a statement reflecting his current optic were ignored. So were efforts to obtain an on-the-record comment from Democratic California Senators Barbara Boxer and Diane Feinstein.

Government is like a whorehouse; the prostitutes come and go, the institution endures.

Writing about then-presidential contender Barack H. Obama, Nikolas Kozloff, of the North American Congress on Latin America, said:

"For a candidate who talks the talk on human rights, Obama has had little to say about the infamous School. [He] likes to employ soaring rhetoric when discussing human rights. But he failed to take a strong position opposing the SOA. When pressed, he said that he wanted to continue to evaluate the institution. What more information could Obama possibly need to reach a final decision on the matter? An Obama spokesman said the senator 'has not committed to closing down the school [now renamed Western Hemisphere Institute for Security Cooperation], but will take a hard look at the program and the progress it has made once he is elected.' To put this all in perspective, Obama has staked out a position to the right of Ron Paul, many members of Congress, and mainstream labor and Church organizations. Given widespread public disgust towards torture and the like, Obama's meekness on WHINSEC is perplexing. In the wake of the Abu Ghraib prisoner abuse scandal, many U.S. citizens have soured on the War on Terror. Meanwhile, the prisoner detention center at Guantánamo Bay, Cuba, has become an international eyesore. Even President Bush and Defense Secretary Robert Gates have publicly said they'd prefer to close the facility. Obama also supports closing Guantánamo, which makes his statements on WHINSEC all the more befuddling. In the present political climate, what does the Senator have to lose by coming out against the former U.S. Army School of the Americas? Perhaps he fears the GOP might accuse him of being weak on defense. But Republican nominee John McCain is not likely to use torture as ammunition during

the campaign -- it hardly seems a winning electoral issue for the Arizona Senator. What's more, many voters are oblivious to WHINSEC and have little knowledge of, or interest in, U.S. policy towards Latin America. No, it's not fear of GOP retaliation on the campaign trail that keeps Obama quiet on WHINSEC. What the Senator is really concerned about is offending the movers and shakers within the military-industrial complex. Closing WHINSEC would demonstrate that the United States has no interest in dominating the peoples of Latin America by military means. Obama however is reluctant to make a clean break from the United States' imperialist past."

After more than three years in office, President Obama has yet to declare his position on the issue, let alone define a coherent strategy.

Politicians speak like poets during electoral campaigns and act like surgeons when they get into office.

Others were not as coy.

"I can think of no earthly reason why our government should [continue to] use taxpayers' money to support the SOA," said Rep. Sam Farr (D-California). The only two Democratic presidential contenders who expressed unambiguous opposition to the institution were long shots former Alaska Senator Mike Gravel and Ohio's Dennis Kucinich. Republican Ron Paul said he too would shutter the school. Strange assurance from an anti-war candidate who has pledged to abolish both the CIA and the FBI to "protect individual liberties" while his flaccid and hopeless presidential campaign is being funded by Peter Thiel, founder of Pay Pal and head of Palantir Technologies, a defense contractor that profits from government espionage work for the CIA and the FBI, and which was caught organizing in 2011 an illegal spy ring targeting opponents of the U.S. Chamber of Commerce, including journalists, progressive activists and union leaders. There is no hint, so far, that Thiel's dealings with the CIA have changed Paul's position on civil liberties.

What Kucinich, Farr and others were referring to were grudging admissions by the Pentagon that torture had routinely been included in the School's curriculum. Founded in Panama in 1948 and now billeted at Fort Benning, Georgia, the SOA would sire a large number of thugs. Hundreds of high-ranking graduates have since been charged in the wholesale abduction, torture, murder, rape and "disappearance" of hundreds of thousands of peasants, activist clergy, trade unionists, teachers, students, human rights advocates and journalists. Many were also implicated in drug-running and money laundering schemes. Typically, the U.S. overlooked their crimes when the perceived common hemispheric enemy was communism.

In an unprecedented move to placate a growing number of SOA detractors in and out of government, and perhaps to deflect attention from a CIA mired in scandal and controversy, the Pentagon released seven SOA training manuals. The declassification puts an end to years of speculations about the School's pedagogic objectives. It also establishes an airtight cause-and-effect connection between the SOA and the atrocities some of its best students committed during the bloody Central American conflict of the 1980s.

In language devoid of ambiguity or paradox, the primers teach soldiers how to torture and execute guerrillas; pay bounties for enemy dead; use "motivation-by-fear;" intimidate the press; sequester "enemy" intelligence assets and their families; subvert and control rural populations; use blackmail and administer injections of sodium pentothal -- "truth serum" -- to extract information.

So much for the "democratization" of Latin America. Predictably, the Patriot Act, Abu Ghraib, "extraordinary rendition" and "enhanced interrogation techniques" were not far off.

Characteristically, what the Pentagon did not do is apologize. Nor is the SOA eager to comment. Nonplused by the Pentagon's disclosures, it steadfastly rejects any hint of wrongdoing. It continues to cling to a revisionist rendering of reality that goes beyond selective amnesia. I call it exculpation by vehement denial.

HIS GRAY EMINENCE

Any lingering doubts that the inmates had taken over the asylum would be dispelled with the nomination by President George W. Bush (and the virtually unopposed confirmation by Congress) of John Negroponte as Ambassador to Iraq. A Foreign Service veteran -- former envoy to Vietnam, Honduras, Mexico and the Philippines, permanent representative to the United Nations and Director of National Intelligence -- Negroponte would be entrusted with the "pacification" and "democratization" of a nation that has never known nor understood democracy and which is now at war with itself. His mission would end in dismal failure.

Described as a "career diplomat devoid of convictions, only unflinching loyalty to the body politic," Negroponte stands accused of concealing from Congress human rights abuses in Central America. While ambassador to Honduras from 1981 to 1985, Negroponte directed the secret arming of Nicaragua's "Contra" rebels and is charged by human rights groups of overlooking a CIA-funded Honduran death squad -- the infamous Battalion 3-16 -- while at his post in Tegucigalpa.

Although Negroponte steadfastly denies any knowledge of the atrocities, declassified documents and disclosures by former death squad members cast doubt on his sincerity. A former embassy information officer who spoke on condition of anonymity told me that Negroponte, who professed to be a staunch advocate of human rights, was indeed involved in human rights, "but not quite the way he claimed." The embassy official added that "dispatches about the human rights situation in Honduras [under Negroponte's watch] were so sanitized that cadres at the embassy in Tegucigalpa joked that they were written about Norway...."

José Miguel Vivanco, director of Human Rights Watch/Americas, called Negroponte "the ostrich ambassador: He never saw anything wrong. He never heard about any human rights violations. It was like he was living on a different planet."

The hasty expulsion from the U.S. of several former death squad members had also raised thorny questions. The men, who'd been granted asylum in the U.S. and Canada in exchange for their discretion, were expelled to Honduras within days of Negroponte's nomination to the U.N. post.

One of them, General Luis Alonzo Discua Elvir, who served as Honduras' deputy ambassador to the U.N. until the State Department revoked his visa in 2001, went public with details of U.S. support for the death squad he co-founded.

At the time, Democratic presidential hopeful, Sen. John Kerry, a member of the Foreign Relations Committee, accused Negroponte of being "at the center of a clash over deep disagreements we had about the role the U.S. should play in Central America and, more importantly, the way -- often secretive or, at best, unclear -- in which policy was being conducted."

Kerry had added that "new information suggests that the U.S. Embassy in Honduras knew more about human rights violations than was communicated to Congress and the public."

In 1981, President Reagan sent Negroponte to Honduras, the "banana republic" Washington commandeered as a base for covert military operations against the leftist Sandinistas who controlled neighboring Nicaragua.

On several occasions Ambassador Jack Binns, Negroponte's predecessor in Honduras, had warned the State Department that violence against political opponents of the puppet Honduran government were on the rise. He first got the cold-shoulder treatment then was summoned to Washington and reprimanded by Assistant Secretary of State Thomas Enders for reporting human rights abuses through official channels.

"He [Enders] was afraid it would leak and make it more difficult for us to continue our economic and security assistance to the contras," said Binns, now retired. Binn's stint at ambassador lasted only a year, ending shortly after protesting the violence in Honduras.

At Negroponte's behest, U.S. military aid to Honduras ballooned from $4 million to $77.4 million. He also helped orchestrate a cabal now known as the "Iran-Contra Affair," during which arms were funneled through Honduras to help the contras overthrow the constitutionally elected Sandinista regime in Nicaragua.

Negroponte looked the other way when atrocities were committed in Central America. In light of stinging revelations of prisoner abuse at the hands of the U.S. military at the Abu Ghraib Detention Center in Iraq and at the prison in Guantanamo, one wonders what kind of message the Bush administration was sending about human rights by posting Negroponte to represent the U.S in Baghdad. Worse, what kind of message did Mr. Bush send about his own moral values?

A man with skeletons in his political closet, Negroponte, a long-time protégé of former Secretary of State Colin Powell, [he can be seen seated behind Powell, a faint grin animating his face as the deluded Powell told the U.N. General Assembly that Saddam Hussein was stockpiling weapons of mass destruction] spent 37 years in the Foreign Service. Like all has-beens, he is now a research fellow and a lecturer.

•

It took six months of negotiations ably mediated by a mutual contact in Honduras to locate an SOA alumnus willing to talk. It took nearly as long to finalize the rules of engagement. Because the subject categorically denied ever receiving anything but "classic war college instruction," it became obvious from the outset that ruminating on the errant CIA training manuals would be fruitless. And, since the more sinister exploits of SOA graduates had been copiously rendered by the media -- including by this writer -- I also reluctantly agreed not to dwell on any specific aspect of subject's military career. It was that or nothing.

Lt. Col. (Ret.) Roberto Nuñez Montes first attended the Panama SOA campus in 1963 as a cadet. He returned in 1965 and took military intelligence courses. A former Military Intelligence Chief, Nuñez was cited by an America's Watch Report as the alleged mastermind in 1987 of a raid on the household of a Honduran Congressional deputy. I knew nothing else about the man before we met. Intuition and conjecture in the face of history did little to help fill the blanks after we parted (though far more serious allegations against Nuñez would since surface).

What the taped interview (here stripped of small talk) lacks in incriminating detail is more than offset by Nuñez's candor and ferocious convictions. His rhetoric is anchored in unbending soldierly doctrine: However abhorrent, atrocities in wartime are unavoidable, often justified. His arguments offer a stark insight into the military soul. His optic also adds a chilling dimension to the mood, legacy and contradictions spawned by lingering Cold War paranoia.

Q: Who were your instructors?

A: Officer-level classes were taught by Latin American SOA graduates.

Q: Did the SOA offer courses in human rights?

A: I don't remember.

Q: Did some SOA graduates commit acts of barbarism?

A: Warring sides give different labels to the tactical components of a military operation.

Q: *Military operation?*

A: Yes. We were at war.

Q: Against your own people? Civilians? You weren't defending against foreign invasion.

A: Civilians subverted by outside influences can destroy a nation.

Q: Old men, women, children?

A: All part of a communist insurgency.

Q: Are you calling clergy, teachers, students, journalists, peasants, and trade unionists, "communist insurgents," thus justifying....

A: Yes -- communists! They threatened the public order and national security. Ours was a war fueled by outside ideological forces intent on subverting the whole region and....

Q: ... thus justifying the murder of priests and labor organizers because their vision of hope for the poor clashed with the interests of the plutocracy? Some were executed face down in the mud....

A: So what?

Q: ... justifying the rape and slaughter of nuns who taught children how to read and write? Justifying the "disappearance" of thousands of civilians? Justifying the massacre of 900 peasants in El Mozote, and gunning down an archbishop and six Jesuit priests who championed the powerless against the powerful?

A: I don't care if they were the Pope. War makes titles, status or celebrity quite irrelevant. They were communists. All the damned lot! They had to be neutralized.

Q: ... or throwing people out of helicopters several hundred feet above ground? Or using private houses as detention and torture chambers?

A: Yes, yes, yes! Madness! No one pretends that war is pretty. There was no other way. The main moral question is what was the *right* thing to do under the circumstance, not who did it, or how. Many good policies are promoted for morally dubious reasons and many bad policies are advanced with the best of intentions.

Q: Good intentions and an unshakable conviction in the morality of a cause do not make such a cause moral, do they?

A: Philosophers must decide, not soldiers. Ultimately, we must ask to what extent the military actions of a debtor nation are driven by the policies and objectives of its creditor.

Q: Nations that depend on superpowers for their survival can never be free -- is that what you're saying?

A: It's one way of putting it.

Q: Is there democracy in Central America today?

A: No. What we have are amorphous societies run by improvisation, governments that have no national conscience, no doctrine, no vision, no plan. They have lost sight of the priorities. When everything is important, nothing gets done.

Nuñez saw fresh signs of conspiracy, "as vast and wicked" as the ones that set fire to the region in the 1980s. His was an imported and stubbornly articulated minority view, not just the nostalgic musings of an old warrior. He found comfort in the notion that the men whose orders he and fellow SOA alumni issued are at large, some chairing large corporations, others basking like sated iguanas, among fellow U.S. expatriates, their cozy retirement in Central America and the Caribbean subsidized by those they helped to positions of military or dictatorial power.

Nuñez also delights in the irony that the punishment called for by a small number of U.S. congressmen for convicted war criminals may never be meted out. In the tug-of-war of accusations and counter-accusations, prosecution of SOA alumni for war crimes, he believes, would "backfire and bring instant and unwelcome scrutiny" on the School, the CIA, the DEA the National Security Agency and the Pentagon, not to mention the Reagan and copycat Bush I and II administrations.

•

Titled, "Janitor's secret past: a death squad," a *Los Angeles Times* article published on October 26, 2006 revealed the clandestine life and arrest in L.A. of a former SOA-trained Salvadoran army officer, Gonzalo Guevarra Cerritos, convicted of killing six Jesuits. The hypocrisy of U.S. authorities -- claiming that they were investigating human rights violations -- is troubling. Fact is the U.S. engineered these atrocities and, in some cases, participated in them. Guevarra is small fry and was probably paid off to shut up about the details of the murders, then offered sanctuary in some safe haven where thugs are retired with all the comforts of home.

So much for the "democratization" of Latin America.

•

Last I heard, Col. Nuñez is still convinced that communists are hard at work in the Isthmus. He claims to see signs of conspiracy, "as vast and evil as the ones that set fire to the region in the 1980s." His is a prevalent and forcefully articulated view, not merely the nostalgic musings of an aging soldier.

One of the paradoxes of democracy is that it tolerates in its midst the existence and propagation of antidemocratic ideas. It is that very trait, some argue, that gives democracy its unmatched vigor and nobility. It is also what makes it so appealing to individuals, groups, clans and dynasties that owe their supremacy to autocratic control, a system of governance steadfastly endorsed by U.S. policy and further bolstered by its military surrogates. Another incongruity impossible to explain, let alone expiate, is that in the name of freedom, democracy and human rights, the U.S. has sanctioned despotism, disappearances and death squads.

Speaking on condition of anonymity, a retired U.S. intelligence analyst told me that, guided and backed by the CIA, SOA-trained cadres "systematically abetted the transplantation of military structures into, and facilitated the propagation of military power and objectives against, legitimately installed civilian governments or fledgling democratic institutions. These structures are so solidly entrenched, they wield so much power and enjoy such intimate and mutually compromising relations with the U.S., that it will be neither possible, nor profitable for the U.S. to dismantle them."

What SOA supporters must grapple with, as its alumni's reputation spreads like blood in bath water, is whether keeping the school open sends the wrong message, both in the U.S. and abroad -- namely that power struggles, particularly those engineered by others for reasons of geopolitical hegemony, sharpen plutocratic dominance, end in abuse and hasten the sacrifice of the innocent.

•

Made public after my interview with Nuñez, the report of the independent Historical Clarification Commission acknowledges that the U.S. funded and trained the Guatemalan military during that country's 36-year genocidal war against the indigenous Maya. The report challenges years of ardent denial by the U.S. that it advocated and sanctioned wholesale torture, kidnappings and executions of thousands of civilians. It confirms the CIA's participation in a blood bath that resulted in the death of nearly 400,000 people -- a role the agency had heretofore zealously, if vainly refuted. The report concluded that U.S. support for right-wing governments in the Isthmus and the training of Central American military cadres [at the U.S. Army School of the Americas] played a pivotal role in "aggressive, racist and extremely cruel violations that resulted in the massive extermination of defenseless people."

The Commission points fingers at military intelligence and blames with shameless effrontery "bellicose Central American government policies" for a decade of illegal detentions, torture, disappearances and extra-judicial executions. It fails to name the guilty or argue in favor of justice. It perfunctorily recommends reparations for the victims and advocates "reconciliation through truth."

Moving beyond the horrors of war is salutary. Admitting (and apologizing for) U.S. backing of "military forces that engaged in violence and widespread repression," as President Bill Clinton did before he left office, is praiseworthy. Arguing for "truth" in the abstract while shielding the guilty adds villainy to hypocrisy. Implicit in this artifice is that for the good of society, victims of barbarism should not only abstain from revisiting the past, they should in fact pretend that it never took place.

Oddly, nowhere was this doctrine more forcefully articulated than in Honduras. Whereas Guatemala is visibly struggling with its inglorious past, Honduras, a nation that gleefully collaborated with the U.S. and demonstrated great skill in meting out its own brand of "anti-communist" justice, continues to seek absolution by promoting collective amnesia.

"Let bygones be bygones," Col. Nuñez pleaded. "The dead are buried and their killers are now old men. How long must we regurgitate the past?"

Poor choice of words from an old soldier to a Holocaust survivor whose family was denied the privilege of old age; fiendish reasoning from a former intelligence officer who calls for a return to military rule and equates any form of political dissent with "terrorism" and "communism."

"You admit there were killers among you."

"We had a job to do."

"The war is over. You're anxious to get on with your life, aren't you? Why not cooperate and help bring the guilty to justice? If you don't, Honduras will not only 'regurgitate' the past, it may well choke on it."

"It's not our job to cooperate. Let the courts handle the matter."

"You know damn well the courts have no *cojones*."

"That's not my problem."

Nuñez is right. With very few exceptions, Honduran tribunals, in the name of "reconciliation," have either looked the other way, conducted pro forma hearings on cases that never went to trial, masterminded the defection of military thugs to safe havens abroad, or simply engineered their release on the grounds that they lacked "sufficient evidence."

While human rights abuses by the Honduran military pale in comparison with their Colombian and Salvadoran counterparts, proportionately they exceed those of the Guatemalan armed forces. Grievous and as yet unpunished, they merit reexamination. SOA graduates implicated in various war crimes, as was Col. Nuñez, are still free and living the good life. They have bought their freedom from and are being shielded by an apathetic and mercenary judiciary accustomed to coddling the rich and the powerful.

●

Some former death-squad members have since branched out into organized crime. Others have invested in "legitimate" businesses. The proverbial "long arm of the law," stunted and collusive, continues to short-change the victims. In so doing, it not only defiles justice, it adds fuel to the flames of national discontent.

There is no statute of limitation on war crimes. War criminals are prosecutable and punishable. So are the intellectual authors who sanction or orchestrate atrocities from the safety of their office. Asking survivors of violence to look the other way while their persecutors are still free is an affront to justice. It is also an invitation to further discord and social conflict in nations scarred by dynasties of thugs.

●

Predictably, the SOA, which has trained, supplied and coddled the "internal security forces" of 17 Latin American and Caribbean Basin nations, and whose alumni continue to bask in the benevolent glow of immunity, has so far evaded what would be a fatal *in vivo* dissection. The world -- and U.S. taxpayers who have footed the bill for over half a century -- may have to wait for an actual postmortem to view and get a whiff of the SOA's malodorous entrails. Now renamed, and with the hot winds of jingoism sweeping America, the school has yet been granted a new lease on life.

●

The CIA, like some mythic deity, has behaved as if it is accountable to no one, as if self-empowerment (when no one looks) and impunity (when no one cares) are the just entitlements of zealots waging the good war of the Sons of Light against the Sons of Darkness. Left to its own devices, "the company" has time and again justified corrupt means to amoral ends, all in the name of "national security." Worse, instead of keeping watch against America's real enemies, it has usurped power not its own and tried to manipulate and control American foreign policy. In defiance of U.S. law, hiding from public scrutiny like a vampire from the rising sun, it has manipulated Congress into granting it powers to wage economic warfare, sabotage, subversion and murder. It further cloaked itself in secrecy by forcing its operatives to sign irreversible non-disclosure oaths.

The CIA also lied through its teeth. When the agency engineered the overthrow of the popularly elected Mohammed Mossadegh in Iran in 1953, his ouster was reported as a "popular uprising." The U.S. government did nothing to amend the report. The CIA then shredded all evidence of its own involvement.

When President Eisenhower ordered the agency to foment a bloody coup against the leftist regime of Guatemala's Jacobo Arbenz in 1954, Henry Cabot Lodge, Ike's ambassador to the U.N. dismissed the action as a "revolt of Guatemalans against Guatemalans." Secretary of State John Foster Dulles, who would order British, French and Israeli forces out of Egypt in 1956 for having acted "unilaterally" (translation: without America's consent) to reopen the Suez Canal, claimed that the Guatemalans were "quietly handling the situation themselves." Quietly indeed. Hundreds of thousands of dead and "disappeared" made very little noise.

Four years after Guatemala, CIA pilots flew missions against Indonesian President Sukarno's forces. The agency then covertly backed a coup in Chile in 1973 and attempted to murder Fidel Castro and Congolese head of state, Patrice Lumumba. Castro survived. Lumumba didn't.

In 1995, the CIA was forced to admit that it had hired SOA alumnus, Col. Juan Alpírez, the torturer and murderer of American lawyer Jennifer Harbury's husband, Guatemalan freedom fighter Efrain Bámaca -- and that it had covered up the crime for months on end. It also conceded that it had authored torture manuals. The CIA officer who blew the whistle by informing U.S. Rep. (later Senator) Robert Toricelli about the incident was fired.

Since 1947, when the venerable and highly effective OSS was transformed into the present-day CIA, the agency has hired and sheltered Nazi war criminals and even brought some to work in the U.S. It subsidized and strengthened the regimes of undemocratic but submissive client states. And, in blatant violation of the law, it snooped on U.S. citizens, tampered with their mail, bugged their phones and tested mind-bending or lethal chemical and biological agents on hundreds of unwitting Americans. It also worked hand-in-glove with the U.S. Army School of the Americas in a symbiosis akin to incest that has spawned unspeakable monsters, many of whom still lurk among us, free, unhindered.

THE MANUAL

Like pus oozing from a festering sore, the CIA's public expiation of past trespasses in Latin America may have had an emetic effect on its conscience. But it came too little, too late, couched in the clinical language of remorselessness and lacking any hint of self-prosecutorial intent.

Documents released by the CIA confirm that the agency taught mental torture and physical coercion techniques to the "security forces" of at least five Latin American states in the early 1980s. The documents also allege to have "repudiated" such training in 1985. A 1983 CIA manual teaches foreign agents the art of extracting information from people without yanking out their fingernails, burning the soles of their feet with the business end of a lit cigarette or hanging them from meat hooks. Claiming that physical torture is counterproductive, it advises against such methods. It suggests, instead, the use of fear, exhaustion, solitary confinement and other forms of psychological duress designed to induce intense anxiety and to "destroy [the subject's] capacity to endure" long periods of interrogation.

"While we do not stress the use of coercive techniques," the manual says, "we want to make you aware of them and the proper way to use them."

These techniques were implemented during President Ronald Reagan's first term, when his administration's anti-communist covert activities relied on the CIA-trained armed forces of El Salvador, Honduras and Guatemala, Nicaraguan Contras, elements of Costa Rica's militarized "civil guard" and, indirectly, the armies of Argentina and Panama. These forces killed, illegally detained, tortured and "disappeared" thousands of suspected "enemies," most of them civilian, during the last decade of the cold war.

Under Congressional pressure, the CIA's role in training its Latin American surrogates was reviewed behind closed doors. In late 1984 and early 1985 leaks to the press and signs of growing public indignation prompted the agency to rewrite the manual and excise passages dealing with coercive interrogation procedures. In October 1984, the agency was rocked by public disclosures of another CIA manual that encouraged Nicaraguan Contras to kidnap and kill elected leftist officials, blackmail citizens and raze entire villages to the ground. Nonplused, the CIA blamed the manual on an "overzealous freelancer" on its payroll. It neither apologized nor withdrew the manual from circulation.

The 1983 manual on interrogation techniques and the 1985 addendum banning coercive tactics were made public in response to a Freedom of Information Act request filed by the *Baltimore Sun* which published a series on the CIA's relationship with Honduras' infamous death squad, Battalion 3-16, whose ranking members were trained at the equally notorious U.S. Army School of the Americas.

The CIA public affairs office acknowledged for the first time that its manuals contained, then excluded, the protocols on psychological torture. Headed, "Coercive Techniques," a section of the 1983 manual advised against "direct physical brutality, as is can create resentment, hostility and defiance" in some prisoners. But it added, "if a subject refuses to comply once a threat [of violence] is made, it must be carried out." With chilling detachment, the manual further counsels:

> *"Torture is an external conflict, a contest between subject and tormentor. The pain which is being inflicted upon [the subject] from outside himself may actually intensify his will to resist. On the other hand, pain which he feels is self-inflicted is more likely to sap his resistance."*

The manual recommends forcing the subject into rigid positions,

> *"... such as standing at attention or sitting on a stool for long periods of time,"* adding that *"the immediate source of pain is not the interrogator but the subject himself."*

The manual also suggests that physical and psychological harassment be combined with

"... persistent manipulation of time -- retarding or advancing clocks, disrupting sleep," all designed to disorient the subject and subvert his will, and to drive him deeper and deeper into himself until he no longer is able to control his responses in an adult fashion."

Some of the passages in the 1983 manual parallel the protocols found in a 1963 CIA primer on interrogation of spies and Soviet agents. Compiled before the agency became subject to congressional oversight or public scrutiny, the work includes a clause requiring prior approval from headquarters to use physical torture, electric shocks and the use of psychotropic drugs. It is not known if such consent was ever sought. Events in Latin America suggest that they were either never denied or that the mandate was simply ignored.

In 1985 the CIA adopted a formal policy against inhumane interrogation. "Experience indicates that the use of force is not necessary to gain cooperation," the policy statement said. It also cautioned that use of force is a poor technique, that it yields unreliable results and that adverse publicity and/or legal action were likely to ensue.

"However," it added, "use of force is not to be confused with psychological ploys, verbal trickery and other non-violent and non-coercive ruses against reticent or uncooperative subjects." Perhaps like waterboarding.

Designed to whitewash past transgressions and to insulate against future ones from prying eyes or accusatory fingers (such as the solitary sequestration of suspected Taliban and al-Qaida operatives), the CIA's injunctions had little effect. Pupils did not heed the teacher's admonitions. Atrocities committed by U.S.-trained Latin American military cadres were recorded long after they were circulated. It's all "gringo rhetoric" based on fake empathy aroused by fear of embarrassment, not humanitarianism; a clear case of the CIA covering its backside.

Meticulous liars tell either plausible or undetectable lies. Only cynics spread preposterous lies.

•

Despite an order by former Attorney General John Ashcroft to "expeditiously declassify and release to the families" information about the fate of victims of torture, disappearances and assassination in Central America, it is unlikely that such order was ever obeyed. The mandate gave federal agencies up to four months to "find" the data, and up to three months after that to "determine" whether it should be released or not. In his order, Ashcroft also reminded the agencies of the president's authority to withhold information that "could impair foreign relations, national security, the deliberative processes of the executive, or the performance of the executive's constitutional duties." Upheld by President Obama, this loophole dashes any hope of transparency on the matter.

RELATIVITY REVISITED

*"There are generations in the world,
there are people whose faces we do not see,
who have no homes.
They wander... like crazy people."*
The Popol Vuh

Separated by three centuries, philosopher Baruch Spinoza and physicist Albert Einstein both studied relativity, the first by exploring the metaphysical realm, the second to postulate immutable cosmic laws. They reached broadly similar conclusions, among them that perception depends on vantage point.

Spinoza buoyed his argument by proposing an intriguing conundrum: Visitors from a faraway planet land on Earth: They're taken to a magnificent palace. Ushered into the king's chambers, they notice scores of people bowing and kneeling before the monarch. Some place their foreheads upon the king's golden robes. Others kiss his feet. Impressed, the space travelers conclude that their host must be a great and saintly man, a benefactor of humanity, or else why would his court engage in such displays of servile adulation?

The visitors are then taken to a coal mine. There they see men with blackened faces hunched over the unyielding rock, toiling from dawn to twilight in the bowels of Earth in suffocating darkness. Surely these men must be evil, the extraterrestrials reason, or else they would have been spared such wretched existence.

Much of human consciousness is based, not on fact, Spinoza teaches, but on how we are conditioned to interpret the occurrence of *being*. There are no wrong answers, only divergent views blurred by conformity to a particular belief. Truth is in the mind's eye of the beholder.

Einstein went several steps further. He suggested not only that reality is what the self perceives, but that perception can actually alter the experience of reality. I had an opportunity to test this strange concept, not in the perfect geometry of space, nor in the sterile labyrinths of Cartesian logic, but in two equally dissimilar yet contiguous regions of the human condition.

Several years ago I attended a reception at a posh hotel in Guatemala City. I crossed paths with bejeweled women, most of them painted to camouflage the ravages of time. I shook hands with sweet-smelling, self-important men in elegant double-breasted suits, silk ties and snake-skin shoes. I engaged in small talk and endured the syrupy banter between those who had come to be seen and those who insist on being heard. Wealth, influence and power all vied for attention as fragrant wines and succulent finger foods traveled on silver trays carried by white-gloved lackeys. Such ostentation, I remarked, must be evidence of great virtue, the well-deserved entitlements of the just, the righteous, the uncorrupted.

Early the next morning, on my way to Zone 3, where the uncorrupted never venture, I came upon sleepy-eyed children pulling heavy loads, sweaty *campesinos* packed like sardines in rickety trucks belching noxious fumes, half submerged under the provisions they'd brought to market from their distant mountain hamlets.

In the stifling shade of an abandoned hallway, young boys in tattered clothes sniffed glue -- one way to escape reality. Further on, resting on a bed of filthy rags near the gutter, a woman slept with an infant at her breast while an older child, disheveled, wiping an ever-running nose on her sleeve, begged for scraps of food. And when I entered the *Basurero,* the sprawling municipal garbage dump, under the limpid blue of a sky black with vultures, I found toddlers and young teens feeding on garbage. Below, knee-deep in steaming mountains of waste and competing with the odious birds of death, another group of youngsters rummaged for a meal, perhaps a discarded toy to brighten an otherwise joyless childhood.

Alien to this netherworld, I asked myself what monstrous sins its denizens had committed to be cursed with such ignominious fate. Gliding on the wings of a sudden gust, a crumpled, lipstick-smeared paper napkin landed at my feet. I recognized the gilt monogram of the hotel where the reception had been held the night before. I felt like screaming.

Back on fashionable *Avenida Reforma*, I met a living ghost. She had no name. Homelessness robs people of all identity. Madness, in her case, further sharpened the alienation, the anonymity. She had no name and she would pass in this dimension and from this life unnoticed. Surely, a name, a vulgar moniker, would give her substance, legitimacy. But she'd been forgotten. Insanity and amnesia had mercifully yanked her from the clutches of reality. But she was real, irritatingly so, the symbol and victim of the society that spawned her. Shunned, loathed, she inspired revulsion, not pity, for she seemed unrepentant, defiant in her grotesque cardboard palace, amid the debris, the scraps of metal, the offal on which she fed, the useless memories that haunted her still, come rain or come shine, come hell or high water.

Her partner-in-grime, ageless, toothless, feral and mad, too mad to erect her own shelter, sat by her companion's side or stole forty winks on the naked pavement. Wielding a yard of rubber tubing, or an old broom, she chased after man and specter with equal fury, a menacing fist raised against oncoming traffic and snickering children, striking the ground with anger and bewilderment -- no, with exasperation, spitting at passers-by, pelting them with invectives. Sometimes rage crested like an open flame and a torrent of tears drenched her grandmotherly face. She then calmed down, tuned in briefly on the world around her and resumed her silent vigil, a lifeless gaze now focused on an all-consuming void.

One morning, the police came and destroyed the paper, string and plastic scaffolding her friend had erected. The woman put up a fierce battle but the cops prevailed. Trampled by uncaring feet, the decimated remains of her flimsy abode were carted away. She was allowed to bed down on the bare sidewalk and fend for herself.

Up the road, in the narrow, windswept slop-splattered alley that hugs the flanks of a church, a man writhed in drug-induced agony. Frothing at the mouth, his eyes on fire, he crumbled to the ground and let out a blood-curdling wail. Wallowing in waste, he clawed at the demons that tormented him. Thrashing about, he rolled into the gutter and narrowly missed being hit by a passing car. Safe in their pews, the faithful were being treated to the grand spectacle of a mid-day mass. *Dominus vobiscum*, chanted the priest. *Et cum spiritu tuo*, the faithful responded, unmindful of the pervading godlessness that surrounds them.

Around the corner, a group of cripples flaunted their grotesque infirmities on the very steps of City Hall. Unruffled, passers-by stepped over them like so much debris. Across the street, a young woman breast-fed her newborn as three older daughters, sired by three different men, plied the beggar's trade.

Who are the mad, I reflected, and who are the meek who inherit the wind? As I pondered the question, I learned that the cadavers of several street children had been found, face down, in the municipal garbage dump. They'd been bound and gagged and shot, gangland-style, in the back of the head.

The only thing that separates "God" and his creation is a dissimilar perspective. Relativity prevents either from switching places. On planet Earth, where heaven and hell coexist in perilous proximity, right and wrong are less sharply defined. For the powerful, the privileged, the favored, the free, truth remains the stronger of two or more conflicting views. For the poor, the disenfranchised, the voiceless, the forgotten, the truth is a useless paradox, like relativity. Don't look for justice, I kept telling myself. Don't look for civility. All you will find is nature, cruel and unmoved, and the aggregate interests of the dominant power base.

•

The UNICEF Press Award ceremony at the Foreign Ministry in Tegucigalpa provided a surreal counterpoint to a week-long barrage of angry threats by the Honduran media against children's rights advocates in Central America. The event also offered a stark contrast in personalities, rhetoric and relativistic justifications.

UNICEF's exhortation that media "should focus on the positive, not on the negative," was in keeping with the organization's "non-confrontational" approach to human rights violations. After all UNICEF donors want to read about happy, well-fed children, not starving, abused outcasts.

Nobel Laureate, Rigoberta Menchú Tum, the *"autodidact peasant,"* who presented the awards, spoke with the riveting eloquence accorded someone who saw half her family massacred right before her eyes by Uncle Sam's Guatemalan pawns.

"The role of the media is to educate, inform, to shed light where there is none, or where the light is filtered. No society is safe without a passionate, incorruptible press."

"Ms. Menchú," I asked, "how would you react to reports that minors are illegally incarcerated with adults in virtually all of Honduras' penal institutions?"

"I have difficulty in English but I understand what you say. Tell the world." She squeezed my hand knowingly, smiled softly and moved on.

I later put the same question to the late President Roberto Reina's envoy, Vice President Guadalupe Jerezano. She reacted with controlled indignation and recited the official catechism.

"This is a complex economic problem. We have repeatedly argued that we just don't have the funds to build separate facilities for adults and for minors. At this time we face obstacles and priorities of a higher magnitude and urgency than the separation of minors and adults in jails and prisons."

"Are you saying that the welfare of children is not a priority?"

"You're putting words in my mouth and trying to embarrass Honduras by making unfair inferences."

"Madam Vice President, you're embarrassing yourself and your government by disregarding your own laws. A year ago, President Reina issued a decree banning the jailing of kids with adults, but judges have stubbornly ignored the ban. Why? Three separate articles in the Honduran Constitution specifically prohibit the incarceration of minors with adults, yet the two are routinely confined in the same small, crowded cells. Why?"

"You forget that Honduras is a very poor country," pleaded the vice president, who had come to the reception in a chauffeur-driven Mercedes-Benz limousine and sported several pieces of diamond jewelry.

"Honduras is not a poor country," I retorted. "It has great natural resources. You receive millions upon millions of dollars in foreign aid and yet you continue to extend the hand of beggary. Where does all that money go? It surely doesn't seem to reach the people."

"Look, this is the wrong time to discuss our problems." Ms. Jerezano reached for a glass of wine, took a long sip, nodded her head and bid me a frosty good evening.

A foreign diplomat who'd witnessed the exchange chided me for my lack of tact.

"I'm not running for office. Freedom," I responded, quoting George Orwell, "is the right to tell people what they don't want to hear."

When the stories I write give me nightmares or insomnia, it's time to wake up and invade the cozy sleep of the unaware or the unmindful.

FRANCISCO'S NEW SHOES

Francisco's new shoes are scuffed, caked with prison slime. They're the relics of freedom divested, pride reviled, the symbols of impermanence, the vestiges of a modest reward granted him for exposing evil with an unassuming eloquence that would come back to haunt him.

Francisco knows this odious place, the turf, the vile smells, the hideous faces of human jackals who prey on the weak, the lonely. He's mastered the survival schemes, the tricks, the scams. He's faced fear, hopelessness, and the immutability of time. Staying alive at the San Pedro Sula penitentiary is no small feat. It's not so much the unbearable heat, the overcrowding, the biting insects, the vile food, the bedlam, the unspoken rage, the shrieks of despair in the dead of night. It's the fear of going mad. Like the vultures circling overhead in satanic formation, psychosis waits its turn as other malignant emotions sap confidence and exhaust the very will to live.

Two years ago, accused of petty theft but never charged, Francisco and his twin brother -- they were 16 -- were jailed, illegally, for more than 18 months in a compound occupied by hardened adult felons. Corrections officers and older inmates alike took turns bullying and beating them. They also witnessed the rape of young prisoners by guards and trustees, an indiscretion they paid for by spending two weeks in a five foot square torture cell, along with a several other prisoners.

When Francisco and his brother were returned to the prison's general population they discovered that the key to their locker had been stolen. They confronted a fellow prisoner. High on drugs, the prisoner lunged at Francisco with a knife, wounding him and killing his brother instantly.

In October 1997, following months of charges and counter-charges between him and Honduran authorities, Bruce Harris, Casa Alianza's Executive Director, presented this latest case in a long series of abuses to the Inter-American Human Rights Commission in Washington.

Called to testify, Harris presented evidence of endemic atrocities committed against minors in the country's 24 penal institutions. He called for swift punishment of the perpetrators.

Accompanying Harris to Washington were various dignitaries, including the Honduran representative to the Organization of American States, Honduran Ambassador Marlene de Talbot, and Honduran Public Defender, Linda Rivera. Undoubtedly, the most important member of the delegation was Francisco himself. In riveting testimony to the Commission, Francisco described in detail his experiences as the San Pedro Sula prison. He spoke of the abuse, physical and sexual, that adult prisoners inflict on minors and he sketched a stark image of the terrible living conditions they are forced to endure. He told his galvanized audience about the torture chamber in which he and fellow inmates were herded and where they slept standing up in the intense heat; about the plastic bags in which some foul meal was served once a day and into which prisoners were forced to relieve themselves. Choking back the tears, he recounted how guards would come by at night, throw buckets of water into the cell then attach live electric wires on the metal grating against which the exhausted men were leaning.

"The guards were amused. They enjoyed the spectacle of sweating, hungry, tired, humiliated men squirming in pain every time they sent another jolt of current...."

When Francisco returned to Choloma, his north Coast hometown, Casa Alianza bought him two pairs of shoes. It was to be a good luck gift, his send-off on a steadier course, a more auspicious road ahead. But he had become something of a celebrity and, from hereon in, the easy target of an unrepentant and vengeful judiciary.

Predictably, Francisco was re-arrested in November and remanded to the same penitentiary on trumped-up charges, hearsay and circumstantial evidence that would have been summarily dismissed had Honduras' inquisitorial system not prevailed. Months of investigations and dozens of writs of habeas corpus filed by Casa Alianza's Legal Aid Office were routinely ignored. Francisco was still in jail when I last paid him a visit. Casa Alianza's attorney, Gustavo Escoto, Public Defender, Hector Arzu and this writer spent a day poring over Francisco's files at the Third Judicial District in San Pedro Sula. None found any proof of wrongdoing. Worse, Francisco had yet to be charged. Naked revenge by the State for his testimony in Washington and for the ensuing embarrassment Honduras suffered in the court of public opinion could not be discounted. An appeal was filed.

Shy, not given to idle chatter, his eyes and thoughts turned toward Choloma where his mother and young brothers and sisters awaited his return, Francisco spit in his fingers and rubbed the shoes' once lustrous leather face. Some of the former sheen yielded briefly to his gentle strokes but the elements and neglect are unforgiving and the gray dullness soon reappeared, as if to mock him, hastened by the burning sun and the hot swirling dust at his feet.

His selfhood impugned, his faith in human institutions shaken, Francisco waited for justice. In Honduras, in very special cases, innocence alone will not buy freedom or redeem a stained reputation. In his case it cost him his life. His bullet-riddled body was discovered in a vacant lot shortly after his release from prison. Corrections officers are on a short list of suspects. None will ever be prosecuted.

CATCH A FALLING STAR

*"Children are like stars. They are lost in the flesh
of the night; but they can be found because they shine.
It is when they become the blackness, that we cannot see them,
that they cease to be children, that they are lost...."*
Guillermo Yuscarán -- Son of Esquipula, Points of Light

Chusito's star is larger than life but its radiance is fading. He will not be reborn from its embers.

"Things could be worse," he says with an untimely sense of predestination. "Life could be forever." Such blighted hope is inexplicable in someone so young. Chusito's cynicism is finely tuned, deeply felt. He's seen the dark side, endured the vulgarity of survival, faced the demons. He's 13.

By day Chusito's world is the carbon copy of a hundred Caribbean seaports: Sweltering heat, sparse touches of grace and opulence on a canvas of squalor and misery. There are unkempt beaches and scum-covered canals in which float, half-submerged, the cadavers of indifference -- trash, human waste, broken-down appliances. Grubby side streets are lined with sleazy bars where locals chug beer and engage garishly painted harlots; darkened pool halls where drug deals are made, and fast-sex bordellos.

La Ceiba, a city of 300,000 continues to spread, fatigued and imperiled, without a plan, without a vision. Like a once-pretty woman, it is now compromised by the elements, ravaged by age, neglect, apathy. Many buildings are cracked, teetering on the brink of collapse. A few eventually crumble in heaps of worn brick and mortar, raising storms of acrid dust in their final agony.

An incessant stream of Diesel-fueled vehicles emits lung-crunching fumes and produces a dissonance of intolerable pitch that assaults the ears, grinds nerves. Dodging each other, motorcycles, Lilliputian taxis and overloaded carts pulled by emaciated mules jockey for space on crowded, unregulated thoroughfares. The frenetic pace only heightens the feeling of weariness, the exhaustion that such momentum creates. It's a city driven by reflex, surviving on hidden reserves of energy akin to frenzy or exasperation.

It's also a city that begs to be loved, for the people have endearing traits, but it also elicits impatience, annoyance and revulsion. Small parks where young lovers meet to steal kisses are littered with trash. Benches are encrusted with guano. Loitering aimlessly, spitting dejectedly, old men wait for the passage of time, as if time were a destination, not a conveyance. A pervasive smell of decay, excrement and death wafts on the wings of intermittent seaborne breezes.

This is Honduras' third largest city. Most travelers pass through on their way to the open spaces and cooling zephyrs of the Bay Islands. At night, after the sun's copper disk has set the sea on fire, La Ceiba turns into a den of Gomorrahan depravity. No lust, however vile, remains unquenched for very long. Here, demand feeds supply. Drugs and human flesh are the commodities of choice, and purveyors abound.

Chusito knows this all too well. Abandoned by his parents when he was six, addicted to the shoe glue *Resistol*, he succumbed to the vile commerce, to survive, to cheat reality. There is no shame and degradation when hunger beckons and hopelessness warps all reason. But Chusito is paying the ultimate price for clinging so passionately to life. He's dying of AIDS.

La Ceiba is one of the hubs for child prostitution. Tourists regularly come to Honduras to exploit minors. While there is no organized child prostitution, networks exist that supply children to pedophiles. Many of the girls are well under 16. There is a street for boys, too. Carnivals and other events attract large numbers of visitors who exercise great stealth, pay cash and command the silence of their accomplices.

At least 300 minors live on the streets of La Ceiba. Most are between the ages of 10 and 16. Most are boys. Illiteracy, poverty, alcoholism, irresponsible paternity are all at work. Most families have not a gram of conscience when it comes to procreation. Use of *Resistol* among the kids is widespread. Produced by H.B. Fuller, the

Minnesota-based manufacturer of adhesives, paints and solvents, it's sold freely throughout Central America. Pimps and sex tourists often pay the children with cans of the deadly glue. It's a case of turpitude further debased by criminal indifference.

In the shelter where he is being cared for, Chusito drifts between excruciating awareness and merciful stupor. Eternal night waits. He will soon be free. Outside, mumbling incoherently, a madwoman, bedraggled, froth caking the corners of her mouth, exchanges stones and insults with vagrants who taunt her. Hoping to squeeze the last traces of pity from a parade of self-absorbed amblers, a cripple displays his horrible deformities. Crying with a studied constancy and resonance, a beggar exposes a newborn at her naked left breast.

Feral dogs, traumatized by hunger, rejection and loneliness, respond to a friendly whistle or the offer of a caress with sidelong glances filled with sadness, mistrust, fear. Head low, tail tucked between their legs, they have surrendered to forces heretofore unimagined, now braved with stoic resignation. They do not have the energy to bark.

In the distance, standing legs wide apart for maximum balance in the shade of a big old tree, a policeman stares catatonically in the void to stay cool, conserve energy, perhaps to guard against the incongruity that surrounds him.

On the street corner, near the Colonial Hotel where I spent the night, a man beckons. "Anything you want, man: Weed? Coke? Girls? Young kids? Name your pleasure."

I describe him to a policeman but the officer stares at me blankly, his eyes-half shut. He waves me off. It's nearly lunch-time. In the noonday heat even duty takes a siesta.

IN XIBALBA'S ENTRAILS

Pleasure is as personal a sensation as pain. No one feels pleasure in quite the same way, or endures pain with the same degree of forbearance, dignity or poise. With irrefutable wisdom, nature has deemed fit to trigger or prolong pain, alerting to the presence of trauma or warning of illness. And with perverse irony, nature has also found it useful to abridge the most intense of all physical pleasures -- orgasm -- to ensure that once discovered, ephemeral ecstasy leads to anticipation, that memory stimulates repetition. It's all tediously simple: We eat so we can get hungry yet another day. Survival manipulates the palate; procreation drives the sexual urge. Were it not for a fleeting spurt of indescribable bliss, would anyone engage in intercourse? Reduced to its primeval core, life combines the pursuit of pleasure with the conscious avoidance of pain. If pleasure delayed is pleasure enhanced, pain unheeded is pain augmented. Only in the most aberrant cultures, among a small remnant of penitent monks, or to the most unrestrained masochists does pain have any redeeming virtue. Pain does not ennoble. In the best of cases, pain is a distraction; in the worst, it's an incomprehensible and cruel ordeal.

These were the thoughts, jumbled and ill-defined, that coursed through my mind when I broke a metatarsal bone in my right foot in the picturesque village of Copán Ruinas, Honduras. Losing my balance as a loose slab of concrete disintegrated under me, my foot lurched violently sideways in a split-second mishap that produced instantaneous and searing pain. Feeling stupid and angry at myself, I limped toward the El Sesteo Restaurant, intent on keeping my date with Don Crescencio.

•

Discretion, cunning, stealth are useful commodities even in the best of times. To Don Crescencio, they're essential virtues, the very tools of survival in a realm where the wrong word, credulity and imprudence will kill.

We huddle at a table, side by side, facing the wall in the darkest corner of the *El Sesteo*. Throbbing with pain, my foot swells and turns a dark shade of blue. We first talk about this and that like neighbors across a picket fence. Then I mention Xibalba.

Don Crescencio stares at me, unknowing, his eyes narrowing with suspicion. He's never heard of Xibalba. But the word, the abstraction, the fullness of its Mayan resonance, awaken a strange clairvoyance of time past and kindles intuitive images of teachings now lost, ancestral wisdom submerged under centuries of alien doctrine and hostile rule. His copper features soften.

"Xibalba, you say?"

"Yes." I draw closer. "It's a place where misery, suffering, disease and death reign, where tears turn to rivers and the laughter of children is seldom heard. The Spaniards call it *infierno*. I hear there is such a place not far from here."

Don Crescencio smiles without pleasure. The abstraction is all too real. He leans into me, speaking in a low, raucous voice, his hand at my back, his lips burning my cheek, his breathing labored from chain smoking, chronic bronchitis, perhaps worse.

Xibalba is a circumstance, not a place. It reaches across a hundred hamlets, a thousand communities; it casts its pall on nearly a million people in these parts. Don Crescencio hopes that the truths he will help me unearth do not fall on deaf ears.

"What your eyes see, your mouth must speak."

It's a tall order.

"Hasta mañana, a la diez," he says. I turn briefly to pay for the soft drinks. Don Crescencio vanishes like an apparition.

●

Don Crescencio is punctual; it's an oddity in these parts. We have coffee. I sip mine; he gulps his down. He's anxious to get going. He feels ill at ease and does not like to dawdle in Copán. After all, it is here that his *compañero*, the charismatic and beloved Maya chieftain, Cándido Amador Recinos, was brutally, senselessly murdered. Don Crescencio swears he can still smell the blood.

I'm in considerable pain. My foot is tightly bandaged. I fashioned an old broomstick into a makeshift crutch.

"Frontera, frontera! Guatemala, Guatemala!" exhorts a young boy atop a pickup truck, his voice hoarse from a regimen of daily broadcasts to *campesinos* and backpackers. Don Crescencio flags the vehicle.

"Climb in, sit and be quiet. You don't know me," he instructs, looking the other way, his lips barely moving.

"Where do I get off?"

"At the junction, by the schoolhouse, one kilometer before the border."

"What about you?"

"Just go."

I comply and straddle a wheel well. There are 13 of us, men, women, patriarchs and small children, two bicycles, an old tire, several rolls of barbed wire, a handful of scrawny chickens that cackle plaintively, and a whimpering suckling pig in a canvas sack. We all huddle in reluctant intimacy, the wind in our hair, dust scouring our faces. It's about six kilometers to the junction and my coccyx will ache for days but the scenery is stunning and I hang on for dear life as the truck navigates the winding, bumpy road ahead like flotsam on a stormy sea.

●

The truck screeches to a halt. Several riders disembark and scatter. A toothless old man who'd been napping lifts the brim of his sombrero, arches his eyebrows and signals for me to get off. I comply. The truck groans back into gear, gains momentum and hobbles out of sight behind a hairpin turn on its final leg to the Guatemalan border.

I'm alone. An eerie silence prevails. I look for Don Crescencio but all I see is a ribbon of road and the mountains. In the distance, vultures ride the thermals against a blazing sky.

Two young men leap out of the bushes and, with unsettling urgency, beckon me to follow. I hesitate.

"No te preocupe. Don't worry. Don Crescencio is waiting." I relax. Meet Paulino and Adám García, my guides. The trail we take is fringed with heavy scrub. Paulino leads, setting a brisk and cadenced

stride. Adám takes the rear. It's about two kilometers to El Carisalon, on foot, mostly up steep, winding inclines and dizzying slopes littered with sharp rocks and gouged with depressions that jar every bone in my body. Panting, bathing in sweat, my foot throbbing, I stop. Paulino points to a tree.

"Sit in the shade, rest." A cooling breeze wafts through the foliage. I shut my eyes briefly. I reopen them. Bending over me, a young boy -- one of many lookouts posted strategically along the way -- hands me a grimy tin cup filled with water of very dubious origin. I cringe.

"Don't worry. It's well water."

It's the cup I worry about but I drink anyway.

•

Waist-high in a field of yellow and blue flowers, we proceed under a merciless sun. On either side, as far as the eye can see, green meadows and fertile pastures stretch from ravine to towering escarpment. But the meadows are fallow and not a single beast can be seen grazing the rich grasslands. Suddenly, several bursts of gunfire shatter the silence and reverberate from peak to peak. Glancing at each other knowingly, Adám and Paulino quicken their pace. I try to keep up.

•

In the one-room adobe schoolhouse, an elder learns the ABC. He strains against the darkness and the dancing shadows as shafts of light dart through an opening cut into the mud wall. The heat and the humidity are oppressive.

My eyes adjust to the dim light and I spot Don Crescencio. He must have wings, I muse. There are a dozen men and women, all sitting stone-faced on crude wooden benches, their arms folded upon rough-hewn school desks that have seen better days. Don Crescencio rises and introduces me. Everyone looks at me with a mixture of lethargy and circumspection. Mesmerized, several children, barefoot and forever wiping the amber slime that oozes from their noses, peer through the doorway at the bizarre gathering.

Don Modesto García Oaxaca, the El Carisalon tribal chief, speaks first. He tells of his people's wretched *"vida de subsistencia,"* of periodic famine, of disease, of broken government pledges to protect against police brutality, to silence threats by landowners, to counter the demented claims of title to wells and acreage by Guatemalan ranchers, to defend against intimidation by the dreaded Cobra Commandos.

Tribal counselor Juan Manuel Mansia agrees. "We're in a no-win situation. Japan donates a million dollars to help us. The money evaporates in a bureaucratic maze and none of us ever sees a centavo. We ask for an audit but all we get from the government is double-talk and more empty promises. Meanwhile, the cattle people are out to rob us of our lands -- at the point of a gun if need be."

José Alberto Martínez, another counselor adds: "A sinister argument being advanced to justify the expropriation of our lands is that we -- the Maya -- are Guatemalan and therefore not entitled to our lands. History and legal documents prove otherwise. Yes, Copán was founded by Maya from the north but our families have lived here in Honduras for generations. Yet, most of our lands are occupied by Ladino cattle ranchers, tobacco and corn farmers, and coffee growers."

Dario Fo, the Italian satirist, calls expropriation "a euphemism for thievery." I quote Fo but no one laughs. In lean times, the obvious is a superfluity. The others speak out.

"Look at us."

I too sit on a hard wood bench, further traumatizing a sore rear-end, but I look, transfixed, at the unadorned face of poverty -- abject, all-encompassing. I look at frail men and women in tatters, disquiet and despondency adding age to their years. Everyone is coughing. Coughs give way to uncontrollable spasms. Spasms yield thick secretions that are unceremoniously regurgitated on the schoolroom's dirt floor. Could it be tuberculosis?

●

A visiting professor from the National Teaching University reads from the International Labor Organization's Convention 169, a document outlining the inalienable rights of indigenous and tribal peoples. Ratified by Honduras in 1994, the compact states that native people are entitled to possess lands they have lived on and, if insufficient for their needs, to acquire new ones. As with other covenants entered into by Honduras, ratification is a perfunctory formality devoid of guarantees.

"What rights?" exclaims the old man who is learning to read. "So long as we depend on the government, the only right we have is to be poor, ignored, marginalized, lied to, harassed and killed."

The truths Don Crescencio had asked me to convey scream at me: alienation, insecurity, fear, bitterness. Four hundred people live in El Carisalon; one hundred and fifty are children, naked, wallowing in mire or hanging at the breasts of pregnant mothers. Disease, despondency and humiliation fester in a setting of idyllic beauty, all suffered with equal doses of numbing apathy and resentment, endured with God's help and, when God is not looking, with the shaman's incantations and the otherworldly exhalations of burning *copal*, the ceremonial aromatic resin used as incense by the Maya and said to please their gods.

•

Photographing the women and children becomes a science, a marriage between patience, opportunity and luck.

"The women are timid, the children wary," I remark.

"They are," says Don Crescencio. "Too many stories about abductions by gringos."

"But these stories are false."

"I know. But the others believe."

"Why don't you tell them the truth?"

"It's better this way. It keeps the community on its toes."

Taking photos is also an intrusion, a breach of privacy -- a threat. Photos rob people of their soul. Thus purloined, the soul wanders aimlessly after death, forever lost in a two-dimensional abyss from which no one can escape.

•

"Chronic bronchitis, dengue fever, diarrhea, dysentery." Don Crescencio enumerates the scourges as we begin our slow descent toward the well. "Cholera is never very far. We need more potable water. We need latrines, health centers, nurses. There's no money for doctors and, when there is, we can't afford to buy medicines. We need to educate the adults. The beautiful land you see around is mostly fallow. There's no money for seeds. Tools are scarce. We're afraid to work the fields. We're shot at almost every day from the higher elevations. We're exposed, vulnerable. You will tell the word, won't you? And you will tell those who want to help us to keep away from government agencies, go-betweens, negotiators. We yearn for self-empowerment, not charity. International aid makes for great headlines but it leaves the legitimate recipients holding an empty bag. Help the people at the bottom. One by one. Hamlet by hamlet. Directly. The shortest distance between two points," Don Crescencio reminds me, "is a straight line. Any other path is the Devil's geometry."

•

It is the fate of Mayan ghosts to roam among the living, unseen and aloof but not unfelt. If you know how to listen, you can hear their ageless lament. Wafting on the wings of a sudden gust, their whispers echo through the giant old trees, causing leaves to shiver, grackles to shriek and take flight, heads to turn and eyes to wander as if roused by some strange and irresistible call. Soon the breezes subside. The rustling ceases and a deafening stillness descends. It's been twelve centuries since the last sacrificial victim was decapitated on a temple terrace and its headless body hurled onto the plaza grounds below. An air of deep melancholy now hangs like a shroud over the ancient valley.

Before me, relived in cryptic iconography and faded hieroglyphics is the colossal spectacle of genius exhausted, splendor humbled, enlightenment dimmed by a headlong rush toward cultural extinction. Conflict, ferocious blood-letting rituals, an obsession with death, overpopulation, deforestation, hunger, disease -- all conspired to bring to a close an epoch of fabled artistic expression and agonizing self-inquiry. The meteoric magnificence of the Maya is chronicled in the lichen-covered tabernacles, in the austerity of age-worn temples and ball-courts, in the enigmatic stares of petrified kings and demi-gods. The calamity that befell this city-state is witnessed in the bleak anonymity of unfinished stele and abandoned stonework that lay scattered on the forest floor. Spectral vestiges of a powerful dynasty that began with Yax K'uk Mo in the fifth century C. E. and ended in flight and dispersal four hundred years later, they may also be seen as a metaphor to the passion and the agony of a dispirited and leaderless posterity -- the modern-day Maya.

How much do these time travelers have in common with their fabled forefathers and what sort of future awaits them?

•

Flashes of anxiety and circumspection dance in Ernesto Súchite's steely eyes. Nervous energy animates his stride. Diminutive, almost frail, endowed with sharp Maya features, he speaks softly, with a passion born of misery endured, hopes dashed but not surrendered. A respected tribal counselor, he has taken on a desperate and costly mission: to give slain Cándido Amador's work legitimacy and continuity by helping buoy the ethnic identity and destiny of his people.

Every Sunday Súchite, fellow advisors and dozens of men and women from outlying communities, converge on Rincón Del Buey, outside Copán, to discuss perennial concerns: health care, sanitation, education, irrigation, political representation. The small, austere structure where they assemble was built with Japanese funds. Benches, wobbly chairs and tables were also donated. In one corner of the room, stacked from floor to ceiling, are unopened sacks of colza and yellow corn, cooking oil from the European Union, huge bags of refined U.S. rice and flour, and crates of canned Norwegian mackerel in tomato sauce.

I ask one of the men about the mackerel. He wrinkles his nose, shrugs his shoulders and bares a toothless smile. Charity has its incongruous side. Marshmallows were once delivered to famine-ravaged Biafra.

The Maya are having a tough time preserving their culture, upholding their rights. Linked by a common ancestry and memories of a shared historical past, they derive dignity from their roots but they have drawn no strength from them. Powerless against acculturation, ill-equipped to take part in let alone survive the caustic crucible of Honduran politics, they feel cast out.

"Ours is a rudderless vessel on a stormy sea," says Súchite.

"incapable of charting its own course; denied safe passage on a route accorded indigenous people by international statutes. The government disregards repeated appeals for compliance on non-negotiable issues such as land, water rights, education and health. Pleas for protection from expropriations, threats, intimidation and increasing violence, including assassination, fall on deaf ears. And when we mention culture, identity and tradition we're denounced as anarchists. We have two choices: sit still, wither and perish, or drift toward assimilation."

•

More than anything, it's the absence of a source of ethical authority -- other than the loose tribalism that still binds them as a people -- that has led the Maya to feel abandoned. One might have expected them to find such guiding light in religion or at the hands of an honest and enlightened state. Force-fed and socially coercive, alien and antagonistic to their ancestral beliefs and practices, the white man's religion offered neither redemption nor emotional fulfillment. Instead, it estranged the greater Maya family from its past, discredited its history, disparaged its customs. Consigned to a spiritual twilight zone, they are now aliens in their own land.

God must be an equal-opportunity fraudster; he deceives everybody.

"For its part, the state has been unresponsive at best, hostile at worst," says my friend, Adalid Martínez Perdomo, a social scientist and author. "By misrepresenting or dodging the life-and-death issues facing the Maya, the state has provided an ideological justification for dominance."

Parallel but culturally incompatible societies can never merge. They are doomed to coexist, for a time, in mutual distrust and antipathy. Only assimilation, an ethnic adulteration forced by the strong upon the weak, can ever raise coexistence to full societal coherence -- but at a heavy price. For the Maya, as is the case among thinning aboriginal groups worldwide, assimilation is another word for ethnic suicide. It is the very inevitability of this somber course that has the Maya scrambling to delay it. Like their ancestors, they witness the sum and substance of their peoplehood grinding to a stupefying halt. Tinged with perceptible horror, the passion and the agony that is their lot are indelibly etched in their inscrutable gaze. As Charles Gallenkamp writes in *Maya:*

> *"The Maya remain suspended between two contrasting worlds ancient and modern -- clinging stubbornly to threads linking them to remote depths of antiquity, to those unfathomed mysteries buried in the shattered jungle-shrouded cities of their ancestors."*

WHO KILLED CÁNDIDO?

*"Their work was to bring disaster upon men,
as they were going home, or in front of it,
and they would be found wounded,
stretched out, face up, on the ground, dead...."*
-- The Popol Vuh

Wafting over the denuded carcass of this formidable Mayan city-state of yore is an immense pall of silent desolation. Scarred by time and neglect, jealous of the past, unwilling to bare their cryptic soul, Copán's temples and stele, sacrificial altars and mausoleums preside in mute stupefaction over barren esplanades and dusty plazas once teeming with life.

It is in the shade of a centenarian tree overlooking the ball court, and under the watchful eye of several Maya lookouts posted strategically nearby, that Juan, a trusted informant, asked to meet me. Juan is not his real name. There's a price on his head. He knows too much but several visits with his people and two exposés I published in Honduras, he affirms, attest to my loyalty and discretion.

"Secrets, like rumors, have a long shelf life," Juan quips as he surveys the landscape below. Mixing metaphor and gruesome actuality, he adds, bowing his head, "and the truth is always the first casualty. Its remains are hastily buried. So it was with Cándido."

A symbol of ethnic pride revived, Cándido Amador Recinos, the charismatic Maya tribal counselor, knew he was a marked man. His activism and fiery rhetoric had earned him countless enemies. Unheeded, subtle hints gave way to explicit warnings. Warnings turned to threats. Cándido first confided in the council of elders. He then shared his fears and suspicions with the leaders of a federation of indigenous groups.

"Cándido told me that several wealthy landowners in the Copán River valley, "had vowed to kill him," Juan whispers in my ear, a slight quiver in his voice. He named names.

Someone did. On April 12, 1997, as night draped the village of Copán in a mantle of darkness, Cándido, a champion of Indian rights and a rising star in the Maya leadership, was brutally, senselessly murdered on his way home from Copán to the neighboring community of Corralitos. Unsolved and unpunished, his assassination would plunge indigenous communities under a pall of fear and suspicion. In galvanizing Honduras' ethnic minorities, the crime -- one of many against indigenous leaders -- also put an end to decades of silence, irresolution and self-restraint. Cándido's death had re-awakened tribal pride, buoyed ethnic unity and fed a tide of resentment and impatience against Honduras' arcane justice system. Frequent and increasingly large demonstrations in Tegucigalpa, added both substance and poignancy to their collective plight. They also helped expose the nation's sluggish civil and human rights apparatus.

Born in 1958 in a hamlet a few kilometers from Copán, Cándido spent much of his childhood in Morazan, a town in the northern department of Yoro, where his parents had moved in search of work. Cándido was a good student. Focused, quick-witted and inquisitive, he'd taken an early interest in his people, past and present. After graduating, he returned to Copán and went to work at the Archeological Institute as an antiquities restoration technician.

It was in 1995 that the Maya, spurred by the energetic Cándido, began to organize and formulate strategies that clearly infuriated the local power structure: The restitution of lands from which his people had been displaced or coerced to sell; ethnic selfhood through political empowerment. In August 1995, Cándido attended his first intertribal meeting. His dynamism soon earned him a full-time seat in the elders' council, and he resigned from his job at the Archeological Park. A year later, he represented the Maya during a demonstration by members of the eight Honduran indigenous tribes. Dubbed "Our Roots," the gathering was sponsored by a government agency charged with channeling foreign aid to impoverished indigenous communities. Publicly, Cándido called the rally "a meaningless government self-promotion ploy." In private, he accused the agency of skimming large sums of money.

"The media were misinformed or bribed," Juan alleged. "Cándido was not slain on the outskirts of Copán, as reported." He was killed at or near the home of a landowner [later referred to as the "prime suspect" in the presence of three accomplices -- an artist specializing in cheap replicas of Mayan inscriptions; a cattle rancher; and a tour-guide operator. Evidence of a fifth accomplice, as yet unnamed, would eventually surface. All were alleged to have been paid by the prime suspect and others angered by the Maya's claims to their lands.

According to Juan, Cándido's lifeless body was then removed and dumped on the road to Corralitos, where he was found. Two days later, Eduardo Villanueva, a district attorney in charge of ethnic affairs, discovered blood and hair evidence at the prime suspect's home. It is believed that Villanueva withheld this evidence. I later spoke to Villanueva. He admitted to have held on to crucial details, contending that he was awaiting the results of an FBI forensic exam. An FBI source familiar with the case declined to confirm or deny Villanueva's claim. Villanueva refused to reveal what had drawn him to the prime suspect's home in the first place and the FBI agent in charge would not say why a U.S. domestic spy agency had taken an interest in a crime committed on foreign soil.

It would later be alleged that Villanueva had only gathered evidence found near the door of the prime suspect's home. "Had he gone inside and inspected the rest of the house, he would have found more clues. But, as soon as Villanueva left the house, domestics hurriedly mopped the floors and tidied up the premises. Several people heard Cándido's screams. He was begging for his life."

The prime suspect's car was then heard speeding toward Corralitos. One witness said he heard gunshots not far from where Cándido's cadaver was discovered. A spent .22 caliber shell was recovered at the site. The autopsy confirmed three .38 mm bullet wounds. Cándido's body also bore multiple stab wounds. The medical examiner could not say whether they'd been inflicted before or after he was shot. Cándido, who wore shoulder-length hair, had also been scalped.

Landowners and cattle ranchers took paid ads in several newspapers in support of the prime suspect. The ads asserted without offering a shred of evidence that Cándido had been robbed of a large sum of "foreign aid money" with which he'd been entrusted and then killed. Landowners then allegedly conspired with the police to implicate two common crooks. Drunk when arrested, the pair first confessed to the murder then recanted, claiming they'd been paid hush money. The duo were jailed briefly and released. They were never heard from again. A lawyer representing a group of Copán hoteliers, restaurateurs and tour operators threatened to sue me and the editor of the paper in which my exposés were published. Under Honduras's inquisitorial system, as it is in other Latin American countries, telling the truth is no defense against a charge of libel.

Cándido's murder was condemned by Honduras' indigenous communities. It remains unsolved to date. The Maya, who describe the investigation as "a travesty and a monumental hoax," have not forgotten and continue to demand justice.

"We want our enemies to know that Cándido's death has made us stronger and more resolute in our struggle," Juan said as we parted, his hands on my shoulders, his inscrutable Mayan black eyes burning into mine.

"Make sure they get the message."

•

The press called Cándido's death "a contemptible murder," but stopped short of naming names. Human rights groups also criticized the National Agrarian Institute, arguing that Cándido would still be alive had it provided his people with legal title over lands that were legitimately theirs to claim.

Redoubling their efforts to deflect further scrutiny, Copán landowners went on a counteroffensive, accusing Juan of killing Cándido in a leadership power struggle. The police cleared Juan. This did not prevent Juan from weeping in my arms when we met again a couple of months later by the venerable old tree. He then took a crumpled square of paper out of his pocket, unfolded it slowly and handed it to me. It read, in part:

"Our ancestors took a wrong turn and followed a course so

errant that they painted themselves into a cultural dead-end. I will not allow their posterity -- our people -- to be subdued and led to final extinction by today's conquistadors. I know this will earn me enemies. I know I might die at their hands. If I do, make sure everyone knows the truth...."

Written in Spanish, the note was signed by Cándido and dated April 10, 1997. He would be murdered two days later.

Fifteen years have passed since Cándido's violent death. Evidence of foul play, incontrovertible and damning, continues to pile up, baffling some, turning others to stony silence. Dozens of Maya activists would be killed over land disputes in recent years. Juan would be next

•

Few, if any, believe that Cándido's death, as infomercials planted in various dailies soon after the killing implied, was "engineered to fabricate an indigenous martyr," or was the result "of intra-ethnic disputes," or the culmination of "insurmountable personal problems."
"Next, they'll say that Cándido died of self-inflicted stab and bullet wounds, and that, for dramatic effect, he also scalped himself," quipped a demonstrator at a human rights rally in Tegucigalpa. Instead, as maturing evidence suggests, Hondurans have quietly concluded that Cándido was eliminated by landowners and cattle ranchers who felt threatened by his firebrand activism.

"Since colonial times," said Juan, "foreigners have plotted to silence our past and usurp our future. They plundered our resources and deprived us of our hereditary rights. Not only did they snatch and parcel out among themselves the ill-gotten booty -- gold, arable lands, wells, water rights and large stretches of pristine riparian and coastal areas -- they also stole and commercially exploited territories traditionally inhabited by our people."

Contrary to assertions made in the press, the Maya have only grudgingly endured the "passive role" imposed on them by tourism. Cándido had characterized tourism as "a mercenary commerce controlled by the state and local landed gentry, and 'sewn up' by foreign developers assured of government cooperation and afforded significant economic incentives and political leverage."

Cándido is also quoted as having asked: "What? [tourists] will trudge up the mountain and gawk at the 'quaint Indians' and take pictures of our grass huts and womenfolk and children, and commiserate with our elders, perhaps buy a few trinkets? Or they will marvel, for an hour or two, at the tattered vestiges of the 'mighty Maya' before retiring to air-conditioned hotels and guest houses -- none of which we own -- and dine in eateries none of us can afford to patronize? We've never seen a *centavo* from the proceeds collected at the Archeological Park or a fraction of the tourist dollars spent in local establishments."

●

Cándido knew that his rhetoric could cost him his life. He accepted the risks and often publicly declared that he was ready to die for his people. Maya activism, Cándido had warned, would be met with intimidation, threats, illegal arrests and detentions, evictions, arson, calumny, fraudulent lawsuits, even assassinations, all designed to quell legitimate dissent and dismember his people.

His prophecies came true.

●

For the past fifteen years, indigenous groups have demanded that Cándido's killers be apprehended and tried. The Maya also appealed to five successive chiefs of state to heed "our urgent call for justice and to help us in our struggle to regain our ancestral lands -- two of the causes for which Cándido Amador sacrificed his life." Their pleas fell on deaf ears.

Juan's revelations, aired in my articles but without attribution, would inflame passions and reanimate the debate. Juan had wanted more. In addition to the killers, he'd called for "the intellectual authors or abettors of this heinous crime" -- allegedly some members of Honduras's Congress -- "to be unmasked and brought to justice." This would prove to be a formidable mission in a nation where politics, bribes and secrecy drive justice, where might, not right, speaks loudest.

•

Tribal counselor, poet, activist, trusted informant and friend, Juan, with whom I'd met a fortnight earlier, wrote me a long note. Entitled, "Letter from Xibalba," it would be his last communication. Set in pencil in large cursive script on unlined paper, his words lost neither their lyricism nor their chilling premonitory character. Intertwined in Juan's cadenced discourse, elegy and prophecy merged in a reaffirmation of faith through fatalism, tenacity through despair. I reread it often and grieve.

> "We keep meeting, you and I, like thieves or hunted beasts, in the anonymity of an ebbing throng or in some darkened corner, two ghostly shadows merging in the night. Inevitably, our thoughts turn to our fallen brother, Cándido. We mourn him still. The night of 12 April 1997 is a date now branded on the collective memory of our people. It continues to burn our souls. Our lives were shattered, our hopes dashed. Centuries of pain and humiliation surged in our throats, like some foul bile. For all of us had in some way been shot, stabbed, disfigured and dishonored that fateful day and left to rot on the side of the road.
>
> "Everyone wept. Despair and fear and disbelief fed tears and the tears irrigated the parched April soil. Men, women, children, fists clenched, eyes fixed toward the heavens, all cried out: 'Cándido, you are gone! Cándido, great is our loss. But fear not. We shall rise and cry out: Never again without land, without food, without health, without education. Your spirit and that of our ancestors will shepherd us along the way. We shall prevail.
>
> "Cándido's executioners are still free. Tell the world that we face extinction, that democracy, the voice and tool of freedom, has betrayed us. Tell the world that indigenous people are being dismembered, that we are rapidly sinking into the abyss.
>
> "The gods are angry. Great is their wrath. We shall emerge

from the depths of Xibalba and the wicked shall at last countenance the horror of their ways. And Cándido's martyrdom shall not have been in vain. Say all that, compañero, over and over so that you and I may one day walk arm-in-arm, our heads held high."

•

A month after I received Juan's haunting letter, I learned through a mutual friend that Juan had been killed in an ambush near the mountain village of El Carisalon. His body, riddled with AK-47 bullets, had been dumped in a garbage-strewn ravine. Vultures were feeding on him when he was found.

•

Embargoed until I was safely out of Honduras, an investigative report detailing the circumstances of Cándido's assassination and including portions of Juan's letter was published prematurely in the now-defunct *Honduras This Week*, forcing me to decamp from Copán in great haste.

On the morrow of its publication, the article, like a trail of blazing gunpowder, ignited the Maya communities around Copán. Led by elders and tribal counselors, hundreds of men and women with babies in tow seized and occupied the Archeological Park for several days, barring access to tourists and costing the Park several thousand dollars in lost revenue. Newspapers ran photos of large clusters of Maya gathered in prayer at the foot of the ancient tabernacles their ancestors had erected. Many were brandishing rolled-up copies of *Honduras This Week*.

Where you can't impose your presence, make yourself scarce.

COPÁN: BEHIND THE FAÇADE

There's nothing like bad news from afar to spoil a well-earned sabbatical and coax a reporter back into the fray. Take the July 10, 1999 slaughter in a Copán *pulperia* (grocery store) that claimed five lives and scorched the soul of this quaint and somnolent village habituated to intermittent violence and accustomed to looking the other way.

Five people. Was it an accident? Was it vengeance? Were they the victims of mistaken identity? Were they felled in a drunken rapture, as one outlandish report alleged, by giddy outsiders celebrating a soccer victory? Or were they targeted for assassination in a drug deal gone bad? Speculation was rife. When the smoke lifted, dozens of spent AK-47, 40mm- and 9mm-caliber shells lay on the ground, silent witnesses in a drama that began and ended with lightning speed in the rain after dusk. The discarded shells offered few clues. Everyone is armed in these parts.

Nor is there anything like a community that hurriedly mops up the blood, plugs up bullet-riddled walls with cement and seals its collective lips in a terror-driven reflex that blunts one's sense of well-being. Nothing like a craven and dimwitted constabulary -- the murderers got away and the leads grew cold -- to cast grave doubt on the probity of Copán's police and resurrect rumors of criminal collusion. Nothing like a timid, controlled press -- mainstream dailies buried the story on their back pages -- to raise doubts about a nation's health and moral fiber. Nothing like yet another senseless crime in a country long tormented by lawlessness, traumatized by the greed, arrogance and ineptitude of successive regimes, and disgraced by the ceaseless suffering of its people, to explain why visitors are scarce and a vigorous tourist trade is but a distant dream.

•

In 2006, speaking on condition of anonymity, a retired CIA analyst and former faculty member at the Johns Hopkins School of Advanced

International studies with whom I'd worked in the mid-80s (he was until recently a consultant on terrorism and bio-chemical warfare) offered this sobering assessment:

"Unemployment, poverty, violence, human rights abuses and political lethargy all risk taking Honduras to the brink of civil disorder. Only swift and massive reforms can reverse years of corruption, government incompetence and apathy, and decades of elitism and plutocratic dominance."

Six years later, Honduras would be declared "the most murderous nation on earth."

Corruption is not the most vexing problem in Honduras; it's the arrogance and impunity that attend it, inspire it, feed it. Groomed to inherit by political incest, power, prestige and economic sovereignty, tomorrow's ruling families, like yesterday's, will contrive dynastic careers and trade favors and divvy up realms of authority and influence and parcel out old and tirelessly replenished wealth while demanding time and patience from a bleeding nation.

Time is a commodity Hondurans do not have. Putting off the reforms the country so desperately needs has resulted in irreversible economic slippage. The potential for discontent and frustration to turn to violence should never be taken lightly. Even the placid, patient, pliant Hondurans have their boiling point. This is a country that can't reform but evolves in miasmic inertia, like a volcano, until the magma boils over. Meanwhile, as the cauldron of unrest and discontent heats up, Honduras remains a dangerous place for Hondurans and for those like me who were once in search of El Dorado.

•

Understandably, many readers especially those protective of their commercial interests, were outraged by my articles. The truths they bared and the conjectures they occasioned left some positively livid. In an effort to deflect attention from the incident in Copán, or to rationalize it, many people, as if on cue, pointed at the April 1999 Columbine School massacre and other aberrant acts committed by troubled American teens, some of whom had the wisdom to surrender, others the civility to take their own lives. The thugs who sprayed the *pulperia* with assault rifles were incapable of such gallantry. Worse, the Copán police characteristically ran the other way and the incident was given suspiciously marginal coverage by the local press. This speaks volumes about the integrity of Honduras' criminal justice system and the entrenched cowardice of its media.

In journalism, like in "show-biz" one is only as good as one's last offering. Whereas a bad script or a weak performance is eventually forgotten, a journalist earns acclaim -- or calumny -- less for his adherence to form than for his devotion to substance. So long as he steers clear from the truth, or "sanitizes" it, he has nothing to fear, not the ire of some readers, not the long arm of a very corrupt and very ruthless "law."

Fickle and self-serving, the public entombs what it need not remember and enshrines what it doggedly refuses to forget. Anyone familiar with my work knows that I'd tried hard to temper my polemics. I'd applauded, rhapsodized, commiserated with, and wept for Honduras. In words and photos, I'd once elegized Copán. *"The good that men do...."*

The drive-by shooting, I'd vainly tried to explain, was symptomatic of the turmoil gripping Central America. The very fact that it had taken place in normally "laid back" Copán was all the more alarming and inadmissible. Notwithstanding the half-truths, innuendoes and outright fabrications dished out in a complaint by several members of Copán's business community against me, I stood by my article, my sources and my instincts.

•

Site of impressive Maya monuments and a popular transit for Guatemala-bound travelers, Copán, once an essential, if remote destination in Honduras, now ranked, along with San Pedro Sula, Tegucigalpa, the north coast, Olancho and Santa Barbara, as a dangerous locale.

Earned in small and fitful increments, this reputation stiffened with the as-yet unsolved murder of Cándido Amador. To the more astute observer, and for all its undeniable allure, Copán is eerily reminiscent of a theatrical backdrop, an all-too-perfect *trompe l'oeil*. At first glance its unassuming charm, the kind envisioned by poets and set designers alike, is enthralling. Surrounded by lush highlands of daunting beauty, it nestles, seductive and unruffled, a few square blocks of old Spanish colonial charm seemingly untouched by time. There's the ubiquitous clip-clop of horses' hooves on cobbled streets, old Padre Roque's whitewashed little church, the village square where vacant-eyed villagers doze off in the noonday sun and peddlers hawk their trinkets. There's the redolence of grilled *carnitas* wafting from under the parasols of ambulant food vendors; the cooling evening breezes, the graceful dawn-and-twilight flights of snow-white egrets over lush, mist-covered uplands; the crisp, starlit nights.

Behind this idyllic setting, unfold dramas unimagined by tourists, ignored or squelched by the press and warily entombed by the locals, some fearing risky entanglement, others eager to protect their business interests against a tide of bad publicity. Less than a kilometer from the legendary temples, sacrificial altars and cryptic monuments, rises a pyramid of deceit, collusion and intimidation under whose shadow villagers live in sham unconcern. Aiding and abetting in a conspiracy of silence and obfuscation are the police, all of whom are said to be deep in the pockets of Copán's landed elite -- better known colloquially as "the local mafia."

Servile freeloaders or opportunistic bottom-feeders driven by harsh economic reality, Copán's cops have a history of looking the other way, mishandling, adulterating or destroying evidence, falsifying arrest records and turning against obstinate plaintiffs.

When it comes to bad news, *Copanecos* react with robotic conformity. Silence being the simplest form of disinformation, they say nothing or change the subject. If pressed, they deny the very events that give them nightmares. It's gossip in reverse. Endowed with a capacity for infinite permutations, this denial-by-justification of indisputable facts becomes a skillfully knitted filigree of extenuation, distortions and absurd rationalizations, all artfully interlaced to befuddle the curious or the inquisitive.

When tenacious probing and astute conjecture meet with stony silence, when doors slam shut, when friendly smiles turn to scowl, the truth, hideous and foul, is surely lurking underfoot like a viper squeezing beneath a rock. Asking too many questions in a hamlet accustomed to pulling in its sidewalks at dusk is as perilous an exercise as it is brazen. Attempts to shed light on the Cándido affair had driven this point home and forced me to make a hasty retreat back to the States. I'd since ventured back into Copán, this time by crossing into Honduras from the Guatemalan border village of Chiquimula, disguised and escorted by two Maya bodyguards. Efforts to pursue leads in that most recent carnage were similarly thwarted by people who would otherwise be the first to benefit from a crime-free Copán.

In what would be one last burst of cheek, and now at an age when most men coddle their grandchildren or tend their herb garden, I turned over sealed documents detailing Candido's murder to a member of Honduras' National Congress who said, "We never met; I haven't heard a word you said," handed back the documents as if they'd burned her hands and abruptly terminated the interview.

Wherever due process is inconsistently applied, where authorities show neither respect for justice nor the will to enforce it, where the privileged and the politically well-connected deem themselves above the law and the search for truth is rewarded with hostility, what you have -- even here, in lovely, secluded, deceptively tranquil Copán -- is a climate of controlled fear and a recipe for anguish and woe. I call this fascism.

Visitors to Copán come and go like the tide. They take with them memories that dull with each passing day. Copanecos stay and keep the myth alive. They must. They have no other choice.

HONDURAN ARMY ABUSES NO SECRET TO CIA

Throughout the 1980's, while the U.S. government was bucketing millions of dollars in military aid into Honduras, Honduran armed forces went on a rampage against its own citizens. So said the CIA after years of silence and duplicity.

According to newly declassified documents, internal investigations by the CIA reveal that although agency operatives in Honduras knew that the military operated a U.S.-funded right-wing assassination squad, the officers' sloppy or evasive reports concerning human rights issues left senior CIA brass "unaware of their seriousness and magnitude." Lies.

In fact, the CIA deliberately fed misleading information to Congress, downplaying Honduras's involvement in abuses so as not to jeopardize that country's U.S.-mandated support for rebels fighting against Nicaragua's Sandinista regime.

"CIA briefings [to Congress] in the early 1980's underestimated Honduran involvement in abuses," the report stated. By the mid-1980's, the CIA provided more detailed information, but some of it was inaccurate."

A redacted copy of the 211-page document of the Inspector General was released to Honduran Human Rights Commissioner, Leo Valladares, and was later made public by the Washington-based National Security Archive. The document was heavily redacted by the CIA, with large sections blacked out entirely.

The report states that the CIA had specific and detailed knowledge of widespread abuses but told Congress that transgressions by the Honduran armed forces were being exaggerated by their ideological foes. Predictably, the agency's former station chief in Honduras denied that U.S. intelligence officers knew anything about the crimes perpetrated by Honduran death squads, or that they had failed to report what they knew about them. Hypocrisy turned to scabrous comedy when the station chief asserted that "the Honduran military was a very benign kind of military...."

CIA internal inquiries into the matter began in earnest in response to a series of investigative reports by this writer and others in various media in Baltimore, Atlanta, Boston and Miami, as well as in Honduras, Costa Rica and Panama. The articles asserted that the CIA trained and supported the Honduran military, including secret army intelligence units that were kidnapping, torturing and murdering thousands of suspected leftists -- among them students, teachers, clergy and union organizers.

At the time, the CIA station in Tegucigalpa served as a command center for the Nicaraguan war and grew to be the agency's largest anywhere in the world. For officials who served at the U.S. Embassy, including John Negroponte, the overriding priority was to ensure that the Honduran government and its powerful, often independent military hierarchy continued to support the war effort. To that purpose, the intelligence branch of Honduras's paramilitary security forces maintained a secret unit known as the Honduran anti-Communist Liberation Army. The unit's role was to fight Honduran leftists, including a fledgling dissident army that was backed by both the Nicaraguan government and Salvadoran rebels. The unit's operations *"included surveillance, kidnapping, interrogations under duress, and execution of prisoners who were Honduran revolutionaries."*

Other military abuses have been linked to members of CIA-funded death squad Battalion 3-16, the brainchild of SOA-graduate, the late General Gustavo Alvarez Martinez, which tortured and assassinated suspected political opponents. Nearly all the members of Battalion 3-16 were trained by the SOA, first in Panama, later at Fort Benning, Georgia.

Again, the CIA failed to investigate, and inform Congress that the Honduran military extra-judicially executed a large number of prisoners. One of them was American Jesuit priest, James G. Carney. The army officer who masterminded Carney's death, General Alvarez, was awarded the Legion of Merit by President Ronald Reagan, "for promoting democracy in Honduras." Some of Carney's former colleagues believe the award is evidence that then U.S Ambassador to Honduras, John Negroponte, authorized Carney's killing.

If deposed President Mel Zelaya is ever to account for the white-collar crimes he is accused of committing during his presidency, then scores of high-ranking Honduran military officers, most of them graduates of the infamous U.S. Army School of the Americas (some in blissful self-exile in Florida, Georgia and Louisiana, others "retired" on their *fincas* in the wilds of Honduras) should also stand trial and pay for the horrific blood crimes they committed and the wretched drug-running schemes in which they were complicit. Among them:

• **Nelson Willy Mejía Mejía,** responsible for the "disappearance of 7,000 people. He was appointed Director-General of Immigration in the interim coup-led government of Roberto Micheletti.

• **Napoleón Nassar Herrera,** who became leader of the General Department of Criminal Investigation, high Commissioner of Police for the northwest region in the Manuel Zelaya government, and one of the Secretary of Security's spokespeople in the *de facto* government of Roberto Micheletti. According to Andrés Pavón of the Committee for the Defense of Human Rights in Honduras, *"there are stacks of proof regarding the role Nassar and other former Intelligence Battalion 3-16 members played.... but that Nassar and the others were not convicted of any crimes because they received State protection and impunity before a compromised judicial system."*

During Ricardo Maduro's presidency (2002-2006), Nassar was leader of the General Department of Criminal Investigation (DGIC). Under his command, agents from the DGIC put Feliciano Pineda, a community leader who'd been stabbed and wounded on his face, neck, back, sides and hands by paramilitaries into chains and imprisoned him in Gracias.

• **Billy Fernando Joya Améndola,** (known as **Billy Joya**) is a former military officer and member of Battalion 3-16. He was national security adviser in Manuel Zelaya's government, a post he has retained. Billy Joya is one of the at least 18 members of Battalion 3-16 who trained at the SOA. Joya fled legal proceedings in Honduras when accused of torture and forced disappearances, and sought political asylum in Spain, which was rejected. Joya voluntarily returned to Honduras in December 1998 after receiving promises of special treatment. He was jailed but freed in August 2000 after a judge said there was not enough evidence to continue his detention.

• **General Luis Alonzo Discua Elvir,** who, after the State Department revoked his visa to the US, went public with details of US support for the death squad he co-founded and whose operations he commanded.

• **Gen. Romeo Vasquez,** who led the coup in which President Zelaya was ousted, now head of the scandal-ridden Hondutel communications conglomerate.

• **Col. Marco Tulio Ayala Vindel,** involved in the disappearance of Amado Espinoza and Adan Avilez Funes. Although the judge issued an arrest warrant, Ayala Vindel failed to appear before the court. Ayala Vindel was head of Battalion 3-16 in 1984.

• **Capt. Pio Flores,** whose house was used as a detention and torture center.

• **Col. Amilcar Zelaya,** from whose country home -- used as a detention, torture, and killing center for Battalion 3-16 -- muffled screams were regularly heard.

In this writer's opinion, no "reconciliation," can take place until deceased SOA graduates and Battalion 3-16 members who are known to have committed human rights abuses and other crimes -- and their U.S. handlers -- are posthumously tried and convicted in public, and their names and deeds chronicled in detail in history books for future generations to contemplate.

Fat chance.

THE TOXIC NORMALITY OF CORRUPTION

In a recent editorial warning of Honduras' "impending existential threat," *Honduras Weekly* [the successor to the now-defunct Honduras This Week] was dead-on in its assertion that narcotrafficking, a lucrative worldwide enterprise, is the source of mounting violence in Honduras. It was less than precise, perhaps even a tad glib, in its haste to blame America's insatiable addition to drugs for Honduras' self-inflicted calamities. The commentary's brevity, the dearth of specifics, may even have diverted attention from the climate of sleaze and collusion that underprops and empowers the drug trade -- from turncoat police to crooked lawyers and judges, to the highest echelons of Honduras' political hierarchy. One brief chapter in a sordid narrative of collusion and crime can now be told.

Three years ago, I was subpoenaed by a U.S. Immigration and Naturalization judge in a case involving a petition for political asylum filed by a former Honduran narcotics detective. Six months earlier, I'd been contacted by his American attorney and asked whether I'd be willing to testify on his behalf as an expert witness. I agreed.

Enrique Granados (nor his real name) was a model cop, a shrewd detective and a rising star in the criminal division of the Public Ministry of Honduras. In 1996, he was promoted to detective by the *Direccion de Lucha Contra El Narcotrafico* (DLCN), an agency overseen by the DEA and the U.S. Embassy in Tegucigalpa. In 2000, according to Granados, the DLCN was suborned by criminal elements whose influence stretched from the Ministry of Security to the Honduran National Congress.

Acting on tips from informants, Granados did old-fashioned gumshoe work that led straight to his DLCN unit commander. According to affidavits submitted by Granados, in which the commander and other key players are named, Honduran court records revealed serious discrepancies in the fines that were being assessed against known drug traffickers. It was clear, Granados said in his deposition, that the commander was taking bribes. Granados reported his findings to his supervisor. Within days, and without explanation, he was transferred to the Customs Department at San Pedro Sula's Ramón Villeda Morales International Airport.

"This was both a demotion and a warning," Granados told me just before the hearing in correspondence forwarded by his attorney.

Six months into his new assignment, Granados found the evidence he'd been looking for. "Every 15 days," Granados testified, "an unmarked truck drove to the airport's loading docks and made a delivery. Invariably, the unit commander instructed stationed Customs officers to move to another location as the truck was being unloaded. The cargo: narcotics rerouted through the airport without detection and destined for shipment by land, air and sea to points north."

Again, Granados confided in his supervisor. Asked to name his informants, Granados declined. Instead, skipping the chain of command, he requested a private audience with his unit chief and the DLCN director. The request was denied. Granados was transferred to a desk job.

"The atmosphere at work became increasingly stressful and hostile," Granados recalled. "Unable to pursue my investigations, I told some of my fellow officers that I would go directly to the DEA."

On vacation in Tegucigalpa, Granados was intercepted by "several individuals" who offered him $50,000 in exchange for his silence.

"They told me I was the only person who hadn't yet been paid off. I was also warned that it would be 'wise' to accept their offer." Granados, declined. Two days later, he received a letter informing him that, owing departmental cutbacks, his employment at the DLCN had been terminated. The next day, ads offering officer positions at the Customs Office ran in at least one newspaper.

"In 2002, driving through San Pedro Sula," Granados testified at his hearing, "I realized I was being followed, then shot at. One of the pursuers was a fellow cop." The name of that officer appears in Granados' asylum request statement.

Fearing for his life, Granados took flight, first to the north coast, then to one of the Bay Islands. Back on the mainland, this time in Comayagua, he was pursued by a group of men, later identified as policemen, who fired at him but missed. Armed with the visitor's visa his mother, a naturalized American citizen, had obtained for him, Granados fled Honduras and sought refuge in the U.S.

It was when Granados' final visa extension expired and he faced deportation that his case came to the attention of a court-appointed immigration attorney and, later, of a U.S. Court of Appeals which promptly granted his motion for asylum on the evidence submitted on his behalf.

•

Corruptibility is the mother of all vices. Without it we'd live in a fantasy world of virtue, love and justice. It's as powerful a drive as the procreative urge or the survival instinct. Because we're human, we're all susceptible to its siren song. Some of us can be suborned by praise; others prefer cold cash.

In some countries -- particularly among the poorest but by no means confined to them -- corruption is the bedrock in which business and governance are anchored. It's become a habitualized, ritualized, institutionalized reflex. It's part of the social fabric. People have become so inured to it from youth that they no longer recognize it for what it really is: the process of putrefaction by which nations decompose or lapse into insignificance.

There is a direct link between how people are empowered in their societies and their leaders' propensity to lie, take bribes and engage in the wholesale sellout of their citizens. In crypto-autocratic nations such as Honduras, where wealth and political power are confined to small, all-powerful elites, people have a nominal voice, but no clout, especially where their vital interests -- life, liberty and the pursuit of happiness -- are abridged and further compromised by endemic poverty, crime, violence and the appalling indifference and incompetence of their leaders. *El Querido Pueblo* simply doesn't count. Those who protest are either ignored, their grievances lost in the murky corridors of bureaucracy, or they risk harassment, persecution and even assassination.

"We've been reduced to turning our heads and looking the other way," a Honduran judge working in the southern city of Choluteca told me on condition that I withhold his name. "We overlook corruption;

we tacitly condone it because doing otherwise will have grave consequences. To be perceived as incorruptible is to stand out. In these parts, principled men don't die of old age."

One of the subtleties that prevent people from listening to their conscience is the stupefying realization that their elected officials, given their own venality and the tangled cabals in which they engage are so inextricably ensnared in shady activities that they couldn't fix the problems they created even if they tried.

There are two types of corruption: corruption of opportunity and corruption of necessity. The first has existed since the Earth cooled. It will thrive as long as humans rule the planet. The second festers when, reduced to their primal state and unable to survive by any other means, decent people do bad things. The synchronism between the two is not coincidental. The poorer the nation, the wealthier the governing elite, the more capital is concentrated in the hands of a few, the greater the temptation and opportunity to be corrupted.

Corruption doesn't occur in a vacuum. It's a system of values and behaviors that straddle public and private spheres: the corrupted are always faced with a corruptor, often originating with those able to buy influence. It is also characteristic of the politics of so-called developing countries, like Honduras, that never seem to "develop" beyond a feudal society in which only plutocrats and criminals -- many of whom are one and the same -- continue to thrive.

Granados has kept in touch with this writer since his petition for safe haven in the U.S. was speedily granted three years ago by a U.S. Court of Appeals. Although he takes no pleasure in it, what he says about his country is damning. What drives his disclosures, after several years of self-imposed silence and stealth, is what he calls, "the unexplored potentiality of hope" -- hope that Honduras may have reached critical mass.

"The country faces two choices; radical change or an inevitable tumble into chaos."

Granados doesn't mince words. "Honduras is a 'narcostate' run by 'narcocrats' whose power and influence reach beyond its borders." Lethargy and a culture of corruption are only part of the problem, he says. Poverty, despair, lawlessness and the lure of easy money all help lengthen the tentacles of Honduras' drug hydra. Granados blames the "ostrich-like attitude" of his countrymen for the dishonesty of their elected representatives.

"What we have is a collective conspiracy of silence. If they know something, they don't talk. Or else they beat around the bush."

In 2009, shortly before Granados' asylum was granted, the French and U.S. ambassadors publicly declared that Honduras had become a major narcotrafficking hub. They also hinted that high-level officials in the government and police were complicit in a colossal scheme to profit from the trade -- an allegation Granados had vainly tried to make a decade earlier and which nearly cost him his life at the hands of fellow cops.

The ousted former President Mel Zelaya -- who naïvely claimed (or was it artful evasion?) that "if it isn't reported, it didn't happen" -- was enraged. He accused the French and U.S. envoys of deliberately sullying the image of Honduras and threatened to take "measures" against them. He called their comments offensive and intrusive. He took no action to verify their claims, however, thus lending further credence to anecdotal reports that he entertained known drug lords on his vast Olancho estate, and giving rise to various charges of corruption -- later dropped in a puzzling covenant with his successor, current President Porfirio Lobo.

A number of prudently penned investigative reports in the Honduran press, probably based on leaked classified U.S. Embassy documents, cited information that supported the ambassadors' statements. Several journalists were subsequently assassinated.

Earlier that year, in the wee hours of the morning, members of the Atlantico cartel, a band of thugs engaged in murder-for-hire, drug-running and auto theft, were ambushed and captured by police in Santa Barbara. Illegal weapons, including MPSs, U.S.-made M-16s, 9-mm and 38-mm handguns, shotguns and two AK-47s, as well as 13 bulletproof SUVs were also seized. Despite objections by one of the arresting officers, a police commander present at the scene ordered his men to return the weapons to the criminals and set them free.

The commander was soon relieved of his duties by the Minister of Security but no charges were brought against him.

Says Granados: "The cartels do cops favors. They provide them with disposable cell phones, they grant protection, offer large bribes and 'pull strings.' Cops reciprocate by keeping them informed of police operations, surprise roadblocks and impending raids. The cops are paid in U.S. dollars or, more often now, in various quantities of narcotics worth their weight in gold which the cops sell at a profit. Drug runners who are nabbed in staged arrests are promptly released and their confiscated assets returned on orders of suborned judges."

Granados alleges that the state of Copán, which borders Guatemala and El Salvador, is the last stop in the "corridor of the trade," a well-traveled road that stretches from the Caribbean coast of southeastern Lempira to Copán and also known as *El Camino de la Muerte* -- the Death Road.

"Recently cleared mountain passes linking isolated communities armed to the teeth, frequent overflies by private helicopters, the free flow of U.S. dollars and careless displays of wealth among previously needy villagers, all indicate the tools -- and fruits -- of a brisk drug-based commerce. Yet neither the *Dirección de Lucha Contra el Narcotráfico,* nor the *Grupo Espécial Antinarcótico* has intervened.

According to Granados, the Copán Ruinas Airport, constructed against the wishes of many Copanecos, was developed with "funds raised among the 'local mafia.' The general aviation facility is uncontrolled; it provides no communication frequencies or runway conditions and issues no NOTAMS (notices to airmen). Drug shipments transit through this airport. Why have there been no arrests, no indictments, no lengthy prison sentences, no extraditions?"

Its pious name notwithstanding, El Espíritu, also in the province of Copán, is a hamlet of about 3,000 boasting elegant villas, luxury cars, pricey flat-screen TVs, state-of-the-art security systems and a team of heavily armed men who patrol the streets and adjoining roads day and night. El Espíritu is a refuge for a branch of the Sinaola crime cartel. Its chief, the now legendary Joaquín Archivaldo Guzmán Loera, aka Chapo, whose prowess is said to have eclipsed that of the late Pablo Escobar -- and who is now on the FBI's most-wanted list -- is said to be operating in Honduras. He's suspected of having liquidated local cocaine distributors. Despite the price on Chapo's head, Granados doubts he'll ever be captured.

"He has so much money, so many connections in high places and so much dirt on them that he can bribe his way out of any situation."

Despite recent all-out offensives on violent crimes by the armed forces of Honduras that targeted mainly slum neighborhoods, the number of murders and assassinations continues to rise in Honduras, now the nation with the highest homicide rate per 100,000 population: Someone dies a violent death every two hours in Honduras. According to human rights watchdogs, many of the homicides are state-sponsored extrajudicial executions of youth suspected of gang activity. So much for due process. The rising rate of deaths among women is blamed on misogynous domestic outbursts. Most of the killings, according to Granados, are vendettas or targeted assassinations, paybacks against snitches and meddlers by police brass and high level government officials -- "including at least one former president, a number of congressmen, lower-echelon provincial administrators, and some elements of the DEA."

Granados hasn't stopped asking questions. It's his countrymen, he says, who've abdicated their right to ask.

AT WHAT PRICE SILENCE?

It was on a visit to Paris that I remembered the words. Uttered years earlier, they echoed with singular resonance as I gazed at the baroque building that had once housed my school. I was a teenager -- a would-be journalist armed with little more than a presumption of talent and an affectation driven by romanticism not purpose -- when I first heard the chancellor's caustic exhortation:

> *"We can't stoke, let alone ignite, the sacred pyre that must consume you, enslave you from within. Journalism is a calling. We can't sell you inspiration. At any price. Nor can we instill the greatest of all virtues -- an unqualified reverence for truth and the dogged determination to find it, sublime and uplifting or hideous and vile, wherever it may hide."*

I'd traveled to Paris on a whim, hoping to wash away the stench that clung to my pores, to stifle the screams of anger and frustration that scorched my throat, to resurrect, in a week's time in the City of Light, my beloved hometown, the Quixotic verve, the exhilaration and the sense of purpose that had once sustained me. And as Paris unfolded before me like a springtime bouquet, I knew that I'd been forever changed, no, damaged by the very events I'd witnessed and felt duty-bound to chronicle, by the hopeless causes I'd so impetuously championed. The obscenity and filth I'd retreated from in search of catharsis would be softened by distance, assuaged by the loveliness of Paris, by the sweet scent of lavender wafting in the air. But the malaise lingered, fed by the images of death and destruction that still danced in my head and sustained by the nausea they induced.

> *"If you want to say it well, say nothing,"* the thinker advises. *"If you want to say it better,"* the doer counters, *"say it out loud."*

•

Weeks earlier, I'd interviewed Tegucigalpa's newly elected mayor, César Castellanos, a large man with big ideas and an infectious energy to match. Things were looking up for Tegucigalpa and everyone banked their hopes on a better tomorrow. Then came a Hurricane named Mitch and a helicopter "accident" that reeked of criminal negligence or worse. And the big man who everyone knew would have clinched the presidency, *El Gordito,* as he was affectionately nicknamed, was no more, and his ideas and the enthusiasm he infused in his fellow Hondurans died with him, overwhelmed by cataclysmic forces and submerged under a tidal wave of collective inertia.

In the riverbeds, hiding a scarred terrain where cadavers half-buried in the muck were still being plucked by the dozens, now grew sparse patches of wild grasses and stinkweeds. Circling overhead, their eyes trained earthward, squadrons of hungry vultures spied their next meal. A scouting party swooped past me, sending shivers down my spine. Agitated, hungry, the birds alit and scrambled through tangled masses of garbage and offal, scratching warily for some succulent morsel. The rest, waiting their turn, perched on roofs and treetops. Surveying their surroundings, they commanded a view of a city enfeebled by nature's merciless bouts of folly and compromised by a climate of sloth and indifference that gripped the nation long before the monster storm touched down.

On the Comayaguela side of town, from the old bridge straddling the Choluteca River, a thin, meandering run of pestilential sludge, men relieved themselves with an unconcern bordering on exhibitionism. No one seemed to care.

Parque Central, a microcosm convulsing for air and space -- and a symbol of the contradictions that characterize Honduras -- throbbed with a visceral cadence perilously akin to agitation. The square was little more than a grimy tract encrusted with bird excrement where idleness exalts indolence at the altar of ennui. One comes to *Parque Central* to kill time. Literally. Along with peanuts, candy, sliced green mangoes dipped in salt and lime juice, ice cream and lottery tickets, can also be enjoyed crude entertainment by doleful circus clowns and would-be jugglers, and the promise of a hereafter by amateur evangelists and raving madmen.

Conditioned to believe that salvation can be attained by osmosis, beggars, cripples, drunks, vagrants, grimy toddlers and horrible harlots whittled away the hours huddled against the walls of St. Michael's Cathedral. Missing an arm and a wing, deprived of his spear, a statue of the dragon-slayer stood atop a waterless fountain, staring uncomprehendingly at an evil beast that would not die, while shoeshine men furiously polished shoes that can never stay clean.

In the *peatonal*, the bustling pedestrian walkway where the tout-Tegucigalpa eventually converges, vacant-eyed, inspiring neither respect for the law nor their person, diminutive policewomen -- often dwarfed by the pistol resting on their hip -- clustered in the shade, perusing comic books or flirting with their male colleagues as mischief and mayhem went unnoticed.

Cabbies, enamored of noise, blew their horns at prospective fares, unmindful of the odious din their collective cacophony produced. Emitting acrid diesel fumes, trucks and buses ground their way through dusty narrow streets cratered with potholes and lined with crumbling sidewalks while kamikaze drivers, unmindful of pedestrians, did not hesitate to run them over to gain an inch.

Still fresh in the memory of city folk, many of whom kept coming back to the site to gawk and cavil, the collapse of a temporary metal viaduct, a Bailey bridge erected in the wake of Hurricane Mitch by the U.S. Army Corps of Engineers, typified the scandalous scorn that Hondurans have for codes, discipline and the immutable laws of physics. Accustomed to disasters, they are wont to call "acts of God" the predictable consequences of their own lack of foresight. After all, who will litigate against God -- and win?

"Culture, your know," Mayor Castellanos had told me days before he died in a suspicious helicopter crash. "My people, God bless them, they are incorrigible." He'd raised his eyebrows, looked heavenward and shrugged his shoulders. "Our nation cries for radical and swift reforms yet we move at a snail's pace. Progress is viewed with suspicion; mistrust leads to inertia. Politicians who keep their promises discomfit their opponents and baffle the voters. Besides, you won't let us manage our own destiny," he'd added without hostility. By *"you"* he'd meant the United States.

Amid the chaos and confusion, frenzied commercial growth had given Tegucigalpa a deceptive appearance of urban dash. Yet another stately hotel was rising, this time a stone's throw from the presidential palace -- one wonders why and for whom, as tourists were as scarce as clean tap water.

For the people, "the pitiful pawns of history," as my friend and colleague, the late Erling Duus Christiansen (1940-2000) aptly called them, very little had changed. "Their fate does not hinge on whether they eat bread or tortillas," he'd argued. "It rests on their willingness to take on the challenges of democracy. Where such will is lacking despotism and bondage will rule." While most of us accept the notion that what cannot be changed must be endured, Duus had insisted that what cannot be endured *must* be changed. It is this defiance of all odds, this bold challenge against sloth, indifference and timidity that come across in his writings and his personal ethic. He inspired, galvanized, jolted and even shocked his way into our consciousness.

Meanwhile, shanties kept growing like purulent warts along the higher elevations as more people from the provinces converged on a city stretched beyond its limits and resources. Many dwellings had collapsed and many more would slide downhill when the next heavy rains rolled in from the east and drenched the city.

"We Hondurans have no problem recognizing reality. We just lack the resolve to change it," a cab driver observed as he tossed a banana peel out the window on our way to the airport.

It's against this backdrop of chaos, antagonism and fear -- much of it attributable to colossal government ineptitude, corruption, indifference and disdain for its own laws -- that I'd headed to Central America, first in Guatemala, then in Honduras and the rest of the isthmus. The somber visions recorded during a marathon 18-hour journey in the dreary streets of Tegucigalpa, later augmented during subsequent visits, had blossomed into several cover stories. A gutsy, budding English-language publication, *Honduras This Week*, now defunct, had run my columns uncensored. Given a nation inching unsteadily from autocracy to semi-democracy and still cowed by decades of authoritarian rule -- military one day, pseudo-civilian the next -- the editor, an American expat, had taken enormous risks. He'd later have reason to curb his enthusiasm and dampen my own. His boss, the publisher, unschooled in English, more interested in circulation and advertising sales, had never read a word I'd written. The message this small, underfed, struggling newspaper sent by publishing my exposés -- that one of the obligations of a free press is to point fingers -- did not fall on deaf ears. But this was still a largely alien concept. Predictably, I was swiftly denounced as a gadfly, an iconoclast and a mischief maker, and the publisher was sternly reprimanded by his clients for allowing "a gringo journalist to 'calumniate' the fatherland."

Later, a series of reports on the assassination of Maya chieftain, Cándido Amador Recinos, would also be greeted with threats of legal action. For its part, the Honduran government reacted to the reports with apathy, if not stupor. Made public, threats against me were likewise ignored or dismissed by the mainstream Spanish-language press. A culture of intolerance toward truth was being exalted by indifference toward the gringo that I am.

In May 1999, I filed a report titled, ***Central America and Genocide: The Seamy Side of Reconciliation***. The original draft contained a list of 22 high-ranking retired Honduran military officers, all graduates of the U.S. Army School of the Americas, all implicated in crimes against humanity. Unlike the Cándido chronicles, which were based on personal research and augmented by intelligence from informants, the miscreants named in the report were already well known, in and out of the region. They'd been cited by *The Atlanta Constitution*, *The Boston Globe*, *The Miami Herald*, *Newsweek*, and *The New York Times*, and by watchdog organizations, such as Amnesty International, Human Rights Watch, the Inter-American Commission on Human Rights and the Center for International Justice and Law. Their crimes are now a matter of public record.

First published two years earlier, the list, and a brief account of documented offenses ranging from narcotrafficking to torture, kidnapping and illegal detention, disappearances, assassination and mass murder, was this time willfully excised from the main story text. Journalists, this one included, zealously and justifiably protective of their status as independent observers, question the very concept of an editor suppressing verifiable fact. As it is, newsmen working in Central America face harassment, intimidation, a weak judiciary and governments that view the media as dangerous meddlers. Scores of journalists have been silenced because of this presumption. The lucky ones were merely fired or demoted. TV networks had their licenses revoked; their anchors were dragged to court to face trumped-up charges of libel and slander. Maverick publishers found their offices padlocked, their printing plants demolished and their paper supply deliveries suspended. Hard-nosed journalism and legitimate dissent were discarded in favor of sensationalism, gore and banality.

Tactically expedient, the motive offered by the editor for deleting a previously circulated list of thugs -- that *"some of these men live a spit's throw away from my house"* -- would prove strategically unsound. It was also a harbinger of things to come. I later submitted several articles on the soaring rate of crime and violence in Honduras. The articles were inspired in part by Cándido's assassination and by the gangland-style, drive-by rub out in Copán that had left five people dead. The articles raised a storm of protest and triggered an avalanche of vituperations against me. They also earned me scores of anonymous threats, many of them traceable to Copán hotel, restaurant and tour operators.

Originally approved and scheduled for publication, a sequel probing Copán's corrupt political machine was suddenly put on hold. Owing the gravity of my disclosures and the potential for legal action (or more serious forms of retribution) I was asked to edit the piece and soften the pitch. Fearing that substance would be seriously eroded by the absence of detail but anxious to get the story out, I reluctantly complied. The text was further heavily "sanitized." Names were deleted. Other litigious elements were muted or expurgated. Notwithstanding these adulterations and a craven retreat from naked truth to adumbration, the editor, expressing concern for life and limb, declared the piece "still too hot to publish" and scrapped it.

Dumbfounded, defenseless against skullduggery, I ended what had been a long and often stormy relationship with the paper. Published after some delay, my letter of resignation, which I'd insisted be made public, was doctored. Among the deleted passages was a reference to threats against the paper by Copán hoteliers and restaurateurs to suspend all advertising so long as I was being published. The article on violence, the riposte its vicious reception elicited and the banned Copán massacre exposé were eventually circulated on the Internet and later published in Panama and the U.S. Six years later, friends still advise me to stay out of Copán.

•

In open societies, a free press is both an asset and a facilitator of democracy. In other parts of the world, it is still viewed as a threat to oligarchies and other deeply entrenched power structures. This attitude has created a self-view by the press that predisposes it to silence. Empowered by the elite, indebted to them, governments add insult to injury by looking the other way. A nation that controls its media or fosters a climate of fear and intimidation that cows them into self-censorship -- or silence -- can only be called a nation of gangsters.

•

Gazing at my old school building on *Rue de Rennes*, across the *Église Saint-Germain des Près*, and remembering the great lessons learned along the way that day in Paris, I was reminded that it is in censorship that the seeds of suspicion, fear and social disquiet grow best. When the truth is sacrificed at the altar of political correctness, the consequences are incalculable. As Spanish philosopher Miguel de Unamuno (1864-1936) warns, "To be silent is to lie." Unamuno was right. Silence invites more injustice, more deaths. Armed only with words, journalists wage an ill-balanced and often fruitless war. The other side has guns, greased, loaded and aimed at the truth by a triumvirate of collusive interests. The first seeks to gain global control by establishing a chimerical "new world order." The second is keen on opening new markets for the bulimic corporate juggernaut. At the bottom are the reactionary political structures of compliant debtor nations that salivate, like Pavlov's dogs, when the bell of foreign aid rings.

"It's amazing that, historically, words have prevailed," says prize-winning essayist and author, Roger Rosenblatt. His may be an ontological perspective. Words endure in the impersonal, two-dimensional realm of the printed page, but they do not *prevail*. Instead, they leave a wasteland of lofty rhetoric that has done nothing to change human nature, chill passions and curb hatred. Some horrors *are* too deep for words or, as deconstructionist philosophy suggests, writing is a dangerous substitute for living as it is likely to betray personal experience.

•

Ebbing passion and waning romanticism in the presence of horror produce a different kind of desolation, one felt deeply in an inaccessible region of one's soul. For years I thought that one way of erring on the side of justice was to side unerringly with the victims of injustice -- the vanquished, the dispersed, the humiliated, the persecuted, the forgotten. Behind prison walls. At mass graves and hurriedly dug sepulchers. Wherever voices of dissent and cries for freedom had been hushed. Amid the anonymous bones scattered about the steaming earth. Pogroms, exile, occupation, torture, war, genocide, ethnic cleansing: They've all become a blur in an unceasing tempest of human agony. Shocking prime-time images of man's inhumanity to man don't lie. Our world, the evening news reminds us, is a sewer in which we wade, knee-deep, in the blood of martyrs. Gathered at the dinner table, we watch them die or fade away like ghosts. "Past is prelude," we declare with scholarly condescension. We owe it to our fragile, overtaxed psyches to forget an endless stream of atrocities -- the Crusades, the "Holy" Inquisition, Shoah, the near-extermination of native Americans, the wholesale slaughter of Armenians, Biafra, the killing fields of Cambodia, the intertribal carnage between Hutus and Tutsis, the bloodbath in Chiapas and the Guatemalan highlands, the 64-year-old blood-letting between Israelis and Palestinians, Iraq, Afghanistan and Syria; the wanton murder of street children.

Distance, racial differences, cultural incongruities, all help intellectualize other people's suffering. We endure it by perfunctorily purging our souls after each infamy. "You can't change human nature," we pontificate, as we partake of dessert. In a pinch, a mind-numbing sitcom will help set our minds at ease. We survive the truth by looking the other way.

The heavy capital of idealism and exuberance I'd invested in unmasking and impaling vampires had by now steadily dwindled. The reason for this lassitude was not a lack of energy or a diminished commitment to justice, but the cumulative effect of disillusionment and disgust at people crippled by sloth and inertia. I'd spent nearly two decades fighting their battles as if they were my own, my activism exhausted in a futile effort to agitate the popular conscience, to stiffen backbones weakened by despotism and exploitation. In so doing, I'd finally hit a brick wall and the stars the impact produced in my head showered me with an insight of blinding clarity. At long last, I understood that mine was a puny and hopeless contest against formidable foes. I realized that the people of Central America would never change, never rebel, not on the streets, not at the polls. A short memory and a weak character will do that to people. Neither alienation nor profound discontent will spur them to shake the political dustbin. Fearful of change, unnerved by serious reformation, they will choose to be seduced by the echo of old, hackneyed words rather than awakened by the unsettling resonance of their own reality.

Passive, submissive, Central Americans never look back, except to reminisce about a blurry and irretrievable past. They are too busy existing and procreating like lemmings to realize that they're being fleeced, that they're being led to slaughter then devoured by the very shepherds entrusted with their care. Occasionally, they give in to knee-jerk reactions, a primordial reflex now reduced to feeble tics that are promptly stilled by police truncheons. Feeling the sting of injustice and institutionalized villainy, they will succumb to a brief and atypical act of defiance that horrifies the flock and is then swiftly swept under the rug of public indifference. Anticipated and tolerated by the oligarchy, these random displays of exasperation are then loudly flouted as the undesirable byproducts of a free society, instead of being flagged and deplored as the warning signs of grave social ills.

For lack of a cohesive voice, Mesoamericans -- apathetic if not inert -- will continue to put into office people who know how to stir their nations' messianic hopes of deliverance from the status-quo but who spend their term polishing the next speech instead of cleaning up the shit, which is what they were elected to do in the first place. Most will be content to live with slogans instead of awakening from the stupor of their political gullibility. Democracy does not work in a vacuum. It demands active participation by all. Its tender shoots will wilt so long as people continue to bask in the feeble light of hope. A basic right of democracy -- and a key responsibility -- is to make politicians accountable for their words, responsible for their broken promises. Long overdue is an upsurge of nausea, a loud, collective spasm of revulsion at the vampires impaled at their throats. Time has come to slam the shutters open and exclaim loud and clear: *"We're mad as hell and we won't take it anymore."* Not the potholes and the crumbling sidewalks, not the garbage, the foul air and polluted water, not the power outages, unregulated traffic, police corruption, influence peddling, drug running, and money laundering, not the gangs and child prostitution and human trafficking, not the inept and fossilized bureaucracies, not the Byzantine red tape, usurious bank rates, lofty explanations, limp excuses, words, words, words.

But such outbursts are dramatized on television and in cinemas where the people purge themselves on a Saturday night out -- never in the streets -- or in the saloons where the national bile is habitually drowned. At the polls, where the democratic process has been reduced to a thoughtless ritual, there will be no surprises. It will be business as usual. Voters will opt for the "least worst" and hope for the best. This is the safe way out. Convictions are easily subverted by sheepish conformity. In the rush to find someone to blame for their woes, the good people of Central America will ultimately exorcise and exonerate their tormentors.

There is comfort in perpetuity. It helps deaden hopeless dreams.

•

What happened to the idealism, the zeal, the élan that once inspired me? Why have disgust, rancor and indifference replaced empathy? Is it age? Is it the realization that I'd been screaming at the deaf and gesticulating before the blind and petitioning the heartless? Is it the pervading squalor, the immovable plutocracies and rampant corruption in nations so lacking in self-respect, ambition and initiative that they wallow in their own excrement and keep smiling? Is it the sudden awareness that I was speaking to myself? Imagine how much time, effort, passion and paper and kilobytes were wasted in the process, how many words uttered in vain.

"Tout passe, tout lasse, tout casse," say the cynical French. Everything slips away, everything tires, everything breaks. Battle-weary, shell-shocked, I lay down my weapons. Nature's laws are immutable. There are those who eat. And there are those who are eaten. I was tired of sorting through the leftovers.

In time, back home, rested, cleansed and eager to find them, I would uncover other depredations and, with them, fresh pretexts for one last hurrah of rabble rousing, one prolonged final burst of fury that would bring on criticism, censorship and subtler forms of rebuke and disaffection, this time not in some backwater Third World nation but in the mythical land of the free and the home of the brave, the Grand Master of corruption, the *capo di tutti capi*, the United State of America.

PART FOUR
THE OPEN SEA

In hindsight

WHERE THINGS ARE NOT

Downstream, as they near the end of their journey, rivers take on a certain solemnity. But beneath the glassy surface, turbid, silt-laden vortices churn with restless vigor. It is there that memories of a distant beginning lay submerged, roiling in a state of suspended animation until the current wrenches them free and delivers them to the open sea. Fond of allegories I seize upon the metaphor. I'm stunned by the bewildering brevity of time. "Time," said Henri Bergson, "is what hinders everything from being ceded all at once." His was an optimist's perspective. Time is a thief: it takes back everything it bestows -- itself included.

Writers spend half their lives dreaming, the other half trying to remember their dreams.

•

Pity the chronicler. His travail is dissonant, his art off-key, his output seldom more than the disfigured fragments of a straying spirit in search of its worldly self. I seek no comfort or recompense by disrobing the past. I only want to fondle the moods and emotions I unearth as I wander along the maze. Anxious to rummage through a drawer full of memories, or a pile of junk, I fondle them, suck on them, so to speak, with equal doses of lechery and reverence, as if they were the Muses' breasts. In short, I milk them dry to set them free. It's the moods these transfigurations convey, the dismay, the outrage they might possibly elicit, that makes me reach for a pen, not some vainglorious urge to inform, enlighten or entertain. I shall ventilate the shadows, stir the foulest exhalations, but I promise no light, no wisdom, no eternal truth. I conform to no particular communion. I'm afflicted with an exquisite curse: I was baptized in ink. It is in the blackness of night, where memories incubate, that ink runs swiftest and deepest of all. I know; I've been swept in its ebbs and flows, never sunk, willing to risk drowning again and again with each pen stroke. To reminisce is to return to the embryo, where unborn reality gestates.

To evoke the past is to break loose from reality endured, to bypass a realm vast and limitless where monsters, mythic and real lie in wait. The voyage is fraught with perils; the path is uncharted. It is the very nature of such journeys that compels those who embark on their gossamer wings to ask themselves, sooner or later, whether it was wise to abandon hearth and home when the old armchair feels so good, when the winds of conformity sing alluringly upon the moonlit waters of the inlet, there before them. For they are apt to discover on arrival at some uncharted port-of-call, as I did when I first arrived in America, that there had been no compelling reason for them to make the trek in the first place. For when all is said and done, at the very conclusion of their aimless peregrinations, weary and confused, they will wisely conclude, as I did, that some ideals are not meant to be aimed at, let alone exceeded.

Buoyed by parental qualms about the future, catapulted by curiosity, immaturity and armed with a colossal disregard for the consequences of my actions, I'd done the unthinkable. I'd crossed the Atlantic, not to flee from persecution or seek my fortune, but to survey the penalties such expedition might levy. In hindsight, I could have found cogent reasons to stay in Paris but my arguments, stunted by immaturity and held back by wanderlust, lay fallow within me, insufficiently parsed, unvoiced. My ability to follow an idea to its logical conclusion would often be sapped by restlessness, corrupted by haste, undermined by the urge to get to the "other side." Inquisitive, I'd spent my childhood exploring the universe around me. Eager to unlock their secrets, I'd taken apart -- and ruined -- clocks, radios, telephones and other devices. I'd played Frankenstein, splicing worms and grafting the thorax of one insect onto the abdomen of another. I'd set fire to unexploded ordnance, just to see what would happen; a piece of shrapnel that lodged in my calf had to be surgically removed. I'd pilfered and sold scrap metal, doctored an I.D. card to gain access to an R-rated movie, injected a pet tortoise with cortisone and shown off my father's speculum to girls foolish enough to play patient as I avidly studied their anatomy. I would rush into adulthood, tempting fate, quelling doubts and overlooking fear in exchange for the trials of involuntary expatriation, military service, matrimony, fatherhood and the ordeals of marital discord, adultery, divorce and depression. And I would pursue an endless stream of occupations, some mind-numbing, others that took me halfway around the world as I chased after my own tail in pursuit of Nirvana.

Daunting and beguiling, New York, the fabulous city I openly vilified and secretly adored, would witness these contests with a detachment that deepened the exasperation and heightened the passion. I blame New York for making self-exile and alienation strangely bearable. I blame myself for letting it hold me in its dizzying embrace as the years spent ambling in its vast labyrinths turned to decades. I also blame myself for being deaf to its siren song: I should have run the other way while there was still time. Or I should have surrendered to it body and soul. I did neither and found myself meandering in a limbo of my own creation.

•

So much had happened since I'd first arrived in the U.S. My uncle had fled Romania and settled in Paris, where he turned to writing and art criticism. His mother (my grandmother), was now by his side. Meanwhile, my parents too had crossed the Atlantic, ostensibly to be near me. Like me, both had been dazzled at first by America's bounties but the love affair was short-lived. They would both bitterly regret leaving Europe. And, like me, they allowed force of habit, relative ease, inertia and old age to entrap them like flies on fly paper in a country where they would never feel at home.

My father had passed the difficult English-language medical boards and was promptly hired by Mount Sinai Hospital in New York. Likening the facility's maddening tempo and impersonal atmosphere to "assembly-line medicine and piece-work healthcare," he quit in disgust after less than a month.

My parents then moved to a small Ohio town where my father had obtained work at a state-run psychiatric hospital. Determined to humanize the institution by enriching the lives of the patients, many of whom had long been victims of antediluvian and cruel treatment by doctors and nurses alike, he made enemies. He became enraged when a staff physician placed two mentally challenged inmates -- a man and a woman -- in solitary confinement and deprived them of "privileges," including dessert for two weeks for having attempted to copulate behind some bushes. To his horror, my father discovered that the couple, institutionalized for life, had been chemically sterilized.

"We aim to foster Christian principles," the physician had protested in defense of his actions. "Fornication and other lewd acts are frowned upon in this country, Dr. Gutman."

"This is a hospital, not a monastery," my father retorted. "And this is the twentieth century, not the Dark Ages. Your job is to make patients' lives as comfortable and sweet as possible, not to punish them for being human and for seeking affection and intimacy."

My father would have other run-ins with his staff and, eventually, with the State of Ohio. He kept a diary documenting medical malfeasance and acts of cruelty against some of the patients. This disquieting document, which incriminates several of his former colleagues -- all of them probably dead by now -- and points an accusatory finger at Ohio's snake-pit approach to psychiatry, is now in my possession. I have been itching to make it public.

Uncompromising in matters of conscience and medical probity, warned not to meddle with "established practice," my father resigned. A month or so later he was appointed Senior Surgeon at the Syracuse Hospital in upstate New York. He held that position until my mother's death in 1973. New York State, he discovered, was no less strait-laced in matters of sex and religion than Ohio, but found most of his colleagues and senior management somewhat more receptive to his egalitarian views. He chronicled a number of bizarre cases involving abuse of authority, the enforcement of absurd blue laws and the illegal experimentation of psychotropic drugs on unsuspecting patients, some of them minors. His notes -- should I choose to publish them -- would add new dimensions to ghoulish leaks in the press (and subsequent corroboration by the U.S. government) that thousands of Americans had been unwittingly exposed to radioactive, chemical and biological agents from the 1940s into the 1970s. As I would later point out in a series of widely circulated articles, the government's tardy and uncharacteristic expiation-by-confession of past trespasses showed more than just a willingness to lay bare a tarnished conscience. It was nothing short of a ploy to keep far more sinister secrets frozen beneath the thick ice of official censorship. Like an iceberg, U.S. complicity in the rewiring, robotizing and subversion of the minds and bodies of thousands of unsuspecting Americans runs far deeper than imagined. And, because such trickery -- allegedly dictated by the need to thwart equally demonic cold war threats -- calls for absolute secrecy, the government almost succeeded in keeping a tight lid on this ultra-covert component of its war machine. *Almost.* Small leaks would eventually spring from the warlocks' overflowing cauldrons. Most were swiftly swabbed clean. A short memory and a phlegmatic unconcern for the inscrutable ways of government helped appease America's scruples and dissipate the telltale noxious fumes from its delicate nostrils.

•

As these events unfolded, I was trying to survive, skipping from one dull job to another, moving from one rooming house to another in a futile and self-deceiving bid to find some permanency in my life. It was around that time that I met Suzy Levine, the daughter of a fish monger in the old Fulton Fish Market in downtown Manhattan. Suzy had short kinky hair and almond-shaped eyes. She reminded me of Leslie Caron. A dance student and a pupil of choreographer Martha Graham, Suzy liked to fuck almost as much as she enjoyed going into demented twirling-Dervish trances during which she pirouetted across the room in an exhausting quest for perpetual motion and Dionysian rapture. I would jump out of my skin as she suddenly snapped into bizarre and convulsive poses in the middle of an otherwise quiet tête-à-tête. She called them "contractions," modern ballet exercises developed by the eccentric and surly Miss Graham herself.

Suzy's parents had taken a liking to me, inviting me to spend weekends at their home in Yonkers. It would not be long before they ceased looking at me as their daughter's boyfriend and began treating me as a prospective son-in-law. I had no intention of marrying Suzy but I was having a good time and eating several square meals a week. One day, yet again out of work, Suzy's father, Harold, a kind and generous man, offered me a job "in the family business." He called it a "career move." After four months of twelve-hour days spent ferrying frozen halibuts from the Hudson River piers to the store, gutting, rinsing, trimming, weighing and wrapping fish, peeling and de-veining shrimp, loading the trucks, taking orders on the phone, canvassing prospective customers and following up new leads in the afternoon wearing a suit and tie, I bid Suzy farewell. I owe an aversion to fish and a leeriness of dancers to this life-altering experience.

•

And then, one day, I saw my mother die. I was 34. No, she didn't die suddenly. She'd always done everything with prudence and reflection. It took months of pain -- constant, searching, tenacious. She turned yellow, lost her hair, shed half her weight and slowly lost her mind. I witnessed this irreversible transformation with disbelief, helplessness and anger. Lies had kept her hoping, fighting at first. Then she learned the awful truth and she gave up. One day, when the others left the room to stretch their legs after an all-night vigil, I touched her face and called her name.

"Mama, mama, don't go."

She winced and her eyelids parted ever so briefly. I knew she'd seen me, felt my presence, heard the words. She expired that evening. June was young and the air was filled with all of spring's fragrances. And every vestige of childhood in me died with her. Only the dreams she'd dreamed for me survived, some unfulfilled, some beyond reach except in the limitless regions of a mother's love. I remember cursing her, hating her. No one understood the rage that surged within me when she died. I felt betrayed, lost. Taken for granted, often unnoticed in life, longed for in death, my mother would have been the first to grasp this paradox. No one else did, except my father who, familiar with the contradictions of the human soul, discerned in my calumnies the brittle fragments of a broken heart. Heeding her last wishes, she was cremated and we buried her ashes in a family plot outside Paris, where my grandmother and uncle would later be laid to rest. It rained that day. It would rain without fail every time I visited the cemetery. And I would grumble every time because my shoes got wet and caked with mud.

W. E. Gutman

It is in the nature of coincidence to contain hints of irony.

•

I would be greeted by rain upon my return to New York. A monotonous downpour drenched Manhattan with chilling persistence. Broadway stretched before me, a dank canyon in which a million lights flickered through the sulfurous mist. They were all there: drunks, vagrants, hawkers, doomsday prophets and reformers, the homeless and the transient, visitors and commuters, and beautiful girls so well disguised that they looked as though they'd spent the day typing. It was the West Side and men with upturned collars and vacant expressions walked right into me, as if I wasn't there. Creatures of all genders trapped me in their staring game and I didn't know if their eyes conveyed hate, lust or defiance. I didn't want to miss a single nuance so I stretched my gaze to the limits of peripheral vision until I found a new pair of eyes up ahead. And the contest resumed. I reached Forty Second Street, the outer rim of a funnel through which stirs a backwash of humanity. The light turned red. I stopped. At my feet lay the puddles, like bottomless black lagoons in which shimmer all sorts of eerie reflections. Everything around me seemed to reinforce life's constrictions. **STOP. ONE WAY. YIELD. NO PARKING. NO STANDING. NO RIGHT TURN. NO LEFT TURN. WALK. DON'T WALK.** Uncle Sol, the only blood relative who drove a cab for a living, and who'd read everything from Anaxagoras to Zola, once described life as "nothing but a fucking traffic jam." His erudition notwithstanding.

•

Grand Central Station. I remember a nun begging for alms at the bottom of a steep, interminable subway escalator. She sat on a folding chair, night after night, gazing at the hordes that spilled at her feet. She nodded, slowly, rhythmically. Her lips moved but the roar of the trains engulfed her incantations. She may have been reciting the rosary, the paternoster, an endless mantra of benedictions, or she may have simply said *"Welcome to hell, welcome to hell...."*

Redemption, she knew, can be bargained for with a little kindness. The generous ones, few as they were, only gave on Fridays. The others pretended not to see her. Underground, where commuters surrender to a numbing daily cadence -- hurry to work, hurry back home -- life seems thin and fitful, snatched in haste, endured with wariness in guilt-ridden anonymity by a transient mob that barely tolerates itself. And there seems to exude from this pulsating, throbbing, scurrying mass of people a smell of hostility and fear and boredom, all of it skillfully concealed behind a million expressionless eyes.

Sooner or later, I noted, everyone made a special effort to diminish the guilt. So the nun waited. And hell got more crowded every day.

•

There are two kinds of solitude: the one we eagerly seek and the one that trespasses when there's no one left around to disturb it.

My mother's death put an abrupt end to my father's career. He said, "fuck medicine," and retired. He was 69. Heartbroken, embittered by the shortcomings of his craft, he withdrew into a world of self-imposed solitude in the company of an irascible cat, Minou, a stray he'd rescued as a kitten on a bitter winter night. This once vibrant man survived my mother by 14 years, now a recluse given to neurasthenia, sudden fits of anger and weeping. On September 9, 1987, after suffering a series of fainting spells, he was admitted for the last time to St. Luke's Hospital. On the 16th, his doctor summoned me. My father was dying, he said. It was a matter of hours. I remember taking his hand into mine and squeezing it gently. He squeezed mine. I had no words. I knew this was the end but I could not bring myself to say anything. My father abhorred the immodesty, the banality of empty words, especially in moments when silence speaks with greatest eloquence.

My mind raced back in time and I remembered the war and tales of a man in a white frock over a silver-braided black uniform, a Reich's officer paid to experiment on thousands of unwitting human guinea pigs. They called him *Herr Doktor* but his stethoscope was cold and he sneered as you shivered before him. He used to shove the tongue depressor so far down your throat that you retched and your nostrils filled with vomit. His injections were painful. The glass syringe was enormous, it seemed, and he held it up to the light like a sacred object, transfixed by the amber droplets of serum gushing from the gleaming needle. You heard yourself pleading, begging. *"Herr Doktor*, will it hurt?" Embarrassed but in desperate need of reassurance, you shed your pride and dropped your pants before the sharp, tugging stab made an answer quite superfluous. You winced and he laughed like a drunken burgher at an Oktoberfest village fair. Nazi wit has a way of reducing obscenity to bestiality. Nothing mattered anymore, the nausea, the sores, the blinding headaches, the chills, the fevers, the dizzying descent into madness. There was plenty of stale bread and thin leek broth on the stove in the infirmary, and he granted seconds to repeat volunteers. In the end, if his injections or his scalpel or the foul salves he applied on your festering wounds didn't kill you right away, he invited you in for more until they did or until insanity finally yanked you out of his clutches.

I looked at my dying father, born poor, of humble origins, a simple man filled with compassion, an honest country doctor, a healer who had shed bitter tears when his first patient died. He seemed to be at peace. At about six that evening, he opened his eyes and looked at me with the same tenderness that had lit his gaze when I was a little boy and he'd pick me up in his arms.

"It's such a short journey from the source to the open sea, son," he said softly. My father had never been big on symbolism. He considered it a subterfuge, an evasion from truth, a descent into mawkishness. He closed his eyes and whispered, this time in French.

"Ne cherches pas midi à quatorze heures." This was an advice he'd often repeated. Loosely translated, the injunction cautions against *seeking things were they are not.* He expired moments later and I knew that, at last, he'd found his "place," an abode not made by human hands, a realm not found on maps that had eluded him all of his life. Would I find mine, I wondered, as I buried him at the New Montefiore Cemetery in Long Island in a simple pine casket, naked and swathed in a shroud, as he'd stipulated in his will.

Like me, he never ceased to long for Paris.

Several years later, after much soul-searching, I wrote a tribute to my father. Careful not to dwell on our personal relationship, the belated eulogy focused instead on the physician. The essay was published by *The Wall Street Journal* on January 31, 1996. Entitled ***A Magnificent Misfit***, it reads:

> *My father did everything himself without benefit of nurses, clerical staff or drafty assembly-line consultation cubicles. He took your temperature as you sat face-to-face on white enameled swivel chairs -- rectally too, if necessary, in which case you weren't sitting. He even drew blood from your finger and let it run up a thin graded tube as you marveled at the strange powers of capillary action.*
>
> *This wonderful man had his own centrifuge, a gleaming autoclave and an old Roentgen that hummed with imperturbable omnipotence in a bright, cheerful room that always smelled of iodine and clove. When he administered injections, he would deaden the point of impact with a dry little slap, and he would talk about this and that with neighborly solicitude long after the needle was out.*
>
> *You were never surprised to learn that he'd pedaled several kilometers at night in the rain to deliver a baby on an old kitchen table or in a big brass bed, or to hold the hand of a dying village patriarch as family and friends looked on. Sometimes it lasted until morning. He'd go straight back to his office looking tired but he'd smile, put on a fresh smock and patch up scraped elbows and knees and he'd even ask how Aunt Lucy or Uncle Charlie was feeling these days. And he never forgot to stuff your pockets with eucalyptus candy and lemon drops.*
>
> *"How much do I owe you, doctor," I would often hear his patients ask.*
>
> *"Oh, I don't know," he'd answer, staring at his feet, clearly embarrassed by the question. "Whatever you can." Then he'd quickly add, "don't worry if you're short. You can pay me next time." He always assumed his patients were impecunious -- most of them were -- and he could never bring himself to demand prompt payment of his very modest fees. Money made*

him feel uncomfortable. He had an almost prudish disdain toward it.

"There is something incongruous about charging money to heal, relieve pain, save lives," he once told me. "I shall never get used to it." This was a remarkable ethos for a man who, by his own admission, had embraced medicine to escape the abject poverty of his childhood and was forced to wash dishes, wait on tables, tutor dunces and donate blood to pay tuition.

"It all happened in dissection class," he recalled in a rare moment of wistful introspection. "I wept at the sight of my first cadaver. He was so very young. Who is this wretched mass no one will claim, I asked myself. Has he no family? Is there no one to mourn him? Surely he was somebody's son, somebody's brother. He was alive, he felt pleasure and pain, joy and sorrow. He had dreams. Did he love? Was he loved in return? Did he suffer? Could he have been saved? Did poverty deprive him of good health or rob him of a decent funeral?"

A pre-med student once asked my father what he considered to be the three cardinal medical taboos. My father replied without hesitation: "Do not operate unless such procedure is clearly in the patient's interest. Do not overmedicate. Never charge patients more than they can afford. Ignore the first two taboos and you are merely unprincipled. Break the third and I shall call you a vampire."

The student now boasts a Fifth Avenue practice, a New Canaan estate and a yacht at anchor in a secluded cove on some Pacific coral archipelago. It takes three months to secure an appointment. He does not handle emergencies. He makes no house calls.

I miss my father. He was incorruptible. He had no time for sophistry, no patience for equivocation, no room for the shaded areas separating right from wrong. Compassion was his only guide, his patients' health and welfare his sole mission and reward. He lived frugally -- "how much does one really need to live with dignity," he once asked a wealthy colleague who found the question contentious. My father died poor but debtless.

I wish I had a dollar for every patient this 1935 graduate of the Paris Faculty of Medicine treated for nothing, for every paté de foie gras or leg of lamb or kilo of butter or basket of eggs he accepted in lieu of honorarium, for every debt he forgave, for every prescription he paid out of his own pocket. I would have had a neat little sum, more than enough to pay for the thorough checkup doctors denied me when I lost my job, when unemployment benefits ran out and I could no longer afford medical insurance.

Will I find a doctor like my father when I retire and my meager writings barely cover the cost of a pine casket? They say it's cheaper to die than to live. My father devoted his career to deconstructing aphorisms. He was the magnificent misfit lesser men do not have the courage to be.

A week or so later, I received a phone call from David Asman, then an opinion page editor at *The Wall Street Journal* (now an anchor on the Fox business network).

"Willy," Asman said, "The White House called. President Clinton read your piece. He wants to respond. May I give your mailing address?"

"Yes," I answered, dumbfounded. "Yes, of course."

A couple of weeks later, the postman delivered an envelope bearing the White House seal. Inside was a note, personally handwritten and signed by the president:

Dear Mr. Gutman --

Several weeks ago I read your very moving tribute to your father in The Wall Street Journal. It impressed me so much that I cut it out and carried it around, re-reading it from time to time. My grandfather, who had barely a grade school education, was much the same kind of man. He ran a grocery store in a poor Southern town before food stamps. He sold food on credit to poor and working people he knew could never repay him when he knew too, that they were doing their best. I have been trying to start a discussion in the country on what we owe each other on the edge of a new century. Your wonderful piece certainly will help. Sincerely, Bill Clinton.

Clinton's letter, unexpected and heartwarming, restored my faith in the vigor and amplitude of idealism. Surely, I thought, such accolade from the president of the United States would translate into reshaping and redirecting political institutions heretofore created by the elite, for the elite.

But that was not to be. Good intentions are often subverted by opportunism, self-interest or, in his case, political expediency. Time and again, Clinton was forced to set aside his campaign pledges, capitulating to the guardians of the status quo, signing bills favoring Republican agendas that bolstered the already colossal might of America's corporate elite.

In his second inaugural speech -- as he had in his letter to me -- Clinton used such rousing buzzwords as "a new century" and "a new millennium." But deeds failed to echo the rhetoric. His stated antipathy for the "evils of capitalism," and his commitment to a "radical redistribution of economic and political power" were soon forgotten in favor of "bipartisan" symmetry. Hard as he tried, his presidency offered no stalwart program to provide Americans a health care system unfettered by extortionist insurance schemes. Instead, like his predecessors (and successors, including Obama), he continued to serve the rich, the mighty and the well connected to the bitter end. His feeble and irresolute commitment to social causes was further sapped by his administration's dependence on militarism and war.

Words sabotaged and distorted by political misinformation can have a disquieting effect on our timorous psyche. Take "socialized medicine." Americans take Social Studies in school. Their parents teach them social graces. Hostile to any form of social contract (except social engineering) many, influenced by social Darwinism, claw their way up the social ladder. Having reached the top, they hire social secretaries to handle social calendars brimming with social obligations. Overly sociable, some come down with social diseases. All eventually become eligible for social security.

Somehow, no one takes umbrage at the word *"social"* except when twinned with the word "medicine," which, Great Zeus, suddenly transmutes it into some ungodly, un-American obscenity. Never mind that other civilized nations provide their citizens with cradle-to-grave affordable, quality healthcare and low-cost, effective over-the-counter medicines. But Americans must not be roused from their naiveté. In a society that willingly sacrifices the individual at the altar of corporate profit, the predatory agendas of the medical lobby and the colossal greed of the pharmaceutical and insurance industries shall not be imperiled.

So, my essay had moved the president of the United States but it failed to touch the sympathetic nerve of the medical establishment. I received scores of choleric letters from physicians around the country. I was branded a gadfly, a meddler, a whiner, and a communist. I was also accused of "opportunism," "romanticism" and "mischief making." How sad when homage to a man who selflessly and valiantly upheld the Hippocratic ethic elicits such a tide of indignation, especially from fellow physicians. This ugly barrage was tempered by half a dozen letters, many from sons and daughters of "country doctors," all echoing the same deep and stirring longing for a more intimate doctor-patient relationship. Yes, doctors are now subject to enormous constraints and proscriptions virtually unknown at the height of my father's career. The craft has been over-bureaucratized. Having said that, I can't help but hearken to a kinder, gentler era when a doctor was also nurse, midwife, pharmacist and confidant, and the honorarium for such versatility and skill was dictated by what the patient could afford, not what the "market" commanded.

TWILIGHT IN THE MOJAVE

Heretics are given us so we might not remain in fancy.
-- St. Augustine

In 1999, I set out on a five-day, 3,000-mile westward drive across America. Its vastness and awesome beauty filled me with exhilaration and appeased for a while the emptiness within. The emptiness returned when I reached the California desert. Behind me was the narrowing perspective of an arrow-straight road merging into the horizon line. Ahead lay a barren, petrified expanse. Alone in its vast, sallow bosom, overwhelmed by the immensity and desolation around me, I stopped, got out of the car and looked at the limitless blue vault above, at the tawny, arid earth at my feet. Everywhere, clumps of sparse, stunted shrubs and contorted Joshua trees clung stubbornly to life in this lifeless citadel. I felt lost. I wanted to scream. The scream died in my throat as I set eyes on a lone yellow poppy, its dainty petals quivering in the breeze. I remembered the wild blood-red poppy fields of Abu Gosh, outside Jerusalem, where I'd gamboled as a boy, taking in their heady aroma, napping under a blanket of undulating crimson blossoms and dreaming Technicolor dreams. I remembered the wistful French song of my youth, *"Comme un petit coquelicot,"* (Like a little poppy) made famous by Mouloudji. I remembered being swept in a stream of indescribable emotions every time I heard it. Poppies are still my favorite flowers -- the blood-red ones of my youth. And I remembered Paris. Words, images, colors and aromas danced inside my head, faint, disjointed, stranded at the limits of consciousness. I felt my tongue forming silent thoughts, like prayers or mantras. Emboldened by self-discovery, delivered from their cerebral bonds, the words gushed out. I let out a monologue of stupefying candor and pathos, part confession, part supplication, words driven by longing, by despair, by a fear of madness, words one only dares to utter in the desert's deafening silence. I looked at the sky.

Then I looked at the poppy and the babble ceased. It had wilted in my hand. But its subtle, intoxicating scent still lingered on the tip of my fingers, in my nose, on my lips.

"I should have never plucked it. I should have never set eyes on it." Then I heard myself asking the same question I'd asked at dawn, on January 30, 1956, as the USS Constitution sailed into the Port of New York:

"What the fuck am I doing here? Is there no end to this senseless peregrination?"

And then I heard myself sobbing as my eyes now strained against the milky glare of day.

I was 62.

•

In the spring of 2000, I went to work as a copy editor for the Antelope Valley Press, a privately owned daily covering the vast "High Desert" region of Los Angeles County, and a self-avowed vector of arch-conservatism. In time, I would also contribute essays, features, news analyses and opinion pieces.

In October 2001, I published a three-part article detailing the history of chemical and bacteriological warfare, the global proliferation of biochemical weapons -- which nations had them and which were shopping for them -- and describing the effects of various agents on the human body. Readers lashed out, calling me a doomsayer and accusing me of deliberately creating a climate of fear. No one protested, in hilarity or outrage, when "Homeland Security" -- as America readied to go to war against Iraq -- ludicrously urged Americans to protect themselves against deadly chemicals and pathogens with duct tape and plastic sheeting. (A codicil, an updated version of a previously published feature chronicling the illegal experimentation by the U.S. government of toxic substances, including LSD, on unwitting Americans, was rejected by the AV Press.)

In November, two months after the tragic events of September 11, and in a climate of fervid nationalism, I wrote *"Our College for Killers,"* an essay supportive of a demonstration that had just taken place at the U.S. Army School of the Americas in Georgia. Protesters had come by the hundreds as they do every year from all corners of America, students and sexagenarians, professionals and blue-collar workers, young mothers with infants in tow, veterans festooned with combat ribbons, priests and nuns and agnostics with an unambiguous lust for justice. They had come as they do every year to denounce state-sponsored terrorism and to demand the closing of an institution that for the past 60 years had trained and coddled, at U.S. taxpayers' expense, a rogue gallery of dictators and thugs. They had come to awaken and revitalize America's sluggish conscience. They had converged on Fort Benning, where the School (now rechristened the Western Hemisphere Institute for Security Cooperation) is billeted, to pay homage to the hundreds of thousands of victims of political repression, dispossession, wrongful arrest, unlawful imprisonment, torture, extrajudicial executions and "disappearances." They had gathered to be arrested if need be, as scores do every year (actor Martin Sheen among them) in a show of defiance against the existence and preservation of a college for killers. And they had assembled, this time, to urge the Bush administration not to allow our neighbors to the south to use the dastardly assault on America as a pretext for committing atrocities against their own people. It is human nature, I reasoned, to recoil against injustice. It was my duty, as a journalist, to revisit the scene.

Few readers shared my perspective. Days later, I learned through the grapevine that my piece had been greeted with "extreme displeasure." Someone in the front office had sent word that "persons drawing a paycheck from the Antelope Valley Press are not entitled to voice opinions that conflict with those of management." I never found out who had issued this directive but I took it as a warning and I lay low for a while. Subsequent columns wisely expressed centrist views on issues that either transcended party politics or clearly met "bipartisan" criteria for political correctness.

Self-censorship, which the press had exercised in one form or another in America, was now in full swing.

In April 2002, I responded with unusual petulance to a guest commentary written by Janice Hall, a local college professor, in which she attacked "the corrupting influence of leftist thought" on education in America. Her citation of literary works she may or may not have read but deemed suitable for young minds unpolluted by "socialist propaganda," reeked of conceit and pomposity and came off as a gratuitous display of erudition, the kind that bulimic egos need to flaunt. The works Prof. Hall extolled and those she panned were poles apart: the former well to the right of center, the latter predictably well to the left. Her casuist attempt to politicize the decline of academic excellence in America by blaming it on "liberal agendas," I felt, was spurious and abhorrent. Yes, I conceded,

> "... Schools keep breeding successive generations of marginally cultured, not to say semi-illiterate, adults, but no, this is not the result of some sinister liberal cabal. If the masterpieces of yore are neither taught nor read, it's because few in this sunbaked fortress of conservatism -- teachers and students -- have the intellectual capacity to recognize their greatness, let alone savor the messages they send. If anything, the anti-intellectualism that permeates this "Valley" is inspired by diehard obstructionists fearful that free thought and enlightenment will subvert the conservative core. Prof. Hall's tirade echoes those on the far right who would freeze the free flow of ideas, foster a world view filtered through the thick lenses of conservatism, prevent inconvenient un-beliefs from interfering with ossified convictions, in short, keep society in the miasmic darkness and stifling conformity of reactionary doctrine."

Don't tamper with Shakespeare unless you ARE Shakespeare.

Petulance gave way to open hostility in response to Prof. Hall's fatuous deprecation of Elie Wiesel's oeuvre and, by extension, of the Holocaust. Wiesel, a survivor of Auschwitz, and a Nobel laureate, I argued, had been an unassuming but tireless champion of human rights. His books had been hailed around the world. By dismissing *Night*, the third in Wiesel's acclaimed trilogy about the bestiality of man, as "undeserving a place in world literature," Prof. Hall, I declared, "makes a mockery of all scholarship." I concluded by suggesting that far too many people on this windswept desert plateau shun the truth for fear that it may interfere with the perpetuation of America's "feel-good" mythology.

> *"There are those among us who cling to an idealization of America that is as flat, saccharine and fake as a Norman Rockwell painting. Sadly, these love-it-or-leave-it flag-wavers are bent on diverting the current of thought, arresting the free flow of ideas and fostering a world view filtered through the narrow-mesh netting of diehard ideology."*

Prof. Hall never responded. Petty demagogues tend to shoot off their mouths in the sanitized vacuum of an obliging public forum but they rarely defend their own pronouncements when challenged. They get even. It should have come as no surprise when my next column, slated for publication in an upcoming edition, was first delayed than scrapped without explanation.

•

Extreme displeasure in the front office turned to indignation. A week later I was "laid off." The reasons given were so vague, and so outlandish that I did not bother to contest them. Both the editor and the owner/publisher had reasons to silence me. My views, openly counter-cultural and disquieting at a time of scorching patriotic fervor had apparently irked large numbers of readers and advertisers. The editor had obliquely and in long-winded perorations rebuked what he perceived in my irreverence to be the result of vexing socialist leanings. I made no attempt to challenge this faulty assessment but I would come to work the next day in my black-and-red CCCP T-shirt, a souvenir of my travels to Russia, just to piss him off.

"Gutman," he would say with a hint of annoyance in his voice, "I always knew you're a pinko."

"Let's just call it a paler shade of red."

Neither portrayal was accurate, not his of me, nor mine of myself. Lacking the capacity or the urge to embrace, let alone champion, any political cause, I was content to agitate against the rigidity of all extreme convictions, whether from the right or the left. Character, upbringing and circumstance had protected me from entrapment by irrevocable doctrines. Patriotism, *"the last refuge of scoundrels,"* however, was an incongruity, a hideous emotion from which I recoiled. Truth is I never felt the remotest allegiance for any state, prince or potentate. I love France the way a child loves to rummage through a toy chest, with wonderment and anticipation. I love Paris with every hedonistic fiber of my being. But this infatuation is wholly Epicurean, not tribal. It evokes no special loyalty or feelings of indebtedness. To this day, ancestral Romania, where I lived for four years, elicits distant and disturbing memories of a vacillating, mercenary nation given to political harlotry. Israel, where I spent five gloomy years as a teenager, inspires no feelings of kinship. I resent its theocratic power base and deplore its leaders' inability (or unwillingness?) to make peace with the long-suffering Palestinian people. Cosmopolitan, sophisticated, maddening and electrifying, New York, where I meandered for 40 years, has done little more than contribute to an "Americanization" of habit and convenience. Like Paris, New York fascinates, titillates, captivates and bewitches. Like Paris, it kindles the senses and galvanizes the intellect. But I would never fully embrace it, feel a part of it. It could never be, it never was *home*. On those rare instances when I'm asked to disclose my origins (or allegiances), I respond, without affectation, that I'm "stateless." No swagger or romanticism is implied, only an admission of alienation from the world's constituent parts. In this self-view is encapsulated a fierce rejection of any form of nationalism. Of all synthetic human emotions, chauvinism frightens me most. Deep inside me linger indescribable and omnipresent sentiments reaffirming a Jewish identity. But I have no religion and the feeling, nebulous, impalpable and unlikely to culminate in some exalted state, must die with me. For reasons I cannot explain, my "Jewishness" is personal, not communal. I admit feeling sorrow at this alienation but since the core values of Judaism rest on a belief in deity (I don't believe) and on the shared observance and celebration of its laws and traditions (I don't observe or celebrate) there is little hope for me of a transformative epiphany.

My sons, born in America, hopelessly assimilated, maddeningly "American," overwhelmed by life's labors and constraints, will not likely return to their roots. I recognize this insensitivity, this detachment from ancestral values for what it is -- a sickness of the soul. I take no pleasure in this infirmity.

●

Dennis Anderson, the AVP editor and I got along well. I knew him to be a decent human being even if he seemed wed to a set of convictions that, by their very nature (or the manner in which he articulated them), betrayed a fossilized right-wing view of reality. Conservatives rarely defect, I reckoned. It's against their nature. Whenever they do, it's usually to assume an even stiffer rightist stance. Who knows, perhaps Anderson, a former AP writer and a man of culture whom I genuinely liked, secretly shared my freethinking views. Perhaps careful not to bite the generous hand that fed him, he, like the RCA dog, dutifully echoed his master's reactionary voice. Juggling mortgage payments, feeding a family and sending kids to college are incompatible with ideological adventurism.

When he summoned me to his office, claiming to be at the mercy of "fiscal constraints" beyond his control, he said something about "economic Darwinism" making my layoff inevitable. I accepted the empiricism of this dastardly doublespeak as readily as I endorse the Theory of Evolution. But I argued that Darwin's premise, freed from its "survival of the fittest" equation, also accounts for adaptation and acculturation in the face of challenge and opportunity.

"It's one thing to lob off an atrophied or gangrenous tree limb. It's quite another to prevent a healthy bough from producing more and juicier fruit," I said.

Anderson didn't bite. I knew that the paper was replacing its archaic computer hardware and software system, and was making a multimillion-dollar investment in a new desktop publishing network. I also knew that "fiscal constraints" notwithstanding, no one else on staff had been laid off. I was being lied to, or royally bamboozled, and I was mad as hell.

I wrote the National Coalition Against Censorship in New York and subsequently spoke to Jeremiah S. Gutman (no relation) a noted attorney specializing in First Amendment issues. Quoting from A. J. Liebling, Gutman, now deceased, reminded me that *freedom of the press belongs to those who own the presses.* Inherent in such freedom, he added, is the right to filter, sanitize or exclude any material that does not harmonize with a publication's doctrine or agenda, or to sack anyone who openly challenges that doctrine or agenda.

> *"A private publisher can publish what he likes and censor what he does not like and, in our capitalistic structure, either you work for him and play the tune he calls or quit and sing your own lyrics and tunes. The First Amendment protects and entitles a publication to promote only those opinions it adheres to and not provide a forum for anything else."*

Fair enough. In a subsequent telephone conversation, Gutman conceded that freedom of expression is a self-limiting standard. It includes the freedom not to publish -- or to *abridge* or *impede* the free flow of ideas.

> *"There are risks in this subterfuge but in these times of 'controlled' free speech and shameless allegations that dissonant views can hurt business, even the high courts would side with your employer, not you."*

In June 2002, two months after I'd been laid off, and as mysteriously, I was rehired and went back to work on the news desk. The OP/ED Page editor, once overtly supportive of my views, was enjoined to keep me out of his lineups. Mortified and apologetic, he complied. I didn't add to his discomfiture by asking him to reveal who had issued the order. It didn't matter.

It was a sad epigraph for someone who'd spent a lifetime excavating the ugly truth to discover that even in America-the-Beautiful there are those who will forcibly keep the ugly truth entombed. Free speech, susceptible to erosion when it's most desperately needed, is no match for the calumnies, innuendoes and outright falsehoods peddled by the merchants of myth. There is great irony in the eagerness to immolate constitutional principles even as the U.S. grants itself the right to impose them on others in the name of democracy.

•

"The whole aim of practical politics," H. L. Mencken, the acerbic social critic wrote, "is to keep the populace alarmed by menacing it with an endless series of hobgoblins, all of them imaginary." The "liberal" press, PBS, the National Endowment for the Arts, the American Civil Liberties Union, Planned Parenthood, the Democratic Party, the Washington Post, Maureen Dowd, Michael Moore, the welfare system, "socialized medicine," Cuba, Amnesty International and Human Rights Watch figure prominently in a bestiary of menacing bugaboos. By focusing on them, by fabricating or exaggerating the threat they allegedly pose, newspapers like the Antelope Valley Press stubbornly aim to conceal or whitewash America's failures and excesses.

In brief and measured communications with Anderson during my layoff, I'd argued that one of the roles of journalism is to enumerate the threats to peace, social justice, national independence and freedom, and to support the defenders of these principles. An open-minded journalist -- as opposed to a lip-server of government-warmed-over versions of the truth -- must at all times attempt to demystify the manipulative power of the state and expose the collusive docility of the media.

"Is it so unusual for a journalist to turn to activism," I asked. "We all champion certain causes from time to time. We all have our threshold of tolerance to bullshit. Objectivity in print journalism is a fable. Only the camera's lens is witness to ironclad reality, if and when it's allowed to focus, zoom in and pan on the naked truth without editing and photo-shop fudging."

Anderson, an ex-paratrooper, never quite forgave me for vilifying the U.S. Army School of the Americas and, by extension, the entire U.S. military establishment. In lieu of an answer, he launched one of his famous orations and succeeded, as he was wont to do with a tortuous logic raised to messianic status by his booming basso voice, to drive me to near-numbness. I'd tried to cultivate a dialogue. Instead, I was being filibustered and, in the process, suavely dismissed as a radical, a red.

•

In November, saddened and troubled by the death on October 25 of Minnesota Senator Paul Wellstone, his wife, daughter and five other people, I wrote a commentary questioning the preliminary results of the National Transportation and Safety Board investigation.

Defying an injunction that I refrain from submitting anything, I handed the piece, entitled *Post-Election Musings: What Killed Paul Wellstone?* to the OP/ED page editor, with a copy to Anderson. It read, in part:

> *Among legislators running for reelection this year, he alone risked the ire of Republican opponents and the disaffection of a faint-hearted, fence-straddling Democratic confederacy. He alone cast the dissenting vote against the resolution granting the U.S. carte blanche to attack Iraq. He voted his conscience, believing his views would bolster his chances for reelection, not weaken it.*

The accuracy of his instincts, I went on, was now a matter of conjecture. Predictably, conspiracy theorists, truth-sleuths and iconoclasts would be asking: Was Senator Paul Wellstone's death an accident?

There may yet emerge a rational explanation for the plane crash. After all, airplanes do fall from the sky from time to time. But nagging questions remain. Both pilots on the ill-fated aircraft were experienced. The captain had an air transport rating. His first officer was a commercial pilot. Equipped with two separate de-icing systems, the plane had been inspected and certified airworthy. Weather conditions were less than perfect -- icing and freezing rain were reported -- but two smaller planes had landed uneventfully at the same Minnesota airport two hours earlier. Visibility was marginal but the runway, under a 700-foot ceiling, was in full view of the crew.

Had the political climate at the time been different, it might have been possible to dismiss the crash as a tragic mishap whose origins could be traced to the complexities of aerodynamics and the vagaries of meteorology. But the death of Paul Wellstone took place at a time when America was veering sharply -- and boastfully -- to the right. It also came two years almost to the day (October 16, 2000) after a similar mishap killed another Democratic Senate hopeful locked in a tight election contest: Missouri Governor Mel Carnahan. The mainstream media promptly noted the "eerie coincidence" but, characteristically, went no further. In hindsight, what I'd written was not so much an account of probable events but, given the political climate at the time and America's penchant for assassination, a hypothetical reconstruction of what might have happened. I offer no apology for my speculations.

In 2001, two leading Senate Democrats, Majority Leader Tom Daschle and Judiciary Committee Chairman, Patrick Leahy, received letters laced with anthrax. The Justice Department -- headed by conservative John Ashcroft (who lost to the deceased Mel Carnahan in the Missouri contest) failed to apprehend the culprit(s). It is interesting to note that no Republican was the target of such lethal mail.

Wellstone was engrossed in a hotly contested reelection campaign, but polls showed him overtaking his Republican opponent, Norm Coleman. With the Senate controlled by Democrats, the loss of even one seat would shift control [as it did] to the Republicans. The immediate effect of Wellstone's death, later borne out by the elections, would be to deprive the Democrats of a majority and hand the Republicans the clout they needed to push for legislation that would benefit the wealthy and pamper corporate America. Some suggested this objective more than justified the "neutralization" of pesky adversaries.

The reactionary elements in and around the Republican Party had shown their scorn for democracy, first in the dogged campaign to scuttle the Clinton administration, then in the barefaced piracy of the 2000 presidential election. They were now preparing to sacrifice young American lives -- and tens of thousands of Iraqis -- to grab control of the second largest oil reserves in the world.

Another curious and suggestive detail had emerged: Virtually every day, the administration issued vague warnings of terrorist assaults on domestic infrastructures. Americans were being drilled like Pavlov's dogs to pin any act of violence on al-Qaida. Yet no one dared suggest that the crash of Wellstone's plane was the result of terrorism.

In a climate of war, shrinking rights, reactionary gloating and the erosion of democracy, it was not unreasonable to ask whether Wellstone might have been the target of a "purge." Under the circumstance, I closed,

> *"... it is tempting to suggest that investigators will conclude that Paul Wellstone was the victim of some inscrutable event -- perhaps an 'act of God.' This should give Bible-thumping diehards endless joy."*

Before submitting the piece, and after much inner debate, I excised a paragraph in which I implied that the timidity and flip-flopping posture of leading Democratic presidential contenders toward the war in Iraq could be reflexive, that they might be fearful for their own political necks. The oft-repeated bromide, "... we shouldn't have gone in but now that we're there, let's finish the job," I had also put forward, was "odious double-speak and rank hypocrisy designed to protect these legislators' career -- if not to prevent them from meeting a fate similar to Wellstone's." This last-minute redaction had been made in hopes that it might somehow enhance the essay's chances of being published. My impudence that day was exceeded only by my naiveté. I'd disobeyed orders and aired heretical views. Word came, anonymously, as front-office pronouncements do, that I better cease and desist, this time for good -- or else. Caught between a rock and a hard place, even the OP/ED page editor demurred with an indulgence born of friendship.

"You know, if it were up to me..., but...."

"Say no more. I understand."

In December, permanently banned from its pages, demoralized, burned out, challenged by a newly installed and unintelligible computer system, and no longer able to weather the grueling evening shift, I resigned from the Antelope Valley Press. I was determined to sing my "own lyrics and tunes," all of which found a receptive audience in several independent newspapers in the U.S. and abroad. A number of articles would be devoted to the telltale language of (media) silence and the lies it conceals.

A year later, in a moment of extraordinary gallantry and candor, Anderson admitted that "the business side," resentful of my political views, had steadfastly frustrated any attempt on his part to grant me a more creative voice. Knowing what I knew about the paper's "business side," namely that it is wed to ultra-conservative causes, gave Anderson's belated but welcome apologia the veracity and legitimacy it was meant to convey. Anderson and I have remained on cordial terms -- from a distance. Our mutual goodwill, sustained by an unspoken tolerance for the divergence of our political views, is tempered by the reality of our respective lives. I'm now retired, living in another town, a free agent, at liberty to carp and cavil and heap insults, unafraid to make enemies along the way. He's still working for a living. I fear that the "business side," which had been breathing down his neck during my brief stint at the paper, would find ways to make life difficult for consorting with the likes of me. I'm grateful to Anderson for giving me a job and putting up with the eccentricities of a fractious old man.

●

A new kind of inquisition was now sweeping America. Less grisly but no less ill-omened than the demented witch-hunts that convulsed Medieval Europe for more than two centuries -- and apart from methods and severity of results -- this latter-day pursuit of heretics had put on a fresh visage. Writing in *From Dawn to Decadence*, historian Jacques Barzun said,

> *"In the United States at the present time the workings of 'political correctness' in universities and the speech police that punishes persons and corporations for words on certain topics quaintly called 'sensitive' are manifestations of the permanent*

spirit of inquisition."

Liberties relinquished are difficult to reclaim. Vulnerable in times of crisis, they become easy prey when "national security" concerns are invoked. They have since been curtailed. The government now detains immigrants; it spies on electronic communications, invades on-line privacy, regulates media coverage of the news and crushes dissent. In the wake of the September 11 attacks (later deleted from official transcripts) Bush White House press secretary Ari Fleischer's admonition that Americans ought to "watch what they say" speaks volumes about the lightning speed with which constitutionally protected dissent suddenly turns into disloyalty and treachery. In California, Representative Barbara Lee, who had voted against congressional authorization for retaliatory military action, was the subject of death threats and had to retain the services of a security detail. Congressman Jim McDermott (D-WA), a vocal critic of American foreign policy in Latin America -- I'd interviewed him in Guatemala in 1994 -- has repeatedly come under fire for advocating restraint and expressing strong reservations about America's military adventurism. Academics, students, labor leaders, members of clergy, journalists had also come under attack for questioning the need and wisdom of war. TV talk-show host Bill Maher and critic Susan Sontag were excoriated for their humanist views. The Dixie Chicks, probably one of the most "down-home" American country music groups, were reviled and boycotted by rubes bloating with patriotism.

Humor was being greeted with the same clodhopping sanctimony when the cartoon, *Boondocks*, by Aaron McGruder, was yanked from syndication for accurately suggesting that the CIA had helped train Afghan rebels, including Osama bin Laden, and that the U.S. had funded the Taliban when they were fighting the Soviets. Everyone knew that the U.S. had engineered Saddam Hussein's rise to power. And everyone knew that the U.S. was aware of the atrocities committed by Saddam's troops in Iran -- when it was strategically expedient to play one thug against another. Saying so out loud, however, was now being deemed unpatriotic, if not treasonous.

At California State University, Chico, students heckled a professor who criticized U.S. foreign policy. News coverage of the event unleashed a barrage of hate mail from around the country. Writing in *The Chronicle of Higher Education*, Robin Wilson and Ana Marie Cox reminded readers that during the "Red Scare" of the 1950s and during the Vietnam War, tenured professors had been dismissed and even jailed for espousing views many considered anti-American. The authors bleakly observed that,

> *"The current test of academic freedom emerges in what some have called a culture formed around the notion that no one should have to listen to ideas or even facts that upset them."*

Inflexible convictions render men blind, arrogant and, carried to the extreme, insane.

•

Then came the Patriot Act, a sinister piece of legislation hastily enacted 45 days after the September 11 assault on America. Giving the president broad powers to fight terrorism and rammed through with virtually no debate, the Act rescinds checks and balances on law enforcement and threatens the very rights and freedoms enshrined in the Constitution. The FBI, without warrant or probable cause, now has the power to snoop on private medical records, library files and student transcripts. The Act also puts the CIA back in the business of spying on Americans. Once gleaned, the information can be shared without a court order.

To fully grasp the wickedness of the Patriot Act, it is useful to recall one of the most shameful chapters in recent history that led to restrictions on the CIA. Until the mid-1970s, both the CIA and the National Security Agency secretly and illegally eavesdropped on Americans. The emergence of a New Left, perceived to be, no less, "Marxist-Leninist-Maoist in structure and objective," fueled Cold War paranoia and resulted, as early as 1970 in the formulation, by Nixon administration insiders, of a cabal reminiscent in concept and scope of the Patriot Act. A secret memo approved by Richard Nixon recommended increased domestic electronic surveillance, monitoring of international communications by Americans, and relaxation of restrictions on mail interception and "surreptitious entry." The memo also advocated planting informants on college campuses, and the creation of an "Interagency Group on Domestic Intelligence and Internal Security" to be controlled from the White House. An addendum recommended that the Internal Revenue Service be enlisted to spy on and harass think tanks and other tax-exempt organizations considered hostile by the Nixon White House -- among them the Brookings Institution and the Ford Foundation. Most of these schemes were appendages of government activity conceived during World War II but gradually rescinded in the postwar years.

Despite the statutory provision in its charter prohibiting the CIA from taking part in law enforcement of internal security activities, the CIA spied on as many as 10,000 Americans. Dubbed *Operation Chaos*, these activities involved surveilling people who opposed the Vietnam War, student activists and militant African Americans. *Operation Chaos* orchestrated a massive information-sharing program between the FBI, the CIA and other agencies. The FBI turned over all of its intelligence on the peace movement -- 1,000 documents per month by June 1970, according to a report issued by the Senate Select Committee to Study Governmental Operations with Respect to Intelligence Activities. Also known as the [Sen. Frank] Church Committee Report, the dossier revealed how simple passive information-sharing from other agencies to the CIA turned to sanctioned spying on lawful political activity protected by the First Amendment. The report stated that,

> *"The mechanics of Chaos, both in performing the mission undertaken by the CIA and in servicing the FBI's needs, involved the establishment of files and retention of information on thousands of Americans. To the extent that information related to domestic activity, its maintenance by the CIA, although perhaps not itself the performance of an internal security function, is a step toward the dangers of a domestic secret police against which the prohibition of the charter sought to guard."*

It was only after these abuses were exposed that the CIA's domestic surveillance and data collection activities were curtailed but never suspended.

The Patriot Act, which exempts the government from scrutiny, also helps shroud in absolute secrecy the proceedings of military tribunals where defendants can be gagged and the press shut out. When a defendant and his accusers are gagged during covert hearings, the public is denied the right to know what the government is doing and why. First Amendment attorney Charles Sims observed:

> "Secret trials have no place in a free society. Secret justice is no justice at all."

In a New York Times editorial dated November 16, 2001 responding to a government tightening of freedom of information rights, historian Richard Reeves wrote:

> "With a stroke of a pen on November 1, President George W. Bush stabbed history in the back and blocked Americans' right to know how presidents (and vice presidents) have made decisions. Executive Order 13223 ended more than 30 years of increasing openness in government. From now on, scholars, journalists and other citizens will have to show a demonstrated, specific 'need to know' in requesting documents from the Reagan, Clinton and two Bush presidencies -- and all others to come. And if someone asks to see records never made public during a presidency but deposited in the National Archives by a former president, the requester will now have to receive the permission of both the former president and the current one...."

The inmates have since taken over the asylum. First we learned that literary selections in the New York English Language Art Regents exam were being routinely censored. Works by Isaac Asimov, David McCullough, Annie Dillard, Isaac Bashevis Singer, Howard Zinn and Anton Chekhov, among others, were butchered to launder or altogether extirpate passages deemed "unfit" by the Regents.

Infringements on academic freedom and intellectual honesty would soon find new life in an Orwellian program cooked up by Vice Admiral John Poindexter for the Defense Department. Known as Total Information Awareness (TIA) electronic "data mining" would allow the government to harvest and scrutinize private information on virtually every person in the U.S. Alarm bells began to ring among civil libertarians over the program's inquisitorial nature, its potential for abuse and its ability to freeze speech. Journalists and legislators questioned the integrity and suitability of its architect, a man who had played a dominant role in the murky Iran-Contra Affair.

Adm. Poindexter would be indicted in 1988 on seven federal felony charges stemming from an arms-deal scandal. Counts included participation in a criminal conspiracy with Col. Oliver North, Air Force Maj. Gen. Richard V. Secord and Albert Hakim; conspiring to obstruct official inquiries and proceedings; two counts of obstructing Congress; and two counts of lying to Congress. Poindexter and his accomplices were convicted on all five counts in 1990. The retired admiral was sentenced to six months in prison on each count -- to be served concurrently. In the fall of 1991, a three-judge appeals panel overturned Poindexter's convictions on the grounds that his testimony before Congress -- which was given under immunity -- may have influenced the testimony of prosecution witnesses. The decision was appealed but the Supreme Court refused to hear the case. Poindexter rationalized his actions with chilling self-justification:

"I made a very deliberate decision not to tell the president [Ronald Reagan] so that I could insulate him from the decision and provide some future deniability for the President if it ever leaked out."

That too was a lie but Reagan's waning "memory" of events he'd orchestrated or tacitly endorsed would prove a convenient exculpatory defense.

Writing in the November 14, 2002 edition of the New York Times, William Safire warned:

"... Every purchase you make with a credit card, every magazine subscription you buy and medical prescription you fill, every Web site you visit and e-mail you send or receive, every academic grade you receive, every bank deposit you make, every trip you book and every event you attend – all these transactions and communications will go into what the Defense Department describes as 'a virtual, centralized grand database. To this computerized dossier on your private life from commercial sources, add every piece of information that government has about you -- passport application, driver's license and bridge toll records, judicial and divorce records, complaints from noisy neighbors to the FBI, your lifetime paper trail plus the latest hidden camera surveillance -- and you have the supersnoop's dream: A 'Total Information Awareness' about every U.S. citizen."

In response to widespread protests, members of Congress put the brakes on this abomination. The outcry against the invasion of Iraq and emasculation of civil liberties at home was deep and far-reaching. There was strong bipartisan support to dilute the program and place it under congressional supervision. Undaunted right-wing Republicans moved to toughen the Patriot Act and give it immutable status.

Then news came that the FBI was collecting information on the tactics, training and structure of antiwar demonstrators. The Bureau, a confidential memo revealed, had advised local officials that they should spy on protesters and report any suspicious activity to counterterrorism squads. Bristling at any suggestion of impropriety, FBI officials insisted that the intelligence-gathering effort was aimed at identifying "extremist elements" plotting violence, not at monitoring the political speech of law-abiding protesters. They would not say by what criteria the two factions -- the "anarchists" and "sanctioned demonstrators" might be told apart. Civil rights groups and legal scholars countered that the program had all the earmarks of the abuses of the 1960s and 1970s, when J. Edgar Hoover headed the FBI and his goons routinely swooped on political dissidents, among them comedian Lenny Bruce ["pardoned" posthumously in December

2003 by New York Governor George Pataki], poet Allan Ginsberg, Dr. Martin Luther King Jr., singer John Lennon, and others in the arts, entertainment and academia. Eventually, abuses by Hoover, Senator Joseph McCarthy and others led to restrictions on FBI investigations of political activities. But these restrictions would be relaxed when Attorney General John Ashcroft, citing the September 11 attacks, issued guidelines giving agents authority to infiltrate political rallies and other public events. The FBI proceeded to target Americans engaged in lawful protest. In so doing, it blurred the line between terrorism and legitimate civil disobedience.

•

Shortly before I resigned from the Antelope Valley Press, one of my colleagues on the news desk casually quoted the late Supreme Court Justice William O. Douglas, who said nearly half a century ago:

> *"Restrictions on free thought and free speech are the most dangerous of all subversions. They are the one un-American act that could most easily defeat us."*

Douglas was the quintessential liberal [free-thinking] member of the Warren Court -- he proclaimed a constitutional right to privacy, championed environmentalism and opposed the Vietnam War. He became a hero of the intellectual left, the only haven of sanity in which a threatened and shrinking centrist minority could take refuge.

Passing by the news desk at that moment and disregarding the sobriety and profound wisdom of Douglas' words, a senior editor known for his diehard views, dismissed Douglas as a "womanizer and a drunk." We all shook our heads.

"Better a progressive drunk and a womanizer than a narrow-minded pedant," I said with discernible annoyance and aiming to be heard. I was heard all right. A day later I was advised to stop "making waves."

•

I began my journalistic career ferrying copy at the late great New York Herald Tribune and sharpening pencils for the likes of legendary sportswriter Red Smith, theater critic Walter Kerr and film columnist Judith Crist. I ended it by polishing the syntax of uninspired scriveners who earned awards for twaddle that would have ended in the trash bin had it not been for the combined talent and diligence of my fellow copy editors. I was pondering the irony of it all when the Bush administration handed the nation's mightiest media conglomerates a mid-year bonus that was bound to focus media ownership in yet fewer hands. Indeed, on June 2, 2003, the Federal Communications Commission, run by Republican Michael Powell -- son of Colin -- ended long-standing federal checks and balances on corporate media influence. Once the rules are out of the way, there will be more mergers and buy-outs of radio and TV stations and networks, and major newspapers. A single conglomerate will now be able to control most of a community's major media outlets, including cable companies and broadband Internet service providers. Unless opposed, right-wing powerhouses are also inevitably likely to grow stronger, more vocal, more strident. Rupert Murdoch had his eyes set on Direct TV, the country's most powerful satellite service. Others could be expected to follow suit.

The proposed FCC rule changes further weakened the ability of mainstream journalism to serve as a critical public safeguard. Soon reporters would have to "watch what they say," especially if their papers were to be absorbed by TV empires not looking for objectivity but for a reinforcement of their own opinions and agendas. Advertising and "brand-washing" would be the end-all of all communications endeavors. And America would find itself increasingly short of moral gatekeepers.

Coverage of the war in Iraq, later of the Afghanistan fiasco, illustrates the extent to which U.S. media companies are loath to provide a serious field of analysis and debate. Clearly supportive of the military campaign and keen on lavishing sympathy and reverence on U.S. soldiers, "embedded" reporters -- undisguised handmaidens to the government -- continue to offer a unilateral, if not myopic, version of events. Their reporting sounds more like cheerleading for the war than a sober and wide-angle view of events. News outlets and prime-time TV networks pay obscure retired military officers handsome fees for engaging in endless and often inane conjecture, whereas journalists regurgitate pre-digested Pentagon propaganda and dispatches carefully sanitized to coat America's weak stomach for blood and gore. Duty-bound to chronicle the evils of war while "supporting our troops," television anchors churn out officially sanctioned banalities and redacted snippets of reality. Surely, there seems to be greater honesty in the contentious extremist rhetoric than in the fence-straddling oratory of a mainstream press averse to antagonizing the government and demoralizing the citizenry. But the double-speak would fail to persuade America that victory can ever legitimize war. In time -- pictures don't lie and government assurances ring false -- the press would also fail to convince the nation that the war can ever be won. Mounting casualties at the front, growing antipathy against the U.S. and the rapid coalescence of disparate terrorist factions willing to die in what they perceive to be the infidels' latest Crusade against Islam, would further dash any prospects of a decisive military or political victory in Iraq. Coerced to endorse -- if not applaud -- America's newest "intervention," the mainstream media would soon degenerate into a template of what is *sayable* and what is not. George Orwell, I thought, must be doing somersaults in his grave.

•

The world is full of naked emperors. Pointing fingers at their nudity, I suppose, is never fully appreciated, least of all by the multitude of bare-assed little Caesars parading in imaginary gilded garments. Forcibly undressing sacred cows makes slaying them a more festive occasion.

Free to sing my own tunes now that age and a lifetime of polemic and agitation had decisively and permanently alienated me from mainstream America, I would indulge in an orgy of denunciations. Ferocity, defiance, and rancor often guided my pen. I was waging a frontal assault against orthodoxy, laissez-faire, nationalism, dogmatism, credulity, ignorance, hypocrisy, obscurantism, and lies. Like the vitriolic right-winger Westbrook Pegler (1894-1969), whose style I relished infinitely more than his politics, I claimed the right to rankle the conformist rabble, not because I identified with it, but because I found in this vast, self-absorbed, silent mass all the seeds of humanity's misfortunes.

I'd forsaken the "middle way to enlightenment," veered from the idealized but seldom traveled *"holy eight-fold path,"* -- discernment, dignity, poise, probity, discretion, restraint, tact and constancy. Instead, now fixed in an adversarial mindset, I would continue to lob incendiary devices that imperiled me more than those at which they were aimed.

LOST IN AMERICA

I went looking for myself.
--- Heraclitus (c. 500 BCE)

Somewhere at the edge of a gray town, a cookie-cutter copy of a thousand gray tank towns, on a gray street senselessly named after some tree or flower, deep inside a gray room adorned with mementos and frozen glimpses of time misspent, the self-probing continues. I'm not in Paris but in a gray town far away across the seas. I'm out of range from the ultimate cause so I seek answers in the gray dancing shadows on the ceiling and hang on to rapidly dissolving shreds of memory.

America. Fifty-six years spent chasing after my own tail, lurching from a brief state of wonderment to one of exasperation, disillusionment and unease as I stumbled one by one on the desiccated fragments of discredited myths and embalmed fiction, trying to fit in, hopelessly out of step, out of tune. Yes, I am a restive stranger, an untamed renegade, ill at ease not in my own skin but in everything that touches it, an interloper in a realm I still do not fully comprehend, outwardly housebroken, inwardly raging and defiant and aching, treading unfamiliar waters, lost in the blinding light of day. Fifty-six years: Two billion heartbeats pumping life into an out-of-soul experience, each pulse adding to my estrangement and perplexity.

•

Where am I? I rewind my life. January 30, 1956. New York towers above me, gray, dank, alien, menacing, as I shiver on the promenade deck of the U.S. Constitution. I try to make sense of this latest disembodiment; I resent my parents who sent me here -- for my own good, they assured me; I'm ashamed of the docility with which I acquiesced to this exile. Driven by an age-old momentum, in search of new horizons, convinced that permanency can only be realized through change, I join the Navy in a failed attempt to resume a life of blissful itinerancy. I find myself marooned instead on the unfriendly shores of a racially divided military town that hates the military, hates foreigners, hates Jews, hates blacks. An overactive libido and imbecility intrude on my horizons and I get married at the age of 24, woefully unprepared for the demands of matrimony and the constraints of fatherhood. Now entombed in a dungeon of my own creation, I die each day a little as I grasp the folly of my actions.

I turn the pages and peel memories like an onion. America. 1956. Industrious. Affluent. At ease with itself, secure in its hypocrisy and crippling illusions. Elvis Presley scandalizes the puritan elite with his hit single, *Hound Dog*, but no one objects when, fiercely opposed to racial integration, ninety-six members of Congress sign the *Southern Manifesto*. Nor would anyone be outraged to learn, after his death in 2003, that Senator Strom Thurmond, the self-confessed racist who co-authored the manifesto, had fathered a child with his black maid. Schools, lunch counters, toilets and water fountains are segregated. Blacks must still ride in the back of the bus. They're often lynched, arrested on trumped-up charges wrongly convicted and imprisoned, humiliated and dehumanized. Many, after spending years on death row, are executed because white justice is not color-blind. But what the hell, if you're white and have a steady job, it's the *Life of Riley*. Relaxed, playful, upbeat, frivolous, given to good-natured inanity -- as witnessed by the dimwitted feel-good movies it released that decade -- America bares its soul and hints at the anxieties, the fretful self-inquiry to which it would later succumb as the world began to unravel. Hollywood turns introspective: *East of Eden. Rebel Without a Cause. The Blackboard Jungle. The Bad Seed. The Wild One. Marty.* Orwell publishes his prescient dystopia, *1984*. They all echo feelings of uneasiness first articulated in the internal dialogues of a nation stirring from complacency to vigilance, from presumed invincibility to perceived vulnerability, and willing, a least for now, to shed its ill-fitting and deceptive disguise. But the small screen, which holds the bulk of America captive, retaliates. The strong, silent, bronc-bustin' pistol-packin' cigarillo-chompin' Bourbon-chuggin' enforcer is still king. *Gunsmoke, The Virginian, Wagon Train, Rawhide, Have Gun:*

Will Travel and *Bonanza* all remind audiences of America's heroic past and reanimate nostalgia for those senselessly brutal days.

•

The sixties and seventies usher an era oxygenated by the rise of an ebullient counterculture. Emancipated from the phony Puritanism of the finicky Fifties, cursorily cleansed from the obscenity of McCarthyism, sickened by the Vietnam War, the Kent State massacre, the Watergate scandal, America welcomes the Beatles, lets its hair down, burns draft cards and the flag, sets fire to ROTC buildings and dons bell-bottom pants, Nehru jackets, dashikis and beaded necklaces. Malcolm X electrifies his people and shocks white America. Black Panther leader Eldridge Cleaver and comedian Dick Gregory, the eloquent drum major for civil rights, parlay acerbic tongue and mordant wit into a brand of social activism that bolsters black America's self-identity. Back from Paris where he was embraced and cheered, James Baldwin rises from obscurity to become a commanding figure in American literature. Also back from Paris where she blossomed and honed an emergent sense of justice, Sartre scholar and once one of the FBI's Ten Most Wanted Fugitives, Angela Davis, takes America by storm. A cultural phenomenon, Alex Haley's *Roots* offers for the first time a black perspective of life in Africa and unerringly records the bestiality of slavery. In *Kunta Kinté* are incarnated the horrors and heroism of the black experience. Lenny Bruce, Mort Sahl and George Carlin turn humor on its head. Their irreverence and biting political satire challenge an outwardly strait-laced but dissolute society and helps redefine and broaden free speech. Jack Kerouac, the leading chronicler of the "beat generation" -- he coined the term -- shocks America with autobiographical sketches that reflect deep social angst assuaged by drugs, alcohol, spiritualism and scorching humor. His leading apostle, Allen Ginsberg, vents his rage against materialism with a tortured lyricism kindled by LSD. Flower children preach love, not war. *Oh! Calcutta*, memorable for its brazen display of frontal nudity, male and female, and *Hair*, America's tribal love-rock musical, open to rave reviews. The plays enthrall audiences for years to come. This is an era of rebellious sex and drugs and freedom from the shackles of conformity, a time of nascent impiety and suspicion toward the political structures that Americans take for granted and trust, an epoch long remembered and still reviled by the conservative core that lived through it and died a little.

I watch these transformations with a relish that does not foster a desire to partake. I inwardly rejoice at the consternation these upheavals seem to wreak upon America's squeamish psyche, but I espouse none of the causes they champion or spawn, at least not openly. I will not let my hair grow until long hair becomes passé. I cut it short the moment manes are back in vogue. I sport a beard when facial hair goes out of style; I shave it off as soon as hirsute faces outnumber beardless ones. I adopt none of the fashions or affectations of the time -- polyester leisure suits and wide psychedelic neckties and bandannas and high-heeled clogs and anti-bomb peace symbols. I use none of the jargon, neologisms and mannerisms typical of that era. I "drop out" on my own time, at my own pace, disinclined to assert my individuality by rushing to embrace someone else's conformist eccentricities. Purely academic, my fascination for the politics of dissent remains voyeuristic. I refuse to get involved for fear that doing so will compromise my spectator status.

Inevitably, I experiment with marijuana and hashish but soon shun the demented and slovenly atmosphere of pot parties. Fed up with the inane laughter, the tangential, off-the-wall conversations, the brutish sex, the narcoleptic sleep, the Dionysian junk food binges, I get high alone in semidarkness and utter silence, plumbing the musings, images and moods the psychedelic high produces. Bored with a steady diet of "altered states," sickened by the immoderate craving for food they produce, tired of sinking into an abyss of depression as the effects wear off, I give up the weed and move back uptown. I surrender to it briefly twenty years later when my first marriage begins to unravel.

Marriage is a prison in which one lands without trial, in which one tarries without pleasure and from which one escapes destitute.

Emulating Baudelaire, Cocteau, de Maupassant, De Quincey and Poe,

I compile under the influence the first notes of a work that would take twenty years to complete. Enigmatic and disturbing even to me, the book teeters dizzyingly between allegory, surrealism and madness. In it, I dissect a world in which the obvious and the cryptic are willfully commingled. Implicit in this cautionary parable is a haunting but strangely tenable ethical question, a premise no doubt issued from my growing malaise with the paradox that is America -- sublime on paper, less than perfect in its incarnate totality, bursting with lofty ideals, ready to rescind them when deemed expedient. Imagine a society, I submit, that censors dreams, a realm in which "unauthorized" musings, nightmares and chimeras, whether seized in one's sleep or evoked in a wakeful state, are rebuked and recidivist dreamers are reprogrammed or permanently disabled. I argue that because knowledge of the world is inextricably shaped and conditioned by the opinions we inherit or perfunctorily manufacture along the way, dream and reality are rival symptoms of the same disease; reality is incurable. A complete understanding of reality lies beyond the limits of rational thought. Iconoclastic, honed to stun, the crypto-novel warns against absolutism and the tyranny of inflexible ideas. Stomached by a few, misunderstood by most, reviled by those who manage to read it in its entirety, the book is a dismal commercial failure. Unsold copies still languish at the bottom of a closet, the mute reminders that nobody wants to be scandalized, even when the affronts are painted in the pastel hues of allegory and narrated in the language of dreams.

•

The 80s and 90s bring fleeting professional successes, prolonged setbacks, and personal ordeals. I divorce my wife of 23 years. Five years later I remarry. We travel. I write. Good jobs and good money give way to lengthy periods of unemployment and penury interrupted by brief stints at dull or profitless occupations. Joblessness soars during the Reagan years. In 1982, 30 million people are out of work. I'm one of them. Along with 16 million Americans, I lose my medical insurance. At 45, I feel the sting of "over-qualification." The specter of chronic joblessness looms ahead, menacing, pitiless. Unemployment benefits dry up, pushing untold numbers of Americans to the brink.

As working America struggles to survive, huge sums of taxpayer money are raised to finance wars. In defiance of a law prohibiting the U.S. from supporting, directly or indirectly, military and paramilitary operations in Nicaragua, the Reagan administration flouts the edict and finds ways to secretly fund the "Contras," looking for "third-party" support, namely from Iran. Reagan himself solicits funds from Saudi Arabia to the tune of $32 million. Guatemala and Honduras serve as conduits in the traffic of weapons to the anti-Sandinista rebels. Israel, a major debtor, also participates in this conspiracy.

Then the Soviet Empire collapses. U.S. foreign policy, no longer forged in the crucible of Cold War paranoia, is now animated by a fear of incipient foreign nationalism and rebellions fueled by ethnic and religious factionalism, poverty, government corruption and apathy, and deepening despair. Noam Chomsky writes:

"The appeal to security [is] largely fraudulent, the Cold War framework having been used as a device to justify the suppression of independent nationalism."

Indeed, nascent foreign nationalism is a threat to no one but a few -- Anaconda Copper, United Fruit/Chiquita Banana, Dole, International Telephone and Telegraph, Coca Cola, PepsiCo, General Electric, Aramco, IBM and other giant multinational corporations and lending institutions that enrich themselves and their stockholders by systematically "hooverizing" -- sucking -- the economic marrow out of poor nations.

Meanwhile, in Central America, my old stomping grounds, the human rights picture grows dimmer even after years of peace and an era of coerced "reconciliation" in which abusers are pardoned and victims are forgotten. Hopes of change in El Salvador, Guatemala, Honduras and Nicaragua yield little or nothing. No viable political opposition emerges and grass-roots organizations that mushroom during the conflicts wither or vanish. Instead, old dynastic political structures succeed one-another. Impunity reigns. Kidnappers, torturers and assassins bribe their way out of jail. High-ranking military officers who'd engaged in murder and drug trafficking are acquitted and absolved in the name of "national reconciliation." Poverty festers as economies based on coffee, sugar and the sweatshop *maquila* industries fail to compete in the global economy. Heads of state are incapable, or unwilling, to deal with crime, violence and soaring delinquency. They respond instead with a loudly trumpeted but resoundingly ineffectual "zero tolerance" policy that triggers orgies of social cleansing. "Undesirables" are liquidated, among them street children and homeless adults. In Panama, Colombian refugees crossing the border are sent back with the knowledge that they will most likely be executed. In Costa Rica, undocumented Nicaraguans are rounded up, manhandled, and deported. It's a mess and I dutifully report what I see. I liken the situation to a cease-fire rather than peace because the problems that caused the wars are still in place -- inept and corruptible plutocrats and a depraved eagerness by the U.S. to tolerate them so long as they dance to America's music. I urge governments to reflect the aspirations of the people they rule only to concede that the people are ungovernable and, like sheep, are devoid of tangible aspirations. Apathy is the opiate of the masses. It prevents them from grasping the abject irrelevance of their lives.

Damned if I don't, damned if I do; in Guatemala and Honduras I'm seen as a meddler, threatened with expulsion by one, forced to bolt from the other -- or forfeit my life. In the U.S., my views are dismissed as subversive by the right, culturally insensitive by the left.

The flower children and the anti-war protesters of my youth have since grown into flabby, self-absorbed sexagenarians. The voices of dissent, the cries for peace are but feeble whimpers. I lament my cynicism and neutrality at a time when young Americans voiced their revulsion toward injustice and chicanery, as they marched against ignoble wars, pouring scorn on ignoble leaders while other young Americans died far from home as lies and colossal fraud were being heaped on a nation too smug to care.

What happened to America's conscience? As Pete Seeger once asked -- "Where have all the flowers gone? When will they ever learn?"

•

"Aren't you a bit too old to play paladin," my uncle asks one day. He fears for my safety. His question startles and irks me.

"I feel younger than my years. Isn't that the secret of eternal youth," I parry, now on the defensive. "I'm conscious of my age only when I look in the mirror." It's a lie. The little aches and pains, the syndromes and anomalies that sneak up on aging men, the vague but persistent cues all remind me that I'm not immortal.

He stares at me as if assessing the veracity of my words, tilting his head sideways, raising his eyebrows and fixing his gaze upon mine with avuncular cynicism.

"I wish you a long and healthy life, my beloved nephew. But don't you think time has come to let younger men carry the torch for a change?"

"I'm not that old," I protest, stung by the unbidden notion that others do not see me the way I see myself. Part of me itches for new tussles. My other self yearns for tranquility. But tranquility, I fear, is another word for surrender and inertia, an admission of defeat, and I bristle at the thought that the flesh will ultimately overwhelm the spirit.

"I'm not that old," I repeat, this time with far less conviction.

My uncle dies six months later at the venerable age of 87.

•

A new century dawns, a new millennium begins, full of illusive promises and fanciful auguries. The American Dream, I discover bit by bit, is a vast exaggeration, a myth invented by and marketed for a privileged and resourceful few who know how to play the game, pull strings, milk the system and sell, sell, sell. Once a middle class country with professed core values of hard work, opportunity and fair play, the U.S. was now being swept by a tsunami of right-wing economic, political and religious influences. The victim of corporate greed, its middle class was frittering away. With the explosive growth of the radical right -- fueled by fears generated by economic dislocation and demonizing conspiracy theories -- white "Christian" hate groups proliferated and vented their bile against changing racial demographics and, notably, the election of the first African-American president. An angry backlash against what political and religious conservatives perceived as the "socialization" of America spawned the monsters of Islamophobia, anti-intellectualism, censorship, racial profiling and concomitant police brutality, and a form of jingoism that openly condones or cheers the use of torture on suspected terrorists. Conducted in 2009, a Pew Forum on Religion & Public Life survey revealed that the more often Americans go to church, the more prone they are to applaud the use of "renditions" and "enhanced interrogation" techniques.

In turn, rabid opposition to same-sex marriage, immigration, the social and cultural advances of non-Caucasians and the upward mobility of women exposed an image of America that belies its self-view. Despite the strident propaganda, America is not:

-- Invincible. The U.S. lost in Korea, Vietnam, Somalia, and Iraq; it "triumphed" against tiny Grenada and Panama; it is being held hostage in Afghanistan. A stalemate will prove worse than defeat. Meanwhile, covert operations -- drone strikes, electronic surveillance and stealth engagements led by black units, mercenary armies and terrorist groups -- are becoming more common as tools of U.S. foreign policy than conventional warfare or diplomacy. Michigan University Prof. Juan Cole calls the new face of America's conflict resolution strategy "shadow power." [Obama's] shadow government, he warns, "masquerades as a way to keep the U.S. strong, but if it is not rolled back, it could fatally weaken American diplomacy" and lead to further erosion of civil liberties at home.

-- The guarantor of democracy; the U.S. ranks 20th after Norway, Iceland, Denmark, Sweden, New Zealand and Australia.

-- A beacon of spiritual objectivity. Americans ignore or abet the incestuous tryst between the body politic and the dinosaurs of the religious right. Considered the single greatest threat to church-state separation, the nation's largest Religious Right organizations continue to amass political power and wealth while stimulating and sharpening conservative anxiety. Together, these groups raise more than a billion dollars annually and invest large sums toward injecting religion into public schools.

-- A paragon of chastity. Americans wallow in a steaming cauldron of promiscuity, corruption and vice.

-- A model of enlightenment and evenhandedness. John Q. Public denounces abortion but cheers when a man is hanged, roasted or injected with a lethal cocktail of drugs.

-- The custodian of a free press. What we have is a faint-hearted mainstream media beholden more to advertisers than inconvenient truths; a press that won't challenge the evisceration of civil liberties; won't protest against the enfeeblement of the middle class; won't acknowledge that a huge number of Americans barely survive on starvation wages; won't denounce the consolidation of wealth into ever-narrower circles of power; will decry neither racism, the right wing's blitz against labor, nor the soaring price of food and medicines or a dysfunctional and predatory healthcare system ranked 37th after Costa Rica, Saudi Arabia and Malta!

Runaway capitalism would also reinforce America's incestuous relations with autocratic or marginally democratic nations around the world and stoke war fever. To maintain the juggernaut's momentum while doubts over the purpose and direction of conflicts widened, the Pentagon would address a growing recruitment problem by spending billions of taxpayer dollars on programs designed to deceive, seduce and capture the youth of America. All in all, U.S. conduct at home and abroad would contribute to the mounting suspicion that it talks with a forked tongue and acts solely in its own political and hegemonic interests.

The result of a glut of media-driven mythmaking, the rift between reality and reporting would end. Widening, the credibility gap, according to Sonoma University sociology professor Peter Phillips, "turned into a literal truth emergency ... the result of phony elections, illegal preemptive wars, torture camps, doctored intelligence and issues that intimately impact our lives at home, from healthcare to education." Clearly, this truth emergency stemmed from the failures of the Fourth Estate to serve as the free and outspoken conscience of America.

●

A lesser dream exists for those who have nothing left but dreams to sustain them. They all know that what separates them from the greater dream is America itself. They lack America's killer instinct. America is the love child of lofty idealism corrupted by persistent, obsessive sloganeering and the diktats of unrestrained capitalism. The flag; the Pledge of Allegiance; God's ubiquitous intrusion into affairs of state; an air of coyness and moral superiority; a pugnacious, confrontational streak; an annoying propensity to see itself as stately and principled -- all prop up the insolent pretense. Shibboleths are carved into America's hide. They help perpetuate an iconic national self-image that conflicts with its actions.

Of course, America has its amiable side. So long as I *behave* like an American -- or pretend to -- America grants me the right not to *feel* like one. This is a transcendent dispensation, one not conferred, if at all tolerated in many parts of the world. But there is an art to *being* American, a subliminal skill that can be acquired only at birth then honed in the crucible of America's self-promoting culture. *Becoming* an American is much more difficult. For some, the effort required and the inevitable transformations that ensue are their own supreme reward. Others, like me, get lost in the shuffle. The moorings that once connected me to my past -- where my selfhood resides -- are frayed. Surrendered to a wasteland of unending transience and irresolution, I'm reduced to mimicking the world around me. I follow the script, mouth the lines, control my inflection and trim my body language, all with sham self-assurance but without the slightest conviction. It's quite an act. I shall not fault America for having failed to match a set of fanciful assumptions brought to these shores by a wide-eyed adolescent and clung to because they once fit his model of El Dorado. Hard as I tried to resist America's enticements by looking the other way, I've become habituated to all its creature comforts and extravagances but none of its conventions. Perhaps this is all there is to *being* an American -- an unstudied acquiescence to things as they are, a piecemeal accommodation with the subtle inhibitions and tempting inducements that are part of the American experience. Yet something's missing. At the end of the day, after an exhausting trek through assorted minefields, I go backstage, wipe off the greasepaint, tuck away the libretto and sink within myself like into a soft, cozy armchair. Once ensconced in this familiar setting, reverting to the common idiom in which I address myself, now safe in the lap of retrospection, I survey my inner world, thankful it is still there, neighborly and obliging. Some of the greasepaint, like the ink in a tattoo, may never come off. Could I have become, by default, *malgré moi,* an American? The question and the implications its raises would leave me perplexed. I still cheer the America of the Patriots, the Whigs, the Sons of Liberty; I cannot abide the America it has turned into: a nation of self-righteous, flag-waiving, war-mongering xenophobes.

•

The images fly fast and furious and I catch them one by one in the net of memory. Ashen in the luster of fall, almost gloomy despite its great beauty, as if strangled by shadows, Paris, my lover, reemerges from the haze. It's not that night gives it a somber visage. In fact, the *Grands Boulevards* are all aglow with Christmas fever, and glittering ornaments hanging from invisible wires hover in festive formation over crowds of shopper and revelers below. It's just that I need to negotiate other memories and traffic, at best, is chaotic.

Stopped by a red light at an intersection, I spot a lone balladeer strumming a tinny guitar, his songs swallowed by the sound effects around him. In the City of Light no one seems to see him. So he keeps on singing. *Paris, je t'aime.* It was on *Rue du Pont Neuf* that I first made her acquaintance, barely out of the womb and already lusting after her as I lusted after her street girls when the time came. I never stopped loving her and yet I hardly know her anymore. Only memories animate the yearning so I partake of her with the circumspection owed a childhood dream. Paris may now belong to my past but she has become the immovable anchor I cling to when reality intrudes, when other dreams turn prosaic. It is on such occasions that I let go. My eyes glaze over and my ears tune out all sounds but those that drift in through the doors of memory. I take flight and Aznavour, Bécaud, Brassens, Ferré, Montand, Piaf and Trenet break into song for me. These are not just idle hankerings or aural mirages but real sensations, everyone a wistful replay brought on by *mal du pays,* a homesickness so intense that I seek refuge in their poetry, in the very timbres of their distinctive voices. Diminutive, a cigarette butt dangling from his lower lip, Aznavour knows how to say "I love you" a hundred different ways without ever repeating himself. His smoky, raspy, plaintive voice speaks of seduction and heartbreak, exultation and sorrow with an innocence and verve that sparkle in his feverish gaze. In his songs I can hear rain dancing softly on a canvas of slick slate roofs glistening in the shadow of the *Sacré Coeur*. I can replay summer breezes and feel them wafting through the chestnut trees as sweethearts stroll in the *Tuileries* gardens and children play admiral to vast armadas of toy galleons in the boat basins' turbid waters. I can even see night draping the City of Light in a dazzling display of shimmering radiance, the Eiffel Tower an incandescent lace spire rising heavenward like hands joined in prayer. I can do all that as morning descends, remote and aloof after a sleepless, dreamless night. Dissolving in the blinding desert light, Paris takes on the pallid hues of a silent film. The Paris I rediscover on increasingly rare visits, or when my reminiscences deliver me into her arms, is an old lover transformed by time and circumstance. She does not seem to age. I find her more desirable than ever, especially when we part. It is I who, in her absence, slowly turned from dashing suitor to decrepit Dorian Gray. Every wrinkle, every blemish, every battered emotion compressed and deferred within me ravage my features and scar my soul. The intimacy we once shared, I fear, can never be reclaimed.

    Held in check or doggedly concealed, my nostalgia is all-consuming. Reality is a vast, pervasive happenstance. Paris is not so much a flight from reality as a side-trip to another very tangible universe that belongs at once to an irreducible past and an as-yet unrealized potential. I accept my "reality" because it is the one that nourishes the very last seeds of hope. Without this reality, there can be no other. Perhaps I'm fated, as I spin on this dizzying merry-go-round, never to catch the brass ring; for doing so would rob me of the illusions that sustain me. Yes, it is the journey, not the destination. *"Getting there is half the fun,"* an old TV airline commercial once trumpeted. *Arriving* infers a state of finality, a climax, the conclusion of a crossing circumscribed by time and space -- the end of the line.

The longing keeps the impossible within reach.

A man of culture can't remember everything. He has the couth to forget the superfluous.

●

It is night that I must cross swiftly, like a turbulent river, not sunup. Fear and uncertainty seem to merge and fuse as darkness, like a black hole, chews up the scenery and swallows it. When morning returns, bringing with it the glare of day, I put my makeup back on, mentally rehearse my lines and get back on stage where men hold court and betray one-another and in whose limelight, predisposed as I am to indocility, I find beguiling and terrifying inspiration.

●

I turn on CNN. The face of evil is not always hideous to behold. Sometimes it assumes a wretched countenance, a visage so cleaved by discomfiture and incredulity that it conceals the malevolence in its deep, gloomy furrows and, for an instant, against all odds, it manages to inspire pity.

So it was when I glimpsed that bizarre feral creature that filled my television screen. But when arrogance and deceit resurfaced on his craggy features, when cunning reanimated his restless gaze with flashes of egocentricity and malice, pity turned to disdain for I recognized a man who knew no compassion, a heartless tyrant who had drenched his nation in blood and martyred his people into submission.

As I watched, transfixed, I remembered the corpses, thousands of them -- Iranian villagers -- men women, infants twisted like disembodied marionettes, frozen in place by death's grotesque choreography. The spectacle still haunts me. VX [nerve] gas is mercifully swift. Mustard gas is slow and agonizing. It blisters the skin, then blinds, then scorches the trachea, bronchia and lungs. Death comes when organs turn to mush.

I then remembered the Scuds raining on Tel Aviv where my son Ron lived at the time. He was nearly killed when an adjacent building collapsed as he ran for shelter.

I revisit battlefields and torture chambers where thousands of Kuwaitis, Jordanians, Kurds and Shiite Iraqis lost their lives. And my eyes fill with bitter, angry tears as I learn of the senseless death of yet another young American in a hostile, alien land Americans can never tame.

There is a feature of evil that escapes scrutiny in times of tragedy, or in moments of mindless national jubilation. Sometimes evil gestates in the alchemist's crucible, awaiting its maker's pleasure. So it was with the hirsute beast that emerged from its lair. For many years the Butcher of Baghdad had been "our man in Iraq." So long as it served our interests, we let him loose against his people and his neighbors. The geopolitics of hegemonic advantage has since shifted. He was tried and executed for war crimes, crimes against peace and crimes against humanity. Hurrah! But shouldn't his Western overseers and handlers be indicted for begetting, then failing to abort, this ghastly miscreation? Will they ever be? The answer, like the question, is the stuff of allegory. There is truth in metaphor but no justice.

Absolute evil is unconquerable. It sired and survived the Crusades, the "Holy Inquisition," the 30-Years War. It spawned the likes of Attila and Hitler, Stalin and the Shah of Iran, Pol Pot and Ceausescu, Franco and Pinochet, Milosevic and Osama bin Laden, to name a few. It continues to breed U.S.-backed despots in Africa, Asia and Latin America, all of whom, given the right political imperatives, will engage -- as they often do -- in acts of monstrous sadism against their own people.

To paraphrase Nietzsche, evil is "human, all-too human." Like the phoenix, it will be reborn of its own ashes and endure long after the man from Tikrit is forgotten.

Much of what I hear and see on the news, and all that is left unsaid or that escapes the camera's unerring eye, suggests less than a perfect future. Wars rage on in nearly every quadrant of the globe. Mankind's appetite for violence is beyond measure. You can't kill large numbers of people except in the name of virtue. So the carnage continues.

●

The mercury tops 105 degrees Fahrenheit. The blinds are down and the shades are drawn but the scorching sun sneaks through the slenderest crannies like meddlesome fingers of light in the cool semi-darkness of my living room. I choose silence over speech, solitude over fellowship, contemplative inertia over aimless motion, simple meals in my kitchen over a full-course dinner in some crowded eatery. In limbo, I see two people struggling for dominance: an embittered old man graced with diminishing convictions, consumed with resentment and anxiety, and a boy in an old man's skin still aiming at the stars. Melancholy, a predator, pits one against the other. It conquers by dividing. My demons lurk in the shadows, always ready to pounce. I know how the psyche works, how brittle a mechanism it is, how prone it is to breakdown. But I also learned that neither psychotherapy, nor miracle potions can do, even collectively, what a stiff dose of will power, determination, impatience and disgust will achieve. When I'm down, I have two choices: marinate in my own toxic juices -- and pay the psychosomatic price of despair -- or snap out of it and collect the dividends of self-conquest. I can't afford to surrender to melancholy; its intrusions infuriate me. Melancholy is an expensive, narcissistic and debilitating extravagance in which only the idle and self-absorbed can luxuriate. Wonder drugs may do wonders for the mentally ill. The emotionally skewed, the existentially maimed, I tell myself, must learn by strength of character and sheer force of will to exorcise the ugly specters. But the more one tries not to be like one's father, the more one is fated to resemble him. Hard as he tried, my father never found his "place." I don't expect to find mine. Perhaps such sanctuary can only be glimpsed when one is not looking. We must both have looked too hard where things are not.

•

Some places escape concealment or disguise. They are there in plain sight, stripped of all allegory, like the corner butcher store or the cobbler's. The commodities they trade, however, can neither be eaten nor worn. They rise, banal and smug, monuments of idolatry amid a wasteland strewn with graven images. They are the temples of falsehood in whose sanctum sanctorum are manipulated the fears and obsessions and hopes and chimeras that haunt us all. Freedom from dogma is bondage, they insist, absence of faith is a sin, they warn, and so sinners and slaves flock to their altars to be released and cleansed. I do not have to look far for these places. They teem and multiply, while school buildings crumble, hospitals shut down and concert halls go silent, in a frenetic contest against the wickedness and corruption that thrive unchecked in city council chambers and on the thoroughfares of the bustling bedroom community in which I now live. There are, in fact, more churches on this "high desert" plateau than crabs up a whore's ass but there's very little religion in these holy abodes, only unbending credos and every sect's ironclad conviction that it alone knows the path to "God's Kingdom." Their billboards, like movie marquees or roadside election-campaign posters, all proclaim to be serving Christ the Savior. All promise grace through communion, but their parishioners would rather burn in hell than pray in ecumenical unity. Factional differences, some trivial, others colossal, hinder the advent of Christian oneness. It is easier to idolize Jesus than to walk in his footsteps. Living by example, free from coercive codified doctrine, is infinitely harder than surrendering to spirited emulation. This is why they all meet to watch each-other sit and stand and kneel and cross themselves and bow their heads and swing their arms in ecstasy and mindless synchronicity. Hallelujah! Rituals and repetition reinforce the illusion of harmony and commonness of purpose. The fervency of their performance earns them the sham esteem of their peers and, provisionally, the clean conscience they crave.

Man is seduced by histrionics; he responds to gestures, not reason.

On Sundays, arrayed in their finest apparel, pious souls spill out of freshly waxed cars and gather in solemn formations in their respective houses of worship to chant in vacant-eyed monotones words so often uttered that they have been stripped of all meaning. When services conclude, a few of the faithful mosey on to the local 7-Eleven for a cold drink, a snack, a pack of cigarettes, perhaps a paper or periodical. These model citizens, their ears still ringing from some exalted homily or sacred hymn, reconnect with the profane world but they are safe, at least while on the premises, from the vulgarity and degeneracy that fester outside. For one, the erotic publications that once graced the racks of this convenience store are gone. If religion is divisive and exclusionary, it is not devoid of aggregated interests. Canonical differences aside, the neighborhood faithful, their innocence imperiled by the First Amendment, got together and forced management to rid the store of all offending titles. They called this auto-da-fé an "application of democracy."

The purge was swift, bloodless, like laser surgery. Overnight, it seems, many publications vanished. With more room on the shelves, periodicals that had never fully shown their faces, but were there, lurking behind the promise of gargantuan tits and peach-skinned buttocks, unfurled their colors now, flaunting surreal covers. **SOLDIER OF FORTUNE. GUNS & AMMO. BOWHUNTER. SURVIVALIST. EXTREME FIGHTING. WRESTLEMANIA.** Instead of leggy sirens and beckoning groins and nipples aroused and vaunting, magazines dish out the bizarre and the grotesque, along with death and gore and bloody faces, smoking firearms and twisted limbs and virtuosos wielding knives that can kill in less time than you can say Jerry Farwell.

Newly crowned dynasties of Elmer Gantries are hijacking America's psyche (while rifling through its pockets), and fresh troops of rapt soul-robbers infiltrate then exploit the coercive power of government. Despite its implied secularism -- *"Congress shall make no law respecting an establishment of religion..."* -- the U.S. is loath to protect against the intrusion of religion into the body politic. Religion is spreading its tentacles ever wider, deeper and tighter into the fabric of governance than ever before. Although the U.S. Constitution also guarantees freedom of religion, *"... or laws prohibiting the free exercise thereof..."* it has spinelessly failed to stop religion from muscling in on the affairs of state.

> "Church and State,
> Greed and hate: --
> Two baboon-persons
> In one Supreme Gorilla."
> **Aldous Huxley**

I look around me. The kingdom of God, I muse, is a place within the heart. It is everywhere. Often, it is nowhere.

•

I buy a long-stem pink rose, secretly delighting in the symbolism, and I retreat home. I sink in my easy chair and listen to Debussy. Dulcet aromas and fragrant harmonies waft like elves on a gentle breeze as the moon pales and Paris stirs from its reverie. Debussy enchants me. His otherworldly music softens the sounds of day. I partake at all hours as if it were an antidote against the dissonance that stalks me now that Paris is but a memory. Yes, Debussy and Ravel and Fauré. In Stravinsky's Firebird, I fumble through the ashes of my own rebirth. In Schoenberg's *Verklärte Nacht*, I seek paths to final transfiguration. Luciano Pavarotti sings *Nessun Dorma* and *Que Gelida Manina*, and I weep. Beethoven's Fifth Symphony overwhelms me with humility and exultation. So does Mozart's *Requiem*. The last stirring phrases of Tchaikovsky's *1812 Overture* fill me with sorrow then elation. I mourn the senseless death of thousands of Napoleon's soldiers as the cannonade drowns out the *Marseillaise*; grieving turns to euphoria as church bells celebrate Russia's victory. Never has a painting, poem or novel touched me the way music does. Music stirs me to the very core of my being. I rate composers on their capacity to enthrall me or make me weep. Seeing people cry also brings tears to my eyes. I watch them crying in Kosovo and Kandahar, Jerusalem and Jenin, Tehran and Tegucigalpa, Baghdad and Bucharest, New York and Nagasaki, Istanbul and Islamabad. Much is happening to make humankind shed tears of woe and bitterness and anger.

PART FIVE
TREADING WATER

Onward to the past

WAITING FOR GODOT

When I worked as a junior editor at a magazine in New York, I befriended an elderly Irish gentleman, Daniel Moran, the advertising sales manager. Dressed exquisitely in silk shirts and ties from Sulka, wearing spats and gabardine suits made to order at Abercrombie & Fitch, and sporting a monogrammed silver-handled cane, Moran was a kind and perceptive human being.

One day, as we were taking a long piss in the men's room after lunch, Moran, with no further preamble, turned to me and, looking me straight in the eye, said:

"Willy, if you don't do it while you're young, you never will."

It took 40 years to realize that "young" is in no way defined by age alone but by the *élan vital*, the creative force that helps move life from a treadmill to a stroll filled with meaning. Moran had been careful not to define *"it"* and I didn't ask. He knew that personal inclination and choice dictate *"it"* and I had enough imagination to seize on the untold potential of a cogent generality.

Moran had often said that he wasn't afraid to die. Instead, he'd expressed regret for all the unmet challenges and opportunities that death would deny him.

"There's so much left to do."

He died a month later of a massive heart attack. He was 70. I was 24.

Moran bequeathed a priceless testament that, to this day, is a source of inspiration and uneasiness. I'm pushing 75. I know that I must do *"it"* **now**. After much inner-debate, I rejected my father's admonition -- *"don't look for things where they are not."* I would like to believe that he hadn't referred to some physical realm but to an abstraction that does not exist outside the self. But his injunction contained an epistemological ambiguity, an inhibiting alternative to the empowering and open-ended exhortation, *"Seek and ye shall find"* that compelled me to abjure it. Like Heraclitus' down-to-earth warning -- *"You will not find the boundaries of soul by traveling in any* *direction, so deep are the measure of it,"* my father's counsel left me with no wiggle room, worldly or transcendent. As such, the advice became its own parody. No one knows where things really are. If I do not seek them *"where they're not,"* I risk never finding them.

•

For over 50 years I wrote about other people. Engaged, impassioned and often combative, my brand of journalism -- enemies of the truth call it muckraking -- focused on the follies, triumphs and absurdities associated with the human drama.

Beginning in 1991, when assignments first took me to Central America, I also dedicated my investigative reports, news analyses and commentaries to an in-vivo dissection of the deep and intractable social ills brought on by dynasties of military and plutocratic civilian regimes that continue to incarcerate minors with adult felons, murder homeless children, engineer the assassination of indigenous tribal chieftains, oversee the expropriation and sale of ancestral lands to foreign developers; regimes racked with political harlotry, corruption, ineptitude; regimes insensitive to widespread misery and discontent; regimes that have revived death squads and slave labor; regimes embroiled in fraud and lies; regimes that keep extending the hand of beggary while the elite lives in Babylonian splendor.

I've since broadened my focus to cover, here in the U.S., what I perceive to be injustice, political chicanery, deceit, greed masquerading as generosity, self-righteousness disguised as faith and crass military adventurism marketed as essential to "national security" or the "establishment of democracy."

I was in my early fifties and involuntarily "retired" (anyone considered "overqualified" understands the sting of unemployment) when I decided to chronicle my life, a story replete with adventures and calamities, and to comment on the world as I saw it, immune from an editor's blue pencil or the ever-present threat of censorship. Satirical, politically incorrect in the extreme, devoid of simplistic rationalizations, what I compiled in more than 20 years of writing and rewriting and agonizing self-doubt is an accolade to independent journalism, an homage to my family, and an honest personal testament of self-scrutiny in which I unabashedly bare my soul with neither pedantry nor false modesty.

No, this was not a burst of male menopausal narcissism, exhibitionism, catharsis or the hope of a ticket to literary fame and posterity. I was driven by a compelling urge to tell all, often with brutal candor and self-deprecation, to relate a personal story that spans four continents and seven decades, and to do so in brushstrokes that deliver an unvarnished canvas of the people, places and events -- reality stripped naked -- that marked my life. I minced no words. I spared no sensibilities. I took no prisoners.

I turned 74 in late September, 2011. I did almost everything I set out to do -- not always as planned. I had an adventuresome, often peril-filled life. I traveled widely, lived in several countries and immersed myself in countless cultures. I was a sailor. I learned to fly. As an obscure journalist more interested in discovery than fame, I must believe that my articles, commentaries and investigative reports -- all inspired by George Orwell's definition of freedom, *"the right to tell people what they do NOT want to hear,"* -- touched, stirred and even incensed someone, somewhere sometime. Finding a funeral wreath propped against my Casa Grande hotel door in Guatemala City several years ago dispelled any doubt that some people would have liked to keep my exposés entombed or, in extremis, to bury the messenger.

My greatest victory, I believe, has been one of self-conquest -- reaching emotional and spiritual independence, shedding absurd beliefs, living in the present and fretting as little as possible about things I can't control. This might not be a "Carnegie" success story. I've amassed no fortune, didn't become a captain of industry. I moved no mountains; nor did I ever aspire to do so. If we measure success in terms of wealth and material possessions, I'm an abject failure. If self-realization is the fruit of self-acceptance, then I've triumphed. Last, I was a struggling agnostic for most of my life. I have since come out of the closet and breathed the oxygenated air of emancipation by proclaiming my atheism.

Begun in 1992, *A PALER SHADE OF RED* went through several permutations, incarnations and title changes. First called *MEANDER-*

INGS, then ***ADRIFT***, to describe a near-lifetime of nomadism, it also took on a life as ***THE ESTUARY***. An estuary is where a river meets the open sea. The confluence of two bodies of water marks both the culmination of a journey -- an end of sorts -- and the beginning of another. The river is life elapsed. The sea, the mighty sea, is the great unknown that lies ahead. An early avatar of this straggling memoir was ***NEVER FAR FROM THE TREE*** as it best summed up what I am: the aggregate of my ancestral parts. In me are bonded the recombined atoms of my parents and grandparents and the genes of their forbears. Ultimately, my self-view, ideologically and politically, and the need to proclaim and defend the values this work propounds would dictate one final change. Under its present title, I've said everything I had to say about a multitude of things and, heeding to grudging civility, refrained from saying infinitely more. I hope readers find my work stirring, if not disquieting. If I left you unmoved, I failed. If I echoed some of your innermost and unspoken sentiments, stimulated you, enlightened you, challenged you, exasperated you, I will have in some great measure succeeded. What I left unsaid was often the heart of the story and the icing on the cake.

•

There exists midway between reason and delirium a narrow space when the hour is still very young. Time suspends its flight and melts, mellifluous and sweet like a star-studded kiss. When my lips brush past it, its nectar transforms me. I find myself at the center of an eternal spring, knee-high in jonquils and crowfoot, fairy tales dancing in my ears, my eyes filled with rainbows. I am child again. I see myself playing hide-and-seek with my shadow. Enraptured by the sudden absence of my other self, liberated from the shackles of reasoned consciousness, I do cartwheels and gambol breathlessly. But childhood is a state of mind that the mind betrays. The illusion is short-lived. Barely hatched from the darkness, I feel myself being transported backwards. Everything flees before me like a movie projected in reverse. Clouds quiver, devour one-another and vanish only to regroup a blink later into billowing and ever-dividing giant masses of white. The sky paints itself with convulsive strokes, now dusky, now fair, here frosty, there ablaze. The momentum that this inverse force generates sucks me within it and lays me to rest in this fragile cocoon woven with dreams where beginnings are born. It is through the eyes of remembrance that I scrutinize myself.

Farther away, I witness my own birth. All is awash in white -- the doctor, whose huge hairy hands yank me out of my uterine abode, the midwife, the ceiling, the walls, the large clock ticking mindlessly, the big swinging doors, the bonneted nurses, the nauseating milk a white teat insists on pumping into my mouth. Even my very first breath seems impregnated with whiteness. I choke on it. White is the light that surrounds me like a shroud. I close my eyes to escape its oppressive monotony. My senses are raw, my thoughts untamable.

"Fetus!" I summon myself. "What are you waiting for? There's no turning back. Dive in. The current will do the rest."

I watch myself pondering the challenge.

"No matter," I answer at last. *"I'm the product of my own optic. There can be no order without chaos, beauty without ugliness, silence without din, peace without torment."*

I cling to this argument as to a life preserver, fearing all the while that I might sink under the weight of its own irrelevance. I close my eyes. The crossing is coming to an end. The metamorphosis is complete. I submit to it time and again in the bosom of night the better to see it clearly, to flee day.

When I reopen my eyes in the morning, after the dreaming, reality dawns. Things take shape around me. I become conscious of time. Weightless in the void of slumber, now awake and knowing, my body yields to gravity. I feel myself being. Inner voices, all vying to be heard, are soon hushed by the sounds of day. Life begins anew.

To ease the discomfort, I weave myself into another dream. I rarely know where I'm headed. I often get lost. But the urge to find my way becomes so compelling that I keep spinning dreams until I do. The journey gets tedious at times and many a vision once indelibly etched in my mind shrivels up and dies a thousand deaths as I uncap my pen. Then night returns to deliver me from day and I reenter the dreamtime. I may be dreaming now even as I tell you this.

•

Before me is the open sea.

"Come hither," it beckons.

I can feel the salty air on my lips. An invisible tide tugs at my being.

"Come. You know who you are. It's time to take the plunge," the sea murmurs as the surf laps at my feet. "What are you waiting for?"

I look over my shoulder. Great rivers spring from humble origins. Like the Nile, the Ganges, the Amazon, the Yangtze, the Mississippi, I know from whence I came but I no longer remember where I'm headed.

Those who have never been anywhere, don't understand nostalgia or live by meaningless clichés remind me with galling smugness, "You can't go back."

"Why not?"

"Well, what you left behind is no longer there. Things change. Entropy, you know."

"But *I* haven't changed. What I hope to find, should good fortune bring me back to the source, is still there, untouched by time, unedited by memory. I'm not chasing after ghosts."

Am I lying, conning myself? Surely, the people I once knew are gone. It's not them that I long for. It's Paris. Paris is still Paris, the City of Light, of stately museums and quaint neighborhood cafés, of timeless monuments and intimate bistros, of majestic plazas and tree-lined boulevards and narrow, winding alleys from which waft the coalescing aromas of exotic cuisines. The neighborhood commons, the playgrounds, flower gardens and sprawling forested parks where I used to gambol as a boy, have not moved an inch. Nor have the small bookstores redolent of aged leather and yellowed vellum paper, the *bouquinistes* selling lithographs and out-of-print periodicals from their stalls along the banks of the Seine. The old-world art galleries and antique shops and inviting *patisseries* and open-air food markets are still there. So are the Romanesque churches and Notre Dame Cathedral, in whose shadow I took my first steps, still gazing at the ageless river below where are reflected its spires and flying buttresses.

I can still smell in my mind's nostrils the indescribable scent of the Metro, the aroma of rain-slick slate roofs and sun-drenched chestnut trees. Forged iron balconies festooned with potted rhododendrons still adorn the cut stone façades of trendy *fin de siècle* town houses. And when I revisit the modest cemeteries and historic necropolises, I find the headstones, simple markers and elaborate mausoleums of Balzac and Baudelaire, Chopin and Debussy, Heloise and Abelard, Eugene Ionesco and Molière, Picasso and Man Ray, Proust, Ravel and Rossini, Sartre and Gertrude Stein, Brancusi and Van Gogh, just to name a few.

Even Samuel Beckett had the presence of mind to die and be buried in Paris.

I still hear the crooners of my youth, their songs embedded in, resonating from, the cobbled streets and stylish avenues in which I once meandered in enchanted fascination. They're all dead and their passing left a gaping hole in France's soul but their music, their poetry, their lifelong love affair with Paris lives after them. They will never be forgotten. Had I dared distract him as he strolled on the Champs Élysées arm-in-arm with a much younger woman, Erich von Stroheim, the enigmatic actor and director now resting at the Maurepas cemetery outside Paris, would surely have reminded me that,

> *"In France, if you write one good book, compose one beautiful song, paint one great picture, direct one outstanding film and nothing else, you are still recognized as an artist and honored accordingly. In Hollywood you're only as good as your last picture. If you didn't have one in production within the last three months you're forgotten, no matter what you have achieved before."*

•

It's April and the poppies are now in bloom. I think of Mouloudji. I scan the high desert mountains that surround me, dwarf me, fence me in and deny me the privilege of a horizon line beyond which deliverance, I tell myself, looms. There are no vultures circling above but predation never takes a rest.

Somewhere in the distance, a car outfitted with monster speakers zooms by like a great booming wall of sound, inflicting an inane song about beer, guitars and sex in the back of a pickup truck on all who share the roadway.

    I turn my gaze heavenward at a searing, implacable sun.

    Then I look at my shoes, caked with brown desert dust.

    Like Vladimir and Estragon, I'm waiting for Godot.

    Waiting extinguishes will and freezes motion. So I just

POSTSCRIPT
THE NAME OF THE GAME

Learn your lines

"ALL THE WORLD'S A STAGE."

Fathers and mothers play the parenting game. Wives and husbands act out roles for which they're mutually unsuited. Children play at being sons and daughters. My teachers played educators. Moses played lawgiver. Jesus played anointed "Savior;" Pontius Pilate played governor of Judea while Tiberius played Roman emperor. Crusaders and inquisitors staged massacres and their victims, mere extras in a cast of thousands, acted as martyrs. Popes and prophets and mystics play at being in a world apart from the human sphere. Kings and queens play at being monarchs; their subjects at being vassals. While Vincent Ferrer and the apostate Solomon Halevy played pious Christians, the Burgos Guzmán clan playacted Christian converts and their Worms descendants played the devout Jews they had never ceased to be. Hitler played Hitler and Mussolini played Mussolini. Stalin and Mao and Pol Pot and Ceausescu and Saddam Hussein played themselves. Joseph McCarthy, a drunkard and a liar consumed with hatred, impersonated a senator. Marylyn Monroe, the beautiful, adorable damaged child assumed any role in which she was cast, except her own. Historians play with the past; soldiers play war; cops and robbers play cops and robbers. Politicians pass for the common man and sell themselves to the highest bidder; they just don't call it prostitution. Bankers play monopoly with other people's money; they just don't call it usury. Clerics play the soul-saving game and their congregants play the salvaged spirits infused with a deaf, dumb and blind God who plays hide and seek from the pinnacles of his nonexistence. *Papa* played doctor and *Maman* played homemaker. People at my father's funeral played mourners. The mourners went home, ate, slept, defecated, copulated and played at life until they too died and grievers attended their funerals. We've honed the art of killing and the angry beast in us roars with greater ferocity than ever. The human race is a multi-headed hydra whose sole function, it seems, is to multiply and, at some distant point in time, to devour itself to extinction.

It's all one big hilarious, heartbreaking, sordid, ghastly act.

•

In the crypt of the Riverside Memorial Chapel on Manhattan's upper West Side, I looked at my father's shroud-wrapped naked body resting in a simple pine casket. His face beamed with the serenity of a sleeping child. The furrows of age, suffering and disillusionment were gone from his brow. A vague impish smile seemed to lift the corners of his mouth. I could almost hear him whisper:

"Don't fret. Take it in stride. It's all just a fucking game."

"It's not fair, *papa*, not fair," I heard myself muttering."

"Fairness? You're looking for fairness? Don't make me laugh. Life isn't fair. Learn your lines and play the game, son! Or else you'll be ignored, stomped on, scorned, trivialized, ostracized, crucified."

I was fifty.

After his interment in the Jewish section of a sprawling Long Island cemetery where the dead forego their sectarian affectations, and for the next twenty years, I went back to playing journalist because I was unfit to play doctor like my father, lawyer like my uncle or even candle maker like my paternal grandfather whose tallow would be turned into soap and his skin into lampshades in one of Hitler's slaughterhouses.

He who walks backwards risks tripping on his future. So I walk forward and keep looking for myself, so great is my fear of getting lost.

ACKNOWLEDGMENTS

I am indebted to my parents, learned, urbane, fair-minded and liberal, for instilling a love of books and an appreciation for music, art and philosophy, for sparing me the enslavement of religious indoctrination and for enduring, if not always endorsing, my wildest antics. To my mother, a selfless, unassuming woman of great culture and refinement, I owe my fondness for beauty and symmetry. From my father, a loving, iron-willed and incorruptible man who abhorred ostentation and pretense, I learned that self-esteem and a respect for truth bestow infinitely greater rewards than money or a good reputation.

I salute my teachers, those I pleased when I applied myself and those I exasperated when I didn't. Their erudition, pedagogical skills and saintly patience for the lazy, unfocused, mercurial and rebellious student I was helped lay the foundations on which I would erect a lifetime career of endless beginnings.

I can never sufficiently acknowledge the immense influence a number of prominent writers, poets and philosophers had on the constantly evolving person I would become and, by extension, on the ideas I would champion. Their prose, verses, insights and eye-opening reflections resonate as intensely today as they did in the days of my youth. Most were French. Of these, one was denied a Christian funeral for penning vitriolic anti-religious polemics; five were imprisoned: one for denouncing the brutality of colonialism; the other for suggesting that the blind can be taught to read through the sense of touch; the third, the son of a prostitute, for vagabondage, lewd acts and "other offenses against public decency;" the fourth, for stretching the limits of literary freedom in tracts that mixed raw eroticism with civil disobedience. The fifth spoke for the common man and rose with uncommon bravery against government and military corruption.

My other mentors wrote in Arabic, English, Dutch, German, Russian, Sanskrit and Spanish. Three hailed from England; one of them did not survive the spurious puritanism of his Victorian milieu. One died insane -- as do many who seek shelter from the battering storm of reality in the haven of delirium. All were freethinkers, rebels and iconoclasts, now long dead, but whose works and the reformist ideas they impart still inspire new generations of radicals-in-training.

www.ingramcontent.com/pod-product-compliance
Lightning Source LLC
Chambersburg PA
CBHW060447170426
43199CB00011B/1123